Sustaining the Divine in Mexico Tenochtitlan

Sustaining the Divine in Mexico Tenochtitlan: Nahuas and Catholicism, 1523–1700

Jonathan Truitt

University of Oklahoma Press
Norman, Oklahoma

and

The Academy of American Franciscan History
Mission San Luis Rey, Oceanside, CA
2018

Library of Congress Cataloging-in-Publication Data

Names: Truitt, Jonathan G., 1977- author. | Truitt, Jonathan G., 1977– editor, author.
Title: Sustaining the Divine in Mexico Tenochtitlan : Nahuas and Catholicism, 1523–1700 / Jonathan Truitt.
Description: Oceanside, CA : The Academy of American Franciscan History ; Norman, Oklahoma : University of Oklahoma Press, 2018. | Includes bibliographical references and index.
Identifiers: LCCN 2017044842 | ISBN 9780806160412 (hardcover : alk. paper)
Subjects: LCSH: Nahuas—Mexico—Mexico City—Religion. | Catholic Church—Mexico—History—16th century. | Catholic Church—Mexico—History—17th century. | Indians of Mexico—History.
Classification: LCC F1221.N3 T78 2018 | DDC 282.7209/031—dc23
LC record available at https://lccn.loc.gov/2017044842

To my parents, Barbara Truitt-Petersen and Allen Petersen
Judy Hand-Truitt, and the late Glenn Hand-Truitt.
Thank you for your love, support, and patience through it all.

Contents

List of Figures and Tables

Abbreviations

AGI	Archivo General de Indias
AGN	Archivo General de la Nación
AHCV	Archivo Histórico José María Basagoiti Noriega del Colegio de las Vizcaínas
AHFC	Archivo Histórico Franciscano de Coyoacan
AHFZ	Archivo Histórico Franciscano de Zapopan
AHN	Archivo Histórico Nacional, Madrid
ANM	Archivo General de Notarías de la Ciudad de México
BNF	Bibliothèque Nationale de France
CSG	Colegio de San Gregorio, INAH
FF	Fondo Franciscano, INAH
FRAF	Fondo Reservado: Archivo Franciscano, UNAM
INAH	Instituto Nacional de Antropología e Historia, Archivo Histórico
NL	Newberry Library, Chicago
UNAM	Universidad Nacional Autónoma de México, Biblioteca Nacional

Acknowledgments

The publication of a book tends to be looked at as an individual's accomplishment. Though it is true that there is a single person at the helm, it is really a team effort. I have been blessed to have an amazing and wide-ranging team of supporters assist me on this endeavor. Its completion would not have been possible without the constant support of family, friends, colleagues, and mentors. Their encouragement, feedback, and assistance have all made this project stronger. For past, present, and future support, I thank them all.

The first incarnation of this monograph was as my Ph.D. dissertation. During that period financial assistance for the research and writing came from many sources. Preliminary research was funded by the Tulane University History Department, a Lurcy Summer Research Grant, the Tinker Foundation, and the Stone Center for Latin American Studies. A Tulane University Graduate School Fellowship helped fund research in Mexico and the United States. The Academy of American Franciscan History provided funds necessary to continue research in Mexico. The Selley Dissertation Fellowship and the Program for Cultural Cooperation between Spain's Ministry of Culture and U.S. universities provided essential support for research in Spain and other parts of Europe. Without the monetary assistance of these institutions, the dissertation would not have been feasible. Since its completion I have benefitted from the generosity of Central Michigan University. The History Department, my former dean, Pamela Gates, and our Office of Research and Graduate studies have provided course releases, funding for research-related travel, and a semester sabbatical, all of which helped me expand on the research and overhaul the manuscript.

From their initial grant the Academy of American Franciscan History has been truly supportive of the project. The times I have spoken with the director, Jeffrey Burns, and told him that the project was almost complete seem innumerable. Each time saw the addition of new research and reworked chapters. His patience and that of the Academy are saintly. I thank them for their patience and the outside reviewers of the press for their insightful feedback. Heartfelt thanks to Alessandra Jacobi-Tamulevich at the University of Oklahoma Press and John Thomas for his fantastic attention to detail.

I have been blessed on this journey by a series of amazing advisors and mentors, official and unofficial. My dissertation advisor, Susan Schroeder, has been a constant support throughout the process. Her depth of knowledge, meticulous attention to detail, and willingness to share her insights, time, and works in progress have made this an infinitely better study. We have both lost count of the number of times that she has read and reread this manuscript. I thank her for her continuing interest in the project, generous mentorship, and friendship.

My undergraduate mentor, Eric Carlson, continued with me on my journey from undergraduate studies to the present. My love of the early modern period and religious history started with his classes at Gustavus Adolphus College. Our conversations since that time have provided me with ample ideas and approaches that have influenced the final project. Every day I spend in the classroom is an effort to pay forward the generosity he has shown me. I fear that no matter how long I spend in the classroom I will still have more to do to pay off that debt. I thank him for his friendship and guidance.

I had the opportunity to meet the late Jim Lockhart in 2002 at the Yale summer Nahuatl course led by Jonathan Amith. When it became clear a few years later that I would be working with an extensive corpus of mundane Nahuatl documents, especially wills and land records, Jim generously helped guide me through their nuances and combed through and corrected my translations. His willingness to share his time and knowledge are greatly appreciated. Beyond his translations, Jim read through the entire manuscript and provided detailed comments that further improved it. This project could not be what it is without the assistance I received from him. He will be missed.

Other scholars have been generous with their time and research. Barry Sell's selfless gift of his translation of the only known Nahua *cofradía* constitution for the chapel of San Josef de los Naturales can be felt throughout, especially in chapter 4. Louise Burkhart has been an unofficial mentor since I started my master's program at Minnesota State University, Mankato. It was her work that first sparked my interest in colonial Mexico. She has responded to countless emails, read chapters, and provided feedback on questions related to Nahuatl since that time. Similarly, Susan Kellogg has read chapters and conference papers related to this work since I started presenting my work in 2007. Her patience with my errors and assistance as I have wrestled with the multitude of ideas related to indigenous women's roles in Mexico Tenochtitlan are greatly appreciated. Fritz Scwhaller has also played a significant role in this project's development. An email to him while he was at the University of Minnesota, Morris, set me down the path of studying Nahuatl. Since that time, he has acted as a sounding board for many of the ideas in the book and has read and reread the entire manuscript. I thank him for his ongoing support.

During my stay in Mexico, several scholars provided many valuable conversations and suggestions. Support came especially from Francisco Morales, O.F.M., director of the Biblioteca Franciscana; Francisco Rodríguez, O.F.M., archivist at the Archivo Histórico Franciscano de Coyoacan (the archive has since been relocated to the Biblioteca Franciscana); and John Sullivan at the Instituto de Docencia e Investigación Etnológica de Zacatecas. I thank them for their time, support, and assistance.

As guardians of the documents needed for so much historical research, specific archives and libraries have proved essential to this work. I wish to thank the entire staff at the Latin American Library at Tulane University. Their support while I was in residence and after I moved away has been remarkable. The staff at the Archivo General de la Nación in Mexico City was fantastic, especially the people in Gallery 4. Genaro Días at the Instituto Nacional de Antropología e Historia's Archivo Histórico was patient and diligent in his pursuit of important documents. Ana Rita Valero de García Lascuráin, director of the Archivo Histórico José María Basagoiti Noriega del Colegio de San Ignacio de Loyola Vizcaínas, took time out of her day to speak with me about my project as well as potential sources. Mercedes Aguilar Lara, archivist at the Archivo Histórico de la Basílica de Guadalupe in Mexico City, provided access to its collections and helped remind me to step back from my research on the colonial period and look at what was transpiring around me. A todos ustedes, digo gracias.

During the spring of 2012, Bill Connell, Barbara Mundy, and I spent one unforgettable day traversing the streets of Mexico City, stopping at every visita chapel and other colonial points of interest. To say I was giddy to walk Mexico City with them is an understatement. Aside from the walk, both of them have been generous with their time and knowledge by reading chapters or providing feedback on various conference panels. I thank them for stimulating conversations and look forward to future walks through Tenochtitlan!

My time in the archives was enriched by a group of fellow colleagues who made the process more enjoyable. Between us we helped to keep our eyes open for sources for each other. Richard Conway, Ken Ward, Tatiana Seijas, Ryan Crewe, and Rob Schwaller all flagged documents for me at some point while we were in the archives. Our numerous conversations over coffee and drinks helped immensely.

A number of colleagues and friends have helped me analyze and examine many of my arguments. Rebecca Livingstone, Adam Beauchamp, Erika Hosselkus, Mark Lentz, Jess Lepler, Lisa Singleton, and Margarita Vargas Betancurt all have provided stimulating conversation over many a cup of coffee at Tulane and in Mexico while we all worked on our projects. R. J. Kelly was incredibly generous with his time and knowledge of Latin; I thank him for his work on three difficult documents on my behalf. For their constant support throughout, willingness to challenge me continually, equally amazing conversations, and assistance I thank Jonathan Amith, John Sullivan, Linda Curcio-Nagy, James Boyden, Mark Christensen, Dana Velasco Murillo, Cory Conover, Thomas Luongo, Stafford Poole, Sujay Rao, and Gertrude Yeager.

In graduate school, the archives, and since, Richard Conway has been a constant presence. Though we have at times found ourselves in competition for jobs and grants, our friendship has always taken precedence. Richard has read through so many versions of this manuscript that I have lost count. His diligence, insight, and friendship are greatly appreciated.

The benefits of having a skilled office professional to assist you and laugh with you can never be overstated. At Tulane the assistance and support of Donna Denneen and Pamela Smith helped to keep me organized and on level ground during my time in New Orleans. Since arriving at Central Michigan University I have greatly benefitted from the skills of Annette Davis. My appreciation of her sense of humor and assistance cannot be overstated. I thank all three of them for all that they do.

At Central Michigan University, I have had the opportunity to work with two outstanding doctoral students, Hugo Zayas and Scarlet Muñoz. Conversations with them about colonial Mexico and religion have influenced aspects of my research. I thank both of them for their time and wish them both the best of luck on their future endeavors.

Friendships are often tested by distance and school. Yet some friends continue the journey with you despite the physical distance. Tim and Mary Wheatley both read sections of the early manuscript and provided feedback and conversation related to my work. Shawn Isenhart and Thistle Parker-Hartog provided me with a necessary loan toward my first Nahuatl course in 2002. That assistance is what ultimately allowed me to follow my dreams. More recently I have benefitted from new friendships. Four years ago I reached out to Jim Hohmeyer for some assistance with musical scores I was examining for my research, and Jim quickly brought Ed Soehnlen in on the conversation. Their knowledge of music, past and present, friendship, and conversation have helped improve chapter 2.

My family, immediate and extended, has been constant in supporting of my interest in history and Latin America from the beginning. They have continually encouraged and listened to me as I talked endlessly about my research. They have also been patient when I became lost in my work and failed to communicate regularly. My late father, Glenn Hand-Truitt, passed while I was working on revisions to the manuscript, but he asked for updates on the work until the end. A special thanks goes to my spouse, and partner in parenting, Tessa, who followed me to New Orleans months before Hurricane Katrina, has supported my wanderlust and extensive absences for research trips to Mexico and Europe, and has made sure that I struck a balance between work and family. Her patience, support, encouragement, and love have sustained me. Since the journey started, our children Braeden and Kai arrived in the world. They have made it clear when it is time to play and when it is time to work. I thank them for reminding me to live life while I study the past.

I have received immense support along the way. Thanks to all named and unnamed (and apologies to the last group!). Any errors or omissions, however, are mine alone.

Introduction

At the start of the sixteenth century the *altepetl* (ethnic state) of Mexico Tenochtitlan stood at the center of imperial authority in Mesoamerica.[1] The Mexica, the indigenous people of that polity, were the military might of the Triple Alliance known as the Aztec Empire, the other two allies being the peoples of Tetzcoco and Tlacopan (Tacuba). Aztec rule started circa 1433 and ended with the Spanish and Tlaxcalteca defeat of Tenochtitlan in 1521.[2] Although the Triple Alliance's hegemony as the imperial authority of Mesoamerica ended, the political centrality of its capital city, now Mexico City, continues to the present.

Because Tenochtitlan was the capital and center of the Aztec Empire, its decrees affected much of central Mexico. To western sensibilities Tenochtitlan was simply a political entity whose religion was wrong; to the Mexica, who built the city, Tenochtitlan was the center of the universe and as much a religious demarcation as a political one. The deity of the altepetl, Huitzilopochtli, represented Mexica strength, and the Mexica position at the center of the empire was religiously significant within the cosmos of central Mexican religion. When Cortés decided to rebuild Mexico City on top of the ruins of the Aztec capital, he reinforced not only a visual political continuity in the region but a religious one, for Catholicism in New Spain was headquartered there. Just as the viceroy of Mexico came to replace the Mexica emperor, so the buildings of the Christian god came to be the dominant representations of religion. As Eleanor Wake argues, "Christianity was not understood [by the indigenous] to be either a new or a different religion."[3] Whereas Spaniards, who had only just arrived in the Americas, viewed their coming and Christianity's as a seismic shift for the natives of the Americas, to the Nahuas and other indigenous groups who had been there for as long as their elders could remember the requirements of life, food, shelter, sex, and care for deities persisted. The Spaniards' decision to position both political and religious authority in the newly built Mexico City maintained the central authority of the island capital as both a political and religious center, despite its new buildings and the replacement of temples with churches.

In precontact Mesoamerican codices the artist-authors used pyramids to represent the various altepetl. This was no accident, for pyramids stood at the center of most ethnic states. Indeed, whenever one group defeated another the chroniclers represented conquest artistically by drawing captives and a destroyed pyramid—though in reality the pyramid continued to stand (fig.

1). After the arrival of the Spaniards and the introduction of Catholicism, churches replaced pyramids as the artistic symbol representing an altepetl (fig. 2). And though the shift from precontact religious iconography to Christian symbolism is indicative of an important change, the fact that a religious structure, a church instead of a temple, continued to represent the idea of the community should not be lost. At a very basic cultural level it suggests that religion continued to be at the heart of altepetl identity. During the precontact period a hierarchy of pyramids, based on deity affiliation, existed within in any given altepetl. Similarly, after the establishment of colonial rule a hierarchy of churches, from smaller and less prestigious to larger and more prominent, developed. The Nahuas built many of these new churches in locations of precontact religious importance within their altepetl.

The pinnacle of power and prestige during the precontact and colonial periods was in Tenochtitlan, later Mexico City, and filtered down, to ever-smaller units, within the altepetl and across the region. Considerable research has been conducted on Spanish Mexico City, but few books have focused on indigenous Mexico Tenochtitlan. Indeed, the majority of the information we have has been inferred from other altepetl. Yet the general trajectory of information sharing during the colonial period was from the capital outward. As early as the 1550s, Nahuas trained in Mexico Tenochtitlan were sent elsewhere in the viceroyalty to educate other natives in Christianity. Examples of *cofradía* (confraternity; religious brotherhood) constitutions and other ecclesiastical documents were sent to various altepetl to help with the establishment of Christianity or to make changes in Church policy, such as the secularization of *doctrinas*, parishes for the indoctrination of indigenous people in a given geographic area.[4] Notably, the only extant cofradía constitution for the indigenous chapel of San Josef de los Naturales is held in the Franciscan archive of Zapopan outside of Guadalajara.

The aim of this book is to take a concerted look at Nahua interactions with divinity in Mexico Tenochtitlan, the heart of the Aztec Empire and the capital of the Viceroyalty of New Spain. Using Nahuatl and Spanish-language sources, this monograph examines the integral role played by the Nahua community in supporting and sustaining the foundation of the colonial divine, Catholicism, in the altepetl of Mexico Tenochtitlan. The focus is not directly on indigenous belief and whether these beliefs were purely Catholic or a syncretism of the precontact and colonial religions; other studies focus on that topic. Although beliefs come into view, the intent is to examine the quotidian interactions, mundane or spiritual, that individuals and the community had with Catholicism. Just as there was continuity between prehispanic Tenochtitlan and colonial Mexico City, as Barbara Mundy's *The Death of Aztec Tenochtitlan, the Life of Mexico City* demonstrates, so there were also continuities between people's encounters with the divine into the colonial period.

FIGURE 1. 1542 image of the founding of Tenochtitlan and military conquests. *Codex Mendoza*, MS. Arch. Selden. A. 1, fol. 2r. Courtesy of the Bodleian Libraries, The University of Oxford.

FIGURE 2. Map of Cuzcatlan, 1580. Courtesy of the Nettie Lee Benson Latin American Collection, University of Texas Libraries, The University of Texas at Austin.

The arrival of foreigners did not change people's understanding of how they engaged with religion, it just changed the religion with which they interacted.

As a central tenet of early modern life for both Spaniards and Nahuas, people necessarily engaged with Catholicism on a daily basis in New Spain. Many of these interactions were centered on belief, for example, confession. Others were more multifaceted. Music is a prime example; indigenous students went to friars to learn European music. But the use of the music did not stop at the walls of the friary. Rather, it went into the indigenous community, thereby connecting audience members with the training efforts of the Catholic Church even though they themselves had not taken music lessons. Another example is found in a pearl diver whose pearls ended up decorating a saint's image in Mexico City. The sale of the diver's pearls allowed a Nahua parishioner to practice her faith in a way she believed important. By using the pearls for a religious purpose, the diver's efforts inadvertently supported the faith. Aggregate small interactions of this sort, by Nahuas and other indigenous groups, such as selling goods to the Church, receiving a religious education, or staging or attending a play at a chapel, among others, ultimately supported the establishment of Catholicism in New Spain.

Simply stated, early modern Catholicism required a lot of accoutrements for any given mass, festival, or ceremony. It may have been possible for a small group of priests to sustain the needs of a Spanish-only flock, but having only Spanish Christians create all of the clothing, incense, candles, musical instruments, books, saints' images, and the like for the proselytization, and later maintenance, of the Native American population of New Spain was not feasible. The Spaniards' desire to have the trappings and the pronouncements of the faith present necessitated a dependence on the indigenous population, and especially its artisans, to produce what Catholicism needed. This research, then, focuses on the way the indigenous population supported the establishment of Catholicism as an institution. It is evident that their physical labor, often forced through labor drafts, was needed for the construction of the religious buildings. Perhaps just as significant was their work to produce religious goods to sell in the marketplace, their support of cofradías, and their work to create saints' images for in-home shrines; these are just some of the things they did to sustain the divine, and thus the growth of Catholcism, at a household and community level. In many ways, Nahuas' support for Christianity is directly connected to their pre-Columbian religious responsibilities and their sense of obligation to the divine.

The Catholic Church considered everyone who lived in Mexico City to be a Catholic parishioner or a *doctrinero,* an indigenous person who was learning the faith. Native Americans formed the cornerstone of Catholicism in Mexico City. By examining the way Nahuas interfaced with Catholicism on a daily basis, we gain a better understanding of indigenous-Spanish relations in

Mexico Tenochtitlan during Hapsburg rule.[5] With a focus on Nahua interactions with the divine, each chapter is organized around a different aspect of indigenous interaction with Catholicism in Mexico Tenochtitlan. By exploring the multifaceted influence of Nahuas on Christianity, this work argues that the spread and growth of Catholicism happened in Mexico Tenochtitlan because of the support it received from its doctrineros, later parishioners, at the community level. Without indigenous people providing the necessary accoutrements, teaching each other, and otherwise embracing the image of Catholicism, the Church would not have been as prominent as it became. Though the religion was introduced into Mexico Tenochtitlan during the 1520s, by 1550 it was pervasive. The residents of the city clearly influenced its development so much that by 1700 they openly fought with religious leaders to present the Nahua view of the faith in their religious dramas.

As the center of Nahua religious faith and practice in Mexico Tenochtitlan, the chapel of San Josef de los Naturales was a constant presence in indigenous life during the sixteenth and seventeenth centuries. The chapel and doctrina of San Josef became the hub of most indigenous activity in the capital, and Nahua parishioners soon came to claim many of the chapel's buildings and ceremonial activities as their own.[6] Through an examination of indigenous testaments and other important sources (e.g., census records, mendicant chronicles, Nahua annals, parish records, pictorial codices, and religious dramas), the significance of women in Nahua Catholicism, the centrality of religious brotherhoods, and the veneration of the saints in colonial life become apparent. Moreover, the book addresses the parish organization of the altepetl and the various religious facilities that were established in it and focuses on the Franciscans' use of three pedagogical tools—alphabetic script, music, and theater—and the spread and adoption of those tools by the community.

This monograph stems from an effort to tell the history of life at a building, specifically, the main Nahua chapel of San Josef de los Naturales in the Franciscan religious compound of San Francisco in Mexico Tenochtitlan. My original goal was to explain more fully what transpired at San Josef during the colonial period, and more specifically how the Nahuas interacted at the religious site. Because it was the largest religious space in sixteenth-century Mexico City, their chapel made the Nahuas very proud. The prominence of San Josef can be witnessed in Francisco Cervantes de Salazar's 1554 account of Charles V's burial memorial in Mexico City. San Josef was chosen for the event over the cathedral because the cathedral was too small to fit the burial monument. Moreover, Cervantes de Salazar relates that the chapel combined with the courtyard of San Francisco was able to accommodate forty thousand people for the event, making it one of the largest public spaces in the city.[7]

Although I found a significant amount of information on the chapel, as is often the case the final product is not what was initially intended but rather the result of the twists and turns of the information provided by the sources. The scope of the research necessarily broadened to include all of Mexico Tenochtitlan, rather than solely the chapel of San Josef, a move necessitated by the available sources and the division of the doctrina of San Josef into four, and eventually six, indigenous parishes. Despite the shift to a broader focus on Mexico Tenochtitlan, the aim continued to be the exploration of Nahua interactions with Catholicism in the viceregal capital. Because of the size and prominence of the chapel of San Josef within Nahua life in Mexico Tenochtitlan and the initial emphasis on its parishioners, there is a definite slant toward Nahuas associated with the Franciscans and the parish of San Josef especially, as opposed to any of the other five parishes or other mendicant orders. Additionally, because of the chapel's prominence there are more sources dealing with San Josef than with other chapels in Mexico Tenochtitlan.

The research for this project draws from an extensive corpus of Nahuatl documentation as well as sources written in Spanish. Prior to this research there were fewer than thirty known indigenous testaments from Mexico Tenochtitlan and Tlatelolco. My research has increased that total for the period under study to ninety (see appendix 4). Written in Spanish and Nahuatl, these wills come from seven different archives in three different countries. These sources are supplemented by additional and equally rare Nahuatl materials, such as a fiscal report on an inheritance dispute (appendix 3) and documents related to the operations of the chapel of San Josef (see appendix 2 for examples). These sources along with the better known chronicles of the colonial period have provided us an opportunity to revise our understanding of a wide range of subjects, including the religious-spatial organization of Mexico Tenochtitlan, the influence of mendicant technical instruction on community life, the role of indigenous women in the community of Mexico Tenochtitlan, the support of indigenous community cohesiveness through religious brotherhoods, and Nahua involvement in the production, sale, and consumption of Catholic paraphernalia. In its entirety the book contributes a new ethnohistory of the Catholic Church in Mexico Tenochtitlan by examining its institutional history and the material culture of Nahua devotion.

In an effort to understand indigenous interactions with the divine in the most cosmopolitan urban center in New Spain, I attempted to limit sources to those from or dealing specifically with Mexico Tenochtitlan. However, at times, for comparative purposes or because of a dearth of source material, I extended the range of documents. The preference in these situations was to look at Tlatelolco, given its proximity (and at times similarity of situation) to Mexico Tenochtitlan, not to mention its position as the northern half of Mexico City. Moreover, on occasion it was either prudent or necessary to go beyond my primary focus, and in these instances special notations are made.

Although the research initially focused on the indigenous chapel, larger questions are considered. How did Nahuas interact with Christianity in greater Mexico City? How was the religion supported and maintained? How did it spread through the community? Who was responsible for the outward expression of the religion over the *longue durée*, the mendicants who introduced it or the Nahuas who practiced it? What role did the Nahuas play in colonial religion? Where possible I sought an indigenous view of events before a Spanish perspective. For certain periods of time, such as the early seventeenth century, this was made considerably easier by the writings of indigenous annalists, especially don Domingo de San Antón Muñón Chimalpahin Quauhtlehuanitzin. At other times, for example, the end of the seventeenth century, there is a dearth of eyewitness Nahua accounts, and for this reason I rely more heavily on other sources, as in the case of the chronicle by the Franciscan fray Agustín de Vetancurt. When possible, I corroborate chronicles and annals of any type with archival sources.

Historiographic Context

Colonial Mexican historiography has not ignored Mexico City and its two constituent altepetl. As the center of power, it necessarily receives mention in many monographs focusing on central Mexico, if not areas farther removed as well. The historiography of the area starts, as with so many other histories of Mexico, with nineteenth-century historian William Prescott's *History of the Conquest of Mexico*.[8] For the bulk of his narrative Prescott depended on Spanish chroniclers and their interpretation of events, especially the conflicts, victories, and losses that ensued on both sides. His interest in Mexico Tenochtitlan was as the capital of the Aztec Empire and its eventual defeat at the hands of Cortés.

Following in the vein of Prescott and his use of Spanish chronicles for primary sources was the early twentieth-century French historian Robert Ricard.[9] However, Ricard also used collected volumes of published primary sources, even publishing some of his own, and Spanish archival materials. Moreover, whereas Prescott focused on the military conflicts inherent in the initial contact period, Ricard examined the history of the Catholic Church and its endeavors in a "spiritual conquest" of the natives of New Spain. More important for this research was Ricard's shift away from focusing on Mexico Tenochtitlan as the capital of the Aztec Empire and looking at it instead as the headquarters of many mendicant endeavors. As a historian of religion and a missionary himself, Ricard focused on both religious preaching and teaching. Although his work expands beyond the scope of Prescott's both geographically and temporally, it concludes in 1572, claiming that a successful "spiritual conquest" of Mexico had been realized by this time. His reliance on Spanish and especially religious sources led to his conclusion. Though biased toward a Spanish point of view, Ricard's work is invaluable as a starting point for information on sixteenth-century mendicant activities in Mexico City and the chapel of San Josef de los Naturales in particular.

Art historians, especially those interested in architecture, have also proved invaluable. Manuel Toussaint pioneered the field in the early twentieth century. But he, like Ricard, focused on Spanish evidence.[10] George Kubler helped to bring the indigenous perspective to greater prominence. Kubler's midcentury work, *Mexican Architecture of the Sixteenth Century*, was, like Ricard's, far more geographically encompassing than Prescott's work. He both traveled to Mexico to examine the architecture and mined the Spanish chronicles and other primary sources to reconstruct buildings that had been prominent during the sixteenth century but were destroyed during the nineteenth century, such as San Josef.[11] More recently, Eleanor Wake's *Framing the Sacred: Indian Churches of Early Colonial Mexico* reexamines indigenous colonial architecture and art to demonstrate that the indigenous understanding and care of religious space speaks of continuity in the midst of change. To use her words, the natives became "the architectural and iconographical embodiment of the Indo-Christian sacred."[12]

Charles Gibson, perhaps more than any other historian of his time, shed light on indigenous life in colonial New Spain. Although his first book, *Tlaxcala in the Sixteenth Century*, was not focused on Mexico City, it is important in the overall historiography of Mesoamerican social history. By using a wide range of sources, Gibson demonstrated that the indigenous government of Tlaxcala had not been subsumed by Spanish dictates but rather had adopted aspects of Spanish culture and altered them to fit its needs.[13] His opus that followed, *The Aztecs under Spanish Rule*, carried his research beyond the important altepetl of Tlaxcala and the sixteenth century. These two studies were pivotal in creating a more comprehensive understanding of colonial Mexican history. For *Aztecs under Spanish Rule,* Gibson used published chronicles and Nahuatl and Spanish-language archival materials.[14] Unfortunately, some of his sources, such as a list of tribute records for the chapel of San Josef held at the Archivo Histórico, Museo Nacional in Mexico City, were lost during the relocation of archival materials to other collections. Because of the loss of the materials, his research has become all the more valuable.

As Gibson's work served to illustrate the need to examine the indigenous perspective of the history of New Spain, the research of James Lockhart, Frances Karttunen, and others helped to provide a real emphasis on indigenous-language documents. Lockhart's *Nahuas after the Conquest* examined the history of the indigenous peoples of central Mexico using philological analyses of Nahuatl documents. Lockhart, as with Gibson, supplied a plethora of information about Mexico Tenochtitlan. His emphasis in regard to Mexico

Tenochtitlan specifically was its position as the center of colonial interaction and language change.[15]

My monograph is a social, cultural, and religious history. It benefits from the work of the scholars mentioned above, but other historians from Mexico, France, and the United States have influenced it as well. The work of historians Miguel León-Portilla, fray Francisco Morales, and Serge Gruzinski, to name a few, have all had an impact. This research is, in a way, an offshoot of work examining the exchange of European and indigenous religious ideas, the most important of which is Louise Burkhart's work *The Slippery Earth*.[16] When Gibson started looking at the indigenous side of colonial Mexican history, other scholars, such as Charles Dibble, looked at the impact of Nahua religion on Catholicism, suggesting that perhaps the Nahuas were not fully converted after all.[17] In 1989, Louise Burkhart published *The Slippery Earth* and refuted the idea of Ricard's "spiritual conquest." She, like Lockhart, focused on indigenous-language materials. She especially examined the Nahuas' precontact and colonial worldview, looking at Nahua understandings of Christianity and the ways in which mendicant friars altered aspects of Catholicism in their educational endeavors. She found that, although the Nahuas adopted aspects of Christianity, their system of belief remained inherently indigenous. The aim of this book is to take the next step and examine how the Nahuas physically and socially interacted with temporal Catholicism.

This research also fits into a growing historiography of colonial Mexico City. Work by Alfonso Caso, Douglas Cope, María Castañeda de la Paz, Linda Curcio-Nagy, Brian Larkin, and Francisco Morales, among others, all help to provide a sense of what life in the capital city may have been like. Susan Kellogg's work, especially, examines indigenous life in Mexico City through the lens of both Nahuatl and Spanish-language documentation. Her *Law and the Transformation of Aztec Culture* uncovers the impact of the Spanish legal system on indigenous society and culture in the viceregal capital. In her research she specifically looks outside of religion to find "patterns of everyday life." While she was conducting her research, she found that, "when ethnohistorians consider cultural change, they focus almost solely on religion." She argues that the Spanish legal system came to serve as a tool of Nahua cultural resistance and one of "cultural conversion and acculturation." She also argues that the extensive use of the Spanish legal system by Nahuas served to weaken and undercut Nahua sovereignty.[18] William Connell continued the exploration of indigenous life in Mexico City with *After Moctezuma: Indigenous Politics and Self-Government in Mexico City, 1524–1730* and found that the actions of the indigenous community supported the growth of Spanish institutions and their increased influence over indigenous governments.[19] More recently, Barbara Mundy's *Death of Aztec Tenochtitlan, the Life of Mexico City* uses colonial era maps, codices, and other ethnohistorical sources to focus on the space that the entities of Tenochtitlan and Mexico City occupied.[20] My research builds on theirs but shifts the focus to indigenous interaction within temporal Catholicism while leaving aside questions of religious belief. The findings suggest that the active celebration of Christianity in Mexico City at the community and household level may not have been sustainable without indigenous efforts. As both Kellogg and Connell demonstrate, the interactions of Nahuas with Spanish institutions supported those institutions' authority over the indigenous population, and this was no less true with Catholicism. Although the Nahuas' work with Catholicism strengthened the Church's position vis-à-vis the indigenous population, this research shows that without the efforts of the larger community, especially women, Catholicism would not have flourished. Despite the Church's authority over religious affairs, the indigenous community maintained control of aspects of its adopted faith, regardless of occasional disapproval from their religious leaders.

Volume Outline

The complexities of indigenous life in Mexico Tenochtitlan are only beginning to be uncovered. Patterns of agency, community, cultural adaptation, education, gender, leadership, and movement (such as among altepetl, barrios, and into and out of Spanish homes) are evident at varying degrees in each of the chapters. Chapter 1 examines the religious organization of Mexico Tenochtitlan briefly during the precontact period and in greater detail in the sixteenth and seventeenth centuries. It treats the initial establishment of the doctrina of San Josef de los Naturales, the division of the doctrina into four parts and then eventually six, and the Nahuas' reaction to the forced redistricting of their doctrina. As becomes evident, the Nahuas participated in decisions regarding their spiritual leaders. Whether rising up to secure mendicant control of their religious instruction or working as a community on behalf of their religious sites, the Nahuas of Tenochtitlan maintained an active position in the establishment of Catholicism within their neighborhoods.

The second chapter treats three aspects of Nahua religious education—literacy in the Roman alphabet, music, and religious drama—and the way the Nahuas interacted with, adopted, and altered them to fit their own cultural needs. Precontact traditions related to literacy, music, and performed religion predisposed the Nahuas to accept similar Christian practices. Regardless of their predisposition, their mendicant teachers were unprepared for the skill and aplomb the Nahuas brought to all three areas. Although each tool stands on its own, they are treated here as a progression as the Nahuas took each one and combined and manipulated them in ways distinct from their Spanish counterparts.

Although women are discussed in all chapters, their role in Nahua Catholicism is specifically highlighted in chapter 3. Considering this chapter alongside chapters 4 and 5, the importance of women to the sustenance and growth of Catholicism within the indigenous community becomes evident. Although they no longer held their traditional positions of recognized authority within the new colonial regime, it is clear that the indigenous community continued to accord women respect and authority at unofficial levels at least until the mid-seventeenth century. Indeed, without their positions in the household and marketplace it is unlikely that Catholicism would have been sustained at the community level.

Chapter 4 focuses on Nahua cofradías in Mexico Tenochtitlan. Though the cofradías were initially organized by fray Pedro de Gante, they seemingly operated independent of most ecclesiastical oversight. The growth and change in the types of cofradías formed during the sixteenth and seventeenth centuries are suggestive of the continuance of Nahua community identity, its continued support of interactions with divinity, and the slow integration of numerous other cultural groups in Mexico Tenochtitlan.

Chapter 5 explores the growth of a market for religious goods in the Nahua marketplaces of Mexico City. This chapter, by virtue of its focus on the goods necessary to support the function of Catholicism on an official as well as personal level, highlights interactions with divinity at its most basic level. It starts by examining the development of an initial market for Catholic goods among Spaniards and follows an increase in their demand with the development of Nahua cofradías and the eventual adoption of iconic saint veneration and the construction of personal shrines in Nahua households. Examination of the space in and around the marketplaces further suggests that women were critical in creating a space for the exchange of religious goods in the colonial marketplace.

In sum, each chapter demonstrates an important facet of indigenous life that coincided with Catholic practice, or the colonial divine, and then came to take on a life of its own within the native community. As a conclusion, "Refashioning Nahua-Divine Interactions" brings everything together to show how Nahuas directed the continuities and changes to their interactions with the divine during the colonial period. The results are as Nahua as their celebrations of the divine during the precontact period.

The timeframe of the chapters concludes around 1700. The chapel of San Josef itself remained an indigenous parish until the second half of the eighteenth century. This timeframe coincides with Hapsburg rule and ties into the new questions raised by the onset of Bourbon Reforms during the mid-eighteenth century. These are important questions, but looking at indigenous interactions with mendicant facilities during the regular orders' decline in New Spain and then examining the native ties to the now secular parishes raise enough questions for another book and so are left for just such an undertaking. Although it does not answer questions in relation to the Bourbon Reforms, the Epilogue fills in some of the seventy-two-year gap and continues to follow the life of the chapel of San Josef de los Naturales and the friary of San Francisco to their present-day remains.

Notes

1. The island of Mexico City comprised two altepetl during the colonial period, Mexico Tenochtitlan (in the south) and Mexico Tlatelolco (to the north). The main focus of this research is on Mexico Tenochtitlan. However, traffic between the two areas was fluid during this period, and at times I use information from Tlatelolco either when no similar material is available for Tenochtitlan or to provide additional supporting evidence. Thus I use the specific place names when I refer to each altepetl. At times reference to the entire island becomes necessary. In these instances I use Mexico City.

2. Charles Gibson, *The Aztecs under Spanish Rule: A History of the Indians of the Valley of Mexico, 1519–1810* (Stanford, Calif.: Stanford University Press, 1964), pp. 17–24.

3. Eleanor Wake, *Framing the Sacred: The Indian Churches of Early Colonial Mexico* (Norman: University of Oklahoma Press, 2010), p. 7.

4. The Spanish translation of "confraternity" is *cofradía*. I opt to use the Spanish term, which I use interchangeably with "sodality" and "brotherhood." To prevent confusion with Jesuit sodalities, I use "congregation," following Jesuit convention in New Spain, when referring to Jesuit indigenous brotherhoods.

5. The term "Nahua" comes from the language, Nahuatl, spoken by the majority of indigenous peoples in central Mexico at this time. Although the book is predominantly concerned with Mexico Tenochtitlan (and, at times, Mexico Tlatelolco), I use the term "Nahua" rather than "Mexica," the name of the principal indigenous group belonging to this altepetl, because of the constant migration of other Nahuatl-speaking peoples from outlying altepetl to the island capital. I employ "Mexica" on occasion, when referencing an indigenous work identified as such. Similarly, when possible, other indigenous groups, such as the Mixtecs and Otomis, are referred to by their proper names when such information is available. I avoid the title "Aztec" except in reference to the precontact empire.

6. When the mendicant orders arrived in New Spain, they established doctrinas for the instruction of the indigenous peoples in Christian doctrine. The term *parroquia* (parish) began to be used around the 1560s. Though *doctrina* and *parroquia*, in this instance, both mean parish, there were initially two different concepts associated with them. Whereas a doctrina was intended to teach Christian doctrine to its parishioners, the members of a parroquia, presumably, already knew the Christian doctrine. I use the term *doctrina* in reference to San Josef prior to the 1560s and *parish* for everything else. The two terms continued to be used interchangeably in the seventeenth and eighteenth centuries.

7. Francisco Cervantes de Salazar, *México en 1554 y túmulo imperial*, ed. Edmundo O'Gorman (México: Editorial Porrúa, 1963), pp. 183–185.

8. William H. Prescott, *History of the Conquest of Mexico* (New York: Modern Library, 2001).

9. Robert Ricard, *The Spiritual Conquest of Mexico: An Essay on the Apostolate and the Evangelizing Methods of the Mendicant Orders in New Spain: 1523–1572*, trans. Lesley Byrd Simpson (Berkeley: University of California Press, 1966).

10. Manuel Toussaint, *Arte colonial en México* (México: Universidad Nacional Autonoma de México, Instituto de Investigaciones Esteticas, 1948).

11. George Kubler, *Mexican Architecture of the Sixteenth Century*, 2 vols. (New Haven, Conn.: Yale University Press, 1948).

12. Wake, *Framing*, 256.

13. Charles Gibson, *Tlaxcala in the Sixteenth Century* (New Haven, Conn.: Yale University Press, 1952).

14. Gibson, *Aztecs.* His use of Nahuatl sources should not be confused with knowledge of the language. The sources he used, such as the Codex Valeriano, often included images or Spanish glosses.

15. James Lockhart, *The Nahuas after the Conquest: A Social and Cultural History of the Indians of Central Mexico, Sixteenth through Eighteenth Centuries* (Stanford, Calif.: Stanford University Press, 1992).

16. Louise M. Burkhart, *The Slippery Earth: Nahua-Christian Moral Dialogue in Sixteenth-Century Mexico* (Tucson: University of Arizona Press, 1989).

17. Charles Dibble, "The Nahuatlization of Christianity," in *Sixteenth-Century Mexico: The Work of Sahagún,* ed. Munro S. Edmonson (Albuquerque: University of New Mexico Press, 1974), pp. 225–233.

18. Susan Kellogg, *Law and the Transformation of Aztec Culture, 1500–1700* (Norman: University of Oklahoma Press, 1995), pp. 213–215.

19. William F. Connell, *After Moctezuma: Indigenous Politics and Self-Government in Mexico City, 1524–1730* (Norman: University of Oklahoma Press, 2011), p. 28.

20. Barbara E. Mundy, *The Death of Aztec Tenochtitlan, the Life of Mexico City* (Austin: University of Texas, 2015), p. 10.

Chapter 1
Nahua Jurisdictions of the Divine in Mexico Tenochtitlan

During the prehispanic period and long after the collapse of the Aztec Empire, the most important indigenous organizational unit was the altepetl. Altepetl could range in size, though they were typically comparable to Mediterranean city-states.[1] When Hernando Cortés arrived in 1519, the most powerful altepetl in central Mexico was Tenochtitlan, situated on an island in the middle of Lake Texcoco. At the time, Tenochtitlan was divided into four divisions, or *barrios,* as the Spaniards referred to them.[2] In order of importance they were Moyotlan, Teopan, Atzacualco, and Cuepopan.[3] Each in turn received a Spanish saint's name: San Juan (Moyotlan), San Pablo (Teopan), San Sebastián (Atzacualco), and Santa María la Redonda (Cuepopan).[4] The ruler of the altepetl was the principal *tlatoani.* Each barrio was also governed by a tlatoani; indeed, the principal tlatoani was usually the ruler in one of the barrios as well. The barrios themselves consisted of smaller units known as tlaxilacalli, and some tlaxilacalli contained their own sub-tlaxilacalli (fig. 3). Responsibilities to the principal tlatoani, such as delivering tribute goods and providing labor drafts, rotated among the barrios.[5]

After the conquest of Tenochtitlan, Cortés and fray Pedro de Gante echoed prehispanic organizational strategies when they ordered the establishment of the Nahua *doctrina* (loosely a parish, but for the indoctrination of non-Christians) of San Josef de los Naturales.[6] The principal chapel was based in the Franciscan friary of San Francisco in the barrio of San Juan Moyotlan and was dedicated to San Josef.[7] The Spaniards also implemented a *visita* system in the four barrios. If the urban visita system operated similar to the rural visitas, nonresident friars walked from their friary to each of the visita chapels to perform their religious duties.[8] Each of the four original visita chapels in Mexico Tenochtitlan was named after the barrio's patron saint. The four visitas were subordinate to the chapel of San Josef de los Naturales in the doctrina hierarchical system. Scattered across the barrios, in the various tlaxilacalli, were the even smaller *ermitas* (neighborhood chapels). The ermitas were typically dedicated to a saint or other symbol of the Catholic faith. The evidence suggests that one of the four original visitas, or the chapel of San Josef itself, oversaw each of the ermitas.

FIGURE 3. Map of Mexico City by José Antonio Alzate, 1770s. BNP MSS Mexicain 150. Courtesy of the Bibliothèque nationale de France.

At its inception, the chapel of San Josef was assigned a chaplain. The chaplain, like other Franciscans in the order, rotated among the friaries, so the Nahuas did not always know their chaplain before his appointment to a particular chapel. For this reason, the Nahua chapel staff was integral to the establishment of a relationship between the chaplain and the community. Although the same individual could hold the same staff position on multiple occasions, the positions tended to rotate among the literate male parishioners. The hierarchy of religious buildings, their placement, dedication to different religious figures, and rotation of positions of authority were all reminiscent of precontact traditions in both the secular and religious spheres.[9] Positions of leadership were prestigious and hierarchical. Nahuas used these positions for social and political mobility.

Because of the similarities between the precontact and early colonial altepetl political and religious jurisdictions, in many instances the Nahuas of Mexico Tenochtitlan were able to adapt their traditions effectively to the new Hispanic system. This chapter examines how initiatives by the Nahua community capitalized on Spanish political institutions and helped to shape the political and religious institutions and landscape of Mexico Tenochtitlan. Specifically at question is how the Nahuas interacted with the established indigenous Catholic hierarchy within the doctrina/parish system, with geographic space, and with the physical buildings of the religion. Ultimately, Spaniards and Nahuas understood the structures of the faith and the space they occupied differently, but it was the Nahuas' use of them on a daily basis that gave them meaning.

San Josef was the most important and populous of the chapels, as seen by its prominence when it came to political decision making. Because of the chapel's importance, my research focuses primarily on the Nahuas' use of it, its multiple visitas, and the Nahua-established ermitas for their own particular religious purposes. The chapter also treats the manner in which the indigenous parishioners of San Josef financially supported and used each site for religious and social advancement. By examining the nature, operation, and support of these areas, the chapter also explores interethnic relations and parishioner-religious interactions. At times, when information is missing for San Josef or when a situation at another chapel more clearly demonstrates what the political, social, or cultural environment was like, I include it, as well as an occasional reference to the northern half of the island of Mexico City, Santiago Tlatelolco.

Although exact figures are uncertain, it is estimated that in 1519 the population of Mexico City numbered between 250,000 and 400,000 inhabitants, making it larger than any European city at the time. Yet by the 1560s the tributary population was around 21,636, with a total population of approximately 75,665. The indigenous population of Mexico City experienced steady decline until the middle of the seventeenth century.[10] Even with a reduced population, however, the Nahuas' dedication to their Catholic chapels continued to expand. They voluntarily worked to increase the number of indigenous chapels and staff members. At times their maneuvers profoundly affected the debate between the secular Church (headed by the archbishop) and the mendicant orders regarding the organization of parishes in Mexico Tenochtitlan.[11]

Tlaxilacalli Space within the Altepetl

The origin story of the Mexica is based on their main deity, Huitzilopochtli. When the Mexica settled on the island of Mexico Tenochtitlan, Huitzilopochtli instructed them to distribute the calpolli gods among the newly formed quarters of Tenochtitlan (Moyotlan, Teopan, Atzaqualco, and Cuepopan; see table 1).[12] The process of distributing the deities among the barrios and tlaxilacalli most likely followed a preexisting hierarchy of gods. This hierarchy may have conformed to the organization of the barrios and tlaxilacalli as well. Indigenous chronicler don Hernando de Alvarado Tezozomoc supports this theory, stating that there were seven neighborhoods, each with the name of a god, such as "Quetzalcoatl, Xocomo y Matla, Xochiquetzal y Chichitic, Çentutl y Piltzinteuctli." Beyond this, each neighborhood also had designated locations of worship for better-known gods such as Huitzilopochtli and Mictlantecuhtli.[13] As suggested by Tezozomoc, religion was very much associated with the geographic and political organization of the precontact altepetl.

In their chronicles, Tezozomoc and don Domingo de San Antón Muñón Chimalpahin Quauhtlehuanitzin (b. 1579) provide the names of the first fifteen tlaxilacalli: Yopico, Tlacochcalco, Huitznahuac, Tlacatecpan, Tzonmolco, Atempan, Tezcacoac, Tlamatzinco, Mollocotitlan, Nonohualco, Çihuatecpan, Izquitlan, Milnahuac, Coatl Xoxouhcan, and Aticpac. Each of the tlaxilacalli were beholden to a specific deity, with the sixteenth, unnamed, belonging to Huitzilopochtli.[14] Typically most altepetl were organized in even numbers, as in the case of the barrios for Tenochtitlan.[15] It is likely that these original tlaxilacalli were a part of the larger barrio units, with four belonging to each. This is suggested by the fact that two of the original sixteen tlaxilacalli names appear in extant documentation, Yopico and Huitznahuac (or Huitznahuatonco).[16]

Alfonso Caso has uncovered the location of multiple tlaxilacalli in Mexico Tenochtitlan. Using an array of additional sources, I have been able to complement his work, as seen in table 1, although doubtless more sites will be known in the future. By knowing the Nahuatl name for these locations it is, at times, possible to understand how Nahuas ordered their precontact life. For example, the *cihuateocaltitlan* (place of the women's temple) may have been a place beholden to priestesses during the prehispanic period. With this

TABLE 1. Tlaxilacalli in the Barrios of San Juan Moyotlan, San Pablo Teopan, San Sebastián Atzacualco, and Santa María la Redonda Cuepopan in Mexico Tenochtitlan, 1524–1700

Barrio/ Tlaxilacalli	*Chapel/ Ermita/Visita*	*Dates of Documentary Appearance*	*Source*
San Juan Moyotlan	San Josef and San Juan de la Penetencia	1564, 1592, 1697	Vetancurt, *Teatro*, pt. 2, p. 69; Bautista, *¿Cómo te confundes?*, p. 283; AGN, Indios, v. 6, e. 341, fs. 91–91v; v. 6, e. 344, fs. 92–92v
Acaztlan	Ermita	1578	AGN, Tierras, v. 39, pt. 1, e. 2
Amanalco (San Diego de)	Ermita	1557, 1563, 1566, 1596, 1632, 1634, 1636–1637, 1697	Vetancurt, *Teatro*, pt. 2, pp. 42–43; AGN, Tierras, v. 29, e. 5; v. 45, e. 3; v. 70, e. 4; v. 1720, e. 7, f. 2v; AGN, Civil, v. 1271, e. 4, fs. 76–83
Atizapan (El Descendimiento de) (Community of Nahuas from Cuernavaca lives here)	Ermita	1565, 1640, 1697	AGN, Bienes Nacionales, v. 387, e. 1; Vetancurt, *Teatro*, pt. 2, pp. 42–43; Bautista, *¿Cómo te confundes?*, p. 299
Atlampa (La Candelaria de)	Ermita and bell tower	1697	Vetancurt, *Teatro*, pt. 2, pp. 42–43
Chichimecapan (San Juan de) (Otomi tlaxilacalli)	Ermita and bell tower	1697	Vetancurt, *Teatro*, pt. 2, pp. 42–43
Cihuateocaltitlan (San Pedro de)		1592, 1697	Vetancurt, *Teatro*, pt. 2, pp. 42–43; AGN, Hospital de Jesús, leg. 298, pt. 1, e. 4; AGN, Tierras, v. 2728, e. 3
Copolco (San Sebastián)[a] (Otomi tlaxilacalli)		1697	Vetancurt, *Teatro*, pt. 2, pp. 42–43
Huehuecalco (Santa Verónica de)		1564, 1565, 1585, 1592, 1594, 1603, 1604, 1612, 1621, 1636–1637, 1697	Vetancurt, *Teatro*, pt. 2, pp. 42–43; Bautista, *¿Cómo te confundes?*, pp. 283, 317; Chimalpahin, *Annals*, pp. 51, 53, 233; AGN, Civil, v. 1271, e. 4; v. 1763, e. 2; AGN, Tierras, v. 84, e. 2; v. 1810, e. 1; AGN, Bienes Nacionales, v. 1455, e. 5; AGN, Hospital de Jesús, leg. 298, pt. 1, e. 4

(continued on next page)

TABLE 1 (*continued*)

Barrio/ Tlaxilacalli	*Chapel/ Ermita/Visita*	*Dates of Documentary Appearance*	*Source*
Hueyastacalco (San Cristóbal)		1636–1637	AGN, Civil, v. 1271, e. 4; Caso, *Los barrios*, p. 12
Necaltitlan (San Salvador de)	Ermita and bell tower	1564, 1586, 1588, 1595, 1697	Vetancurt, Teatro, pt. 2, pp. 42–43; Bautista, *¿Cómo te confundes?*, p. 287; AGN, Tierras, v. 59, e. 3, f. 186
Oquitoco		1551	AGN, Tierras, v. 20 pt. 1, e. 3; pt. 2 e. 1
Quauhchinanco[b]		1578	AGN, Tierras, v. 39, pt. 1 e. 2
Tecpancaltitlan (Santa Cruz de)		1592, 1593, 1599, 1642, 1697	Vetancurt, *Teatro*, pt. 2, pp. 42–43; AGN, Bienes Nacionales, v. 1281, e. 1; AGN, Hospital de Jesús, leg. 298, pt. 1, e. 4; NL, Ayer, MS 1481, F5; BNP, FM, 112
Teocaltitlan (San Felipe de Jesús de)		1578, 1592, 1593, 1634, 1697, 1703	Vetancurt, *Teatro*, pt. 2, pp. 42–43; AGN, Tierras, v. 39 pt. 1, e. 2; v. 1720, e. 7; v. 396, e. 6, f. 18; AGN, Hospital de Jesús, leg. 298, pt. 1, e. 4
Tepetitlan (El Niño Jesús de)		1566, 1604, 1616, 1636–1637, 1697, 1712	Vetancurt, *Teatro*, pt. 2, pp. 42–43; Chimalpahin, *Annals*, p. 85; AGN, Tierras, v. 29, e. 5; v. 101, e. 2; v. 112, e. 2; AGN, Civil, v. 1271, e. 4, fs. 76–83
Tequicaltitlan (Los Reyes de)	Ermita	1564, 1589, 1595, 1612–1613, 1670, 1697	Vetancurt, *Teatro*, pt. 2, pp. 42–43; Bautista, *¿Cómo te confundes?*, p. 237; Chimalpahin, *Annals*, pp. 233, 241; AHCV, est. 9, tab. 2, v. 28, e. 9; AGN, Tierras, v. 55, e. 2
Tequixquipan (La Navidad de)	Ermita de Montserrat	1564, 1589, 1594, 1595, 1636–1637, 1697	Vetancurt, *Teatro*, pt. 2, pp. 42–43; Bautista, *¿Cómo te confundes?*, p. 287; Chimalpahin, *Annals*, pp. 33, 47, 53; AGN, Civil, v. 1271, e. 4, fs. 76–83

(continued on next page)

TABLE 1 (*continued*)

Barrio/ Tlaxilacalli	*Chapel/ Ermita/Visita*	*Dates of Documentary Appearance*	*Source*
Tianquiztenco		1592, 1596, 1615, 1640	AGN, Tierras, v. 70, e. 4; v. 3553, e. 5; AGN, Bienes Nacionales, v. 387, e. 1, f. 15; AGN, Hospital de Jesús, leg. 298, pt. 1, e. 4
Tezcatzonco (San Antonio de) (Otomi tlaxilacalli)		1698	Vetancurt, *Teatro*, pt. 2, pp. 42–43
Tlachquac		1574	AGN, Tierras, v. 22, pt. 1, e. 4
Tlatilco		1558, 1564, 1565, 1587, 1596, 1619	Bautista, *¿Cómo te confundes?*, pp. 291, 303; AGN, Tierras, v. 17, pt. 2, e. 4; v. 54, e. 5; v. 70, e. 4; ANM, Hernando de Arauz #4, v. 7, yrs. 1619–1622, fs. 7–12v
Tlaxilpan (Santiago de)	Ermitas (number unspecified) and bell tower. One ermita named Santiago	1693, 1697	Vetancurt, *Teatro*, pt. 2, pp. 42–43; AGN, Bienes Nacionales, v. 677, e. 8
Tzapotlan (Santo Christo de)		1612, 1669, 1697	Vetancurt, *Teatro*, pt. 2, pp. 42–43; AGN, Tierras, v. 30, e. 1; AGN, Bienes Nacionales, v. 1455, pt. 2, e. 5
Xacalpan		1567, 1605, 1636–1637	AGN, Civil, v. 1271, e. 4, fs. 76–83; AGN, Bienes Nacionales, v. 549, e. 7; v. 965, e. 6, f. 10
Xihuitongo (San Salvador de)	Ermita	1576, 1587, 1589, 1592, 1648, 1697	Vetancurt, *Teatro*, pt. 2, pp. 42–43; AGN, Tierras, v. 38, e. 2; v. 54, e. 5; v. 55, e. 2; AGN, Bienes Nacionales, v. 1766, e. 7; AGN, Hospital de Jesús, leg. 298, pt. 1, e. 4
Xihuitongo [?] (San Juan Bautista de)[c]	Visita de San Juan de la Penetencia	1697	Vetancurt, *Teatro*, pt. 2, pp. 42–43
Yaotlica		1575, 1592	AGN, Bienes Nacionales, v. 1581, e. 6, fs. 65–66; AGN, Hospital de Jesús, leg. 298, pt. 1, e. 4

(continued on next page)

TABLE 1 (*continued*)

Barrio/ Tlaxilacalli	*Chapel/ Ermita/Visita*	*Dates of Documentary Appearance*	*Source*
Yopico (Espíritu Santo de)		1570, 1578, 1592, 1595, 1598, 1697	Vetancurt, *Teatro*, pt. 2, pp. 42–43; AGN, Tierras, v. 30, e. 3, f. 226; v. 39 pt. 1, e. 2; v. 63, e. 2; v. 2728, e. 3; AGN, Hospital de Jesús, leg. 298, pt. 1, e. 4; AHCV, est. 9, tab. 2, v. 28, e. 9
San Pablo Teopan	San Pablo		Chimalpahin, *Annals*, p. 41
Almanalco		1580	AGN, Tierras, v. 49, e. 5
Apepetzapan		1566	AGN, Tierras, v. 48, e. 4
Ateponasco		1629, 1636–1637, 1667, 1691, 1703,	AGN, Tierras, v. 95, pt. 2, e. 8, fs. 465– 465v; v. 109, e. 4, f. 1; v. 163, e. 2; v. 1774, e. 10; AGN, Civil, v. 1271, e. 4, fs. 76–83
Coatlayauhcan[d]		1565	Bautista, *¿Cómo te confundes?*, p. 299
Çoquipan (San Agustín)		1565, 1611–1613, 1636–1637, 1747	Chimalpahin, *Annals*, p. 193, 229, 233; Bautista, *¿Cómo te confundes?*, p. 299; AGN, Civil, v. 1271, e. 4, fs. 76–83; AGN, Tierras, v. 946, e. 5, fs. 1–6
Cuezcontitlan (San Lucas)	Ermita		Caso, *Los barrios*, p. 19; and Morales, "Santoral franciscano," p. 361
Huitznahuatonco		1564, 1636–1637	Bautista, *¿Cómo te confundes?*, p. 221; AGN, Civil, v. 1271, e. 4, fs. 76–83
Iznahuatonco			Caso, *Los barrios*, p. 21
Malcuitlapilco (La Candelaria or La Purificación)	Ermita: La Candelaria	1636–1637, 1644, 1655, 1662–1663, 1673	AGN, Tierras, v. 2776, e. 18, fs. 191, 212; AGN, Civil, v. 1271, e. 4, fs. 76–83; UNAM FRAF, caja 96, e. 1413
Ometochtitlan		1565, 1612–1613, 1636–1637	Chimalpahin, *Annals*, pp. 229, 233; Bautista, *¿Cómo te confundes?*, p. 299; AGN, Civil, v. 1271, e. 4, fs. 76–83

(*continued on next page*)

Table 1 (*continued*)

Barrio/ Tlaxilacalli	*Chapel/ Ermita/Visita*	*Dates of Documentary Appearance*	*Source*
Temascaltitlan		1667	AGN, Tierras, v. 109, e. 4, f. 10; and Caso, *Los barrios*, p. 22
Teocaltitlan (San Hipólito)		1564, 1574, 1594–1595, 1599, 1615, 1648, 1686, 1692, 1694–1695, 1701, 1712	Bautista, *¿Cómo te confundes?*, p. 193; Chimalpahin, *Annals*, pp. 47, 51; *Codex Valeriano*, UNAM FRAF, caja 96, e. 1413; AGN, Tierras, v. 22 pt. 1, e. 4; v. 3554, e. 8; AGN, Bienes Nacionales, v. 1766, e. 7; AGN, Civil, v. 592, e. 1; v. 738, e. 4
Tlacaltitlan		1636–1637	AGN, Civil, v. 1271, e. 4, fs. 76–83
Tlachquac (San Juan)		1564	AGN, Tierras, v. 22 pt. 1, e. 5
Tla[c]hquititlan		1564, 1611, 1667	AGN, Tierras, v. 55, e. 5, fs. 16–17; v. 109, e. 4, f. 10v; Chimalpahin, *Annals*, p. 173
Tlaliçtacapan		1562, 1586, 1589	AGN, Tierras, v. 55, e. 2; v. 1595, e. 4
Toçanitla		1577–1578, 1594, 1639	Chimalpahin, *Annals*, p. 51; AGN, Bienes Nacionales, v. 339, e. 6; AGN, Tierras, v. 42, e. 5
Toltenco		1636–1637	AGN, Civil, v. 1271, e. 4, fs. 76–83
Tucanitlan		1576	AGN, Tierras, v. 37, e. 2, f. 1
Tzoquiapan			Caso, *Los barrios*, p. 21.
Zacatlalmanco (Santa Ana)	Ermita		Morales, "Santoral francis cano," p. 361; Caso, *Los barrios*, p. 21
San Antón de (Santa Cruz)[c]	Ermita: San Antón Abad: Acatlan Chiquito	1564, 1595, 1600, 1613, 1629, 1675	Bautista, *¿Cómo te confundes?*, p. 287; Chimalpahin, *Annals*, pp. 255, 257; AGN, Tierras, v. 70, e. 4; v. 95, pt. 2, e. 8, fs. 465v–466; v. 165, e. 4, f. 14
San Antón de Abad: Tepiton		1629, 1675	AGN, Tierras, v. 165, e. 4, f. 1; v. 95, pt. 2, e. 8

(continued on next page)

TABLE 1 (*continued*)

Barrio/ Tlaxilacalli	*Chapel/ Ermita/Visita*	*Dates of Documentary Appearance*	*Source*
San Antón de Abad: Xoloco, (La Conceción de or San Agustín)	Ermita: San Antón de Abad	1583, 1591, 1593, 1604, 1613, 1629, 1697	Vetancurt, *Teatro*, pt. 2, pp. 42–43; Chimalpahin, *Annals*, pp. 29, 37, 47, 85, 255–257; AGN, Tierras, v. 95, pt. 2, e. 8, f. 465
San Sebastián Atzacualco	San Sebastián		Chimalpahin, *Annals*, p. 99
Acalcaltitlan (San Lázaro)		1595	Chimalpahin, *Annals*, p. 55
Ahuatonco		1572, 1611	Chimalpahin, *Annals*, p. 175; AGN, Tierras, v. 2789, e. 1, f. 7
Atlisocan		1558, 1569	AGN, Tierras, v. 20, pt. 2, e. 4; v. 30, e. 1
Çacatlan		1562, 1569, 1571, 1572, 1584, 1636–1637	AGN, Tierras, v. 20, pt. 2, e. 4; v. 30, e. 1; v. 2729, e. 20; v. 2789, e. 1; AGN, Civil, v. 1271, e. 4, fs. 76–83
Çitlaltepec		1558	AGN, Tierras, v. 20 pt. 2, e. 4
Coatlan		1636–1637	AGN, Civil, v. 1271, e. 4, fs. 76–83
Cotolco		1571, 1595, 1636–1637	AGN, Tierras, v. 35, e. 1, f. 7; v. 58, e. 7, f. 439; AGN, Civil, v. 1271, e. 4, fs. 76–83
Cuitlahuactonco		1569, 1591, 1612, 1615, 1636–1637, 1646, 1719	Chimalpahin, *Annals*, p. 233; AGN, Tierras, v. 397, e. 3; v. 1595, e. 4; v. 3663, e. 3; AGN, Civil, v. 1271, e. 4, fs. 76–83
Teocaltitlan		1636–1637	AGN, Civil, v. 1271, e. 4, fs. 76–83
Tlamagascapan		1636–1637	AGN, Civil, v. 1271, e. 4, fs. 76–83
Tomatlan		1594, 1612, 1636–1637	Chimalpahin, *Annals*, pp. 47, 51, 233; and AGN, Civil, v. 1271, e. 4, fs. 76–83

(continued on next page)

TABLE 1 (*continued*)

Barrio/ Tlaxilacalli	*Chapel/ Ermita/Visita*	*Dates of Documentary Appearance*	*Source*
Tzahualtonco			Caso, *Los barrios*, pp. 26–27
Zacatlan		1712	AGN, Indiferente Virreinal, caja, 1124, e. 25
Xocototlan[?][f]		1691	INAH, CSG, v. 119
Santa María la Redonda Cuepopan[g] (There may also be a tlaxilacalli named Cuepopan)	Santa María de la Asunción Cuepopan		Vetancurt, *Teatro*, pt. 2, p. 83; Chimalpahin, *Annals*, p. 99
Amaxac		1558	AGN, Tierras, v. 17, pt. 2, e. 4
Analpan (Espíritu Santo de)	Ermita	1618, 1630, 1679, 1688, 1693, 1697, 1727	Vetancurt, *Teatro*, pt. 2, p. 83; NL, Ayer, MS 1481, B(3)d; AGN, Civil, v. 1271, e. 4, fs. 76–83; AGN, Tierras, v. 157, e. 7; v. 442, e. 5; v. 2241, e. 12
Apanohuayan		1576, 1587, 1592	AGN, Tierras, v. 55, e. 3; AGN, Bienes Nacionales, v. 293, e. 1; AGN, Hospital de Jesús, leg. 298, pt. 1, e. 4
Atenantitech		1558, 1613	Chimalpahin, *Annals*, p. 241; AGN, Tierras, v. 17, pt. 2, e. 4
Atlampa (San Diego)		1630, 1636–1637, 1697	Vetancurt, *Teatro*, pt. 2, p. 83; AGN, Tierras, v. 442, e. 5; AGN, Civil, v. 1271, e. 4, fs. 76–83
Ayoticpac		1604, 1613, 1615	Chimalpahin, *Annals*, p. 81, 241, 299
Cihuatlan[h]		1615	Chimalpahin, *Annals*, p. 299–301
Cohuatlan		1573, 1586, 1589	AGN, Tierras, v. 22, pt. 1, e. 4; v. 55, e. 2; AGN, Tierras v. 3663, e. 3
Colhuacatonco (San Andrés)		1587, 1592, 1636–1637, 1652, 1688, 1721	AGN, Tierras, v. 55, e. 3; v. 157, e. 7; v. 1595, e. 4; AGN, Hospital de Jesús, leg. 298, pt. 1, e. 4; AGN, Civil, v. 1271, e. 4, fs. 76–83; NL, Ayer, MS 1481, B(3)k

(continued on next page)

TABLE 1 (*continued*)

Barrio/ Tlaxilacalli	*Chapel/ Ermita/Visita*	*Dates of Documentary Appearance*	*Source*
Copolco (de Santiago)		1560, 1587, 1612, 1630, 1659, 1683, 1693, 1697, 1699	Vetancurt, *Teatro*, pt. 2, p. 83; Chimalpain, *Annals*, p. 233; AGN, Tierras, v. 39, pt. 2, e. 1; v. 55, e. 3; v. 442, e. 5; NL, Ayer, MS 1481, B(3)f; MS 1481, B(3)b; MS 1481, B(3)1
Iztacalecan		1587, 1592, 1602, 1621, 1677	NL, Ayer, MS 1481, B(3)e; AGN, Tierras, v. 55, e.3; v. 84, e. 2; AGN, Bienes Nacionales, v. 551, e. 5; AGN, Hospital de Jesús, leg. 298, pt. 1, e. 4
Quauhtepeque	Ermita: Santa María	1577	AGN, Tierras, v. 39, pt. 2, e. 1
Tescatzonco (San Antonio)		1576, 1587, 1630, 1669	AGN, Civil, v. 1271, e. 4, fs. 76–83; AGN, Tierras, v. 55, e. 3; v. 442, e. 5
Teocaltitlan (Santa Clara de)	Ermita	1586, 1590, 1592, 1636–1637, 1657, 1687, 1693–1694, 1697	Vetancurt, *Teatro*, pt. 2, p. 83; NL, Ayer, MS 1481, B(3)a; AGN, Tierras, v. 3711, e. 1, 2; AGN, Hospital de Jesús, leg. 298, pt. 1, e. 4; AGN, Civil, v. 1271, e. 4, fs. 76–83
Tlacuechiuhcan	Principal Franciscan chapel for barrio of Santa María la Redonda	1577	AGN, Tierras, v. 39, pt. 2, e. 1; Caso, *Los barrios*, p. 31
Tlalcozpan (subunit of Teocaltitlan)		1590, 1674, 1693, 1694	AGN, Tierras, v. 3711, e. 1, 2
Tlocalpan		1558, 1587, 1614, 1636–1637	Chimalpahin, *Annals*, p. 271; AGN, Tierras, v. 17, pt. 2, e. 4; v. 55, e. 3; AGN, Civil, v. 1271, e. 4, fs. 76–83
Tolpetlac		1558	AGN, Tierras, v. 17 pt. 2, e. 4
Santa Cruz Contzinco	Santa Cruz		Chimalpahin, *Annals*, p. 245
Toscaminca		1636–1637	AGN, Civil, v. 1271, e. 4, fs. 76–83

(*continued on next page*)

TABLE 1 (*continued*)

Barrio/ Tlaxilacalli	*Chapel/ Ermita/Visita*	*Dates of Documentary Appearance*	*Source*
Tlaxilacalli of unknown jurisdiction			
Texialcocolco (likely belongs to San Juan or Santa María)		1592	AGN, Hospital de Jesús, leg. 298, pt. 2, e. 4
Tolenco (San Francisco)		1592	AGN, Civil, v. 592, e. 1
Purificacion[i]		17th century	AGN, Hospital de Jesús, leg. 210, e. 4, f. 21

Note: Further research is under way on the tlaxilacalli for Mexico Tenochtitlan, but the size and scope of that project rapidly grew beyond the topic of this volume.

a. Vetancurt notes it to be a little run down: "que otro de S. Sebastián Copolco se ha consumido."

b. It is not completely clear that this tlaxilacalli is a part of San Juan. However, all of the other tlaxilacalli mentioned in the document are located in San Juan. For this reason, I tentatively believe that it too was located in San Juan.

c. Vetancurt is the only source that I have encountered that distinguishes between two Xihuitongos.

d. I am assuming that Coatlayauhcan is a tlaxilacalli of San Pablo, because the other three tlaxilacalli on the list are from San Pablo.

e. Acatlan, Xoloco, and Tepiton were all tributaries of the barrio of San Pablo. However, as discussed in chapter 1, the Nahuas of the area of San Antón managed to maintain their tie to the parish of San Josef despite the creation of the parish of San Pablo.

f. This barrio is in Mexico City. The source is a testament recorded at the Jesuit Colegio de San Gregorio. San Gregorio was in San Sebastián. I believe that Xocototlan is in San Sebastián.

g. Chapel of Nuestra Señora del Rosario, principal chapel of the Mixtecos parish. The Dominican friary was in this barrio as well. I have been unable to discover the name of the tlaxilacalli where the Dominican religious compound was located. AGN, Bienes Nacionales, v. 1766, e. 7.

h. In his annals Chimalpahin mentions that within Ayoticpac was another tlaxilacalli called Cihuatlan (Woman's Place) where the nunnery of Nuestra Señora de la Concepción was located. Chimalpahin, *Annals*, p. 299.

i. Likely San Juan Bautista, possibly same as Xihuitongo of San Juan, largely based on information from a will tying it to San Juan Bautista.

knowledge in mind, it becomes possible to compare the precontact and colonial use of the territory and thereby understand who directed the colonial organization of the altepetl, Nahuas or Spaniards.

In his study of the altepetl, James Lockhart postulated the hierarchy of the four barrios of Mexico Tenochtitlan, suggesting that each had four tlaxilacalli that likely subdivided as the altepetl grew.[17] The actual growth rate, development, and political importance of each tlaxilacalli are difficult to document, but tlaxilacalli development and division (into other tlaxilacalli and sub-tlaxilacalli) were surely tied to population growth as well as political maneuvering. The understanding of altepetl growth is best seen in the existence of specific tlaxilacalli for specific groups; at least four, and probably more, of these existed by the end of the seventeenth century. Four in San Juan—Atizapan (a tlaxilacalli with a large population of migrants from Cuernavaca), Chichimecapan (home to Chichimeca), Copolco, and Tezcatzonco—were designated as Otomi tlaxilacalli by fray Agustín de Vetancurt, with Copolco being noted as run down. Additionally, it is likely that other tlaxilacalli within the altepetl came to be associated with other migrant groups. For example, by the end of the seventeenth century San Sebastián was known to have a large population of Filipinos.[18] Had the populations of these groups not been significant, it is likely that Vetancurt would not have noticed them. If population size can be an indicator of tlaxilacalli growth, then the most populous of the barrios would tend to contain the most tlaxilacalli. If this is the case, then the majority of the indigenous population resided in southern Tenochtitlan, in San Juan and San Pablo. It is already established that, in terms of political authority in the altepetl, San Juan was primary, with San Pablo a close second. By the end of the sixteenth century, San Juan comprised twenty tlaxilacalli, San Pablo had sixteen, San Sebastián eight or nine, and Santa María fourteen.[19] By the close of the seventeenth century, the numbers for each barrio had increased (though it may well be that some of these "new" tlaxilacalli already existed during the sixteenth century): San Juan was made up of twenty-eight tlaxilacalli, San Pablo twenty-four, San Sebastián twelve or thirteen, Santa María eighteen, and Santa Cruz Contzinco (which successfully broke away from San Pablo in the early half of the seventeenth century to form its own parish, if not barrio) one or two.[20]

Alfonso Caso altered the José de Alzate map (see fig. 3), expanding on the information Alzate provided (fig. 4).[21] Alzate's map answers some questions on tlaxilacalli location, and Caso's answers others, but both raise additional questions. For example, the central *traza*—an area that was officially Spanish during the colonial period—has only two tlaxilacalli names listed within it, and both are at the very edge and have question marks next to them. This is odd, in light of the fact that at least two tlaxilacalli names, and likely many more, were established during the precontact period. Surely the most

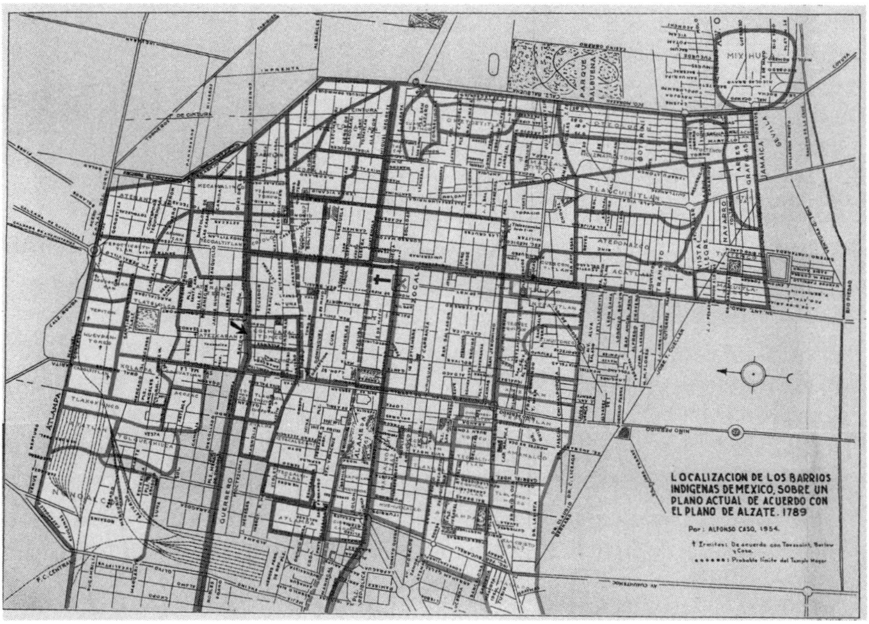

FIGURE 4. Alfonso Caso's map of Mexico City. Alfonso Caso, "Los barrios antiguos de Tenochtitlan y Tlatelolco," *Memorias de la Academia Mexicana de la Historia* XV:1 (1956), plano 1.

important ceremonial center in all of the Aztec Empire had a name associated with it.[22] Based on tlaxilacalli naming patterns, the most likely name for the center of the city was Teocaltitlan (literally, Next to the Temple). Indeed, all four barrios of Mexico Tenochtitlan are found to have a Teocaltitlan.[23] This suggests that the center of the city could have been called Teocaltitlan, with each barrio having its own toehold in the ceremonial center in the middle of the altepetl. Yet it is also probable that each barrio's main temple was built in a tlaxilacalli called Teocaltitlan, as noted in Caso.

Caso's argument is supported by another tlaxilacalli located in San Juan called Cihuateocaltitlan (Next to the Women's Temple). The existence of Cihuateocaltitlan and the four Teocaltitlans suggests that neighborhoods with important religious structures were named after them. So, although it is possible that the Teocaltitlan tlaxilacalli were not contiguous but rather located in different areas in the city, and Alzate's map supports this, it also appears that the neighborhood around the Templo Mayor possessed a name that employed the word Teocalli (God House, or Temple). The importance of the main temple is also seen in the rotation of priests, who, though frequently relatives of the main tlatoani, appear to have had responsibilities at the main temple dedicated to Huitzilopochtli.[24] Whether or not a similar rotation of priests for the barrio and tlaxilacalli temples existed is not known.

Some of the names of the tlaxilacalli clearly denote their location, such as Tecpancaltitlan (Next to the Lord's House); others like Çacatlan (Place of Grass, Weeds) are more difficult to place. That said, there are clear instances demonstrating that the identity and function of some sites in a tlaxilacalli pertained to its precontact name, as noted for Cihuatlan in Santa María la Redonda and Tianquiztenco (Edge of the Marketplace) in San Juan. According to Chimalpahin, Cihuatlan was in the tlaxilacalli of Ayoticpac, making it a sub-tlaxilacalli, but Tianquiztenco appears to be a tlaxilacalli in its own right.[25] The case of Cihuatlan seems logical, for Chimalpahin indicates that the first convent in Mexico City was established there.[26] Beyond the obvious connection, the convent also possessed two other significant ties to the prehispanic past: two granddaughters of Mocteucçoma. Though both women were *mestizas* (women of Spanish and Native American ancestry), they were two of the founding members of an otherwise all-Spanish convent.[27] The larger question is who suggested this as the location for the convent, the Nahuas or the Franciscans. It seems most likely that the Nahuas were the ones acting to maintain the precontact connection, although the Franciscans surely realized its value. The case of Tianguiztenco supports this assumption as well.

A collection of ninety-three wills (see appendix 4) from Mexico City, although closely divided between men (forty) and women (fifty), reveals that the only testators in the extant wills from Tenochtitlan to own shops or even discuss property adjacent to the marketplaces were women (though one, from 1619, mentioned a man owning a shop next to hers). These wills afford valuable information about women in or near their markets and is illustrative of gender relations, financial interactions, their homes, shops, and stalls, property transactions, and Franciscan meddling. For example, a notable element about the houses on the marketplaces is that of the five that were specifically mentioned as shops two had second stories, two had two adjoining rooms, and the final had two rooms but was unspecific as to the design. Three structures dating from 1581, 1619, and 1623 were bequeathed (one to a daughter, one to two nieces, and the other to a Nahua couple), and the other two were sold in 1596 and 1605 as part of testamentary requests.[28] The two that were sold went for 240 pesos (in 1596) and 800 pesos (in 1605), a substantial amount at this time.[29] What is also remarkable about these structures is that they possessed stores as part of their building plan. One testatrix, Petronila María, owned an additional two houses *altas y bajas* (tall and short) next to the marketplace. The homes were adjacent to those of another woman known to have owned at least one shop. On the basis of this information, it is probable that the taller of the two structures also maintained a shop. In 1619, upon her death, she sold these properties (though she bequeathed others to her nieces);

her spouse and a brother predeceased her. The amount her properties sold for is not known.[30]

According to fray Juan de Torquemada, the three markets in Mexico City, though generally open daily, had days assigned specifically to them.[31] Most vendors were women, and they set up their stalls, much as street vendors in Mexico do today, with a temporary awning for shade and a blanket used as a display rug.[32] The women who owned the permanent shops around the marketplace were financially better off than their counterparts in the plaza and likely did not move from marketplace to marketplace to sell their wares. Moreover, their location directly adjacent to the marketplace was ideal for creating foot traffic for their stores, which explains why their property held such high value. Although the women owned their structures, they do not appear to have had carte blanche regarding all transactions. Rather, it appears that the female merchants owned the buildings and enjoyed the right to sell goods on the property, but that the property adjacent to the marketplace in San Juan Moyotlan, at least (and likely in Tlatelolco to the north), was owned by the indigenous community and controlled by its leadership.

The property rights of the women and the Nahua community are most evident in a series of cases concerning Juana Mocel and her two granddaughters, Martina and Clara López. Prior to her death in 1596, Juana Mocel purchased a two-room structure located on the *tianguiz* (marketplace) of San Juan from a Franciscan friar by the name of Gerónimo de Zárate. The building had purportedly been given to the Franciscans by the owner, Mateo Juárez, in his will, with the intent of having prayers said for his soul (the sale of Juárez's property by Zárate is an interesting case and is discussed below).[33] Juárez had used the property to make and sell footwear. After his death, Mocel purchased the property from Zárate for 230 pesos, and in turn when she died she sold the property off to pay debts and to have masses said for her soul. Unfortunately, the executor of this second sale goes unmentioned. Juan García and María Gerónima, two members of the Nahua community, purchased the property.[34]

Juan García and María Gerónima owned the property for some time after Mocel's death in 1596. They sold it, with the permission of the Spanish corregidor of Mexico Tenochtitlan, to Diego Arias Dávila (a Spaniard) around 1601 (the year in which the lawsuit takes place). When Arias Dávila started building a new structure on the property, the indigenous governor, alcalde, and regidores (who had approved the previous sales) stepped forward and issued a lawsuit, claiming that he did not own the property, in spite of agreements between him, García, Gerónima, and the corregidor. The governor, alcalde, and regidores' argument was that the property did not in fact belong to any of these individuals but rather was, and always had been, the property of the indigenous community of the barrio of San Juan Moyotlan, which thus had the rights to distribute the property. Property immediately adjacent to the marketplace belonged to the community, and only its leaders could determine who might use it. Though Mateo Juárez had lived on the land and possessed the right to use the property, he could not sell the land without the community's backing. When Zárate sold the land to Mocel, then, he did so with the support of the indigenous *cabildo* (town council)—or at least the cabildo supported Mocel's use of the property. It was only when an outsider of no significant rank started operating on the property that the community perceived a problem with the land transaction.[35]

At the time of the trial, fray Gerónimo de Zárate was out of the city, which was as unfortunate at the time for the Spaniard purchasing the property as it is for those of us looking at the evidence today. What is not fully known is Zárate's understanding of the sale of the property. Was he cognizant of indigenous property rights or did he believe that the sale of land that he facilitated was done under Spanish customs? Our best source for information on Zárate comes from Chimalpahin. In 1593 the Nahua cabildo successfully petitioned for the removal of an abusive chaplain from their chapel, San Josef de los Naturales. After the chaplain's removal Zárate and another Franciscan were appointed joint chaplains of the chapel. Zárate had worked with the Nahuas of Mexico Tenochtitlan in the past, but this was his first time as their chaplain.[36] By 1612, Zárate too had started to abuse the people. As well as physical and verbal abuse, Chimalpahin relates that Zárate had also been seizing and selling property belonging to deceased Nahuas:

> And he [Zárate] would sell people's houses, the houses of the deceased that are in the various tlaxilacalli; he sought it all out and asked about it. If they told him where it was, he would right away take it from people and sell it, even if it did not belong to the church, and even if there were heirs who were truly the children or grandchildren, he would ignore them and consider them as nothing. He would actually take their houses from them, remove them from them and sell them away from them.[37]

Chimalpahin goes on to state that no one ever saw Zárate perform masses for the dead, nor did he provide anything to the property owners. Even more irritating to Chimalpahin was Zárate's zeal in searching through wills to find property belonging to the deceased that he then sought out and seized. It is not known if Zárate's sale of Mateo Juárez's property to Juana Mocel was among those reported by Chimalpahin, but certain pieces of evidence suggest it. Although Zárate had not been chaplain of San Josef for very long when the land was sold to Mocel, he sold her not one but two pieces of property (both of which were adjacent to the marketplace; the second is discussed below). He is the only Franciscan I have encountered in Mexico City who played the role of real estate agent (though others were executors for wills).[38] A further indictment of Zárate is evidence suggesting that Nahua men, in comparison to women, were much less inclined to purchase masses for their soul during the sixteenth century; rather, they preferred to pass their property and money along to family members (see chapter 3). If Mateo Juárez asked for his property to be sold, it is unlikely that he wanted the proceeds invested in masses for his soul. Whatever Zárate thought he was doing, the greater Nahua community clearly did not agree, for he was eventually relieved of his position as well. What is notable is that in this case three Spaniards (Dávila, Zárate, and the corregidor) clearly did not understand how the property surrounding the marketplace was controlled. As is discussed below, it still is not completely clear.

As noted, Zárate sold two pieces of land to Mocel. The second of these was more typical of traditional Nahua household organization, with three buildings surrounding a common patio. Mocel purchased each house for thirty pesos, for a total sale price of ninety pesos. The price alone suggests a single purpose for the structures rather than the dual-purpose nature of the home/store mentioned above. These buildings were also adjacent to the marketplace; however, Mocel did not sell the structures, she bequeathed them to her three granddaughters (one building apiece).[39]

In 1615 two of the granddaughters, Martina and Clara,[40] decided to sell the land they inherited from their grandmother. The sale document describes the structures as adobe and stone and mentions that both women were still single. A Spanish widow, one doña Leonor Dávila, wanted to purchase the property for 700 pesos. Unlike the previous sale of property to a Spaniard, this one went uncontested. Neither Martina nor Clara needed the money; they both owned additional adobe structures on the marketplace, were *principalas* (women of high social standing) in the community, and at the time of their deaths (in the late 1630s for Martina and 1640 for Clara) possessed a substantial amount of capital. Additionally, both women were identified (and Clara self-identified) as *ladinas*, indigenous women conversant in Spanish, and Clara's testament was written in Spanish.[41]

This second case occurred fourteen years after the first, with its outcome significantly different. In the first case a Spaniard was denied ownership of the property. In the second, ownership was granted to the Spaniard. The Nahuas' control of the land surrounding the marketplace of San Juan prompts a question. Did ownership of or permission to use the property surrounding the marketplace of San Juan depend in part on individuals' status in or usefulness to the community?

Although it is by no means certain, it seems to be the case that they did. Although the only person to hold the title *don* or *doña* was the Spanish widow, the rest of the indigenous people appear to have been of an elevated status.[42]

The property in question sold for a much higher amount than similar properties at the time. Juana Mocel clearly had money, and it is likely that the couple that purchased it had some money, considering what they paid. It is also known that Juana's granddaughters were principalas, and both had a future governor of Mexico, don Juan de Aguilar, act as the executor of their estates. Petronila María, who owned property adjacent to the sisters and had Martina act as her executor, also possessed quite a bit of wealth, yet no title. Additionally, Clara López was a member of four cofradías at the time of her death, and she spent a lavish amount of money on her funeral ceremonies.[43]

The fact that the marketplace was traditionally associated with women may explain why women are more prominent in the property records, though men operated there as well. Additionally, single indigenous women continued to be prominent in the sale and ownership of property in the area until at least 1640 when Clara López died. The question remains, though, why a Spanish doña was allowed to purchase property next to the market when a Spanish man was not? There may have been a policy change or an issue of status, or it may reflect traditional ties between women and the marketplace. The apparent prominence of women's ownership of property adjacent to the marketplace and their role in day-to-day transactions in the marketplace, considered along with their more rapid acceptance of Christianity than their male counterparts (discussed in chapter 3), suggests that Nahua women were crucial in establishing a network of support for the Catholic Church and the paraphernalia needed for its function on official as well as household levels.[44] These ideas are revisited in later chapters.

Mapping the City and Locating the Chapels

The arduous process of building friaries and chapels was prominent in the lives, record keeping, and location of natives during the sixteenth and seventeenth centuries. Philip II's late sixteenth-century Relaciones geográficas, which were maps and inventories of New Spain, demonstrate the centrality of religious facilities in the mindset of Nahua painters. The maps were requested by Philip II in an attempt to provide information about his dominions. As part of the cartography project, Philip distributed a survey containing fifty questions. The project extended across Spain, the Americas, and beyond. For Spain, Philip called upon Spanish cartographers.[45] To map the Americas he appointed two cosmographers, Alonso de Santa Cruz and Juan López de Velasco. They attempted to carry out the king's mandate while remaining in Europe. To help with the process, they sent questionnaires to the Americas, which they hoped would receive numerous responses. What they did not plan on was that the men who responded to their questions were indigenous artists without European cartographic training. These artists responded with maps that reflected

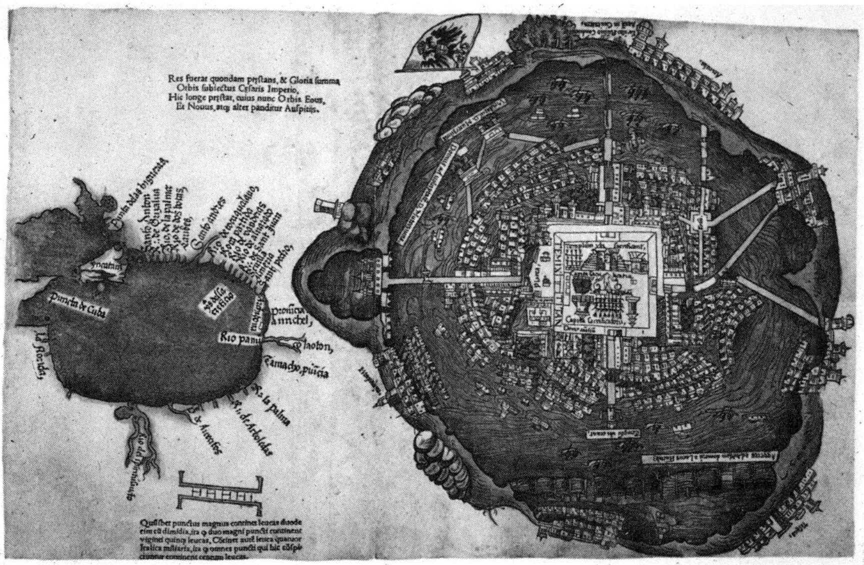

FIGURE 5. Cortés map of Mexico Tenochtitlan, 1524. Courtesy of the Newberry Library.

their perspective of the organization of their altepetl, communities, and countryside.[46] The maps were, to a degree, based on a precontact cartographic tradition, a tradition that incorporated dynastic lineages and pictorial images as representative of aspects of each altepetl. Along with the images were footprints to demonstrate routes of travel.[47] Although similar, in a way, the tradition was very different from its European counterpart (see fig. 2).

The earliest extant map of Mexico Tenochtitlan is known as the Nuremburg map. Its European name indicates where its woodcut was created but does not mention its original author. The map depicts Tenochtitlan as it presumably looked at the time of Cortés's arrival in 1519 (fig. 5).[48] The city is placed in the middle of a lake with causeways leading to it from the mainland. In the center of the island are palaces and temples with what appear to be houses on their periphery. Many of the houses, especially those located on the shores of the island, possess *chinampas*, aquatic agriculture plots.

After the defeat, or surrender, of an altepetl to the Spaniards, churches were generally constructed near the center of the polity. Barbara Mundy postulates that the colonial indigenous towns were organized around friaries and chapels (as in fig. 2). As she explains in her discussion of the Cuzcatlan map, for example, the friary stands in the center with the "subject villages" (or visita chapels) surrounding it, with roads leading to each one. Mundy argues that

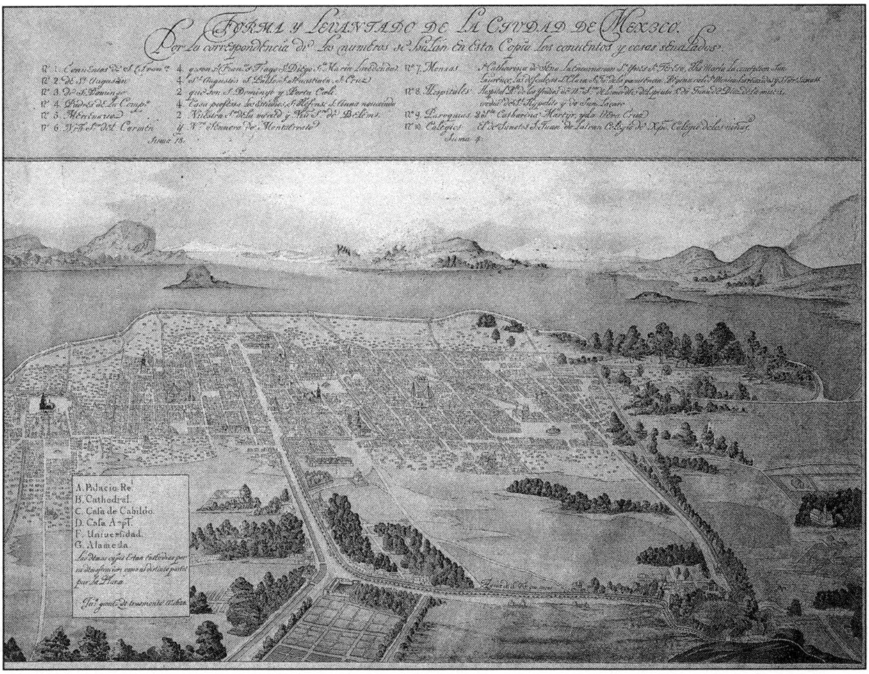

FIGURE 6. Juan Gómez de Trasmonte map of Mexico Tenochtitlan, 1628. Courtesy of the Nettie Lee Benson Latin American Collection, University of Texas Libraries, The University of Texas at Austin.

the "mapmakers' use of the church to symbolize communities was . . . an autonomous choice."[49] Their decision to use chapels to represent altepetl illustrates how pervasive religious architecture was in these villages by the end of the sixteenth century. The physical structure of the church had ostensibly become the religious and social center in the lives of many.

A Relaciones geográficas map does not exist for Mexico City, but the prominence of the friaries and indigenous chapels is illustrated in the seventeenth-century map of Mexico Tenochtitlan by Juan Gómez de Trasmonte (fig. 6). This map, placed alongside the annals of Juan Bautista and Chimalpahin, demonstrates the importance of the Catholic Church to the Nahuas. Additionally, a diagram of the principal chapel of San Josef and its four visitas in the Códice Osuna, 1563–1566 (fig. 7), places San Josef centrally among the four visita churches of San Juan, San Pablo, San Sebastián, and Santa María. The size and central placement of the image of San Josef (with a bell tower) and the image of fray Pedro de Gante firmly establish that chapel's prominence over the other four in a method similar to that used for the Cuzcatlan map. By the beginning of the seventeenth century, however, a hypo-

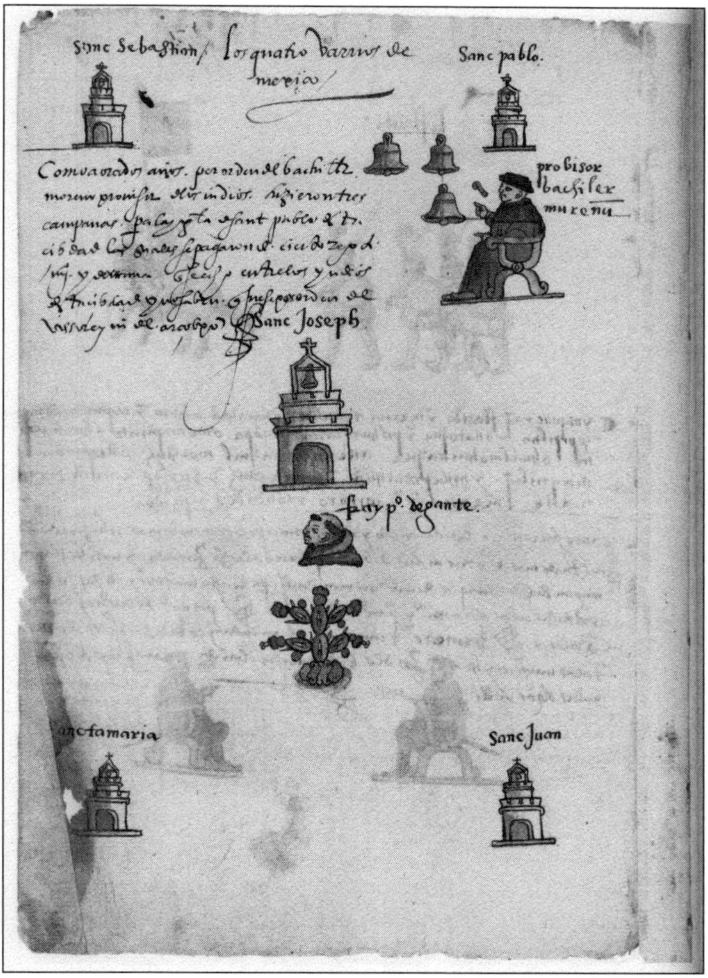

FIGURE 7. Image depicting the chapel of San Josef and its four visita chapels, 1565. *Códice Osuna*, 8v. Courtesy of the Biblioteca Nacional de España.

thetical representation of the same barrios would have shown four different images, with the chapels of San Josef, San Pablo, San Sebastián, and Santa María each at the center of its own parish and the visita of San Juan de la Penetencia still subject to the chapel of San Josef because of the latter's preeminence in the barrio of San Juan Moyotlan. Despite parish redistricting, San Josef's central position remained prominent and extended beyond the city, largely due to its concurrent role as an indigenous school. It is even possible that some of the authors and artists of the documents mentioned above studied, trained, and worshiped at San Josef.

The division of the four barrios into distinct ecclesiastical units was inevitable. When the Catholic Church was sent to central Mexico, the mendicant orders arrived first. The mendicants took oaths of poverty and dedicated themselves to spreading the faith. They were also outside the secular hierarchy of the Catholic Church. Because of their exclusion from the secular Church hierarchy and their strength, in both numbers and establishment in New Spain, controversy arose quickly between them and the bishops as the heads of the secular Church. To make matters more difficult, Pope Adrian VI issued the Omnímoda (10 May 1522), granting mendicants who were at least two days' travel from a bishop the ability to act with the pope's power in all regards except the granting of orders. The second archbishop of Mexico, fray Alonso de Montúfar, especially worked to weaken the authority of the mendicant orders.[50] The separation of the doctrina of San Josef was a part of that effort.

The debate regarding the secularization of parts of the doctrina of San Josef began as early as 1552. In a letter to Charles V, fray Pedro de Gante specifically requested that Charles not allow the secular religious hierarchy control of the Nahuas' religious education.[51] When referring to San Josef, Gante used the term *doctrina*, and the meaning of the term was the focus of some debate.[52] Was San Josef a doctrina, as Gante seems to suggest, or a *parroquia* (parish), as Archbishop fray don Alonso de Montúfar appears to argue? In contrast to Gante, Montúfar employed the term *parroquia* in a 1562 letter to Philip II. Montúfar argued that there should be four indigenous parishes, not one.[53] He was using the Council of Trent's (1545–1563) decrees regarding the division of parishioners into "fixed and proper parishes." His actions demonstrate that he desired clearly defined parish lines, with secular priests (i.e., not of a religious order) as clerics.[54] However, if the religious organization of Mexico Tenochtitlan followed the organizational procedures for other altepetl, there should be only one doctrina for Mexico Tenochtitlan.

In 1562 two religious jurisdictions existed in Mexico Tenochtitlan, a Spanish parish and a Nahua doctrina. Although it took a while, Montúfar eventually succeeded in dividing the doctrina of San Josef into multiple parishes. By subdividing the indigenous parishes along barrio lines, Montúfar had the opportunity to start placing secular clergy in positions of authority in the indigenous chapels. The initial result was the secularization and elevation of the chapel and barrio of San Pablo to its own parish, sometime between 1562 and 1565. Nevertheless, based on an image in the aforementioned Códice Osuna, it appears that the chapel of San Josef was the only indigenous chapel in Mexico Tenochtitlan to possess bells. The presence of bells was significant and definitely helped to enhance the importance of San Josef in the eyes of the Nahuas. The Nahuas themselves appear to have been fond of bells and used them for a variety of functions, including to toll the time of day, burials, calls to worship, feast days, and processions and to launch rebellions.[55]

The immediate elevation in San Pablo's status, then, can be seen in the manufacture and designation of three bells for its chapel. The addition of the bells likely demonstrated the polity's new importance as the principal chapel in its own parish. The Nahuas of San Pablo, then, were justifiably upset when one of their new bells broke shortly after installation and took more than two years to be replaced.[56]

Historian Robert Ricard argues that the battle between the secular clergy and the religious orders was for the financial support that the indigenous parishioners provided.[57] Generally speaking, when a religious order, such as the Franciscans or the Dominicans, ministered to an indigenous group they could benefit from wealthier natives' financial support.[58] The battle between the secular Church and the mendicant orders over congregants lasted into the eighteenth century. The great advantage for the orders was their knowledge of native languages. In 1580 the crown decreed that to receive appointment to an indigenous doctrina in the colonies a priest had to pass an indigenous-language test. The examiners were normally mendicants, possibly making it more difficult for secular priests to obtain their appointments.[59] Another advantage was the dedication of the native population to their clergymen. On occasion, an indigenous group rose up in defense of its ministers, generally in an attempt to prevent their removal. For example, in 1569, in Mexico Tenochtitlan, the viceroy supported Archbishop Montúfar and replaced the Franciscans with secular clergy at several chapels in the city. The Nahua parishioners became so enraged that they stoned the secular clergy and a Spanish judge. Spaniards were forced to defend themselves with swords. It was not until the Franciscans were allowed to return to their parishes that peace was restored.[60] Moreover, in 1584, Archbishop Viceroy don Pedro Moya de Contreras (r. as archbishop 1573–1591, as viceroy 1584–1585) tried to secularize the parishes of Mexico Tenochtitlan again. The Nahua rulers of the four barrios appealed to Moya de Contreras on behalf of the mendicant orders.[61] The mendicants were allowed to retain control of the parishes; however, additional changes in authority happened after this date.

Although there is no extant evidence of Nahua involvement in the initial secularization of San Pablo, it is likely that they were a part of the process. A close reading of some indigenous documents, such as annals, legal cases, and wills, quickly demonstrates the existence of micropatriotism in the barrios of Mexico Tenochtitlan. Each barrio possessed its own secular leadership during the precontact and colonial periods. Before the defeat of Tenochtitlan, each barrio had its own temple and religious leadership below that of the Templo Mayor (Great Temple). The initial mendicant-organized chapel hierarchy, with San Josef as the highest-ranking indigenous chapel, reflected the precontact organization. Then, the four-way parish organization, rather than the doctrina system, firmly established an independent religious hierarchy for each barrio rather than for the altepetl as a whole. It effectively fractured the leadership in Tenochtitlan. During the precontact period the routes to political and religious power in the altepetl were at least parallel if not intertwined.[62] By dividing the doctrina, but not the secular government, Archbishop Montúfar (and his successors) disrupted an age-old hierarchical system. The Spaniards may not have understood this, but the Nahuas certainly did, and religious-political maneuvering ensued wherein each barrio (and at times tlaxilacalli) attempted to gain a stronger religious standing (as they understood it) than their rivals. As is observed below, the Nahuas' involvement in parish jurisdictions and tlaxilacalli decisions eventually came to the forefront.

Little is known about religious jurisdictions and the four barrios for the period 1570–1610. Table 2 provides a list of the indigenous populations for each barrio in 1570. From these figures, one can estimate the financial and spiritual gains that could be made or lost by each of the orders. In 1570 the spiritual leadership of each parish was in question, and it was unclear which order, or if the secular Church itself, would be in charge of any particular parish. Presently, it is not possible to know how much each individual listed in the table gave in alms for each Sunday mass, for each burial, feast day, or marriage, or in requests for masses for the deceased. Nor is the amount of voluntary labor received by the parish priests from the Nahuas known, although such quantities should also be taken into consideration when calculating the financial gain, or loss, each order would receive upon changes in parish jurisdiction. For the barrio of San Juan, the loss would have been in excess of 11,000 people of tribute-paying age.[63] This sum does not include children who may have made small donations or sought to help their religious teachers. The stakes involved in the breakup of the indigenous parish of San Josef are clear. By being in charge of three of the four barrios at the time, the Franciscans were going to suffer a loss, regardless. Because of Archbishop fray Alonso de Montúfar's desire to secularize the parishes, it can be assumed that only secular clergy would benefit, although the Augustinians, Dominicans, and, for a while, Carmelites could have remained neutral or possibly gained from the situation.

The first attempt to use secular priests for the administration of the sacraments in an indigenous barrio in Mexico Tenochtitlan apparently failed. It is not known why San Pablo ceased to be secular, other than that it was transferred to the control of the Augustinian order in 1575.[64] It is possible that the Nahuas of San Pablo clamored for a religious order rather than the secular clergy. The earlier unrest on the part of the Nahuas in favor of the Franciscans, as reported by the Franciscans, may have assisted in this change as well.[65] In 1571, Pope Pius V entered the debate regarding the religious instruction of Nahuas in Mexico Tenochtitlan. In his papal bull he allowed the Franciscans to retain San Juan, assigned San Pablo to the Augustinians, and assigned San Sebastián and Santa María to the Dominicans. Only two of the directives were

TABLE 2. Nahua Tribute Payers in Mexico Tenochtitlan, 1570

Barrio	*Married couples*	*Widows/ widowers*	*Single*[a]	*Order Affiliation*
San Juan[b]	4,091	1,115	2,231	Franciscan
San Pablo[c]	1,274	106/407	373/339	Secular
San Sebastián[d]	2,000	N.A.	1,500/2,000	Franciscan
Santa María[e]	2,700	N.A.	N.A.	Franciscan

Source: AGI, México, v. 336a, ramo 2, doc 104(7). These totals differ from those estimated for the 1560s in Gibson, *Aztecs*, pp. 377–378.

a. Single men over fourteen years; single women over twelve years.

b. The totals provided were not organized as succinctly in these areas, so there is only one number per entry.

c. For an itemized distribution of tribute payments from 1574 (in pictorial and alphabetic Nahuatl) for San Pablo, see *Codex Valeriano.*

d. The total of widows/widowers was not provided

e. Only one total was provided for Santa María. The number is used in reference to tribute payers.

followed, however, for San Juan remained with the Franciscans and San Pablo went to the Augustinians.[66] The Dominicans did not receive either San Sebastián or Santa María.

In 1585, San Sebastián was separated from the parish of San Josef and granted to the Carmelites. Then, in 1608, at the direction of their superiors, the Carmelites relinquished the parish of San Sebastián, and Viceroy don Luis de Velasco II (r. 1590–1595, 1607–1611) turned it over to the Augustinians in that same year. Chimalpahin reports that the Nahuas of San Sebastián "did not give them [the Carmelites] up quickly; they made every effort, for the Atzaqualca did not want to be deprived of their church building." The Nahuas wanted to keep the property, which had been theirs before the arrival of the Carmelites. Initially the Carmelites were going to be allowed to retain the property; to prevent it the Nahuas filed a lawsuit. Chimalpahin does not say how the suit ended, though the Nahuas were allowed to continue going to their chapel for a time, at least; however, they were now ministered to by the Augustinians. It is also probable, based on the unrest mentioned above, that the Nahuas of San Sebastián wanted to retain the spiritual services of the Carmelites.[67] In 1589 the viceroy confirmed the Franciscans' possession of San Juan and Santa María.[68] The doctrina had been split into four parts, but it still differed from the Spanish parish system, leaving the conflict between the secular and mendicant clergies unresolved.

Although Franciscan control of the parish of San Josef was reaffirmed by the viceregal decrees, it seems that the Nahuas decided not to take any chances after the separation of San Pablo and San Sebastián. In 1592 the Nahuas of San Juan Moyotlan donated their visita, San Juan de la Penetencia, to the

Poor Clares for a convent.[69] As part of the arrangement, the Nahuas were promised the right to continue to celebrate certain feast days at the chapel.[70] The donation of the visita at this time had some intriguing consequences. First, by giving the visita of San Juan to the Poor Clares, the Nahuas of San Juan Moyotlan secured the continuation of Franciscan chaplains for their festival celebrations at the chapel of San Juan.[71] The donation of the visita also meant that there was only one other chapel in the barrio large enough for all the Nahuas, the chapel of San Josef de los Naturales. This maneuver was a coup for both the Franciscans and the Nahuas of San Juan. Because the only chapel large enough to minister the faith to the Nahuas resided within the Franciscan compound, it became more difficult for the secular Church to weaken Franciscan control of Tenochtitlan further. Although the Franciscans gave up part of the doctrina, they secured control of the most populous of the Nahua barrios, and they had claim to many of the additional visitas, outside of the main four barrios, that had been assigned to San Josef.[72] And the Nahuas' chapel was now presumably the largest and most prestigious of any indigenous chapel in New Spain. Operationally, San Josef had never been a visita (unlike the chapels of San Pablo, San Sebastián, and Santa María, at the time). The Nahuas of San Juan now claimed *the* principal parish chapel as their main chapel. And, according to Franciscan fray Juan de Torquemada, the Nahuas of all four barrios continued to think of San Josef as the "mother" chapel.[73] Whether or not it influenced the king's and the pope's final decision to award San Juan and Santa María to the Franciscans is uncertain. However, it seems that the friars did not receive official notice from the pope and king until 1597, eight years after the viceroy's decree and five years after the donation of San Juan to the Poor Clares.[74]

The donation of San Juan went beyond social purposes and demonstrated the Nahuas' desire to sustain the divine in Mexico City. An examination of their participation in the city's religious life reveals particulars about their barrio patriotism. Chimalpahin relates that when the nuns of Santa Clara took up residence in San Juan in 1593 the Holy Sacrament was placed at San Juan de la Penetencia, "whereby our lord God greatly favored his altepetl and gave honor and fame to the entity of Moyotlan." A procession of Spaniards and Nahuas commemorated the event, and the viceroy and Audiencia judges were in attendance.[75] Indeed, Chimalpahin points out that "God greatly favored the altepetl" as a whole but that the honor and fame went to a specific barrio, San Juan Moyotlan. The micropatriotism seen here, in the shifting of the parishes, and the devotion to the Franciscans on behalf of the Nahuas of San Juan Moyotlan argue for a group identity among the Nahuas of Mexico Tenochtitlan based on their barrio of residence.

Political jurisdictional changes tied to religious organizational units continued into the seventeenth century. The barrio of Santa María la Redonda became an independent parish in 1609 but remained with the Franciscans. Construction of a new friary and indigenous chapel for Santa María began in 1612.[76] The Augustinians gained control of San Sebastián from the Carmelites in 1607. Although it was clear by this time that the mendicant orders would retain control of the indigenous parishes, Philip III (r. 1599–1621) reissued an order supporting the Council of Trent decrees in New Spain. In it he stated that the bishops and archbishops were to be allowed to check on mendicant-run parishes.[77]

In 1610 the parish of Mixtecos was established for Mixtec migrants from south-central Mexico. Their chapel was based at the Dominican friary of Santo Domingo in the barrio of Santa María. Eventually the parish included other migrants including Filipinos. Unlike the other five parishes, this parish had no physical boundaries and was based solely on ethnicity. The Dominicans believed that based on their ties to Mixtecs and Zapotecs in Oaxaca and knowledge of their language, they should be the ones to minister to them. In contrast, Franciscans and Augustinians argued against the establishment of the parish, stating that most migrant natives to Mexico City spoke Nahuatl. The only extant will from Mixtecos supports the Franciscans' and Augustinians' arguments; it is written in Spanish and borrows only Nahuatl terms.[78] The argument against the foundation of a parish for Mixtecos suggests that other native-language speakers in Mexico City, without their own chapel, had to attend mass and ceremonies in Nahuatl at Nahua chapels. One possible example was the Otomi ermita in San Juan Chichimecapan.[79] Although the Otomis had their own ermita, they were still affiliated with the larger Nahua parish of San Josef. Likewise, other indigenous groups, such as those from Michoacan who were members of a cofradía, appear to have been required to hear Sunday mass and celebrate feast days in Nahuatl, for they do not seem to have possessed their own ermita. Given the existence of the Otomi ermita and other indigenous-language speakers, Mixtecos was even more unusual in that it was both a parish and a chapel, not an ermita in a larger parish. The existence of the Mixtecos parish demonstrates the important role friars played, Dominicans in this case, in indigenous religious and political life. In this instance the friars provided parishioners of Mixtecos with their own community gathering space, independent of the dominant Nahua population. Moreover, with this separation the Mixtecos community in Mexico City was able to have its own religious leadership.

In 1633 a sixth indigenous parish, Santa Cruz Contzinco, was created by combining the southern portion of San Sebastián with a segment from northern San Pablo.[80] The Augustinians also ministered to this parish, although its creation seems to have happened against the wishes of the Nahua nobles of San Pablo. Nahuas of Santa Cruz Contzinco showed their desire for the creation of their parish as early as Easter in 1613, when they petitioned to take their images in procession separately from the main chapel of San Pablo. They received permission from the dean of the cathedral, the secular Church, but not from the supervising religious, the Augustinians. For this reason, one of the nobles of San Pablo, Hernando de San Martín Teucxochitzin, initiated a lawsuit against the Nahuas of Santa Cruz to force them to go in procession with the rest of San Pablo. To avoid such a fate, the Nahuas of Santa Cruz secretly went in procession during the middle of the night.[81] By doing so they broke tradition and gained the right to parade without the cofradías of San Pablo.

The final attempt during the Hapsburg period to reorganize the indigenous parishes of Mexico Tenochtitlan came in 1689 and was spearheaded by Archbishop don Francisco de Aguiar y Seijas y Ulloa (r. 1681–1698). He hoped to create parishes out of established ermita sites, but his efforts did not have the support of the indigenous communities, and despite his ecclesiastical authority he failed.[82] The archbishop's plan was to remove the communities from the established chapels in the various friary compounds in the city. He most likely failed to gain the support of the Nahuas because he intended to remove them from their parish chapels and place them in smaller and less ornate ermitas. The ermitas were already under Nahua control, and establishing them as parish heads would have moved the Nahuas farther from the center of Mexico Tenochtitlan. A redistricting such as the one proposed would have provided no apparent benefit for the natives of Mexico Tenochtitlan.

In the indigenous secular government of Mexico Tenochtitlan, the highest ranked position was that of governor.[83] Alongside his secular duties, in all four barrios, the governor was beholden to be a good Catholic and to take extra care in tending to Christian doctrine and the divine offices at the chapel of San Josef and other chapels in the city, regardless of changing parish lines.[84] This requirement held true over the course of the sixteenth and seventeenth centuries. In most of the long and short guides detailing Nahua gubernatorial duties for Mexico Tenochtitlan, the chapel of San Josef was mentioned.[85] The governor's continuing responsibility to San Josef is interesting since there were eventually six indigenous parishes, and he governed all of them. Yet his main religious responsibilities were at San Josef, such as his duty to appoint a Nahua to keep track of attendance on Sundays and feast days.[86] The oath probably became pro forma as each barrio was turned into its own parish. However, San Josef's presence in the oath and other documents reasserted its position as the most prestigious of the indigenous chapels. In documents regarding religious responsibility in Mexico Tenochtitlan, San Josef was frequently mentioned, and no other chapel made an appearance in the general decrees. The duties of the governor and appointment of the attendance monitor argue for the sustained level of importance of San Josef for the Nahuas of Mexico Tenochtitlan. Additionally, Franciscan matrimonial records from 1659–1668 emphasize the centrality of San Josef in the indigenous chapel hierarchy of Mexico City. The documents refer to the chapel as *esta yglesia Cathedral de Yndios de S. Joseph de Mexico* (this cathedral church of Indians of San Josef of Mexico). The Franciscan chaplain of San Josef, fray Pedro Camacho, signed the records, suggesting that he approved the use of the title. The term appears to be used to set San Josef apart from other indigenous chapels. The phrasing changed to *iglesia parroquial de indios* (parish church of Indians) starting in 1669; the reason for the change is not known.[87]

Indigenous parish organization in Mexico Tenochtitlan was also important in Spanish politics and control in Mexico City. The main parish chapels kept baptismal, burial, and marriage records for their parishioners. If the government needed a population count for labor drafts, tribute payments, or any number of other reasons, it turned to the religious order in charge of that particular parish. This put the mendicant orders in the position of mediator between the Nahuas and Spanish authorities. Also, the relationship of the friars with natives in Mexico City often helped after periods of serious crisis. Their role was evident after the 1692 Mexico City riots, when the viceroy, Conde de Galve (r. 1688–1696), turned to the guardians of the friaries and requested a census of natives who lived with Spaniards (and therefore might be inside the perimeter of the Spanish *traza*, an area where only Spaniards were technically allowed to live that extended about a kilometer in each direction). Each of the six parishes in Mexico Tenochtitlan and the one in Santiago Tlatelolco provided a list and in some cases a letter in support of their parishioners' good behavior.[88] Thus, the friars on occasion were intermediaries between the viceroy and the Nahuas. Aside from helping the viceroy, some of them also vouched for the location of their parishioners during the riots.

Parish Beginnings: Construction and Upkeep

The Nahuas started the colonial period as laborers forced to construct religious and secular buildings under the guidance of Franciscan friars and Spanish conquistadors. They used the stonework and statues of deities from their old temples in the foundations for many of the largest buildings. Though several sites remained the domain of Spaniards, such as the cathedral, the Nahuas also built a large number of chapels under the guidance of friars for themselves.[89] These buildings, in particular, came to hold significant religious meaning for the natives of Mexico Tenochtitlan.

The Nahuas of Mexico Tenochtitlan and other altepetl were responsible for the construction of the friary, San Josef, and their visitas and ermitas.[90] The original Franciscan friary was built on the central plaza of Mexico Tenochtitlan before the Franciscans moved to their final location, which was closer to the Nahua population they served in San Juan Moyotlan. Their move occurred sometime between 1525 and 1527.[91] According to friars Pedro de

Gante and Juan de Torquemada, the site had previously been Emperor Moctezuma II's (r. 1502–1520) aviary. When the Franciscans and Nahuas built the friary on the aviary grounds, they kept much of it intact, leaving many of the birds, fountains, and trees in place.[92] In the Franciscan compound, the Nahuas paid for and constructed the chapel of San Josef.[93] The earliest version of San Josef was finished by 1532. The active process of proselytization on the friary grounds had started by 1527 and probably moved to the chapel within a few years.[94] The chapel was rebuilt after an earthquake in 1547, and in 1574 they tore down the wooden version, presumably to replace it with the stone structure that eventually emerged. The stone chapel had seven naves with seven altars, with the main altar in the center, and all facing east.[95] They added a sacristy to the wood version in 1556 and updated and renovated it in 1587.[96] As noted above, in the 1590s the Nahuas of San Juan gave up their visita of San Juan de la Penetencia and construction started on a new bell tower at San Josef.[97]

Encircling the friary courtyard was a rectangle of ancient trees (as shown in fig. 8), fray Diego Valadés's concept of an "ideal *atrio*," or courtyard. Activities taking place in the atrium were most likely inspired by the manner in which Valadés observed fray Pedro de Gante use the patio outside of the chapel of San Josef de los Naturales.[98] At each corner of the courtyard Nahua laborers built a *posa* chapel, or resting place. Friars and natives probably used the posas during celebrations and as meeting places for cofradías.[99] In the center of the courtyard stood a 200-foot cross, made from an incredibly old cypress tree. Aside from cutting, transporting, and erecting the cross, Nahua artisans carved ecclesiastical motifs on it.[100]

Around 1548 the friary of San Francisco entered a state of perpetual construction, a result of both the friars' purposes and the constant need for repairs. The Franciscans added more rooms, an infirmary, fountains, and bell towers, filled in sunken floors, and replaced rotting woodwork.[101] In 1590 they tore down the church of San Francisco because of structural deterioration and started construction on a new one.[102] Spanish artisans may have executed the most ornate work in the church of San Francisco, but natives were the laborers.

During times of disaster, the Nahuas worked under the guidance of Franciscan friars to help preserve the city and religious buildings. Frequent flooding left the city in a state of almost continual disrepair. To stem an inundation of water in 1555, Viceroy don Luis de Velasco the elder (r. 1550–1564) issued a labor draft for more than six thousand workers. After this incident and others like it, fray Gerónimo de Zárate directed some Nahuas in the construction of a lagoon or pool, twenty yards wide and two leagues in length, four leagues north of the city, to help retain some of the water that came down the mountainside.[103] These protections failed half a century later, on 27 August 1604, when another flood struck. Water and landslides destroyed roads and houses, and churches

FIGURE 8. Fray Diego Valadés's ideal courtyard, based on the church of San Francisco. From Diego Valadés, *Rhetorica Christiana*, Perugia, 1579. Courtesy of the John Carter Brown Library at Brown University.

and friaries were inundated with water. To try to prevent the flooding of the church of San Francisco, as well as other religious buildings, laborers attempted to raise the level of the floors by adding more dirt to them.[104]

In the last quarter of the sixteenth century, many of the Nahuas' chapel-building efforts came of their own volition. At this time, the Nahua secular leadership was attending chapel groundbreaking ceremonies and selling land for ermitas, and the annalist Chimalpahin heralded the construction of San Josef's bell tower.[105] Over the course of the seventeenth century, Nahuas solicited permissions to build, for the purpose of new ermita construction and to repair older chapels. Although Franciscans such as Agustín de Vetancurt are named in the documents, they appear as witnesses verifying the need for repairs or supporting the new construction. Though it is unlikely that the Franciscans would oppose something to their benefit, the documents read as though it was the Nahuas who desired the new structures and repairs, and the Franciscans were witnesses, not agents.

By the end of the sixteenth century, the Nahuas had proved capable of maneuvering in the Spanish legal system. By the close of the seventeenth century, they were apparently operating in it nearly as effectively as the Spaniards. Because of their facility in the legal system, there are at least two ways to look at their solicitations for chapel repair. When the Nahuas requested permission to fix their religious sites, they also provided an estimate of the expenses. The money that went into the renovations could be deducted from the amount of tribute they needed to pay that year. This was the case with a request submitted in 1692 to repair San Josef and its former visita of San Juan de la Penitencia. The petition for San Josef and San Juan was granted with a reduction in tribute payment in the amount of 3,600 pesos. The grant of the reduction is interesting in light of both the arrears Tenochtitlan owed in tribute (in 1687 they were behind by 4,700 pesos) and the amount of tribute collected in 1692 (527 pesos, two reales, and three granos).[106] In 1694 the Nahuas admitted to overspending by forty-four pesos and five reales. Though the chapel of San Juan was attached to the convent of Santa Clara, it appears that, because of structural degradation, the Nahuas were no longer able to use it for their designated feast days.[107]

Knowing that they could receive reductions in tribute, it is possible that the Nahuas sought the repairs of their religious facilities solely for financial purposes. The other possibility, and one that seems more likely, is that the reduction in tribute was an added benefit to help them meet their religious responsibilities, one of which they were certain to take advantage—the community's desire to congregate at the sites. This suggestion is based on a 1693 petition by the community members of the tlaxilacalli of Santiago Tlaxilpa, in the barrio of San Juan, to relocate and build a new ermita dedicated to Santiago. The existing chapel suffered from such a regular inundation of water that they could rarely celebrate mass there. Spaniard Baltasar Pacheco, the mestizo Blas García, and fray Agustín de Vetancurt verified that the chapel needed repairs. Neither the Nahuas nor the presiding Spanish official, Joseph Rubio, mentioned the cost of the new building or the possibility of tribute reduction.[108] The Nahuas in this tlaxilacalli belonged to the parish of San Josef. In the year preceding the petition and the one following it, the Nahuas of San Josef requested a reduction in tribute for repairs to the chapel of San Josef and their old visita of San Juan de la Penetencia. Most likely, the Nahuas of Tlaxilpa were as knowledgeable of legal procedures as the rest of the parish. It is not known why money was not involved in the request. Tribute reductions may have entered the picture later. It is also possible that financial assistance was not available for the renovation of ermitas and was instead reserved for the main parish chapels. If the Nahuas wanted to build or reconstruct the chapel, they probably needed permission and likely had to pay for it themselves. At the very least, major repairs on three separate chapels in three consecutive years demonstrate their commitment to Nahua religious sites and their interest in not paying tribute.[109]

Dedication to a specific chapel played out on a more individual scale as well. In two wills from San Pablo Malcuitlapilco (from 1644 and 1663), the deceased requested masses and burial at the chapel of San Josef, despite living in the parish of San Pablo.[110] In both cases, the *fiscal* (church steward) of San Josef was present. In the testament from 1644, Francisco Juárez had been a parishioner of San Josef before moving to San Pablo. It is not known why the other testator, Francisco Antonio, behaved similarly to Francisco Juárez, though it is likely that his situation in 1663 was similar to that of Juárez.[111] The commitment to a home parish is further strengthened by information found in the 1678 will of Juana Petrona. In the testament she states that her father was buried at San Josef whereas her mother was returned to the parish she was from, Santa María.[112]

If such plans existed for these two Nahuas, it may well have been the case for others, demonstrating that movement of individuals among the barrios could happen and that parish ties, community, and chapel preferences remained strong. It also suggests that barrio lines acted as defining boundaries for each barrio and the authority of the Nahua tlatoani. These territories are what fray Pedro de Gante and Hernando Cortés used to organize the visita jurisdictions. The same characteristics were then used again by Archbishop Montúfar to delineate specific indigenous parishes in the city. Moving away to live in another part of the city for economic or other reasons was one thing, but both individuals decided to donate money, at the time of death, to their home parish, to be buried there, and to entrust their souls to the parish they were from rather than the one closest to where they lived.

Staffing the Chapels: The Teopantlaca

During the sixteenth and seventeenth centuries in New Spain, Nahua parishioners performed many of the duties related to ritual obligations and maintenance at their chapels. The small size of the Spanish population precluded the possibility of Spaniards performing the duties. From a desire to convert the indigenous peoples and teach them respect for the religion, priests had to instruct them quickly in the care of Church buildings, ornaments, vestments, and other items essential to the faith. This required a staff of individuals based on parish population and rank. Positions at indigenous chapels—

teopantlaca—tended to include fiscales, sacristans, notaries, *alguaciles mayores* (constables, in this case, and below the fiscal in rank), *cantores* (singers), and different types of *topiles* (staff holders). At the outset of Spanish contact none of these positions held much importance, but over time some of them grew in importance (such as the fiscal), and additional positions developed, with different levels of prestige ultimately associated with them. The officers and their duties and responsibilities were what kept the chapels functioning on a daily basis. These Nahuas controlled the finances and keys to their chapels. Some held their position by appointment, others by election. Each position could lead to a higher appointment in either the secular or religious leadership of a given altepetl. Additionally, individuals could serve for multiple terms (see appendix 4). Most were important members of the community.

Fiscales

Before the arrival of Spaniards, leadership in the indigenous religious and secular spheres was so intertwined that it is often difficult to tell the two apart.[113] The distinction between secular and religious spheres was more precise during the colonial period, but important offices developed in both areas. Shortly after the construction of the indigenous chapels, friars introduced the position of fiscal. Fiscales acted as local intermediaries between the indigenous parishioners and the priest. Though initially a low-level position (in the eyes of the Spaniards), it came to be the second-highest-ranked position in the indigenous religious and political hierarchies, below the governor. Early on, this roles may have in some way been a continuation of a type of precontact priesthood. But if it was a path that allowed the priesthood to carry over its roles and preeminence, it seems to have ceased by the second half of the sixteenth century.[114]

In his examination of religion in sixteenth-century New Spain, Robert Ricard found that in the countryside the fiscal frequently acted in the stead of an absent priest. The fiscal watched over the moral and spiritual life of the community, maintained and adorned chapels, organized feast days, assisted with marriages, helped with burials, chose names for infants, and collected the fees for all of the above.[115] Mark Christensen's work on religious documents written in Mayan and Nahuatl shows some of the ways rural fiscales were deeply involved in the propagation of the Catholic faith as they understood it. This diversity of understanding by native assistants, many of whom were certainly fiscales, created a diversity of Catholicisms.[116] The fiscales' responsibility for caring for the parishioners was such that fray Alonso de Molina (b. 1513[4?]–1579) may have written his *Confesionario mayor* for both priests (unfamiliar with Nahuatl) and fiscales (who were new converts to the religion).[117]

In her research on Coyoacan, Rebecca Horn found evidence of fiscales as far back as 1549.[118] Ryan Crewe recently uncovered a 1549 Nahuatl document from Tula that was witnessed by a fiscal.[119] Luis Reyes García has encountered a fiscal in Puebla from a 1543 Nahuatl document.[120] Chimalpahin supports an earlier establishment of the position with his claim that don Carlos Ometochtzin, the ruler of Tetzcoco, was also a fiscal at the time he was burned at the stake for heresy in 1539 by Bishop fray Juan de Zumárraga.[121] Note that it is likely that Ometochtzin held the position because of his alliance with the Spaniards, his role as ruler of Tetzcoco, and his wealth rather than because the position of fiscal itself had any prominence at that time. This is especially clear when compared to the two fiscales from Coyoacan and Tula, neither of whom held the important Spanish title *don* in 1549.[122]

The earliest extant record of a fiscal in Mexico Tenochtitlan comes from 1564, a Toribio Vásquez Tlacochcalcatl, from the barrio of San Juan and likely fiscal at the chapel of San Josef.[123] The evidence of fiscales in Coyoacan, Tula, and Tetzcoco prior to 1550 suggests that the position was widespread early on. Fiscales were likely present in Mexico Tenochtitlan even before the position was established in other areas, suggesting a possible late 1530s to early 1540s start at San Josef.

Fiscales existed in San Pablo (and possibly San Sebastián and Santa María) by the end of the sixteenth century. Fiscal positions may even have been established at some of the early ermitas. Three instances involving one fiscal, Miguel de los Angeles, hint at the growing prestige of the position. Although he was from the barrio of San Pablo, in 1589, 1591, and 1592 de los Ángeles was the fiscal of San Josef.[124] By 1589 the Augustinians were already in control of the barrio of San Pablo and most likely needed their own fiscal. So why did Miguel de los Ángeles, who lived in the Augustinian parish of San Pablo, become fiscal at San Josef? Why did he return to the position in 1591 and 1592, a time when construction had begun on a new church in San Pablo, elevating its prestige and creating some excitement?[125] Possibly, as is clearly evident in the 1592 case, another person was fiscal in 1591.[126] But this does not explain why Miguel de los Ángeles left his own parish to attend San Josef instead of remaining a parishioner of San Pablo. There are several possible reasons for his dedication to San Josef, including community ties, devotion to the Franciscans, and the prestige of being fiscal at the first and most important indigenous chapel.[127]

Although the office of fiscal was high among the chapel staff and a station that required literacy, it does not seem to have implied high rank until the early seventeenth century. It was conspicuous by the lack of the title *don*, which marked an individual's place within Spanish society, for most Nahua fiscales during the sixteenth century. The title was normally reserved for people born into the Spanish nobility or gained through elevation to a position of recognized importance. In New Spain, the conqueror Hernando Cortés awarded the title to high-ranking Nahuas as he saw to their baptism, a policy that continued during the colonial period. Individuals in certain positions in the indigenous government could also obtain the title as a mark of their high rank. However, during the sixteenth century many Nahuas did not earn the title through advancement in indigenous governing positions. This is especially seen in the case of Antonio Valeriano (the elder), who held the position of governor of Mexico Tenochtitlan toward the end of the sixteenth century. He was highly respected by both Spaniards and Nahuas and had been trained as a Latinist in the Colegio de Santa Cruz in Tlatelolco. Yet, despite his success and his marriage to an indigenous woman of noble lineage, he was not awarded the title.

At the very end of the sixteenth century, the title began to be used by individuals on the basis of specific positions attained. By 1595, probably because of his position as governor, Valeriano was awarded the title.[128] Fiscales eventually received the title as well. Lack of a title did not mean there was no prestige, but the eventual granting of the title *don* to fiscales at specific chapels denoted those chapels' position within the hierarchy of indigenous chapels. Table 3 provides a list of known fiscales at chapels in Mexico Tenochtitlan. The title *don* distinguishes some individuals.

Until 1611 only three fiscales are known to have used the title: don Antonio Valeriano (the younger), don Miguel García, and don Nicolás Andrés. Valeriano (the younger) was so entitled because of his mother's lineage. He took the position as fiscal at San Josef only briefly before going to Azcapotzalco to become governor there.[129] Don Miguel García and don Nicolás Andrés were different. García was fiscal at San Josef in 1577 and did not use the title. In a document dated 1593, he was an *alcalde* (magistrate) and signed his name with *don*.[130] In 1602 he was again fiscal at San Josef and so entitled presumably because of his previous position as alcalde.[131] Although the documentation is missing, a similar process was likely the case for don Nicolás Andrés. The position of fiscal seems not to have warranted the title of *don* by the end of the sixteenth century, for in 1601 the fiscal of San Josef, Josef Juárez, did not hold the title. However, it is possible that the position was now acting as a step for advancement in the community. Sometime between 1601 and 1624 it became common for the fiscales at the four main chapels of San Josef, San Pablo, San Sebastián, and Santa María to use the title. It is during this period that fiscales also began to work at ermitas, but none used the title.[132] Nahuas generally earned the title, as in the case of becoming a fiscal, or were baptized with it. The acquisition of the title *don* by more prominent fiscales likely enhanced the fiscal position in the chapel hierarchy.

The position of the indigenous fiscal was created during the sixteenth century, but it does not seem to have become a position of particular prestige

TABLE 3. Examples of Nahua Chapel Positions in Mexico Tenochtitlan, Sixteenth through Seventeenth Century

Name	*Position*	*Chapel*	*Year*	*Source*
Toribio Vásquez Tlacochcalcatl	Fiscal	San Josef	1564	Bautista, *¿Cómo to confundes?*, p. 183
Pedro García Temilo	Fiscal	San Josef	1565	Bautista, *¿Cómo te confundes?*, p. 299
Miguel García	Fiscal (acquires *don* in 1593 as alcalde).	San Josef	1577, 1602	AGN, Tierras, v. 42, e. 5; AGN, Hospital de Jesús, leg. 298, pt. 1, e. 4; AGN, Bienes Nacionales, v. 551, e. 5
Francisco de Sandoval	Fiscal (and syndic in 1598)	San Josef	1586, 1587, 1598	AGN, Tierras, v. 54, e. 5; v. 59, e. 3; Chimalpahin, *Annals*, p. 65
Miguel de los Ángeles	Fiscal	San Josef	1589, 1591, 1592	AGN, Tierras, v. 55, e. 2; v. 2728, e. 3; Chimalpahin, *Ocho relaciones*, v. 2, p. 269
Francisco de la Cruz	Fiscal	San Josef	1590	AGN, Tierras, v. 3711, e. 2
Martín Juárez Cozcaquauh	Fiscal	San Josef	1600	Chimalpahin, *Annals*, p. 71
Josef Juárez	Fiscal	San Josef	1601	Chimalpahin, *Annals*, p. 73
Mateo Flores	Fiscal	San Josef	1603	AGN, Tierras, v. 84, e. 2
don Antonio Valeriano (the younger)	Fiscal	San Josef	1611 (January–November)	Chimalpahin, *Annals*, pp. 173, 193
Miguel Valásquez	Fiscal (minor fiscal?)	San Josef	1624	AGN, Tierras, v. 3711, e. 2
don Melchor de Santiago	Fiscal	San Josef	1624	AGN, Tierras, v. 3711, e. 2
don Nicolás de Medina	Fiscal	San Josef	1644	UNAM FRAF, caja 96, e. 1413; AGN, Tierras, v. 101, e. 2
don Mateo Juárez	Fiscal	San Josef	1651	AGN, Tierras, v. 103, pt. 1, e. 6, f. 3
don Martín Alonso	Fiscal (and syndic in 1644)	San Josef	1644, 1655	UNAM FRAF, caja 96, e. 1413
don Pedro de San Pablo	Fiscal (previously alguacil mayor)	San Josef	1664	AGN, Tierras, v. 2776, e. 18, f. 213

(continued on next page)

TABLE 3 (*continued*)

Name	*Position*	*Chapel*	*Year*	*Source*
don Antonio Rodríguez	Fiscal	San Josef	1665	AGN, Tierras, v. 3711, e. 2
don Juan Bautista	Fiscal (in the tlaxilacalli of Tezcatzonco)[a]	San Josef	1665	AGN, Geneología, v. 432, roll 1947, f. 20v
Diego de la Cruz (performed duties of notary)	Minor fiscal	Unknown, likely visita of San Juan Bautista	17th century	AGN, Hospital de Jesús, leg. 210, e. 4, f. 21
Josef Gómez	Sacristan	San Josef	1612	Chimalpahin, *Annals*, p. 195
Diego de Santiago	Sacristan	Ermita: San Gerónimo (Barrio San Juan)	1692	AGN, Historia, v. 413, e. 1, f. 35v
Nicolás de la Cruz	Sacristan	Ermita: San Agustín	1692	AGN, Historia, v. 413, e. 1, f. 36
Francisco de San Juan	Choirmaster	San Josef	1640	AGN, Bienes Nacionales, v. 387, e. 1, f. 15
Toribio Quauhtli	Cantor/topile	San Josef	1566	Bautista, *¿Cómo te confundes?*, p. 145
Francisco Andrés	Cantor	San Josef	1692	AGN, Historia, v. 413, e. 1, f. 33
Pedro Jacobita	Notary of the church (and mayordomo)	San Josef	1586 (1590 acts as witness)	AGN, Tierras, v. 59, e. 3; v. 3711, e. 2
Cristóbal Sánchez	Notary of the church	San Josef	1590	AGN Tierras, v. 3711, e. 2
Antonio Rafael	Notary of the church (and syndic)	San Josef	1601	Chimalpahin, *Annals*, p. 73
Sebastián Bonifacio	Notary of the church	San Josef	1644, 1655	UNAM FRAF, caja 96, e. 1413
Andrés Felipe	Notary of the church	San Josef	1665	AGN, Tierras, v. 3711, e. 2
Pedro de San Pablo	Alguacil mayor (becomes fiscal by 1664)	San Josef	1655	UNAM FRAF, caja 96, e. 1413
Juan Miguel	Teopan topile	San Josef	1624	AGN, Tierras, v. 3711, e. 2

(continued on next page)

TABLE 3 (*continued*)

Name	*Position*	*Chapel*	*Year*	*Source*
Francisco Moreno	Mayordomo of the church	San Pablo	1567	AGN, Indiferente Virreinal, v. 1742, e. 14
don Nicolás Andrés	Fiscal	San Pablo	1592	AGN, Tierras, v. 1774, e. 10
don Juan de Morales	Fiscal	San Pablo	1639	AGN, Bienes Nacionales, v. 339, e. 6
don Juan de Medina	Fiscal	San Pablo	1664	AGN, Tierras, v. 109, e. 4, f. 3
don Francisco Martín	Fiscal	San Pablo	1675, 1686	AGN, Bienes Nacionales, v. 1766, e. 7, fs. 5v, 7v
don Juan Gregorio	Fiscal	San Pablo	Before 1686, 1691, 1692	AGN, Bienes Nacionales, v. 1766, e. 7, f. 7; AGN, Civil, v. 592, e. 1; AGN, Tierras, v. 163, e. 2
don Josef Andrés	Fiscal	San Pablo	1695	AGN, Civil, v. 592, e. 1
don Blas de Santiago	Fiscal	San Pablo	1701	AGN, Bienes Nacionales, v. 1766, e. 7, f. 11
Juan Luis	Minor fiscal	San Pablo Malcuitlapilco/ Ermita La Candelaria	1613	UNAM FRAF, caja 96, e. 1413
Sebastián de Santiago	Minor fiscal	San Pablo Malcuitlapilco/ Ermita La Candelaria	before 1655	UNAM FRAF, caja 96, e. 1413
Diego Luis	Minor fiscal	San Pablo Malcuitlapilco/ Ermita La Candelaria	1655	UNAM FRAF, caja 96, e. 1413
Baltasar de los Reyes	Notary of the church	San Pablo	1686, 1692, 1695	AGN, Bienes, Nacionales, v. 1766, e. 7, f. 7v; AGN, Civil, v. 592, e. 1; AGN, Tierras, v.163, e. 2
don Salvador Mateo	Alguacil mayor	San Pablo	1686	AGN, Bienes Nacionales, v. 1766, e. 7, f. 7v
don Diego de Santiago	Alguacil mayor of the church	San Pablo	1701	AGN, Bienes Nacionales, v. 1766, e. 7, f. 11

(continued on next page)

Table 3 (*continued*)

Name	*Position*	*Chapel*	*Year*	*Source*
Andrés Perez[b]	Minor fiscal	San Sebastían	1625	AGN, Hospital de Jesús, Leg. 210, e. 4
don Andrés Martínez	Fiscal	San Sebastián	1692	AGN, Tierras, v. 155, e. 9
Miguel daYiel(?) de Rojas[c]	Minor fiscal	San Sebastián	1712	AGN, Indiferente Virreinal, caja 1124, e. 25
Pedro Sánchez	Alguacil mayor	San Sebastián[d]	1569	AGN, Tierras, v. 1595, e. 4
don Antonio Rodríguez	Fiscal	Santa María la Redonda	1630	AGN, Tierras, v. 3711, e. 2
don Lucas Francisco	Fiscal	Santa María la Redonda	1659	NL, Ayer, MS 1481, B(3)b
don Andrés Felipe	Fiscal	Santa María la Redonda	1669	NL, Ayer, MS 1481, B(3)1
don Baltasar del Castillo	Fiscal	Santa María la Redonda	1673	AGN, Tierras, v. 157, e. 7
don Agustín Hipólito[e]	Fiscal	Santa María la Redonda	1677, 1679	NL, Ayer, MS 1481, B(3)e; MS 1481, B(3)d
don Juan Lázaro	Fiscal	Santa María la Redonda	1683	NL, Ayer, MS 1481, B(3)F
don Juan Marcos	Fiscal	Santa María la Redonda	1693	NL, Ayer, MS 1481, 1B(3)1; AGN, Tierras, v. 2241, e. 12
don Josef de Santiago	Fiscal	Santa María la Redonda	1699, 1709	NL, Ayer, MS 1481, B(3)1; AGN, Tierras v. 3711, e. 2
don Juan de Santiago	Fiscal	Santa María la Redonda	1721	NL, Ayer, MS 1481, B(3)k
Felipe de Jesús	Cantor	Santa María la Redonda	1691	AGN, Historía, v. 413, e. 1, f. 54
Pedro de la Cruz	Cantor	Santa María la Redonda	1691	AGN, Historía, v. 413, e. 1, f. 54
Juan de los Santos	Cantor	Santa María la Redonda	1691	AGN, Historía, v. 413, e. 1, f. 54v
Andrés Felipe	Notary of the church	Santa María la Redonda	1630 (fiscal 1669)	AGN, Tierras, v. 3711, e. 2
Blas Rodríguez	Notary of the church	Santa María la Redonda	1673	AGN, Tierras, v. 157, e. 7

(continued on next page)

TABLE 3 (*continued*)

Name	*Position*	*Chapel*	*Year*	*Source*
don Blas de San Diego	Notary of the church	Santa María la Redonda	1679, 1683 (receives *don* status 1679–1683)	NL, Ayer, MS 1481, B(3)d; MS 1481, B(3)F
Diego de la Santa María	Notary of the church	Santa María la Redonda	1721	NL, Ayer, MS 1481, B(3)k
Juan Pascual Ventura	Alguacil mayor of the church	Santa María la Redonda	1677	NL, Ayer, MS 1481, B(3)e
don Josef de Santiago	Alguacil mayor of the church	Santa María la Redonda	1699	NL, Ayer, MS 1481, B(3)1
Josef Marcos	Choirmaster	Santa María la Redonda	1677	NL, Ayer, MS 1481, B(3)e
don Felipe de la Cruz	Fiscal	Santa Cruz Contzinco	1692	AGN, Tierras, v. 155, e. 9
Miguel Chimalaca	Fiscal	Santo Domingo (before Mixtecos was created)	1566	Bautista, "*¿Cómo te confundes?*," pp. 147–149
Pedro Hernández	Fiscal	Santo Domingo/ Mixtecos	1648	AGN, Bienes Nacionales, v. 1766, e. 7, fs. 16, 19
Lucas Josef	Fiscal	Santo Domingo/ Mixtecos	1648	AGN, Bienes Nacionales, v. 1766, e. 7, fs. 16, 19
don Juan Diego	Fiscal	Mixtecos	Before 1692	AGN, Historia, v. 413, e. 1, f. 68v
Rafael de los Ángeles	Fiscal	Mixtecos	1692	AGN, Historia, v. 413, e. 1, f. 69

a. In the burial records for the parish of San Josef from 1665, he is listed as the fiscal for this specific tlaxilacalli. I have not found evidence of an ermita in this tlaxilacalli, although his position suggests that there was one. This is the only occurrence of this type that I have encountered.

b. No chapel association or *don* title were provided with this fiscal's name. Because of the lack of a title it is assumed that he was the fiscal of an unknown ermita.

c. This name is hard to make out because of fading. It is also uncertain if he was fiscal at the main chapel of San Sebastián or at an ermita. His name does not carry the *don* title in the document where other witnesses do, so it seems likely that he was a minor fiscal.

d. This information comes from a will from the barrio of San Sebastián. The testator specifically requested burial at the chapel of San Sebastián. For this reason I believe that Pedro Sánchez is the alguacil mayor of that chapel. However, given the date of the document it is possible, and even probable, that he was an alguacil mayor at the chapel of San Josef.

e. A don Agustín Hipólito was also a notary in Santa María Teocaltitlan in 1687. The use of *don* by both individuals suggests the possibility that they are the same person. AGN, Tierras, v. 3711, e. 1.

until the beginning of the seventeenth century. Fiscales acted as intermediaries between the Nahuas and their chaplains, or priests. In a source from 1655, the fiscal don Martín Alonso was sent by the chaplain of San Josef, fray Pedro Camacho, and a Franciscan preacher, fray Sebastián de Olivares, to solve an inheritance dispute in the community of San Pablo Malcuitlapilco. In the letter the fiscal states that he was familiar with the family and the testament. He demonstrates in the document that he knew what was transpiring in the community. In response to the request from the friars to solve the dispute, he measured the property himself and divided it among the two heirs. For witnesses he called upon a former fiscal (jurisdiction unstated) and the fiscal of a nearby ermita.[133] The case suggests the possibility of a hierarchy of fiscales within the altepetl. A fiscal of the principal parish was sent to solve problems with the parishioners, whereas an ermita fiscal was not.

Another document written by fiscal don Pedro de San Pablo of San Josef in 1664 brings to light some of his additional responsibilities. Don Pedro collected the money for a high mass and then handed that money over to the guardian of San Francisco, fray Pedro Camacho.[134] He performed this duty on two separate days. Additionally, he verified that the mass was performed and acted as a witness on behalf of the Nahua community, thereby confirming that the Franciscans fulfilled their requests. As an intermediary between the religious orders and the indigenous community, a fiscal's responsibilities were, at times, of a bit more dubious honor. In 1612 a previous chaplain of San Josef, fray Gerónimo de Zárate, in a grand display of mock humiliation had the fiscal of the chapel tie a rope around his, Zárate's, neck and lead him naked into the chapel in front of the entire congregation, who had been locked in the building to witness the spectacle. Zárate then ordered the fiscal to whip him. The fiscal refused, so Zárate started whipping himself.[135]

The importance and duties of the fiscal appear to have continued to expand through the rest of the Hapsburg period. By the late seventeenth century at least two ranks of fiscales—a *mayor* (principal fiscal) and *menor* (assisting fiscal)—began to appear in altepetl parish chapels with congregations of more than one hundred people, as permitted by the 1681 *Recopilación de leyes*. One section of the law code specifically examined *reducciones*, the relocating of multiple indigenous districts to one location.[136] Although Mexico Tenochtitlan's situation was different from that of the reducciones, there may have been at least one assistant for the fiscal mayor, if not more. William Taylor, in his study of eighteenth-century parishes, found that the position of menor was as an assistant to the fiscal mayor and was often lower in status than other Church officials, such as the sacristan and cantors. The fiscal mayor was also in charge of the fiscales in the visita chapels and, probably, for Mexico City fiscales in the ermitas as well.[137] Although the fiscales worked with their chaplains and were to perform specific duties, the manner in which those responsibilities were carried out appears to have been at the discretion of the fiscal himself. To return to the 1655 inheritance dispute overseen by don Martín Alonso, the friars had not only sent Alonso to deal with the dispute but also sought his opinion about what should be done. It was Alonso and not the priests who put forward the idea of splitting the disputed goods in half, if the inheritors could not reach an agreement.

> And I [don Martin Alonso] said to them [fray Pedro Camacho and fray Sebastián de Olivares], "If they [the siblings] aren't placated [come to agreement], it should be divided, because it [the inherited property] is attached to each other, if it isn't divided, [and then] she and her brother[138] would no longer contend over it, because what she has inherited will be separate and he will not touch it." The two of them, the father guardian and the preacher, said, "Let it be done so; go, inspect it, divide it, so that the priestly ruler will not say that we do not obey him in what he orders us to do."[139]

After his conversation with the friars, Alonso went to speak with the sister, María Francisca, and confronted her brother, Francisco Juárez. Together, with most of the family, they worked out a solution. Along with the resolution they stipulated a punishment, should one of them break the peace, of twenty pesos (which went to purchase olive oil for the Holy Sacrament). When the process was concluded, Alonso ordered the church notary to make copies of the will and the letter of payment. The notary was instructed to read the document to the siblings and provide both of them with identical copies of the original so that if any dispute arose they could be compared. The final orders were written on the back of the original document so all could know what had been decided.[140]

This case demonstrates the level of reliance the friars had on fiscales during the seventeenth century. Friars Pedro Camacho and Sebastián de Olivares had been ordered by the guardian of their order to resolve the dispute. They approached the fiscal with the problem and then let him find a solution. Although the Nahuas could appeal to the Franciscans, as Francisco Juárez initially did at the beginning of the case, the friars did not solve the problem but rather agreed to the fiscal's proposal. In a way, the fiscal was now acting outside the legal process. The increased importance and prestige associated with the office of fiscal demonstrate continued activity at indigenous chapels. By 1613, if not earlier, fiscales began appearing at the small ermita chapels of Mexico Tenochtitlan. At this point, it is clear that the Nahuas provided a significant number of staff members for the main chapels and their ermitas, and by the end of the century, if not sooner, sacristans had joined fiscales at the ermitas.

Notaries of the Church, Alguaciles Mayores, Sacristans, and Topiles

Indigenous notaries started appearing in the Nahuatl documentation for Mexico Tenochtitlan around the time of the Nahuatl documents themselves (c. 1547); notaries identified as *de la iglesia* largely made their first appearance in 1586.[141] This development argues for an increased need at the chapels for their own notaries. Though high-ranking members of society typically held the post of notary for the church, not all used the title *don*. However, James Lockhart has noted that, of the leadership opportunities in the Church, notaries more than others had a tendency to advance to fiscal.[142] This may have been the case with a church notary at Santa María la Redonda. Blas de San Diego was notary at Santa María in 1679 and 1683. In 1679 he was Blas de San Diego; when he returned in 1683 he signed his name with the coveted title.[143]

Another position to appear semiregularly in documents as a witness alongside the fiscales and notaries is that of alguacil mayor. At this time, there is not enough documentation to say when the position developed within the chapels of Mexico Tenochtitlan. The first reference I have to the position appears in 1569, although there may have been church alguaciles before that time.[144] They seem to have served as assistants to the fiscal, and, like the notary, could advance to the position of fiscal. In at least one instance, at San Josef, an alguacil mayor went on to become fiscal (see table 3). In his research on Cuernavaca, Robert Haskett found alguaciles mayores acting as door guards at specific functions and working to make sure that people showed up at gatherings where they were expected.[145]

Sacristans, although not as prominent in the records, also held a central position in the indigenous chapels. These officials controlled the keys to the sacristy, which housed the images, ornaments, and vestments. This was generally an appointed position, and sacristans were also responsible for the care of the chapel and for documenting all of the goods contained therein.[146]

Records mentioning the indigenous sacristans of Mexico Tenochtitlan are relatively scarce. A rare indication of a sacristan at San Josef is from 1612, when sacristan Josef Gómez and two Nahua women reported fray Gerónimo de Zárate to the Audiencia for abusing his parishioners. This report eventually led to Zárate's removal from the position of chaplain at San Josef.[147] Evidence of the continued existence of the position in Mexico Tenochtitlan comes in a 1692 census of Nahuas living in Spanish-owned residences. Two of the parishioners at San Josef are listed as sacristans for two small ermita chapels, San Gregorio and San Agustín.[148] Additional evidence has not presented itself for Mexico Tenochtitlan, but Haskett found a case in Cuernavaca where the sacristan of the main indigenous chapel took some of the images and vestments for use at a local ermita's celebration against the friars' wishes.[149] In this case, the sacristan demonstrated a devotion to his own ermita that led him to act against the wishes of the parish priests. His devotion to his local tlaxilacalli community, and its ermita, appears to have superseded his dedication to the parish.

Separate offices for *alguacil* (constable) and *topile* appear by 1569 in Mexico Tenochtitlan. The alguacil was a mid-level position that probably assisted the alguacil mayor. Lockhart has found that the position of topile seems to have also been a mid-level position and may have been a general term applied to multiple offices. Haskett has encountered topiles helping with the collection of rent and the financing and organization of celebrations in Cuernavaca.[150] At San Josef, there have been two appearances in the documentation. The first reference is from 1624, when Juan Miguel was identified as a *teopan topile,* church staff-holder.[151] The second, from 1655, is for an alguacil mayor *topilecapan,* literally, "where the topiles are." It is possible that Baltasar de los Reyes, the holder of the position, was in charge of the topiles at San Josef.[152] The use of the word *topile* in both cases to reference other titles supports Lockhart's argument of it being a loosely applied title. The topiles at San Josef were probably present through the colonial period, but their specific duties were such that the documents rarely mention them. Another position, possibly of similar responsibility to the alguaciles and topiles, is that of the *mayordomo de la iglesia.* Only two such individuals have been uncovered in Mexico Tenochtitlan. The first appears at the chapel of San Pablo in 1567, and the second at San Josef in 1586. It is likely that their presence at San Josef predates that of San Pablo. Haskett has also found mention of them in the Cuernavaca region, but little is known regarding their official duties, although it is probable that they were a type of church steward.[153]

Choirmaster and Cantores

Though not quite as early as the 1527 formal initiation of baptisms by the Franciscans, instruction in Christian singing started shortly after the arrival of the mendicant friars in New Spain.[154] In a letter to the Holy Roman emperor, Charles V, fray Pedro de Gante claimed that he had trained his students at San Josef to sing so well that they could perform in Charles's personal chapel.[155] By the end of the seventeenth century, towns were legally allowed at least two or three *cantores* (singers). Because of its large population and the number of chapels in Mexico Tenochtitlan, it is likely that there were many more cantores in the viceregal capital than any other place in New Spain. Because of their long training cantores tended to hold their positions for longer periods than other members of the church staff. Their duties included assisting the chaplain with mass, leading the chanting in high masses, and singing at burials.[156] If the choir had a leader, as did the one at San Josef, he was known as the *maestro de capilla* (choirmaster). Both the choirmaster and the cantores had a guaranteed income, based on their weekly duties at mass and at special occasions, such as feast days and burials. I have encountered only a few references to specific cantores and choirmasters in census and ecclesiastical records; however, there are regular requests for them in wills. In one will, choirmaster Francisco de San Juan received five pesos in payment for the music he and the cantores of San Josef provided for the burial of a high-ranking Nahua woman. His acceptance of the money was documented and witnessed by the other cantores.[157]

Overall, documentary references to teopantlaca leadership are scarce. It is possible that positions developed as needed at any given chapel. Duties could be assigned and reassigned. Based on the impressive level of involvement of women in many religious practices, such as cofradías, convents, and hospitals (see chapters 3 and 4), it is likely that they also had some degree of representation among the teopantlaca, though none has appeared yet in the documentation. Over the course of the sixteenth and seventeenth centuries, leadership positions increased and expanded perhaps even more than did the chapels. The Nahuas' interest in filling the positions is indicative of their interest in maintaining a high level of involvement in local religious life.

Holy Sites and Miracles within the Tlaxilacalli

The tlaxilacalli in Mexico Tenochtitlan appear to have been the second-smallest neighborhood units in the capital city. Before the conquest, it is likely that some of the tlaxilacalli contained small temples devoted to the Nahuas' deities. During the colonial period, many of the subdistricts constructed ermitas for their own use. In Mexico Tenochtitlan at least eighteen ermitas existed.[158] The Nahuas used the smaller chapels for community feast day celebrations, although they were generally of a more local nature than a barrio-wide celebration, and for the observance of weekly mass. Some of the sites, such as the ermita of San Antón Chiquito, in the tlaxilacalli of Acatlan, were even associated with the performance of miracles.[159]

Aside from the tlaxilacalli's own legal disputes, the Nahuas also rallied together as a predominantly cohesive unit for the defense of their communities' religious symbols. This is especially visible in land disputes and solicitations for chapel repair. In the cases examined below, the Nahuas of a particular tlaxilacalli (and in one case the entire barrio of San Juan) worked as a group to achieve their desired goals. Each lawsuit indicates a continuation of Nahua community identity until the end of the seventeenth century. In two of the cases, the Nahuas initiated the lawsuits on their own accord. In the third, they worked in tandem with the Franciscans. In another the Nahuas appear to have submitted their own documentation, demonstrating their interest in the proceedings outside of any exterior pressure they may have received from the Franciscans.

The area of San Antón in Xoloco, south of San Pablo, became a place of jurisdictional conflict between Franciscans and Augustinians after the split of the doctrina of San Josef. In terms of its secular government, San Antón was initially, and seems to have remained, beholden to the tlatoani of San Pablo. Established in 1530, the ermita of San Antón de Abad was part of the original doctrina of San Josef.[160] When the redistricting of the doctrina started in the 1560s, it appears that part of San Antón (the tlaxilacalli of Ateponasco) was transferred to the chapel of San Pablo. Three other tlaxilacalli (Acatlan, Xoloco, and Tepiton—the latter potentially a sub-tlaxilacalli of one of the other two) remained with the Franciscans.[161] What prompted the separation and reorganization is not known.

The chapel of San Antón was initially ministered to by fray Agustín del Espíritu Santo, a member of the hospital order of St. Anthony Abbot. After his death in 1624, the Augustinians forcefully occupied the chapel of San Antón, suggesting that they did not want the Franciscans to take control there. The Augustinians were evicted a month later when city officials closed the ermita.[162] The Nahuas of Acatlan and Xoloco, if not Tepiton as well, continued to support their claim as parishioners of San Josef and the Franciscans until the end of the seventeenth century.[163]

The area of San Antón was most likely a rich gem to the Franciscans. Of their twelve known ermitas, two were in San Antón in the tlaxilacalli of Xoloco and Acatlan.[164] Additionally, Chimalpahin credits God's intervention at two sites in San Antón on the Nahua community's behalf. The first account is telling of Chimalpahin's faith and belief in God's intervention and surely that of the surrounding community as well. His second example is supported by a corresponding legal case. It takes place at a location that later became known as the ermita of San Antón Chiquito and shows the Nahua community coming together for spiritual reasons and challenging the individuals who claimed ownership of the land.

On 31 May 1613, "María, a widow and seller of bitter atole, died." She lived behind the church of San Antón de Abad in the tlaxilacalli of Xoloco. According to Chimalpahin, she died from God's anger over her objection to the erection of a cross in a street intersection by the brothers Juan Morales and Bernabé de San Gerónimo. María initiated a legal case, claiming that the land was hers. The brothers were arrested and taken to the municipal building. The chaplain at San Antón de Abad, fray Agustín del Espíritu Santo, managed to intercede on the brothers' behalf and free them. After their release, fray Agustín helped Juan Morales and Bernabé de San Gerónimo gain viceregal permission for their cross. Shortly after the cross was finished and blessed, the widow María and her son-in-law (who supported her claim) died.

In a related case about a holy cross earlier that year, in Acatlan, a Spaniard, Diego de Senete, and his wife, Mariana Rodríguez, opposed a cross that had been erected near their house.[165] Based on Chimalpahin's and the Nahua residents' accounts, the cross had been there for a very long time, "before their parents, grandparents, and ancestors." And, although Diego de Senete and Mariana Rodríguez had been resident in their home for a great while, it was only a short time before the lawsuit that they purchased a piece of land from fray Gerónimo de Zárate, when he was chaplain at San Josef.[166] The property was next to the land where the cross stood. Senete and Rodríguez claimed that the land containing the cross was theirs; the Nahuas of Acatlan filed a suit claiming part of it as patrimonial land and the other part as a fourteen-year-old donation by a Nahua woman named Juana Francisca.[167]

In his account of these events, Chimalpahin omits some items that most likely served to increase the ire of Diego de Senete and Mariana Rodríguez. The Nahuas of Acatlan asked for more than protection for their land; they requested permission to build an ermita around the cross using *un solar y parte de otro* (a piece of land and part of another).[168] I suspect that the *parte de otro* was what initiated the legal argument. According to the petition submitted by the Nahuas, they, the men and women together, had been gathering at the cross on Sundays and feast days (especially the May celebration of the Veracruz) from time immemorial and without fail.[169] For verification they pointed to their connection with the Franciscans and the chapel of San Josef. It was not until the entire tlaxilacalli community, represented by Matías Juárez, Martín Francisco, Miguel Juárez, Martín de San Antonio, Andrés García, Juan Bautista, and the rest of the residents of Acatlan, sought permission to build an ermita on the land that the longtime residents, Diego de Senete and Mariana Rodríguez, objected to their gatherings. Chimalpahin reports that within three days of filing the suit Mariana Rodríguez fell ill and died. The people of the tlaxilacalli claimed it was God's judgment against her opposition to the cross. When the case closed, the Nahuas received the land on which the cross stood and permission to build their ermita.[170]

The community effort on behalf of the holy cross and ermita demonstrates a voluntary and sincere devotion to symbols of Catholicism. The lawsuit was between local Nahuas and Spaniards; friars made only the occasional appearance to confirm information. Nahua belief that God punished the people threatening this site can be taken on Chimalpahin's word, which, though biased, is supported generally by chroniclers' accounts and documents such as those for this legal case. The suit specifically shows Nahuas' dedication to their religious sites; however, they also fought to maintain their association with San Josef.

In 1629 the religious jurisdiction of Acatlan came into question. The Augustinians and some Nahuas from San Pablo, who were heirs to the land in question, wanted a change in parish jurisdiction.[171] The judge used the 1613 legal case as the basis for his decision to leave Acatlan and its ermita with the Franciscans. However, before that decision was made, the Nahuas of Acatlan and Xoloco came together to reaffirm their common affiliation with the chapel of San Josef, demonstrating local community devotion and their desire to maintain their affiliation with the larger parish of San Josef.[172]

Yet another Nahua cross came under threat in 1651. This time both the Nahua community and the Franciscans turned out in its defense. The site was located on a small road that ran along the east side of the chapel of San Josef. According to the Nahuas, the place in question had previously been a small canal that could be used for hauling goods to and from the chapel. Spaniards, however, started dumping their trash there. So the Nahuas together, *los naturales y principales*, with permission from the *contador* (accountant), Nicolás Romero, filled in the canal with rock and mud and turned it into a public road, where they built a cross. They claimed that Francisco de Córdoba (whose title, *capitán*, they omitted) destroyed the cross to build a shed and obstructed the lights in the chapel. The Nahuas argued that the road was theirs.[173]

The Nahuas' suit was initiated by don Pedro Moreno (alcalde), don Juan Tomás (alcalde), don Mateo Juárez (fiscal at San Josef), don Diego de la Cruz, don Martín Alonso, don Diego de Zárate, and the commoners as well as the high-ranking men and women of San Juan. The indigenous governor of Mexico Tenochitlan, don Juan de Aguilar, also became involved on the side of the Nahuas. Although the Franciscans supported them, the Nahuas were against Capitán Francisco de Córdoba, a contador, and doña Ana María de Porras, a widow five times over who argued that the small street was theirs.[174]

The initial suit lasted until 1656, when the road was determined to be public property.[175] Additionally, it was decided that Francisco de Córdoba's building could not be higher than the windows of the chapel and sacristy of San Josef (to avoid blocking the light) or connected to the walls of the friary, and that dumping trash in the street was prohibited. It appears, though, that the Nahuas lost the argument regarding the cross. This suit shows that the Nahuas came together and worked with the Franciscans in defense of their land, the road, the cross, and San Josef. Although only Nahua men were mentioned by name, women participated as part of the larger group.

In the above lawsuits, Nahuas are seen interacting with Franciscans in situations that took place outside the chapel grounds, though religious sites were involved in all three cases. Generally, the relationships were amicable and friendly. Most of the friars came to the Nahuas' aid and supported their claims to their land and religious sites. The case of Zárate selling off land the Nahuas perceived as theirs presents a different aspect of their relationship with individual Franciscans. Zárate had been chaplain at San Josef and was removed from his position, a case initiated by three Nahuas, for cruel actions against his parishioners. The Nahuas dealt with Zárate's abuses on an individual basis and continued to maintain their allegiance to the Franciscans in general, as seen in the Augustinian attempts to seize control of San Antón. The Nahuas needed the support of the friars. In these cases it was the Franciscans who provided that aid, through their position as the Nahuas' spiritual advisors, although it is likely other mendicants would have provided a similar type of assistance for their parishioners. In any case, the dedication of Nahua parishioners to the chapel San Josef and the Franciscan order continued to be significant over the course of the sixteenth and seventeenth centuries, though at times both the secular Church and other mendicants attempted to wrest sections of the parish away from them.

After the defeat of Tenochtitlan, Spaniards worked with Nahuas to organize what became the viceregal capital. By utilizing the Nahua organizational structure, from altepetl to sub-tlaxilacalli, the Spaniards reinforced precontact uses of space within Mexico City. As early as 1524, Nahua laborers began to construct ecclesiastical facilities. The initial process was doubtless a forced endeavor, but during construction or shortly after the Nahuas developed a bond with some of the structures, possibly because the churches were being built on the sites of their temples. Placing the chapels on old religious sites reinforced precontact tlaxilacalli ties and preexisting connections to the divine. The Nahuas embraced the chapels and made them their own. They performed most of the duties associated with their upkeep, including adorning, cleaning, and repairing them. Indigenous leadership positions in the chapels enhanced Nahua status and importance within the Nahua community. Apparently, of their own volition (but with the necessary permissions), Native Americans started to build the smaller ermitas and provided a staff for them as well. During periods of population decline, the number of chapels and the leadership opportunities in them grew. The hierarchy of the ecclesiastical offices in the Church provided a ladder for social and political elevation. By the beginning of the seventeenth century, if not earlier, Nahuas also associated miracles with certain religious sites and went to court, of their own accord, to be able to continue worshiping at those locations.

Initially, the doctrina of San Josef fell under the control of the Franciscans. The Spanish political situation that developed around the redistricting of Mexico Tenochtitlan's doctrina eventually removed half of the city from Franciscan control. The political turmoil that developed as a result demonstrated that the relationship between friars and indigenous parishioners was significant in the politics and social life of the city. In the case of San Josef, the Nahuas provided a much-needed source of income for the Franciscan friars. When the Franciscans were threatened with the loss of their Nahua parishioners, the latter came together to make sure, through violence and other actions, that the Franciscans continued in their roles as spiritual advisors. The Nahuas demonstrated on several occasions that they knew the Spanish system well enough to help effect the desired outcome. In exchange for their support, Nahua parishioners received aid from the Franciscans as spiritual advisors, educators, witnesses in legal cases, and political and social advocates. Although largely devoted to their friars, Nahuas nevertheless challenged individual Franciscans who acted against the best interests of the community.

It is difficult to ascertain with any certainty whether the majority of Nahuas fully understood the theological precepts of Catholicism, but they appear to have embraced what best suited them about Christianity—usually a place for religious worship, social status as officials in the indigenous Church hierarchy, a belief system and set of ritual obligations, social welfare benefits, Franciscans as teachers and protectors, and a seemingly endless series of religious celebrations. In short, they embraced elements of Catholicism when they correlated with expectations of the precontact divine and made slow adjustments from there. The Nahuas used their chapels, especially San Josef, to fulfill their communal religious and social responsibilities. They acted both as individuals and as a community separate from, yet under the protection of, their Franciscan ministers. Over the course of the sixteenth and seventeenth centuries, Nahuas continued to be instructed in the tenets of the Christian faith at the Colegio de San Josef. It becomes clear, however, that rather than simply accept the lessons of their teachers the Nahuas both incorporated and altered the very techniques the Franciscans used to teach them about Christianity.

Notes

A portion of this chapter was presented at the 2007 meeting of the American Society for Ethnohistory. Special thanks to Richard Conway for his help with the chapter title. My thanks as well to John Schwaller for his perceptive comments.

1. Lockhart, *Nahuas*, p. 14.

2. Numerous possibilities exist for what these four jurisdictions may have been called in Nahuatl. The terms *altepetl*, *calpolli* (altepetl subdistrict), *tlayacatl* (altepetl subdistrict), and *tlaxilacalli* (altepetl subdistrict) have all been used. I have seen the term *tlaxilacalli* applied to them rarely. In those cases it tends to be Franciscans using the term and not Nahuas. In two documents from 1695 and 1714, I have seen them referred to as altepetl, suggesting that they were viewed as sub-altepetl to the larger altepetl of Mexico Tenochtitlan. This idea of them being altepetl in their own right is not unique; Chimalpahin uses the term in reference to the five constituent parts of Amaquemecan. The annalist Juan Bautista uses the term *inauhcanpaixti* (its four parts). So far I have encountered *calpolli* only in the writings of Chimalpahin and in a 1569 testament in reference to the smaller neighborhood units normally called *tlaxilacalli* (see below). My use of the term *calpolli* is limited to Chimalpahin's usage, which seems to be as an organizational unit that is moving toward a future settlement.

For more information on Chimalpahin's use of *calpolli*, see Susan Schroeder, *Chimalpahin and the Kingdoms of Chalco* (Tucson: University of Arizona Press, 1991), pp. 143–149. Thus far the best Nahuatl term I have encountered in reference to the largest altepetl subdistricts is *tlayacatl*. And, indeed, Chimalpahin uses the term to describe San Pablo. Moreover, he also uses it on two other occasions, albeit with less specificity. However, the majority of Nahuatl and Spanish-language sources use the Spanish term *barrio*, as does Chimalpahin in his Spanish writings. As a way to differentiate the four constituent parts of Tenochtitlan from the larger entity of the altepetl, I opt to use the term Nahua notaries from Tenochtitlan preferred, *barrio*. Though the term is Spanish and imprecise, it is the most common term used during colonial period by Nahuas. Likewise, the term *tlaxilacalli* is used in reference to the neighborhood subdistricts that made up the barrios. AGN, Bienes Nacionales, v. 1766, e. 7; AGN, Tierras, v. 1595, e. 4; Juan Bautista, *¿Cómo te confundes? ¿Acaso no somos conquistados? Anales de Juan Bautista*, ed. and trans. Luis Reyes García (México, D.F.: Centro de Investigaciones y Estudios Superiores en Antropología Social y la Biblioteca Lorenzo Boturini Insigne y Nacional Basílica de Guadalupe, 2001), p. 256 (The original of this document can be found at the Archivo Histórico de la Basílica de Guadalupe, caja 378, e. 1 sección Antiguedad de Guadalupe); Domingo de San Antón Muñón Chimalpahin Quauhtlehuanitzin, *Codex Chimalpahin: Society and Politics in Mexico Tenochtitlan, Tlatelolco, Texcoco, Culhuacan, and Other Nahua Altepetl in Central Mexico*, 2 vols., ed. and trans. Arthur J. O. Anderson and Susan Schroeder (Norman: University of Oklahoma Press, 1997), vol. 2, pp. 69, 83; Domingo de San Antón Muñón Chimalpahin Quauhtlehuanitzin, *Las ocho relaciones y El memorial de Colhuacan*, 2 vols., trans. Rafael Tena (México: Consejo Nacional para la Cultura y las Artes, 1998), vol. 2, pp. 186–187; Schroeder, *Chimalpahin*, pp. 132–133; and AGN, Indiferente Virreinal, caja 1124, e. 25, f. 13.

3. María Castañeda de la Paz argues for Tlatelolco's consideration as part of the larger altepetl of Tenochtitlan because of its conquest of Tlatelolco in 1473. Though her argument for its inclusion is good, it was treated as a separate altepetl during the colonial period by Nahuas and Spaniards and as such is treated separately here. Importantly, Castañeda de la Paz's research into variations of altepetl establishes two classifications, simple and complex, for altepetl. She posits that Tenochtitlan was a complex altepetl that contained five simple altepetl (of which Tlatelolco was one). My brief examinations of Mexico Tlatelolco support her research in placing Tlatelolco organizationally in closer proximity to the four barrios of Mexico Tenochtitlan than to Mexico Tenochtitlan as a whole. María Castañeda de la Paz, *Conflictos y alianzas en tiempos de cambio: Azcapotzlco, Tlacopan, Tenochtitlan y Tlatelolco (siglos XI–XVI)* (México: Universidad Nacional Autónoma de México and Instituto de Investigaciones Antropológicas, 2013), pp. 83–85.

4. I use the Nahuatl names for the barrios when referring to them during the precontact period and their Spanish names for the colonial period.

5. For more information on altepetl formation and leadership, see Lockhart, *Nahuas*, chap. 2.

6. Gibson, *Aztecs*, p. 372. It is not known how active Cortés would have been in this process; he was in Honduras and later Spain during the formative period of the doctrina.

7. The friary of San Francisco and the chapel of San Josef occupied an interesting space—one of a few locations for natives within the Spanish *traza* (central plaza). Aside from being home to the chapel of San Josef, the barrio of San Juan Moyotlan was also the seat of indigenous government, where there was also a jail and governor's palace. The position of governor eventually replaced that of the principal tlatoani but served similar purposes. See Juan de Torquemada, *Monarquía indiana*, 3 vols. (México: Editorial Porrúa, 1986), vol. 3, p. 228.

8. Gibson, *Aztecs*, pp. 101–102.

9. Frances F. Berdan, *The Aztecs of Central Mexico: An Imperial Society* (New York: Harcourt Brace College , 1982), pp. 130–133.

10. Gibson, *Aztecs*, pp. 377–378.

11. In New Spain at this time there were two principal branches to the Catholic Church—the secular Church, headed by the archbishop, and the regular or mendicant orders. The latter group is referred to as "regulars" for the *regla* (rules) they adhered to upon entering their chosen order.

12. Chimalpahin, *Codex Chimalpahin*, vol. 1 p. 109.

13. Hernando de Alvarado Tezozomoc, *Crónica mexicana* (Madrid: Dastin, 2001), p. 55.

14. Ibid., p. 58; and Chimalpahin, *Codex Chimalpahin,* vol. 1, pp. 81, 109.

15. Lockhart, *Nahuas*, pp. 16–17.

16. There is continued evidence for the existence of Yopico until at least the start of the eighteenth century, when fray Agustín de Vetancurt recorded its name in his book, and of the latter until the 1630s. Agustín de Vetancurt, *Teatro mexicano* (México: Editorial Porrúa, 1982), pt. 2, pp. 42–43; and AGN, Civil, v. 1271, e. 4, fs. 76–83.

17. Alfonso Caso, *Los barrios antiguos de Tenochtitlan y Tlatelolco* (México: Imprenta Aldina, 1956); Lockhart, *Nahuas*, p. 25.

18. The population of Filipinos was significant enough that they joined with local natives to form a mixed religious brotherhood at the indigenous chapel of San Sebastián. See chapter 4.

19. These numbers are approximate, for there are potential discrepancies, as noted on the table. For example, some of the tlaxilacalli that are apart of this count are clearly sub-tlaxilacalli, though what the relationship between a sub-tlaxilacalli and its tlaxilacalli parent entailed is not known. It is possible that the sub-tlaxilacalli was just a smaller geographic space within the larger used to specify a location within. Additionally, there are two tlaxilacalli that I have encountered in the documentary evidence but have been unable to place within their respective barrio.

20. Beyond supporting the evidence of a larger population in southern Tenochtitlan, the numbers suggest one other possible shift—that of the third-place political ranking from San Sebastián to Santa María. If this happened, or when, is not possible to confirm. But if tlaxilacalli numbers are significant, it is suggestive.

21. Though Caso dates the Alzate map to its publication in 1789, the map was probably created in the 1770s since it names the viceroy as Antonio María de Bucareli y Ursúa (r. 1771–1779). Special thanks to Barbara Mundy for giving me her digital images of the Alzate map and for clarifying the conflicting Alzate dates.

22. The lack of tlaxilacalli in the central area could be the result of the sources used, since Caso depended on colonial sources for most of his research. Though I have broadened the base of sources consulted, most of my work is also with colonial sources.

23. Teocaltitlan is the only recurring tlaxilacalli name that I have identified to date.

24. Lockhart, *Nahuas*, p. 18.

25. ANM, Hernando de Arauz #4, v. 7, yrs. 1619–1622, fs. 7–12v; AGN, Bienes Nacionales, v. 387, e. 1, f. 15; and AGN, Tierras, v. 70, e. 4.

26. Asunción Lavrin places the foundation date of the convent at 1540. Asunción Lavrin, *Brides of Christ: Conventual Life in Colonial Mexico* (Stanford, Calif.: Stanford University Press, 2008), p. 359.

27. Domingo de San Antón Muñón Chimalpahin Quauhtlehuanitzin, *Annals of His Time*, ed. and trans. James Lockhart, Susan Schroeder, and Doris Namala (Stanford, Calif.: Stanford University Press, 2006), pp. 49, 299–301. The tie to the prehispanic past is clear in Chimalpahin's annals; he clearly distinguishes on two separate occasions that he does not consider the women to be Spanish. He remarks, "[They] were truly among the beginners and founders when female religious, nuns, were established for the very first time at the said house for female religious. . . . They came from what was called the Colegio de Mestizas. . . . All the others who came from there were just Spanish women." The important implication is that they were not Spanish, and he later states that "the said doña Isabel [de Moctezuma] was buried at the nunnery of Concepción, in the presence of her relatives, who have become Spaniards and are called the Andradas."

28. NL, Ayer Collection, MS 1481, B(1)a; AGN, Bienes Nacionales, v. 965, e. 6; AGN, Tierras, v. 70, e. 4; ANM, Hernando de Arauz #4, v. 7, yrs. 1619–1622, fs. 7–12v; and BNF Mexicain 299.

29. AGN, Tierras v. 70, e. 4; ANM, Hernando de Arauz #4, v. 7, yrs. 1619–1622, fs. 7–12r; and BNF Mexicain 299. It should be noted that Juana Mocel initially purchased the house for 240 pesos prior to 1596. It is not known what the sale price was after her death. However, this property entered into some legal disputes after its sale, discussed below.

30. ANM, Hernando de Arauz #4, v. 7, yrs. 1619–1622, fs. 7–12v.

31. The three Mexico City markets were San Juan Moyotlan, Santiago Tlatelolco, and San Hipólito. Ross Hassig, *Trade, Tribute, and Transportation: The Sixteenth-Century Political Economy of the Valley of Mexico* (Norman: University of Oklahoma Press, 1993), p. 234.

32. Torquemada, *Monarquia*, vol. 3, p. 556.

33. Franciscans take a vow of poverty and therefore cannot own land individually. So presumably Zárate was acting, in name at least, on behalf of the Franciscan order.

34. AGN, Tierras, v. 70, e. 4, fs. 193–228.

35. Ibid.

36. Chimalpahin, *Annals*, p. 43; and Vetancurt, *Teatro*, pt. 1, p. 34.

37. Chimalpahin, *Annals*, p. 197.

38. NL, Ayer Collection, MS 1481, B(3)k.

39. AGN, Tierras, v. 70, e. 4, fs. 193–228.

40. There was no mention of the third.

41. The location of Martina's will is not known. AGN, Tierras, v. 3553, e. 5; AGN, Bienes Nacionales v. 387, e. 1; and ANM, Hernando de Arauz #4, v. 7, yrs. 1619–1622, fs. 7–12v.

42. The elevated status of the women involved in the case is also supported by the location of their property, as illustrated by another woman, Petronila María, who owned property directly between Clara and Martina on the tianguiz, was also relatively well off, and was a member of four separate cofradías at the time of her death in 1619. ANM, Hernando de Arauz #4, v. 7, yrs. 1619–1622, fs. 7–12v.

43. AGN, Tierras, v. 70, e. 4; AGN, Bienes Nacionales, v. 387, e. 1; and ANM, Hernando de Arauz #4, v. 7, yrs. 1619–1622, fs. 7–12v.

44. Property records and testaments for this research point toward indigenous women being the dominant property owners around the main marketplace in Tenochtitlan. More research is needed on land ownership and the marketplace to confirm these early findings.

45. Barbara E. Mundy, *The Mapping of New Spain: Indigenous Cartography and the Maps of the Relaciones Geográficas* (Chicago: University of Chicago Press, 1996), pp. 1–2.

46. Ibid., pp. 11, 23.

47. C. A. Burland, "The Map as a Vehicle of Mexican History," *Imago Mundi* 15 (1960): pp. 11–18.

48. Barbara E. Mundy, "Mapping the Aztec Capital: The 1524 Nuremberg Map of Tenochtitlan, Its Sources and Meanings," *Imago Mundi* 50 (1998): pp. 11–33.

49. Mundy, *Mapping*, pp. 69–73.

50. Stafford Poole, *Pedro Moya de Contreras: Catholic Reform and Royal Power in New Spain*, 1571–1591 (Berkeley: University of California Press, 1987), pp. 66–67, 71.

51. AHN, Diversos Colecciones, v. 23, n. 59.

52. Ibid.; AHN, Diversos Colecciones, v. 24, nn. 35–36.

53. Robert Ricard, "Documents pour l'histoire des franciscains au Mexique," *Revue d'histoire franciscaine* 1 (1924): pp. 228–230.

54. *Canons and Decrees of the Sacred and Ecumenical Council of Trent: Celebrated under the Sovereign Pontiffs, Paul III, Julius III and Pius IV*, ed. and trans. J. Waterworth, facsimile (Chicago: Christian Symbolic Publication Society, 1848), p. 221.

55. For more information on bells, see Michael T. Ducey, *A Nation of Villages: Riot and Rebellion in the Mexican Huasteca, 1750–1850* (Tucson: University of Arizona Press, 2004), p. 39; Chimalpahin, *Annals*; and a likely San Josef cofradía constitution attributed

to Molina found in the Archivo Histórico Franciscano de Zapopan (hereafter cited as AHFZ Constitution). See chapter 4, "Directives of the Colonial Nahua Cofradía," for discussion. Thanks to Barry sell for sharing the document and his translation with me.

56. AGN, Indiferente Vireinal, v. 1742, e. 14; *Códice Osuna: Reproducción facsimilar de la obra del mismo título, editada en Madrid, 1878*, ed. Luis Chávez Orozco (México, D.F.: Ediciones del Instituto Indigenista Interamericano, 1947), p. 196; Ricard, "Documents," pp. 228–230; and Peter Gerhard, *Guide to the Historical Geography of New Spain*, rev. ed. (Norman: University of Oklahoma Press, 1993), p. 181. Thanks to Ryan Crewe for bringing the Indiferente Vireinal document to my attention.

57. Ricard, *Spiritual Conquest*, p. 252.

58. Gibson, *Aztecs*, p. 124.

59. Ricard, *Spiritual Conquest*, p. 51.

60. Gibson, *Aztecs*, pp. 110–111.

61. Chimalpahin, *Annals*, p. 29.

62. Lockhart, *Nahuas*, pp. 210–211.

63. This number is reached by doubling the number under married couples and then adding in the additional two columns.

64. Gerhard, *Guide*, p. 181.

65. Torquemada, *Monarquía*, vol. 1, p. 639; and Ricard, "Documents," pp. 231–232.

66. AGI, Patronato, v. 3; see also AGI, Mapas y Planos: Bulas y Breves, v. 66.

67. Chimalpahin, *Annals*, p. 109; and Torquemada, *Monarquía*, vol. 3, p. 228.

68. Chimalpahin, *Annals*, p. 33.

69. Established in 1212 by St. Clare, the Poor Clares are women who follow the order of St. Francis.

70. AGN, Indios, v. 6, e. 341, fs. 91–91v; and Indios, v. 6, e. 344, fs. 92–92v.

71. The Nahuas continued to use this chapel, under the administration of the Franciscans, even after its successful secularization at the end of the eighteenth century. See AGI, México, 727.

72. Franciscan fray Pedro Oroz, writing during the 1580s, stated that the friars of San Francisco would not have been able to sustain themselves without the alms received by the Nahua parishioners of San Josef. Although it is difficult to know the accuracy of this argument, it does provide the sense of dependence Franciscans may have felt for the financial support of their Nahua parishioners. Pedro Oroz, *The Oroz Codex: The Oroz Relación, or Relation of the Description of the Holy Gospel Province in New Spain, and the Lives of the Founders and Other Noteworthy Men of Said Province, Composed by Fray Pedro Oroz, 1584–1586*, ed. and trans. Angélico Chávez (Washington, D.C.: Academy of American Franciscan History, 1972), p. 366.

73. Torquemada had his biases, but he also provided examples of when the Nahuas of all four barrios gathered together at San Josef for celebrations, such as those of Maundy Thursday and Easter Sunday. Torquemada, *Monarquía*, v. 3, p. 229.

74. Chimalpahin, *Annals*, p. 61.

75. Ibid., p. 45. "yquac quimotlallilico in Sacramento yn oncan St. Juan baptista de la penitencia yc cenca quimocnelili yn ialtepetzin tt^{o}. Dios. yc quimomahuiçotili quimotenyotilli yn moyotecayotl."

76. Ibid., p. 231; and Gibson, *Aztecs*, p. 373.

77. British Library, MSS #13994.

78. Matthew D. O'Hara, *A Flock Divided: Race, Religion, and Politics in Mexico, 1749–1857* (Durham, N.Car.: Duke University Press, 2010), pp. 40–41; Jonathan Truitt, "Revelations on Mexico Tenochtitlan: The 1648 Testament of Nicolasa Juana," in *Native Wills from the Colonial Americas: Dead Giveaways in a New World*, ed. Mark Christensen and Jonathan Truitt (Salt Lake City: University of Utah Press, 2016), chap. 3; Francisco Sedano, *Noticias de México: crónicas de los siglos XVI al XVII*, 3 vols. (México: Colección

Metropolitana, 1974), v. 3, pp. 20–22; AGN, Indios, v. 11, e. 122, fs. 98v–101v; and Vetancurt, *Teatro*, pt. "Tratado de la Ciudad de México," pp. 43–44. Though the parish had no physical boundaries, by 1691 a small cluster of its parishioners resided together in the barrio of San Sebastián. AGN, Historía, v. 413, e. 1, fs. 44r–44v, 49r.

79. Vetancurt, *Teatro*, pt. 2, pp. 42–43.

80. Gerhard, *Guide*, p. 181. The sources demonstrate that the Nahuas in Santa Cruz Contzinco were active before this date. Gerhard's dates are most likely from the official recognition of the parish and barrio.

81. Chimalpahin, *Annals*, p. 345.

82. AGI, México, v. 319.

83. For more information on the governorship and the changing politics of indigenous Mexico City, see Connell, *After Moctezuma*.

84. AGN, Indios, v. 25, e. 9, fs. 7–8v.

85. Ibid.; AGN, Indios, v. 25, e. 113, f. 91v; AGN, Indios, v. 25, e. 442, fs. 306–307v; AGN, Indios, v. 24, e. 485, f. 353; AGN, Indios, v. 23, e. 370, fs. 339–344v; and AGN, Indios, v. 9, e. 272, f. 132v.

86. Charles Gibson found that Church attendance among Nahuas had started to decline during the 1550s and that in 1562 Church leadership believed only one-third of the population of Mexico City was receiving the sacraments. The appointment of a position to observe attendance likely reflects efforts to end parishioner absence. AGN, Indios, v. 9, e. 300, fs. 147–147v; and Gibson, *Aztecs*, p. 111.

87. AGN, Geneología, v. 339, roll 1922. Matrimonial records for San Josef prior to 1659 are missing.

88. AGN, Historia, v. 413, e. 1, fs. 1–74v.

89. Nahuas from across New Spain were brought to Mexico Tenochtitlan to help build the cathedral. The four principal barrios had to provide workers for this endeavor as well. For information regarding labor drafts and tribute payments, see AGN, Reales Cédulas Duplicadas, v. 28, e. 262, fs. 141–141v; AGN, Reales Cédulas Duplicadas, v. 28, e. 303, f. 169v; AGN, Reales Cédulas Duplicadas, v. 28, e. 339, f. 202; AGN, Reales Cédulas Duplicadas, v. 14, e. 7, f. 27v; AGN, Reales Cédulas Duplicadas, v. 20, e. 385, f. 235; and AGN, Indios, v. 15, e. 19, f. 108. This is just a small sampling of the documents dedicated to the cathedral.

90. Vetancurt, *Teatro*, pt. 4, p. 26.

91. Fidel de Jesús Chauvet, *San Francisco de México* (México: Editorial Tradición, 2006), pp. 7–9.

92. AHN, Diversos Colleciones, v. 23, n. 59; and Torquemada, *Monarquía*, vol. 1, p. 303.

93. Gibson, *Aztecs*, p. 124.

94. Chimalpahin, *Annals*, p. 135.

95. Torquemada, *Monarquía*, vol. 3, p. 228; and Kubler, *Mexican Architecture*, pp. 466–467.

96. Charles E. Dibble, ed. and trans., *Historia de la nación mexicana: Reproducción a todo color, Códice de 1576 (Códice Aubin)* (Madrid: Ediciones José Porrúa Turanzas, 1963), pp. 92, 97, 115, 128.

97. Chimalpahin, *Annals*, p. 41.

98. Kenneth Mills, William B. Taylor, and Sandra Lauderdale Graham, eds., *Colonial Latin America: A Documentary History* (Wilmington, Del.: Scholarly Resources, 2002), pp. 150–152.

99. Esteban Palomera, *Fray Diego Valadés, O.F.M.: Evangelizador humanista de la Nueva España: Su obra* (México: Editorial Jus, 1962), p. 306.

100. Samuel Edgerton states that the cross was engraved, although he is unsure of the exact style of the carvings. Samuel Y. Edgerton, *Theaters of Conversion: Religious Architecture and Indian Artisans in Colonial Mexico* (Albuquerque: University of New Mexico

Press, 2001), p. 67; *Códice franciscano: Siglo XVI informe de la provincial del santo evangelio al visitador lic. Juan de Ovando: Informe de la provincial de Guadalajara al mismo. Cartas de religiosos, 1533–1569* (México: Salvador Chávez Hayhoe, 1941), p. 215; Francisco Cervantes de Salazar, *Crónica de la Nueva España*, 2 vols., ed. Manuel Magallón (Madrid: Ediciones Atlas, 1971), vol. 1, p. 338; and Torquemada, *Monarquía*, vol. 1, p. 303.

101. Kubler, *Mexican Architecture*, pp. 464–466.

102. The church of San Francisco was located within the friary of San Francisco and acted as the main Franciscan church for Spaniards.

103. Vetancurt, *Teatro*, pt. 1, p. 34; and Gibson, *Aztecs*, p. 225.

104. Chimalpahin, *Annals*, 79–81.

105. AGN, Indios, v. 6, e. 875, f. 236; and Chimalpahin, *Annals*, p. 41.

106. Connell, *After Moctezuma*, pp. 177–178.

107. AGN, Indios, v. 32, e. 216, fs. 192–193v; and AGN, Indios v. 34, e. 37, fs. 39v–41v.

108. AGN, Bienes Nacionales, v. 677, e. 8.

109. It should be noted that the requests took place either during or shortly after the 1692 Mexico City riots. Based on my research, it does not seem that any of the buildings had suffered damage because of the rioting.

110. The loyalty to one's parish appears to have been reciprocal, at least in the case of the parish in Santiago Tlatelolco. In documents from 1691, the Franciscans at the friary of Santiago Tlatelolco provided a list of their parishioners who lived inside one of the other indigenous parishes of Mexico City. Moreover, it appears that women, and not men, married out of the parish they lived in and into that of their husbands. AGN, Historía, v. 413, e. 1, fs. 56–60v.

111. UNAM, FRAF, caja 96, e. 1413; and AGN, Tierras, v. 2776, e. 18.

112. AGN, Indiferente Virreinal, caja 6493, e. 8.

113. Berdan, *Aztecs*, p. 130.

114. Lockhart, *Nahuas*, pp. 210–211, 533n17.

115. Ricard, *Spiritual Conquest*, p. 98.

116. Mark Christensen, *Nahua and Maya Catholicisms: Texts and Religion in Colonial Central Mexico and Yucatan* (Stanford, Calif.: Stanford University Press and Academy of American Franciscan History, 2013), pp. 16, 259.

117. Alonso de Molina, *Confesionario mayor en la lengua mexicana y castellana* (1569) (México: Universidad Nacional Autónoma de México, 1984), pp. 12–13.

118. Rebecca Horn, *Postconquest Coyoacan: Nahua-Spanish Relations in Central Mexico, 1519–1650* (Stanford, Calif.: Stanford University Press, 1997), p. 245.

119. Thanks to Ryan Crewe for sharing this source with me. AGN, Indiferente Vireinal, v. 2529, e. 1.

120. Lidia E. Gómez García, "Las fiscalías en la Ciudad de los Ángeles, siglo XVII," in *Los indios y las ciudades de Nueva España*, Serie de historia novohispana (México: Universidad Nacional Autónoma, 2010), p. 182.

121. Chimalpahin, *Codex Chimalpahin*, vol. 2, p. 41.

122. Horn, *Postconquest*, p. 245; and AGN, Indiferent Vireinal, v. 2529, e. 1.

123. Bautista, *¿Cómo te confundes?*, p. 183.

124. AGN, Tierras, v. 54, e. 2; and AGN, Tierras, v. 2728, e. 3.

125. Chimalpahin, *Annals*, p. 41.

126. AGN, Tierras, v. 1774, e. 10.

127. There is also evidence supporting a similar pattern for don Miguel García, who lived in San Pablo and was fiscal at San Josef in 1577 and 1602, but the trail of evidence is a bit murkier. See table 3.

128. Nevertheless, Valeriano did not tend to use the title when he signed documents. AHCV, est. 9, tabla 2, vol. 28, e. 9; and Chimalpahin, *Las ocho*, vol. 2, p. 269.

129. Chimalpahin, *Annals*, p. 193. Valeriano the younger returned to Tenochtitlan and was governor there from 1620 to 1624. Connell, *After Moctezuma*, p. 189.

130. AGN, Hospital de Jesús, leg. 298 pt. 1, e. 4.

131. García may have been the fiscal at Santa María in 1602, and not at Santa Josef, but the prominence of San Josef makes it the more likely place. The documentation is not clear. Preceding the dates of his position as fiscal, a literate and politically active Miguel García from the barrio of San Pablo was active in a lawsuit against the indigenous government of Tenochtitlan. Although colonial indigenous naming patterns make it possible that there were three (or more) Miguel Garcías in Tenochtitlan at the time, it seems unlikely that there would have been three extremely literate Miguel Garcías of prominent standing within a similar span of time. For more information on the lawsuit involving Miguel García, see Connell, *After Moctezuma*, p. 37.

132. See table 3. Both Santa Cruz and Mixtecos established positions for fiscales as well, though my evidence for these two parishes and San Sebastián is scarce.

133. UNAM, FRAF, caja 96, e. 1413, fs. 29–29v.

134. Don Pedro de San Pablo is also representative of how attainment of the position of fiscal elevated a person's position in society. In 1655 he had been the alguacil mayor of San Josef and apparently did not have the title *don* (see table 3). His document is transcribed and translated in appendix 2. AGN, Tierras, v. 2776, e. 18, f. 213.

135. Chimalpahin, *Annals*, pp. 199–201. John Chuchiak encountered a case where the fiscales of a chapel in Yucatan were ordered to place human excrement into the mouth of an offending parishioner. John Chuchiak, "Secrets behind the Screen: Solicitantes in the Colonial Diocese of Yucatan and the Yucatec Maya, 1570–1785," in *Religion in New Spain*, ed. Susan Schroeder and Stafford Poole (Albuquerque: University of New Mexico Press, 2007), p. 97.

136. *Recopilación de leyes de los reynos de las indias: Mandadas imprimir, y publicar por la magestad catolica del rey don Carlos II nuestro señor*, 4 vols. (Madrid, 1681), libro 6, titulo 3, ley 7.

137. William B. Taylor, *Magistrates of the Sacred: Priests and Parishioners in Eighteenth-Century Mexico* (Stanford, Calif.: Stanford University Press, 1996), pp. 324–332.

138. See appendix 3 for discussion of *-oquichtiuh*, derived from *oquichtli* (male person).

139. UNAM, FRAF, caja 96, e. 1413, f. 29. See full document in appendix 3.

140. Ibid., fs. 29–30v.

141. AGN, Tierras, v. 59, e. 3.

142. Lockhart, *Nahuas*, p. 218.

143. AGN, Tierras, v. 1595, e. 4; NL, Ayer Collection, MS 1481, B(3)d and B(3)F.

144. UNAM, FRAF, caja 96, e. 1413; and AGN, Tierras, v. 2776, e. 18, f. 213.

145. Robert Haskett, *Indigenous Rulers: An Ethnohistory of Town Government in Colonial Cuernavaca* (Albuquerque: University of New Mexico Press, 1991), pp. 107–108.

146. Ibid., p. 119.

147. Chimalpahin, *Annals*, p. 195.

148. AGN, Historia, v. 413, e. 1, fs. 35v–36.

149. Haskett, *Indigenous Rulers*, p. 119.

150. Lockhart, *Nahuas*, p. 217; and Hasket, *Indigenous Rulers*, p. 117.

151. AGN, Tierras, v. 3711, e. 2.

152. UNAM, FRAF, caja 96, e. 1413. See appendix 3.

153. AGN, Tierras, v. 59, e. 3; AGN, Tierras, v. 3711, e. 2; AGN, Indiferente Virreinal, v. 1742, e. 14; and Haskett, *Indigenous Rulers*, pp. 116–117.

154. Chimalpahin, *Annals*, p. 135.

155. AHN, Diversos Colecciones, leg. 22, n. 13.

156. Taylor, *Magistrates*, p. 333.

157. AGN, Bienes Nacionales, v. 387, e. 1, f. 15. See appendix 2 for transcription and translation.

158. It is probable that more ermitas existed, especially since I have not discovered any for the barrio of San Sebastián. For a more extensive list of the tlaxilacalli, see table 1.

159. AGN, Tierras, v. 95 pt. 2, e. 8; and AGN, Bienes Nacionales, v. 677, e. 8.

160. Schroeder, *Chimalpahin*, p. 11; and Günter Zimmerman, "Chimalpahin y la iglesía de San Antón Abad en México," in *Traducciones mesoamericanistas: Tomo 1* (México: Sociedad Mexicana de Antropología, 1966), pp. 14–15.

161. AGN, Tierras, v. 95 pt. 2, e. 8.

162. Fray Agustín del Espíritu Santo died suddenly from a "stomach ache." BNF, Fondo Mexicains, 220. Thanks to Susan Schroeder for providing me with a photocopy of this document. In 1628 control of the chapel was returned to the order of St. Anthony Abbott at the request of a member of the order fray Juan Pérez Gil. AGN, Indiferente Virreinal, v. 1867, e. 3 Clero Regular y Secular.

163. AGN, Tierras, v. 95, pt. 2, e. 8.

164. For the details of the case discussed here, see Chimalpahin, *Annals*, pp. 251–257. As far as we know, Chimalpahin spent much of his time in Mexico City at this chapel under the supervision of fray Agustín del Espíritu Santo.

165. Although Chimalpahin dates the suit as starting in May, the actual legal case was in March; the suit concluded in May. AGN, Tierras, v. 95 pt. 2, e. 8; and Chimalpahin, *Annals*, p. 255.

166. I have not found a record of this specific land sale, but there is evidence of a similar process in another testament. In Juana Mocel's will, she mentions that she bought her house from fray Gerónimo de Zárate. Unless acting as an executor for a testament, Zárate would not have had any land to sell; his vow of poverty should have prevented it. Yet, as seen from Mocel's will and Chimalpahin's account, he was active in real estate transactions: "ca çā nocalcohual yehuatsin totatsin fray geronimo de çarate nechmonamaquiltilli nicten matlacpohualli omome p°s" (and my bought house, he, our father, fray Gerónimo de Zárate, sold it to me I [paid] 240 pesos). AGN, Tierras, v. 70, e. 4, f. 207.

167. This is a rare situation; we have the actual legal case to compare with Chimalpahin's eyewitness account. The land case seems to be a copy, for it is written entirely in one hand and is in Spanish. The document being written in Spanish is not exceptional, for there were two indigenous translators present, don Pedro de la Cruz Moctezuma (from San Pablo Ateponasco) and Francisco Hernández (from San Antón Acatlan). However, there is a Nahua will in the middle of the document, and it is written in the same hand as everything else and is in Spanish, not Nahuatl. The majority of Nahua wills from this period were written in Nahuatl and then translated to Spanish. There are a couple of notable exceptions, but not until the 1640s. Thanks to Richard Conway for sharing this document. AGN, Tierras, v. 95, pt. 2, e. 8, fs. 465–553v, 574–574v; and Chimalpahin, *Annals*, pp. 255–257.

168. AGN, Tierras, v. 95, pt. 2, e. 8, f. 469.

169. The specification of May is significant, for there were two celebrations of the Veracruz, one in May and the other in September. See table 6 for more information.

170. AGN, Tierras, v. 95, pt. 2, e. 8; and Chimalpahin, *Annals*, pp. 255–257.

171. This was the Augustinians' second attempt within the decade to claim part of San Antón for the parish of San Pablo. In both cases the Nahuas of San Antón sided with the Franciscans.

172. AGN, Tierras, v. 95, pt. 2, e. 8.

173. AGN, Tierras, v. 103, pt. 1, e. 6, f. 3.

174. AGN, Tierras, v. 103, pts. 1–2, e. 6.

175. This same suit has another brief entry in 1744. AGN, Tierras, v. 103, pt. 2, e. 6.

Chapter 2
European Pedagogies and the Nahua Populace

In 1523 three Flemish Franciscan friars, Juan de Tecto, Juan de Aora, and Pedro de Gante, arrived in New Spain to start the proselytization of the indigenous peoples of Mesoamerica. One year later another twelve Franciscans, called the apostolic twelve, arrived on the shores of Veracruz and made the trek to central Mexico. Of the first three only fray Pedro de Gante survived to make a significant contribution to the colonial enterprise in New Spain. Initially, some Franciscans believed that they had very little time to convert the newly encountered peoples before the arrival of Judgment Day.[1] In part because of these views, the Franciscans started the conversion process before surmounting the linguistic and cultural barriers between Europeans and indigenous peoples. Although they organized the doctrina of San Josef (and its visitas) and learned the native languages, the Franciscans employed images as well as theatrical demonstrations to assist in conversion efforts, such as Hernando Cortés's dramatic submission to the apostolic twelve when they first arrived in Mexico Tenochtitlan in 1524, which showed that, even though he overthrew Moctezuma, Cortés was still subordinate to the bedraggled priests of the one true God.[2]

Upon his arrival, fray Pedro de Gante assisted in the construction of the religious community and became closely involved with the natives of Mexico Tenochtitlan. He acted as the first chaplain at San Josef and simultaneously started using the facility as a school to teach the sons of the Nahua nobility. By 1527, Gante had established two schools in New Spain (in Tenochtitlan and Tetzcoco) to instruct Nahua children in the Christian faith. As part of the endeavor, he and other friars transcribed the sounds of Nahuatl into the Roman alphabet and taught his Nahua students how to read and write in Nahuatl, Spanish, and Latin. Spaniards closely watched the Franciscans' efforts to teach the Nahuas, whose accomplishments surprised many observers. When shown a book written by a Nahua, fray Bartolomé de las Casas was amazed by his abilities, stating that he "saw a book that . . . was actually written by an Indian."[3] The thought of teaching Nahuas to read and write, let alone to do so in three languages, surprised Europeans like las Casas, who had experience in other cross-cultural encounters in the Americas.

Noting the theatrical nature of Nahua religion and the Nahuas' love of music, the Franciscans incorporated performance and music into the religious curriculum of their schools. They hoped that the use of these pedagogical tools would encourage a wider acceptance of Christianity. Moreover, the Nahuas took quickly to the new ways of writing, learning Latin, Spanish, and Nahuatl well enough that by the 1550s they were creating documents in all three languages. By the end of the sixteenth century, Nahuas were using their literary skills to engage in the performance, writing, and editing of dramas in Nahuatl, some of which were sponsored by friars, and others written by the Nahuas themselves.[4] European-style music was also included in the Nahuas' daily life. They loved the bells and other European instruments introduced by the friars. They incorporated singing and musical instruments into their plays, festivities, and religious ceremonies. With the friars' encouragement, the Nahuas made many of the elements of their Christian education their own and added them to their traditions.

By the end of the seventeenth century, some aspects of their engagement with Christianity (which they had adopted during the sixteenth century under the guidance of their chaplains) were deemed to have pagan tendencies in them. Ecclesiastics fought to remove these heretical practices, but the Nahuas strove to keep them, citing ancestral tradition. This conflict lends itself to a series of questions: Who was responsible for the cultural expressions of the divine in Nahua Christianity? Was it the ecclesiastics who introduced theater and European music, or did they lose control over Nahua Christianity and the pedagogical tools used in instruction? Or were the Nahuas responsible, as the parishioners, musicians, and actors within Nahua Christianity?

During the colonial period, education was directly tied to Nahuas' interaction with the divine. By virture of who the teachers were, priests, and where instruction was conducted, indigenous chapels, colonial education was tied directly to support of the divine. An examination of how the Nahuas interacted with and incorporated aspects of their religious education into their daily lives teaches us about what the Nahuas chose to adopt and how it changed both the Nahuas' culture and their understanding of their past, their social memory. This is especially evident in the context of religious drama. Nahuas did not have religious theater as a specific genre, in the European sense, prior to 1521. By the end of the seventeenth century they had adopted Christian religious dramas and were acting in formal theatrical performances known as *neixcuitilli* and considered their performance an "ancestral tradition." Theater's acceptance by the Nahuas in this regard as a tradition fits Eric Hobsbawm's definition of an "invented tradition" in that neixcuitilli had a "set of practices, normally governed by overtly or tacitly accepted rules and of a ritual or symbolic nature, which seek to inculcate certain values and norms of behaviour by repetition, which automatically implies continuity with the past."[5] The Nahuas' use of history to justify their interest in neixcuitilli into the eighteenth century supports the argument that Nahuas incorporated those aspects of the pedagogical tools that they found the most useful for their society.

The process of accepting the pedagogical tools of Franciscans further removed the Nahuas from their lived precontact past and altered, however slightly, their culture. As the Franciscans made accommodations for Nahua customs, these changes were made largely by the Nahuas to help them fit into the colonial environment they found themselves in after the fall of Tenochtitlan and Tlatelolco in 1521. Though altered, the new culture was still as definitively Nahua as the precontact one. Looking at Nahua use of Spanish pedagogical tools, we find that they adjusted their culture to fit the constraints of Spanish colonialism and then used those same tools to accomplish their own goals, some of which ran counter to colonial dictates. The teaching techniques used by the mendicants were simultaneously a product of religious contemporary circumstances in Europe and the early colonial experience. The Franciscans sought to comprehend indigenous language and culture in order to encourage Nahua understanding and acceptance of Christianity. In the process Franciscans facilitated the Nahuas' adoption and appropriation of alphabetic writing styles, theater, and music to suit their own cultural and societal needs.

Though I explore writing, music, and theater independently in this chapter, it should be kept in mind that each growing skill built upon the others. Much as foreign-language classes today focus on teaching students through written assignments, songs, and the occasional in-class performance, so the Franciscans employed similar techniques with their Nahua pupils. For example, drama as a teaching tool included imagery, language, and music and used Nahua thespians as teachers, through example, for the rest of the community. Nahuas wrote or translated many of the plays and incorporated music and pictures into them. Their participation in these pieces placed them in a position to teach their peers. The theatrical displays, more than other pedagogical tools, often show the adoption and rejection, through omission, of certain elements of Spanish customs into Nahua culture.

As the primary recipients of Franciscan education, Nahua men received a disproportionate amount of the training discussed in this chapter. Schools created for indigenous women during the early colonial period were short-lived.[6] Nevertheless, the women's exclusion from a formal Spanish education did not preclude them from the pedagogical lessons learned by Nahua men. It is difficult to know at what point and who taught Nahua women the lessons men learned in the friaries. The dearth of documentation has created a void that is difficult to overcome. Some women did, however, use these tools by the end of the seventeenth or during the early eighteenth century.

Although it has been demonstrated that a "spiritual conquest" did not succeed as completely as first believed, the mendicants sincerely believed in their task.[7] Philip II believed that command of the indigenous languages was essential to the evangelization effort and ultimately assisted the friars in their efforts to teach the Christian doctrine and administer the sacraments to the native peoples.[8] Similarly, fray Bernardino de Sahagún explained that his reason for learning Nahuatl and writing the Historia general was to understand indigenous culture and to assist in the proselytization of the Nahuas:

> The physician cannot advisedly administer medicines to the patient without first knowing of which humour or from which source the ailment derives. Wherefore it is desirable that the good physician be expert in the knowledge of medicines and ailments to adequately administer the cure for each ailment. The preachers and confessors are physicians of the souls for the curing of spiritual ailments. It is good that they have practical knowledge of the medicines and spiritual ailments.[9]

The Franciscans desired a greater knowledge of Nahua culture to enable their evangelization efforts to be more productive. Their wish to comprehend both language and culture is visible in the more than 110 ecclesiastical publications that appeared in Nahuatl. This number does not include a selection of dictionaries and grammars developed for the Nahuatl language, nor does it count the numerous works written in the other languages of New Spain.[10] To assist Nahuas in confession and maintain the confidentiality that would have been lost with the use of an interpreter, the Franciscans encouraged them to draw pictures of their sins. Fray Toribio de Motolinia and fray Diego de Valadés noted that the Nahuas used images to show the priests which sin they had committed.[11] Motolinia described a firsthand account of this in Cholula during Lent:

> The number of those who came to confess was so great that I was unable to give them the advice I should have liked to give them. I told them that I could hear confession of only those who would bring their sins written down in figures, because writing in figures is a thing they know and understand, this being their way of writing. It was not to a deaf people I said this, for immediately they began to bring so many writings with their sins that I could not attend to all of them. So they designated their sins with a stick, while I helped them with another stick, and in this way they made a short confession.[12]

Motolinia mentions an attempt to bring Christianity to the Nahuas through precontact communication methods, whether spoken or written, including pictorial script. The friars also used iconographic aids (see figs. 8, 9). Figure 8 displays a layout of what Valadés considered to be the "ideal *atrio*." It depicts many of the uses for which the courtyard of the friary of San

FIGURE 9. Franciscan instructing Nahuas with lienzos. From Valadés, *Rhetorica Christiana*, Perugia, 1579. Courtesy of the John Carter Brown Library at Brown University.

Francisco in Mexico Tenochtitlan was employed. In the upper left-hand corner fray Pedro de Gante instructs natives in artisan trades. He is pointing to a *lienzo* (painted tapestry) that displays different symbols. Across from him, in the right-hand corner, is another friar using a more European image to teach the story of Genesis. Figure 9 portrays a priest at a pulpit lecturing and using a stick to point to lienzos depicting distinctly European pictures. As Louise Burkhart has demonstrated, the Franciscans realized that to reach the indigenous peoples of central Mexico quickly they had to do so using preexisting forms of communication while they worked to learn the indigenous languages.[13] Once the Franciscans learned Nahuatl and improved their own abilities to communicate, they transitioned to more traditional European modes of pedagogy to engage the Nahuas in Christianity.

Roman Letters and Nahuatl Words: The Alphabetization of Nahuatl Writing Practices

Initially Franciscans relied on images to instruct the Nahuas; over the long term, however, they sought to train them in European literacy. To accomplish this they proceeded to codify Nahuatl in the Roman alphabet. The Franciscans then taught the alphabetic script to the sons of high-ranking Nahuas. By the 1540s the Nahuas had begun to incorporate the foreign style of record keeping into their society and culture.

In his path-breaking study on the history of Nahuas and Nahuatl, James Lockhart discovered a process of language adaptation and change that manifested in three stages: stage 1, from the arrival of the Spaniards in 1519 to 1540–1550; stage 2, from 1540–1550 to 1640–1650; and stage 3, after 1640 or 1650. This same framework serves well for examining the Franciscans' instruction of Spanish, Latin, and Nahuatl and the Nahuas' understanding, adoption, and use of the new recording tools. Lockhart notes that during the initial years of contact (and by contact he means "peaceful, person-to-person interactions") several factors worked to keep interaction between Spaniards and Nahuas to a minimum: a dearth of Spaniards; the concentration of that small population in specific urban areas, most notably Mexico City; and a lack of relevant language skills between both populations, among other reasons.[14]

During stage 1, there were at least two groups of Nahuas who found themselves in regular interaction with Spaniards—those who served as servants to high-ranking Spaniards and the aides and students of friars. In both cases, Lockhart argues, the Nahuas were removed from their traditional social context, and because of this "contact between the two populations as such can hardly be said to have existed."[15] The religious training of Nahuas began during this initial period of contact in Mexico Tenochtitlan. Friars and the Mexica then carried successful endeavors to other areas in New Spain. Mexico City possessed the largest population of Spaniards in the new viceroyalty and the most interaction between servants and Spaniards, friars and Nahuas; daily marketplace encounters of poorer Spaniards with Nahuas also occurred here. The education that Franciscans and Nahuas received at the friary, as well as other interactions in the altepetl, were central factors in bridging the communication and cultural divide between the two populations.

During the latter half of the 1530s, the Colegio Imperial de Santa Cruz de Tlatelolco opened in the altepetl of Santiago Tlatelolco. Fray Bernardino de Sahagún claimed that the most able indigenous students at primary schools such as San Josef de los Naturales went to Santa Cruz for further training.[16]

Many of the students became either prominent members of the indigenous government in Mexico City (or other altepetl), such as Antonio Valeriano (the elder), or important aides to prominent friars. By the time they finished at Santa Cruz, many of the students were trilingual in Nahuatl, Spanish, and Latin. The first group of students was trained at the end of stage 1 and the beginning of stage 2. As this select few started to generate documents, it was possibly their choice of words, based on their experiences with Franciscan teachers, that initially shaped the Nahuatl-language documents available to researchers today.

One of the most difficult things about studying stage 1 is not the brevity of the period but the lack of source material from the time. Most of the Nahuatl-language material comes from the two later stages. The only known Nahuatl documents to belong to stage 1 are a set of census records from the Cuernavaca region, dating from around 1535–1545, and another recently discovered 1549 copy of a 1541 document from the Tula area.[17] Still, some other sources exhibit aspects of stage 1. The census records demonstrate that within eight years of the establishment of the school of San Josef de los Naturales (and possibly before training began at Santa Cruz in 1536) Nahuas were actively using alphabetic Nahuatl to record household information in different altepetl (subject to Cuernavaca).[18] Moreover, the Tula document suggests that training in the Roman alphabet had started to spread to other altepetl during stage 1 as well.

The best source of information on stage 1 Nahuatl-language material comes from fray Alonso de Molina's Nahuatl-Spanish dictionary, because much of that information was compiled before 1555. Two other Franciscan-produced Nahuatl publications appeared prior to Molina's dictionary, both Christian doctrines. One, written anonymously, was published in 1548 with two more editions following in 1550. The other, authored by fray Pedro de Gante, was penned around 1547, with a second edition printed in 1553.[19] All three books demonstrate that a dearth of written material from stage 1 does not indicate a lack of activity at the schools during this time. In fewer than seven years Franciscans not only learned Nahuatl but also converted it to the Roman alphabet and taught themselves and their students to read and write in the new alphabetic format. Though the majority of the educational work was performed in Mexico City, by 1535 Nahuas (trained at the chapel of San Josef or a similar school) were traversing the area around Cuernavaca, and possibly elsewhere, for census material. They recorded information in a style that had been completely foreign to them less than a decade earlier. Moreover, as the Codex Mexicanus and Codex Valeriano support, pictorial documents were still being produced and employed for similar purposes over the course of the sixteenth century.

These colonial pictorial manuscripts linked the indigenous precontact and colonial past. Many were created as histories; others, such as the Codex Valeriano, were used for tribute collection.[20] In the early colonial period, indigenous leaders used their codices to demonstrate lineage and land claims. They saw the painted documents as the more authentic histories of the period. In the first half of the sixteenth century, Viceroy don Antonio de Mendoza commissioned an indigenous historian trained in precontact manuscript paintings to solve an inheritance dispute in Chalco using similar documents. Mendoza also likely commissioned the creation of the well-known codex named for him, the Codex Mendoza (1541), at the request of Charles V. Nahuas continued to value pictorial documents during the colonial period and saw them as important sources.[21]

By the 1550s and 1560s, some of the students of the Colegio Imperial de Santiago Tlatelolco, such as Antonio Valeriano (the elder), Pedro de San Buenaventura, Martín Jacobita, Alonso Vejerano, and Andrés Leonardo, were active in Mexico City; they worked in the Franciscan religious compounds, entered altepetl government, or became notaries.[22] It is likely that students from other schools were also active during this time. Nahuas attending Franciscan schools probably learned many of the Spanish nouns that were adopted during the initial years of stage 2, such as *trompeta* (trumpet), which appears in a 1551 entry of the Mixtec Códice Sierra for the purchase of eight trumpets from Mexico City.[23] Additionally, many of the Nahuas probably interacted with Spaniards in Mexico City. The loanwords notaries opted for are probably representative of those used in the vernacular of the surrounding Nahua community, especially words for items traded at the marketplace such as pears, peaches, and axes.

As early as 1547, Nahua aides were working with Franciscans to produce accounts of their precontact culture and society. Both fray Bernardino de Sahagún's Historia general and fray Andrés de Olmos's Huehuetlatolli (Speeches or Pronouncements of the Elders) are a result of this early collaboration.[24] While Sahagún, Olmos, and their aides were producing these materials, Nahuas were creating other texts using a combination of the precontact imagery and alphabetic script. The best known of these sources, and the earliest, is the Codex Mendoza; others such as the Codex Osuna and Codex Aubin also appeared during this period. Though most pictorial practices faded by the end of the sixteenth century, the Nahuas of Mexico Tenochtitlan continued to use iconography to display property measurements well into the seventeenth century (fig. 10).[25]

By the beginning of stage 2, some Nahuas and Franciscans were very well trained in alphabetic Nahuatl. The Franciscans' skills are demonstrated by the more than eighteen Nahuatl works from the sixteenth century alone.[26] The production of these materials also demonstrates the considerable literacy of Nahuas during this period. When fray Alonso de Molina's bilingual *Confesionario breve* and fray Pedro de Gante's *Doctrina Christiana* are compared, the format and language choice are suggestive of the changing literacy of the

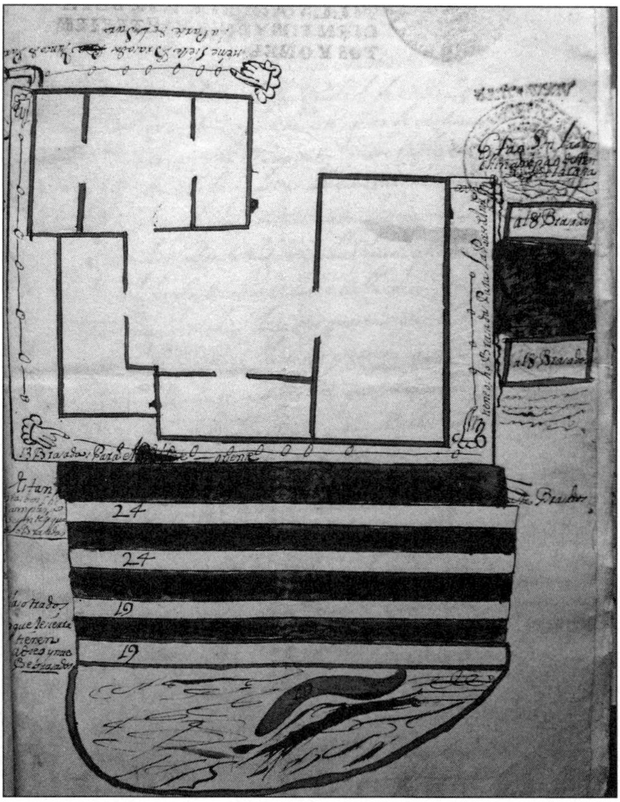

FIGURE 10. Nahua house plan from Santa María la Redonda, 1709. Image shows continued use of indigenous pictorial record keeping into the eighteenth century. AGN, Tierras, v. 3711, e. 2. Courtesy of the Archivo General de la Nación, México.

time. Molina wrote his *Confesionario breve* with parallel columns, one in Nahuatl and one in Spanish.[27] Written in 1565, it was designed to aid priests who did not know Nahuatl to confess the sins of Nahuas. By having parallel columns friars could look at the requisite passage in Spanish and then read the Nahuatl passage aloud. Assuming the priest enunciated the words carefully, the confessant could then presumably state his or her sin. The book probably served indigenous fiscales as well, who may have confessed people on their deathbeds when a priest was unavailable, which was frequently the case in rural areas. Another use for the book may have been Nahua teachers who went afield to help train other indigenous groups, such as the Mexica teacher who traveled to the Mixteca and worked with the *teopannenque* (church people) there.[28]

Gante wrote his *Doctrina* approximately eighteen years earlier. He did not write his book with a parallel Spanish translation of the Nahuatl. Instead, the book was written in Nahuatl with occasional Spanish and Latin loanwords. Because he wrote in Nahuatl, the audience for the book was relatively small, limited mainly to clergy trained in Nahuatl and literate Nahuas. The book was also penned during a period when the Franciscans were trying to train an indigenous clergy.[29] If the text was designed solely for clergy teaching Nahuas, why write a monolingual Nahuatl book? It would have made it difficult for Franciscans, newly arrived from Europe, to use it until they learned Nahuatl. A bilingual book would have been more effective. It is likely that Gante, writing at San Josef, intended that both Nahuas and Europeans use his *Doctrina* in their attempts to convert the native populations of New Spain.

Gante's letter to Charles V in 1532 lends credence to this explanation, for he claimed that there were Nahuas trained as teachers, preachers, and writers.[30] Moreover, the beginning of the *Doctrina* describes a dialogue between a Nahua convert and an unconverted Nahua. The convert is trying to instruct the other individual in Christianity, so he, in turn, can convert others to Christianity. This is potentially a situation an unnamed Mexica teacher from Mexico Tenochtitlan found himself in when he was hired by the Mixtec community of Santa Catalina Texupa.[31] The introduction to the *Doctrina*, in conjunction with the letter to Charles and the Codice Sierra, supports the idea that Gante wrote his book especially for Nahuas.[32] His publication of the text in 1547 demonstrates that he and other clergymen were confident by this time of the Nahuas' abilities in Nahuatl, Spanish, and Latin.

As early as the 1550s, Nahua records included documents in Spanish and Latin. In 1554 members of the indigenous government of Mexico Tenochtitlan, as well as don Pedro de Moctezuma, son of Emperor Moctezuma II, wrote a petition in Nahuatl (with a Spanish translation) to Prince Philip complaining about mistreatment by Spaniards and asking him to intercede on their behalf.[33] Then again in 1556 another two letters were written for relatives of Moctezuma II, this time in Latin, and sent to Prince Philip and the queen of Spain.[34] Both letters requested financial assistance; however, they differ in tone. The letter to Philip emphasizes the strength and power of Moctezuma, calling him the *rex mexicanus* (king of Mexico), and lists the various peoples he had conquered as ruler—twenty-one altepetl in total and the fifteen territories over which he enjoyed dominion. Additionally, it details the good religious work of his descendants (don Pablo Nahaxeo, doña María, don Juan Axayaca, and doña Juana). In the second letter, signed by the same individuals as well as a second doña Juana, the daughter of don Juan Axayaca, the focus is on their deepening poverty and mentions their royal lineage. But, whereas the one to Philip serves as a plea for justice, the second, to the queen, appeals for mercy. The letters themselves, and the differing tones between them, demonstrate that the Nahuas believed they could appeal separately to either Philip or the queen. The fact that the letters were written in Latin suggests that the Nahuas viewed Latin as the language of royalty.[35] The use of Spanish and Latin to petition the monarchy supports an increased level of European education by Nahua elites. They used the language tools they learned from the Franciscans to appeal for succor from their predicaments.

In 1566 a third and longer appeal was written to Philip II, also in Latin. This letter addressed specific land claims and the genealogy of the petitioner, don Juan Axayaca. It was in a different hand and used remarkably fewer loanwords. In the two 1556 appeals, loanwords are typically Spanish with Nahuatl place names. Still reminiscent of Nahuatl linguistic traditions, the writing tone lends itself to the possibility that the Nahuas had the letter translated for them rather than penning it on their own. However, the mood of the 1566 letter is very reminiscent of some Nahuatl documents.[36]

The increase in documents written by Nahuas in three languages during this period also saw a decline in their pictorial codices. In the precontact period the Nahuas painted paper and cloth to detail the history of their altepetl. Their annals speak of dynastic ties and the rise and fall of native polities. Some Nahuas opted to continue their record-keeping traditions during the colonial period. Although individuals sought to keep their history alive, they chose to record it in either the Roman alphabet or a combination of hybridized forms, with distinct European and indigenous elements, as illustrated by the Codex Aubin. Despite their decision to use alphabetic script, some multilingual Nahuas chose to write their annals in Nahuatl, demonstrating their desire to adopt a part of the colonial enterprise without fully abandoning their traditions. The so-called annals of Juan Bautista[37] and Chimalpahin are two of the best-known examples. Generally, higher-ranking mestizos, also proud of their histories, opted to write in Spanish, such as don Fernando de Alva Ixtlilxochitl (a mestizo descendant of the ruling class of Tetzcoco), who wrote at the end of the sixteenth and beginning of the seventeenth century. As with the Nahua annalists, he emphasized the precontact history of his people.

As suggested by these letters and other sources, the Nahuas' language skills were considerable by the end of the sixteenth century, even surpassing those of some clergy.[38] In one account, told by fray Gerónimo de Mendieta, a poorly trained secular priest asked one of the Nahua boys studying at the Colegio de Santa Cruz in Tlatelolco if he knew his prayers in Latin. The student stated that he did and recited the Lord's Prayer perfectly. The cleric then asked him to recite the Apostle's Creed. When the Nahua student proceeded to do it, the priest stopped him to correct a perceived error. The boy disagreed with the cleric, and to prove that his command of Latin was better the boy asked the priest a question in Latin. The priest was unable to respond and

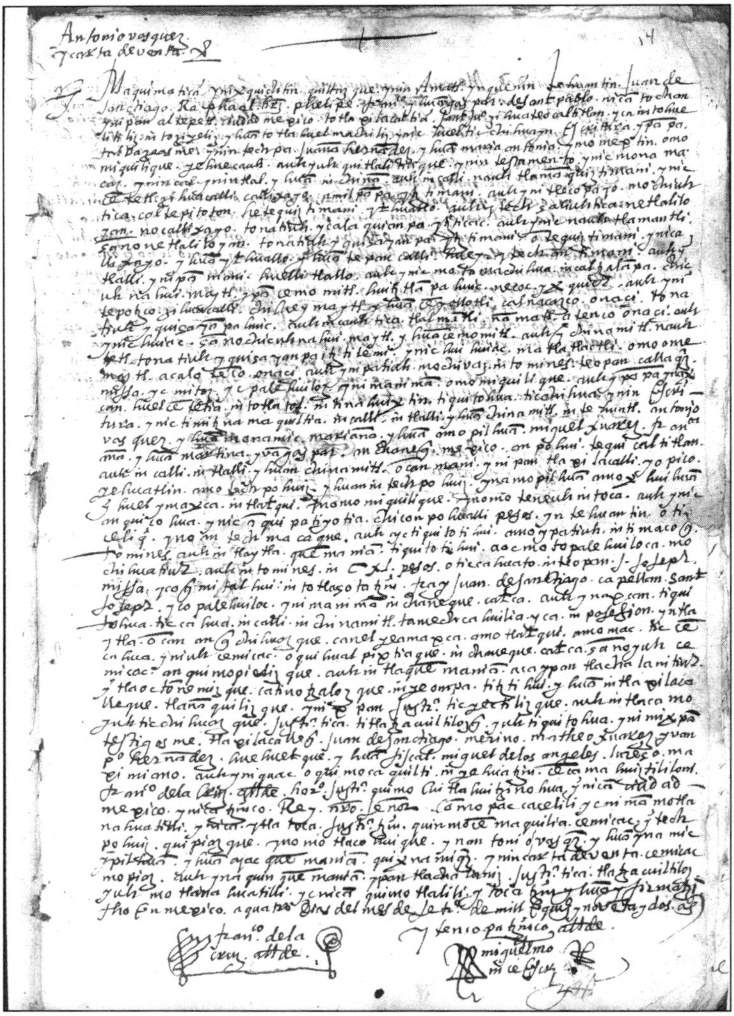

FIGURE 11. Nahua handwriting from 1592. AGN, Tierras, v. 2728, e. 3, f. 14. Courtesy of the Archivo General de la Nación, México.

stormed off.[39] Even if this story did not occur as Mendieta related, it speaks highly of the Nahuas' language skills, or so the Franciscans believed. Antonio Valeriano (the elder) serves as another example. Prior to becoming governor of Mexico Tenochtitlan in 1573, Valeriano was trained at the Franciscan Colegio de Santa Cruz in Tlatelolco. As a student there he received high praise from his teachers, worked on the Florentine Codex, and was eventually known as an accomplished Latinist by Nahuas and Spaniards alike.[40]

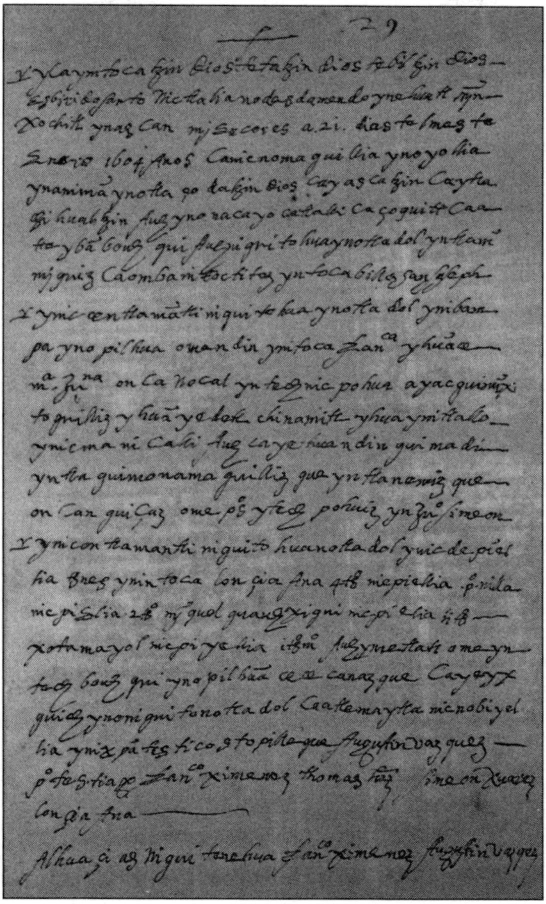

FIGURE 12. Nahua handwriting from 1604. AGN, Bienes Nacionales, v. 1455 pt. 2, e. 5, f. 29. Courtesy of the Archivo General de la Nación, México.

In the sixteenth and seventeenth centuries Nahuas continued to be taught to read and write at the chapel of San Josef. Their training at the friary is reflected in their handwriting. Nahuatl script, by and large, is legible and is usually printed rather than in cursive hand. In most areas this remained true until the end of stage 2; however, it appears to have started a half-century earlier in Mexico City. The handwriting in the documents displayed in figures 11 and 12 demonstrates a change in both form and possibly training. It is impossible to say whether a friar or another Nahua trained the individual writing the 1604 document. But what is clear is that the alphabetic writing was no longer under the same strict guidelines that it had been earlier, and penmanship may no longer have been of paramount importance.

As the Nahuatl written language slowly evolved, so too did the Nahuas' Christian education. As the thousands of pages of legal petitions, religious sources, histories, testaments, and other documents demonstrate, the Franciscan teachers at San Josef were successful in imparting language and writing skills in Mexico Tenochtitlan. Additionally, the Nahuas became skilled enough in written Nahuatl, Spanish, and Latin to take over some of the language instructor positions at the Colegio de Santa Cruz in Tlatelolco at the end of the sixteenth century. They did so in part to keep the school alive; it was declining and in disrepair by the 1570s and functioned only as a primary school with limited class offerings.[41] During the course of the colonial period, indigenous literacy was generally limited to men. By 1724, with the foundation of the indigenous noblewomen's convent of Corpus Christi, some Nahua women were probably literate in Spanish if not Nahuatl and Latin as well.[42] The founder of the convent, Viceroy don Baltazar de Zúñiga Guzmán Sotomayor y Mendoza (r. 1716–1722), wanted to make certain that novices had a minimum of Latin for reciting the divine office, the ability to read and write in Spanish, and the ability to play musical instruments. Because he wanted the women trained prior to their entry into the convent, they likely started lessons with Spanish nuns from San Juan de la Penetencia prior to Corpus Christi's foundation in 1724.[43] Whether indigenous women received any informal training in literacy before then is not known at this time. As discussed below, at least one Nahua woman had probably learned to play a European musical instrument by 1677.

Colonial Nahua Musical Practice

Soon after landing in the Americas, Cortés and other Spaniards held a mass, which was in part chanted by the priest and accompanied by singing and the playing of musical instruments. According to Robert Stevenson, the peoples of the Americas were quite taken with European music and soon began to imitate Spaniards.[44] As early as 1527, fray Pedro de Gante began to train Nahua singers in European music. And music was deemed important enough that fray Juan Caro taught music classes in the Colegio de San Josef designed to improve mass.[45] In 1532, fray Martín de Valencia, head of the Franciscan order in New Spain, wrote a letter to Charles V in which he explained that the Franciscans trained Nahua cantores in two types of vocal music—plainsong, similar to Gregorian chant, and polyphonic, or part-music—and taught them how to sing the canonical hours and help with mass.[46] That same year fray Pedro wrote to Charles V and claimed that some of the cantores at San Josef possessed skills equivalent to those of Charles's personal chapel choir.[47] In 1558, Gante wrote to Philip II and mentioned that, although the friars had success earlier with the nobility by educating their children, the Franciscans' accomplishments were not gained with the "commoners" until he started teaching them Christian songs and allowed dance (incorporating appropriate Christian insignia on their capes) into religious occasions.[48]

The apparent speed with which Nahuas adopted Christian music was aided by their precontact musical traditions. Nahuas typically had percussion and wind instruments. Examples are the *teponaztli* (fig. 13), a slit-drum made from a meter-long section of tree trunk with two holes on opposing sides; the *omitzicahuaztli,* a rasp of wood or bone constructed from a larger serrated piece that was scraped by a smaller stick; the *ayacachtli,* a rattle-like instrument created from a dried gourd; the *tlapitzalli,* a trumpet or flute made from shell or bone; the *quiquiztli,* a conch shell trumpet; and the *huehuetl* (fig. 14), a three-foot-high cylindrical drum.[49] Based on codices and carvings, it appears that indigenous peoples played music to accompany religious and political ceremonies. Bernal Díaz mentions at least two such occasions where Nahua music made an impression on him. One was a political ceremony, at which the Spaniards first dined with Moctezuma, and Díaz reminisces, "There were . . . Indians who told him jokes . . . and others who sang and danced, for Montezuma was very fond of music and entertainment."[50] The other occasion caused great fear in Díaz and may have been a religious ceremony involving sacrifice:

> As we were retreating, we heard the sound of trumpets from the great *cue* of Huichilobos and Tezcatlipoca, which dominates the whole city, and the beating of a drum, a very sad sound as of some devilish instrument, which could be heard six miles away; and with it came the noise of many kettle-drums, conches, horns, and whistles. At that moment, as we afterwards learnt, they were offering the hearts and blood of ten of our comrades to these two idols.[51]

What Díaz likely did not understand was the high esteem in which all of the musicians mentioned above were held. As Amos Megged has found, some acts of sacrifice were referred to metaphorically in musical terms.[52] What is clear is that musicians of the immediate precontact period, at least, were well trained and enjoyed high social rank because of their skills.

According to fray Toribio de Motolinia, precontact indigenous nobility frequently supported household singers, who also composed new songs and dances. Song and dance had central roles in many of the larger public celebrations that occurred every twenty days. Concerts were communal rather than solo affairs and were often accompanied by dancing, singing, and probably a certain degree of pageantry. Musicians needed to know the appropriate routine for each celebration within the 260-day religious cycle and probably spent much of their time preparing for their performances, since mistakes were deemed offensive to the gods.[53] Depending on the celebration, music could

FIGURE 13. Teponaztli. AMNH Anthropology Catalog Number 30.3/2471. Courtesy of the Division of Anthropology, American Museum of Natural History.

start in the early morning and continue until midnight. Both Motolinia and Sahagún state that musical mistakes were not tolerated at religious ceremonies, the offending party's punishment apparently being execution. Sahagún also mentions that boys trained for the precontact indigenous priesthood received musical training as part of their education.[54]

The Nahuas' association of music with religious ceremonies and their enjoyment of music in general, in addition to its position as a communal endeavor, probably contributed to the speed with which they learned and adopted European music.[55] European music, as much as writing, spread across the Nahua community of Mexico Tenochtitlan, and though taught at San Josef it quickly extended beyond the chapel's confines and into the community as part of cofradía processions, feast day celebrations, theatrical performances, marriages, and burials, among other occasions. During the sixteenth and seventeenth centuries, Nahuas requested that music be played at their funerals and sold instruments in their wills.

Indigenous singers met in their chapels daily to practice. In each chapel there were usually fifteen to sixteen singers. They performed for mass and the divine office. Chapels were filled with polyphonic singing as well as the sound of flutes and *chirimías*, an instrument similar to a clarinet. In many areas their performances included dulcimers, oboes, viols, and organs, including some of indigenous origin.[56] During the first half of the sixteenth century, Nahua musical training included both how to play and how to make a specific European instrument. Among the instruments they learned to construct were flutes, trumpets, chirimías, *orlos* (regals), and *vihuelas de arco*, a member of

FIGURE14. A Huehuetl drum and a quiquiztli shell-trumpet are played alongside a Teponaztli and other traditional instruments. Sahagún, *Florentine Codex*, book 8, image 88.

the viol family. They also played cornetts, *bajones* (bass viola or bassoon), and the *rabel* (three-stringed instrument played with a bow). Other instruments included guitars, sitars, *discantes* (small guitars), vihuelas (differing from the vihuela de arco in that a bow is not used), harps, monochords, and possibly trombones.[57]

In the process of learning European-style music, Nahuas were taught how to read musical scores. As with modern sheet music, the paper contained notes and words, so composers must have planned to have a vocal component as well. This also speaks to the level of education musicians needed. The sheet music alone required them to read musical notation and the Roman alphabet (potentially in several languages including Spanish, Latin, Nahuatl, and other European or Mesoamerican languages) and to play an instrument or sing, not to mention the skill to follow the lead of a conductor or choirmaster. A choral miscellany from 1635 (fig. 15) appears to have been used by a Nahua. Although the words from the sheet music are in Spanish (and another sheet is in Latin), the notes in the book itself are written in Nahuatl, suggesting that the work was potentially intended for someone fluent in Nahuatl.[58] The evidence suggests that sheet music was produced by at least 1561 when Mix-

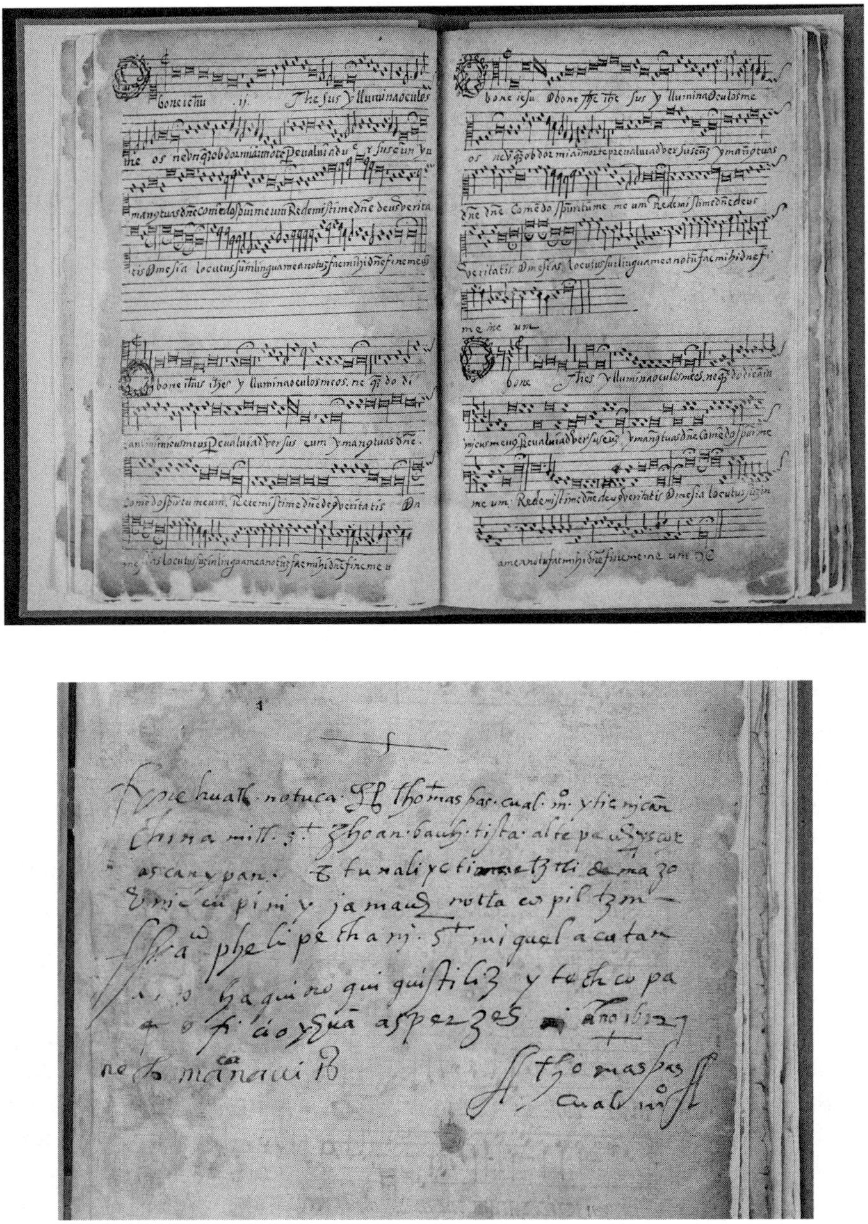

FIGURE 15. Music and notes from Thomas Pascual, "Choral Music Miscellany, 1635." Courtesy of Princeton University Library. Garrett-Gates Mesoamerican Manuscripts, no. 258 (C0744.01), Manuscripts Division, Department of Rare Books and Special Collections, Princeton University Library.

tecs from Santa Catalina Texupa purchased a book of polyphonic music for thirty-two pesos.[59]

By the mid-sixteenth century, friars were scoring Christian psalms, written in Nahuatl, to indigenous music. One such example—of a local Mixtec community's purchase of a hymnal in 1561—is found in the Codex Sierra.[60] The success of these earlier canticles is questionable; Sahagún's frustration with them encouraged him to start work on the *Psalmodia Christiana* between 1558 and 1561, finishing in 1583 (noticeably absent from this work is musical notation).[61] Sahagún wrote (or more likely had Nahua students write) the canticles to encourage them to abandon the old songs they sang to their precontact deities. He wanted his songs, using familiar tunes but different words, to encourage the Nahuas to exalt the Christian god and the saints. He believed that the *Psalmodia* would help in this endeavor and aid priests working to convert indigenous peoples. Before printing the *Psalmodia*, Sahagún circulated the manuscript among the indigenous peoples, presumably to be sure they understood and used it. Moreover, he received the support of three viceroys: don Luis de Velasco (the elder) (r. 1550–1564), don Martín Enríquez (r. 1568–1580), and don Lorenzo Suárez de Mendoza, count of Coruña (r. 1580–1583).[62]

Contemporary with Sahagún's *Psalmodia* is another, anonymous, compilation of Nahua music.[63] The Cantares Mexicanos was created from songs taken in oral testimony from Nahua informants during the second half of the sixteenth century. The work originated predominantly in Mexico City, with a smaller contribution from Azcapotzalco. Many of the songs recorded in the Cantares were based on precontact tradition, but much of their content had clearly been altered to be acceptable to the colonial authorities. For example, a verse from the "Old Man Song" reads: "San Fran^co^ ontlatoa fray pedro ye nechnahuatia nicuicanitl" (San Francisco speaks! And [f]ray Pedro commands me as I sing).[64]

The song also employs the term *Obispo* (bishop) twice and *Dios* (God) three times. Despite the modifications, this song, among others, also contains references to many things that had been precious to Nahuas in the precontact period, including turquoise, flowers, and eagles. Moreover, the "Old Man Song" has numerous references to teponaztli, huehuetl, and gourd rattles, indicating that these indigenous instruments may have been used to accompany the musical piece.[65] Songs used in Moctezuma's palace also contain slight modifications. One of the songs of this genre mentions Dios (three times) instead of an indigenous deity, suggesting that Nahuas attempted to mask the precontact references rather than fully alter the song. Despite this small European influence, the majority of this song refers to important precontact items such as jade, quetzal, eagles, and jaguars, thereby emphasizing its indigenous background.[66]

Despite the friars' attempts to convert precontact religious songs to Christian themes, they allowed some traditional tunes to remain in use through the colonial period. One such song deemed religiously safe by the mendicants (at least after alterations to some of the lyrics) was the *michcuicatl* (fish song).[67] Chimalpahin relates an occasion in 1593 when the michcuicatl was sung in Mexico City at the request of Viceroy don Luis de Velasco. Dancers from different altepetl and tradespeople dressed in their insignia, and *voladors* (natives who, using ropes, descend headfirst from a pole) also took part in the festivities.[68]

The *Psalmodia Christiana*, Cantares Mexicanos, earlier canticles mentioned by Sahagún, and the aforementioned Mixtec-purchased hymnal all used the Roman alphabet. Yet they lacked European musical notation, so the composition of the music in these instances was likely passed along in traditional Mesoamerican fashion rather than European. One of the processes through which this may have occurred is recorded in book 10 of the Florentine Codex:

> The singer [is] one who cries out, who utters clear sounds. He sings full voice, in falsetto; [he is] one who holds a note, who raises [the voice], who lowers it; who composes, who sets to music, originates [songs], gives them form.
>
> The good singer [is] of sound voice. Good, sound [is] his voice; well rounded [are] his words. [He is] of good, sharp memory, keeping the songs in mind; retentive, not forgetful. He sings, cries out, enunciates clearly; [he sings] with well-rounded voice, in full voice, in falsetto. [He sings] softly; he tempers his voice, accompanies judiciously, gives the pitch, lowers [the voice], raises it. He reduces it to medium; he uses it moderately. He practises [*sic*]; he improves his voice. He composes, sets to music, originates [songs]. He sings songs, sings others' songs, provides music for others, instructs others.[69]

Obviously, the job of the *cuicani* (singer) was to do more than just sing; he was also responsible for composing music, memorizing words and musical intonations, and instruction. The expectation that singers would retain and pass on what they knew helped them learn European music quickly, just as, much to Sahagún's angst, it ensured that they continued to share their precontact songs.

During the late sixteenth century, friars attempted to introduce a new element of Spanish music to the mix—musical notation. With the advent of this addition some Nahuas eventually learned how to read musical notes in addition to the Roman alphabet. Based on precontact traditions it is unlikely that all Nahuas learned to read European music, for the choirmaster (a likely candidate for this training) could instruct them in their parts. The need for musical literacy is evident with the introduction of polyphonic pieces with accompanying Nahuatl lyrics. Only two pieces of polyphonic sheet music in Nahuatl are known; they are attributed to Hernando Francisco (possibly a Nahua) and most likely date from 1599. In his thorough examination of the sheet music and historiography of these pieces, Eloy Cruz found that they do not fit with any specific genre of music dating from the period. The two pieces, contained in the Códice Valdés, were clearly designed for four- and five-part vocal music.[70] The lyrics in both pieces focus on the Virgin Mary; they lack the precontact imagery of some of the lyrics found in the *Psalmodia* and Cantares collections; and they may have been intended for use in the cathedral (based on the other liturgical music surrounding the Códice).[71] Its potential use in the cathedral or later provenance may explain the absence of precontact imagery. The combination of musical as well as alphabetic literacy by an indigenous individual holding a position other than choirmaster is evident in the 1677 musical notations of notary Juan Felipe, who placed a hexachord between the end of a testament and its addendum and included more musical notation among his other notarial documents (figs. 16 and 17).[72]

Those engaged in the private use of indigenous musical performances may have maintained ties to precontact traditions as well. This is hinted at in the 1699 will of Melchora de Santiago. In spite of the missing honorary title *doña*, she held a relatively high rank in Nahua society. Her father was don Juan de Santiago, who possessed *cacicazgo* land (land held by an indigenous ruler) in San Juan Cochtocan despite living in Mexico Tenochtitlan. He passed this land, as well as an image of Nuestra Señora de la Purificación, on to his daughter at the time of his death. Similarly, when she died Santiago bequeathed half of the money from the cacicazgo to her adopted daughter and the other half to provide for the holy image, which was left to the daughter once she came of age. The care of the image included money for a high mass, a priest on the saint's feast day, and four reales for singers.[73] It appears that the distance between these indigenous singers and the precontact period had little impact on their societal responsibilities; they still performed for a religious image, and they did so at the request of wealthy, high-ranking Nahuas. It is difficult to state with any certainty how the latter practice may have existed in Mexico Tenochtitlan, but it is known that Nahuas owned personal images of saints as early as 1554.[74]

As a cultural expression in most societies, music has the ability to move across barriers with greater ease than other traditions. As evidenced by Gante's indigenous choir, Spaniards seem to have appreciated this possibility and used it to engage other indigenous groups as well. In 1584 a group of Spaniards traveling to the Philippines initially planned to bring four Nahuas trained to play wind instruments with them (the specific type of instrument is not specified). They reduced the number of musicians prior to departure

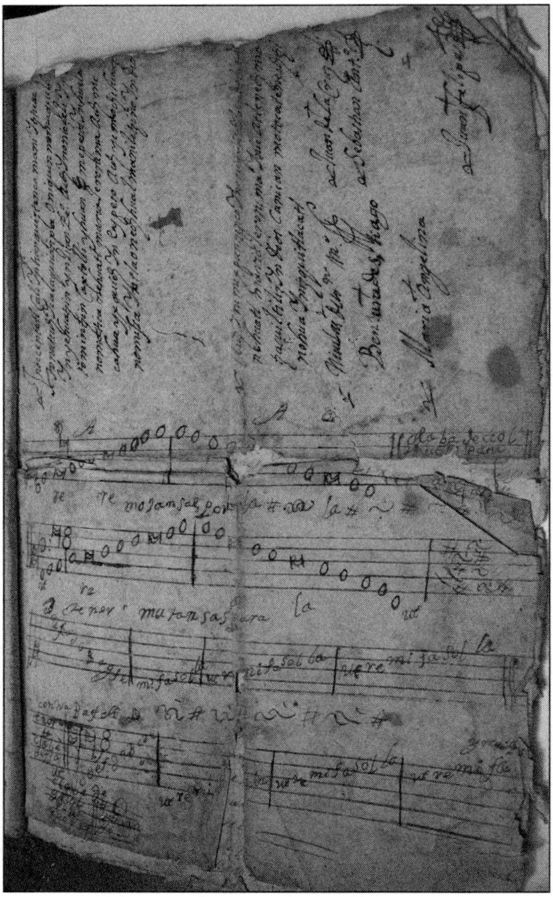

FIGURE 16. Hexachord created by notary Juan Felipe between a will and its addendum, 1677. AGN, Indiferente Virreinal, caja 3873, e. 7. Courtesy of the Archivo General de la Nación, México.

from New Spain to a single Nahua skilled in playing the chirimía. In 1591, when a large group of Tlaxcalteca (natives from Tlaxcala) left for New Mexico, two Nahuas from Mexico Tenochtitlan (most likely a fifer and a drummer) escorted the archbishop, don Pedro Moya de Contreras, to bid them farewell. It is likely that the party took musical instruments with them. But even if instruments did not accompany that group, cornetts, chirimías, trombones, an organ, and bells arrived in New Mexico in the summer of 1609 with two unnamed Franciscans and twenty soldiers. The company also carried other items related to their pedagogical tools such as primers for teaching and European paper.[75] The choice of instruments probably reflects

FIGURE 17. Musical notations found in the 1677 notarial records of Juan Felipe. AGN, Indiferente Virreinal, caja 3873, e. 7. Courtesy of the Archivo General de la Nación, México.

their intended use, to accompany European, and probably indigenous, choirs.[76] Clearly, music continued to be important in Franciscan missionary efforts in the Philippines and New Mexico.

Many of the European instruments were different enough from indigenous instruments that Nahuas eventually adopted their names as loanwords, such as the cornett, chirimía, and organ. *Trompeta* (trumpet) alone appears as a loanword by 1551.[77] The adoption of Spanish loanwords suggests the prevalence of specific instruments in indigenous society. Moreover, the use of specific instruments demonstrates a desire to bring them into the culture.[78]

Music held a central position during celebratory occasions as well. In September 1593, Mexico City leaders organized a festival that brought tradespeople from many of the surrounding altepetl, including Xochimilco and Tacuba. Dancing and singing took place during many festivities, to the wonderment of Spanish officials.[79] The skill of some Nahua musicians was good enough that their services extended beyond the religious and community needs of Nahuas to include Mexico City as a whole. As early as 1531 they took part in celebrations for the arrival of important colonial administrators. Initially relatively small in size, viceregal entry celebrations at their height (1585–1700) witnessed an increase in participation by Native Americans. An example is the 1640 arrival of the new viceroy, don Diego López Pacheco, marquis of Villena. Before entering the city, he stopped at the Chapultepec palace just outside Mexico City where, among other festivities, four hundred indigenous people danced for him, probably accompanied by music. When the viceroy left Chapultepec and entered Tlatelolco, he met Mexico City's most powerful officials; with them were twenty-five Nahua musicians trained in the trumpet, chirimía, and drum. Five additional days of festivities followed his arrival, during which more indigenous music and dancing was performed.[80] The celebrations were secular in nature, but the Nahua musicians employed the Catholic musical education they received at San Josef, or similar schools, to partake in some of the festivities.

That European-style music quickly became popular was no doubt helped by a reduction in tribute requirements enjoyed by indigenous musicians. This likely led many unskilled musicians to take part in performances, too. Motolinia states that many of them had difficulty learning how to use the chirimía. Moreover, in 1555 the colonial Catholic Church took steps to ban the playing of trumpets, flutes, and chirimías inside chapels, except in provincial areas. The vihuela de arco was banned altogether. In 1561, Philip II tried to limit the number of musicians as well; whether this was for the purpose of receiving more tribute, to improve the quality of the musicians, or to protect Spanish musicians from increased competition is difficult to know.[81]

Sixteenth- and seventeenth-century testaments from Mexico City and surrounding areas provide additional information about music. An examination of indigenous wills strengthens the evidence found in the annals of Chimalpahin and Franciscan chronicles regarding the importance of music to Nahua society. During the sixteenth century, instruments appear to have been owned by men, and they sold them in their testaments. Intriguingly, in almost all cases instruments were not bequeathed to an individual but rather sold for the proceeds, suggesting that fathers did not necessarily train their sons to perform, that musical instruments were sufficiently available in the marketplace, or both. The money from the sales went to pay debts or for masses. In only one case in these wills was an instrument bequeathed to another individual. This occurred in Culhuacan when both a teponaztli and a huehuetl were given to the *amiztlatoa* (ward head) for use in public entertainment. Also of note during this time is that the majority of the instruments sold in testaments were drums, although a flute was also documented during this period.[82] In addition, guitars were sold in Mexico City markets by the 1540s or 1550s.[83] The men who owned these instruments during the sixteenth century appear to have had a slightly elevated status; some carried the title *don* or still possessed an indigenous surname. In contrast, some seventeenth-century instrument owners lacked any distinct indication of social status within the community. Unfortunately, a scarcity of sources makes it difficult to provide more than a conjecture on this matter.

The seventeenth century witnessed a number of changes. By 1625, indigenous women in Mexico City owned instruments. In her testament of that year, Magdalena María bequeaths two huehuetl to the teopantlaca. Unfortunately, we do not know if she played the drums or just cared for them. Tellingly, she had three children, two boys and a girl, alive at the time of her death, and she did not pass the instruments on to any of them.[84] The 1677 testament of Micaela Angelina, a woman of some wealth, demonstrates that by the end of the century some indigenous women owned European-style instruments. At the time of her death Angelina requested that three harps be sold. Her husband inherited considerable property and money from her. But he did not receive her harps. Her decision to sell rather than bequeath the instruments demonstrates that they were hers, not his. It is not possible to tell how she came by them, though if other testaments are an example it is likely that she purchased rather than inherited them.

By midcentury, Nahuas in Mexico City, both women and men, had started purchasing and selling European-style instruments, such as the harps and guitars mentioned above.[85] Moreover, some musicians, such as Gaspar de los Reyes, were specifically associated with their instruments. In a 1691 census-like document, de los Reyes is listed as a *guitarrero* (guitar player or maker). This designation suggests at least a degree of proficiency with the European instrument.[86] The association of Nahuas with harps and guitars appears to have been common enough that an anonymous seventeenth-century painting of an indigenous wedding includes both a native harpist and a guitarist.[87] Moreover, as suggested by Magdalena María's ownership of two huehuetl and Micaela Angelina's ownership of three harps, indigenous women supported music in Mexico City and had started playing European-style musical instruments, privately at least, by 1677.

Vocal music also was important during the colonial period. Indigenous cantores, prominent during both the sixteenth and seventeenth centuries, appear to have achieved a degree of independence from their chaplains by the mid-seventeenth, something they may not have enjoyed previously. As mentioned above, the length of time it took to train cantores provided them with a certain amount of job security. They paid half the amount of tribute of other indigenous men and possessed a guaranteed income for their weekly responsibilities at Sunday mass and on other occasions. Yet, although the cantores of the chapel of San Josef were clearly a part of the institution of the Church, they acted independently of the Franciscans to fulfill many of their community responsibilities, as seen in the next case.

In 1640 a high-ranking indigenous woman named Clara López requested that the cantores of San Josef perform at her burial. Her executor, the indigenous governor of Mexico Tenochtitlan, don Juan de Aguilar, arranged her burial with the Nahua choirmaster for 23 July 1640. The choir performed part-singing for a fee of five pesos. The brief document concerning this transaction is revealing in what it does and does not say:

> Yn axcan martes a 23 d. Julio d. 1640 años otictocaque yn tehuantin cantores nican capilla San Juseph yn omomiquili yn itoca ocatca clara lopes chane tianquiztenco auh yn yehuatzin señor Juan de aguilar albasea omochiuh yehuatzin otechmotlaxtlahuili macuili pesos otechmomaquili ynicc omotocac moch ica ynicc omochiuh yn imisa cuerpo preçente mochi canto de organo huel mahuiztic ynicc otictocaque auh yni macuili pesos nehuatl nomaticca oniccuic: nicçeli yn nehuatl maestro nican capilla sanc juseph mochintin yn ixpa yn ermanos cantores auh ynic neltiliztli melahuac nican nictlalia yn notoca yhuan yn nofirma ffecho e mexico
>
> Francisco de San Juan Maestro de la capilla. 5 pesos.
>
> Today, Tuesday the 23rd of July of the year of 1640, we the singers [or cantors] here at the chapel of San Josef buried the deceased person who was named Clara López, citizen of Tianquiztenco. Señor Juan de Aguilar, who was made executor, paid us 5 pesos. He gave it to us for burying her, including the performance of her mass in the presence of the body, complete with part-singing. How we buried her was very splendid. And I the [choir]master here in the chapel of Josef took these 5 pesos in my hand; I received them before the brothers cantors. And [to show] that it is authentic and true I place here my name and signature. Done in Mexico [City].
>
> Francisco de San Juan, choirmaster. 5 pesos.[88]

The exchange was not recorded or even witnessed by a friar or notary; rather, the choirmaster wrote and signed the document in front of Aguilar, and the cantores of San Josef acted as witnesses. This suggests that the choirmaster was in charge of the choir's engagements. It may also be that members of indigenous choirs were literate and could read music, as is suggested by an image from the Florentine Codex (fig. 18). The illustration clearly displays two indigenous singers. One of them holds what may be a musical score. The positioning of the singers, such that they are not facing anyone directly, and location of the speech scrolls around the sheet music rather than in a straight line directed at another person suggest that the two men are in the act of singing.[89] Yet a third source, the musical score found in the Códice Valdés, lends credence to Nahua singers' ability to read.[90] Indeed, as is hinted at by the name attributed to the sheet music, Hernando Francisco (two Spanish first names, suggesting a person of indigenous heritage), and fray Juan de Torquemada's admission that Nahuas copied plainsong and polyphonic music and eventually composed at least polyphonic music, some Nahua musicians were exceedingly literate.[91] This is further supported by the 1677 notarial

FIGURE 18. Cantores. Sahagún, *Florentine Codex*, v. 11, image 43.

documents of Juan Felipe mentioned above. Though many Nahuas likely memorized the lyrics and music for their performances during the early colonial period, women's involvement in music and the musical doodling of a notary in the seventeenth century suggest that musical literacy had spread beyond the confines of the friary walls. Clearly the cantores of San Josef were skilled and able to function independently of ecclesiastical oversight. In addition, the Nahuas knew the songs and could differentiate between musical genres. They had taken the musical education they received from the Franciscans and incorporated it into their culture and society.

Members of the Nahua community played a multitude of European and indigenous instruments and had received training in vocal music. Some Nahuas owned their instruments, but more expensive instruments (e.g., trombones and organs) were probably maintained by the mendicant orders and used primarily for religious ceremonies. Although Nahuas performed for official Church celebrations, they also used their instruments, and traditional songs, for community festivities and larger city celebrations. Finally, music appears to have been a male-dominated field, but by the seventeenth-century some Nahua women cared for or owned their own instruments and may have learned to play them as well.

Music continued to be performed alongside religious and theatrical occasions, as with the arrival of a new viceroy, in both Spanish and Nahua communities during the sixteenth and seventeenth centuries. The incorporation of music into Nahuatl dramas would not have been difficult and was probably facilitated by a similar inclusion in Spanish theater. Moreover, it is possible that the friars approved of the endeavor, for they themselves enjoyed both artistic forms and were frequently responsible for supervising the publication of Nahuatl texts. Regardless of their thoughts on a particular script, instrumental music does not appear to have been a limiting factor in whether or not friars deemed a script appropriate for an indigenous audience.

Staging Catholicism: From Teaching Tool to Ancestral Tradition

In the Americas religious dramas are known to have been written in only two native languages, Nahuatl and Quechua.[92] As a tool of evangelization, religious dramas started to appear after the introduction of alphabetic script and music. The first known play performed in New Spain occurred in 1533 in Mexico Tlatelolco. In general, Nahuas wrote their scripts and conducted performances in Nahuatl, and they eventually used musical cues differently than their European counterparts. This mode of proselytization was especially appealing to the Nahuas because of its similarity to their traditional religious ceremonies, which had emphasized public rituals more than preaching for private worship. Nahua playwrights, working independently of priestly oversight or acting in tandem with friars, penned or translated the scripts. Many of the dramas originated from preexisting Spanish plays. Others were created for the local scene.[93]

Nahuas were accustomed to stylized, staged performances. Many of their precontact religious ceremonies were accompanied by music and were performative in nature. In some rites a person dressed as a deity interacted with priests in an established pattern, often depicting a specific deed attributed to the god.[94] After the conquest, much of what the Catholic priests did at Sunday mass, though shrouded in the mystery of a foreign culture and language, possessed a theatrical quality akin to that of the precontact period. This is seen especially in the specific dress worn by priests and deacons, the props employed (e.g., crucifixes), and the orchestrated movements performed by the priests as they approached the altar. The precontact and colonial tie was emphasized by Nahua feather workers' creation of Franciscan ecclesiastical garments; feather cloaks especially were associated with deities in the prehispanic era.[95] When Nahuas took part in the dramatic enactments of the colonial period, it situated them in a position to "perform" the new religion, or at the very least to act out portions of it. But it also placed the actors (and eventually actresses) in a position to instruct their fellow community members in their understanding of the tenets of Christianity.

As they did with European music, the Nahuas of Mexico Tenochtitlan incorporated European theater into their culture and society. It became a public form of religious expression. Nahuas helped write many of the scripts, copied others, and passed them from barrio to barrio and altepetl to altepetl. By the end of the seventeenth century and the beginning of the eighteenth, the Nahuas had come to view religious drama as part of their cultural heritage. Colonial authorities, however, started to see it as heretical and sought to repress both performances and the scripts.[96] As Burkhart argues, "The performance of plays was . . . one arena in which indigenous communities strove to control their own affairs, their own self-definition and self-expression, enacted in communal ritual."[97]

Plays took place in or next to indigenous chapels in New Spain. These venues, in combination with the courtyards outside friaries, provided a stage for performance and a space for spectators. Audiences consisted of Nahuas, priests, Spanish officials, and at times foreign visitors. As the largest indigenous chapel in Mexico Tenochtitlan, San Josef was especially well situated as a center for theatrical performances. Whereas the incorporation of theater into Nahua culture appears to have happened at a pace similar to that of alphabetic literacy, European music, cofradías, and other institutions, religious drama was eventually a topic of open conflict in the indigenous parishes of Mexico City, with Spanish ecclesiastics on one side and Nahuas on the other.[98]

Background and Development of Theater in Mexico City

Of roughly twenty known Nahuatl plays from the sixteenth century, the majority were the product of the Franciscans' evangelization efforts. Franciscans and Nahuas produced most of the plays at one of their larger religious compounds. Horcasitas found that from 1531 to 1600 there were five documented performances in Mexico City. Burkhart has uncovered an additional play that may have made its debut at the chapel of San Josef in the 1590s. Moreover, by the end of the seventeenth century Nahuas were performing a Passion play annually on Palm Sunday. The 1533 performance of the play, *El Juicio Final*, by fray Andrés de Olmos, is the earliest known example of an evangelization drama in Mexico City.[99] Approximately eight hundred Nahuas took part in the play, and it was watched by Archbishop fray Juan de Zumárraga. Fray Bartolomé de las Casas, amazed by the report of the play, stated that the sixteen Nahua actors with speaking roles were responsible for their own lines, that no one cut another person off, and that their performance was the talk of Europe.[100]

Plays continued to be performed at the request of both Nahuas and Franciscans. The end of the sixteenth and beginning of the seventeenth century saw the introduction of the Holy Wednesday drama.[101] Chimalpahin mentions that on 20 February 1600, the first day of Lent, fray Juan de Torquemada directed a play "as a model for the lives of us commoners."[102] Numerous plays were written, copied, and translated in the seventeenth century, some in Mexico City and others in surrounding areas. Some have no known Spanish predecessors; others, such as those translated by don Bartolomé de Alva, are clearly translations into Nahuatl and at times modifications of Spanish Golden Age drama. Alva himself, a mestizo priest descended from Tetzcocan nobility, provided Nahuatl translations of some of the works of Lope de Vega Carpio and Pedro Calderón de la Barca. Alva translated the dramas to help the Jesuit father Horacio Carochi with his linguistic research into Nahuatl and for performance as well.[103]

Theatrical productions eventually incorporated music. Spanish Golden Age drama used both instrumental and vocal music, as illustrated by stage directions in Calderón's *Great Theater of the World*. Alva included many of the musical stage directions in his translation of the work and often altered some of them. In one instance Calderón's version states simply, "Music plays as two spheres open in half at the same time." Alva's version of this paints a similar scene, but the music differs. His stage directions call for "a song, and music made on an organ."[104] However, a small musical cue similar to Calderón's suggests a possible innovation in Nahuatl theater. The change occurs when the actor playing the part of "Our Savior" exits the stage. In the Nahuatl version "musical instruments are played"; in the Spanish script no music of any type is mentioned. Moreover, there is no scene change or other action mentioned. This is unlike the Spanish cue above that specifies the opening of two spheres.[105] Because of the difficulty of dating Nahuatl scripts, it is not possible at present to say if this was the first occurrence of this type of stage direction. By 1678, as seen in the script for the *Sacrifice of Isaac*, such cues were common for characters entering and leaving the stage. In the twenty-four-page script, twelve musical cues were used.[106] Such directions appear in a majority of the known Nahuatl dramas, though it is difficult to tell when the trend started. Noticeably, musical instruments are absent from the Holy Wednesday drama (ca. 1590), suggesting that this innovation started during the seventeenth century.[107] The descriptions of the cues themselves do not tell us exactly how elaborate these cues might have been. Certain Nahuas' musical prowess and ability to compose scores suggest that amateur musicians did not necessarily perform these cues.

The playing of instruments, including drums and wind instruments, when actors entered or left the stage in Nahuatl theater may have started with Alva. It was certainly in full force among other Nahua playwrights or translators by the 1670s. The incorporation of music, beyond what Spaniards used in their plays, should not come as a surprise given that the Nahuas enjoyed it so much. The Franciscans introduced the Nahuas to Spanish theater and European musical instruments, but by the end of the seventeenth century the Nahuas had made them part of their community traditions.

Neixcuitilli, an Exemplum

Theater in Mesoamerica originated with the Spanish, but Nahuas did not adopt Spanish vocabulary to denote their theatrical productions. Instead they used the term *neixcuitilli,* which initially served to translate Spanish *ejemplo* or Latin *exemplum* (example).[108] The Nahuas continued to prefer this term over the Spanish equivalents, *auto* or *comedia,* suggesting that they saw the Nahuatl theater genre as distinct and separate from its Spanish counterpart. Spaniards also appear to have understood it as a different type of theater, for they had adopted the term into colonial Spanish by the second half of the seventeenth century. When Archbishop don fray Payo Enríquez de Rivera Manrique complained about the Nahuas' "nescuitiles" in Mexico City, in 1673, he did not provide any clarifying remarks, suggesting that anyone who read the document understood what the term meant.[109] The word continued to appear in other complaints in favor of or against Nahua theatrical performances and was used by fray Agustín de Vetancurt in reference to Palm Sunday Passion play performances in his seventeenth-century chronicle.[110]

Sometime before 1673 and Archbishop Enríquez de Rivera Manrique's complaint, Nahuatl theater had diverged sufficiently from its European counterpart to be considered a genre of its own. Many of the scripts were translated and adapted to fit Nahua culture and society. This was especially the case in don Bartolomé de Alva's translation of Spanish Golden Age dramas.[111] The alteration of these plays went beyond changing scripted parts and adding stage directions. The change in the cues suggests that the Nahuas were not only rewriting the performances but also serving as the directors, or at least influencing the directors, of the performances.

The divergence between Spanish and Nahuatl religious drama caused conflict during the last quarter of the seventeenth century. The initial concern was with the Mexico Tlatelolco Nahuas' performance of the Easter Passion play. Complaints eventually included the Epiphany neixcuitilli as well and targeted the additional Mexico City indigenous parishes of San Josef, San Pablo, San Sebastián, Santa María, Santa Cruz, and Mixtecos.[112] The disagreement was over the Nahuas' portrayal of religious characters, the participation of actresses, and the amount of alcohol imbibed by some thespians. Fray Miguel Camacho Villavicencio said he had to remove the actors playing the apostles from the 1697 production because of their drunkenness. He advocated the cessation of such performances, stating that visual spectacles of Christian narratives were not needed since Nahua parishioners could learn by simply listening to the stories. However, both he and the fifteen high-ranking Nahuas who petitioned for permission to continue performing the Passion narrative stated that the play was well established and that it dated back to the early colonial period. The Nahuas described the play as a very old tradition.

In 1704, Archbishop don Juan de Ortega Canon Montañez y Patiño affirmed his predecessor's decree against the performance of the Easter and Epiphany neixcuitilli. He sent his edict to the seven indigenous parishes in Mexico City and had the chaplains sign the document, stating that they both heard and obeyed the declaration. The authorities objecting to the performances do not appear to have been anti-neixcuitilli; they simply were opposed to Nahua women acting onstage and Nahuas playing the part of Jesus, the apostles, St. Joseph, one of the Marys, or other named saints and angels, especially in the Epiphany and Passion plays. The argument over both neixcuitilli lasted for at least thirty years. The agreement eventually reached between the archbishop and mendicant chaplains did not involve the acceptance of indigenous parishioners. Despite Archbishop Ortega Cañon Montañez y Patiño's decree banning the performances, the indigenous peoples of New Spain continued to perform "Passion" neixcuitilli, as demonstrated by an eighteenth-century copy of a Passion play script in Tepaltzingo and the continued performance, to this day, of the Iztapalapa Passion play in Mexico City.[113]

Neixcuitilli continued to be written and performed in spite of their prohibition. Vetancurt, chaplain of San Josef, supported the composition of another neixcuitilli. The play had angels and demons in its cast, but none of them was named, nor were there any female roles. Despite attempts to alter their performances, neixcuitilli continued to come under censure from the Inquisition in the eighteenth century. This disapproval, however, did not prevent the Nahuas from passing the scripts from one generation to the next or from continuing to stage them. Even Passion plays, the target of heated debate, continue to make an appearance in many indigenous villages today.[114]

Why were the Nahuas so tied to using a European medium to express seemingly European religious ideas? The answer to this question cannot be definitively known. However, the changes Nahuas made to colonial era drama may have gone beyond visual and aural differences to include the Nahuas' historical memory of the performances. As Megged explains, "For the Nahuas, commemorating the past in a transcendental manner and through its reenactment required merging the historical, mythological, and godly personalities, as well as the far-removed events of other eras, with the leading figures and circumstances of the present."[115] The neixcuitilli merged the Christian past with the Nahuas' precontact ritual practice. They combined Christian teachings with visual Nahua religiosity. The plays encouraged and allowed the Nahuas to connect the present with the past. In this regard, colonial religious authorities encouraged them. How Nahuas viewed that process was tied to their own cultural understanding. And indeed they appear to have fully incorporated the merger of the present with the past, coming to consider neixcuitilli as a part of their ancestral traditions. Megged goes on to argue that Nahua social memory was directly connected both to the world and the afterlife, such that "the recording, as well as the commemoration of historic or sacred times[,] remained acts tied closely to distinct abodes, where time was continually rejuvenated."[116] Despite the Spaniards' role in introducing Christian religious drama, the Nahuas may have viewed neixcuitilli as a continuation of precontact religious practice and expression. In other words, the idea of drama as a performed piece on a stage arrived with the Europeans, but the Nahuas may have understood it to be literally, rather than figuratively, a part of their ancestral traditions. This would suggest that they did more than simply adopt theater as an expression of religiosity; rather, they incorporated it fully into their present and their past. And in so doing they created a new cultural form.

Alphabetic literacy, theater, and music started as pedagogical tools used by the Franciscans in the hope of converting the Nahuas of New Spain to Christianity. Theater, unlike music and alphabetic literacy, eventually came under censure by ecclesiastical authorities because of the Nahuas' portrayal of key religious figures and their perceived interpretation of the stories. The argument over the neixcuitilli reveals that the Nahuas had adopted this teaching aid into daily life. Their struggle to continue performing theater pieces and their success in doing so, against the desires of multiple archbishops and some Franciscans, reveal a degree of cultural and social autonomy in the capital of New Spain 175 years after the conquest of Mexico Tenochtitlan.

The mendicant orders adapted their conversion tools to fit the needs of New Spain. In the process, they codified several indigenous languages in the Roman alphabet and strove to learn Nahua culture. Their attempt to incorporate aspects of Nahua culture into their pedagogy can be seen in Sahagún's *Psalmodia Christiana* and the use of music and dancing in feast day celebrations. The Franciscans believed that the most effective way to convert the Nahuas was to engage them in the learning process. The Nahuas' adoption of traditional pedagogical tools was indicative of the Franciscans' success. Moreover, the Franciscans' choices in regard to certain teaching aids appear to have been fruitful, for many Nahuas embraced and adopted European writing practices, music, and theater. Essentially, the Nahuas decided to own the tools that provided them with a closer connection to the Catholic faith, thereby supporting their own interactions with divinity.

By the end of the Hapsburg period, the Nahuas of Mexico City had not only incorporated the Europeans' pedagogical tools into their culture but also combined, altered, and added them to their perceived ancestral traditions. In some business transactions the Nahua cantores appear to have acted independently of clerical oversight. In addition, both Nahua men and Nahua women started to purchase and perhaps play European instruments.

We do not know how much musical composition happened away from the watchful eyes of religious teachers, but it is probable that indigenous musical instruction did not remain within the confines of religious compounds. By the 1530s schools for musical instruction, started by Spaniards outside the religious orders, had opened in Mexico City.[117] The creation of these schools, the innovativeness of Nahua society, a notary literate in musical notation, and the existence of a possible female Nahua harpist suggest that Nahuas were instructing each other in European musical instruments by the end of the seventeenth century.

Whereas the musical engagements of the Nahuas of Mexico Tenochtitlan received some independence from ecclesiastical oversight, the theatrical dramas, which they had been performing since the 1530s, came under censure by the 1670s. The argument over neixcuitilli shows the Nahuas' adoption of a tool of evangelization, its incorporation into their society, and willingness by the community to perform neixcuitilli in their own way even in the face of adversity. In many ways, their engagement with neixcuitilli was the most personal interaction with colonial divinity that Nahuas possessed. In writing and maintaining scripts they literally became divine, just as their precontact priests had done. Their ability to campaign successfully for the continued performance of Nahuatl theater attests to an independence of their culture and society at the very heart of the Spanish colonial enterprise in New Spain; it also demonstrates a desire to sustain the divine.

Franciscan friars introduced European music, literacy, and theater to the Nahuas during the first half of the sixteenth century. By the mid-seventeenth century all three pedagogies had taken on a life of their own within the Nahua community. Women, who had been excluded during the sixteenth century, became participants in at least two of the three traditions by the end of the seventeenth. And though the Nahuas came into conflict with Church authorities, they continued to use the tools received from their mendicant teachers to fight for control of their past and to influence their future well into the eighteenth century.

Notes

Portions of the chapter were presented at the 2008 meeting of the Rocky Mountain Council for Latin American Studies. Special thanks to Stafford Poole for his insightful comments. The sections on theater and music were published previously; new discoveries since that publication have been added to this chapter. For more information, see Jonathan Truitt, "Adopted Pedagogies: Nahua Incorporation of European Music and Theater in Colonial Mexico City," *The Americas: A Quarterly Review of Inter-American Cultural History* 66, no. 3 (January 2010): pp. 311–330. Permission courtesy of the Academy of American Franciscan History.

1. John Leddy Phelan, *The Millennial Kingdom of the Franciscans in the New World*, 2nd ed. (Berkeley: University of California Press, 1970), p. 11.

2. Richard C. Trexler, *Church and Community, 1200–1600: Studies in the History of Florence and New Spain* (Rome: Edizioni di Storia E. Letteratura, 1987), p. 578.

3. Bartolomé de las Casas, *Apologética historia sumaria: Cuanto a las cualidades, dispusicion, descripcion, cielo y suelo destas tierras, y condiciones naturales, policías, republicas, manera de vivir e costumbres de las gentes destas indias occidentales y meridionales cuyo imperio soberano pertenece a los reyes de castilla*, 2 vols. (México: Universidad Nacional Autónoma de México, Instituto de Investigaciones Históricas, 1967), vol. 1, p. 327.

4. Barry D. Sell and Louise M. Burkhart, *Nahuatl Theater*, Vol. 1: *Death and Life in Colonial Nahua Mexico* (Norman: University of Oklahoma Press, 2004), p. xix.

5. Eric Hobsbawm, "Introduction: Inventing Traditions," in *The Invention of Tradition*, ed. Eric Hobsbawm and Terence Ranger (Cambridge: Cambridge University Press, 1992), p. 1.

6. Mónica Díaz, *Indigenous Writings from the Convent: Negotiating Ethnic Autonomy in Colonial Mexico* (Tucson: University of Arizona Press, 2010), p. 6.

7. The idea of a "spiritual conquest" was first put forward by Ricard in *Spiritual Conquest of Mexico*. For sources arguing against the "spiritual conquest," see Burkhart, *Slippery Earth*; Dibble, "Nahuatlization," pp. 225–233; and Jorge Klor de Alva, "Spiritual Conflict and Accommodation in New Spain: Toward a Typology of Aztec Responses to Christianity," in *The Inca and Aztec States: Anthropology and History*, ed. George A. Collier, Renato I. Rosaldo, and John D. Wirth (New York: Academic Press, 1982), pp. 345–366.

8. Dibble, "Nahuatlization," p. 227.

9. Bernardino de Sahagún, *Florentine Codex: General History of the Things of New Spain*, 2nd ed., 13 vols., ed. and trans. Charles E. Dibble and Arthur J. O. Anderson (Salt Lake City: School of American Research and University of Utah, 1970–1982), vol. 1, p. 45.

10. Barry David Sell, "Friars, Nahuas, and Books: Language and Expression in Colonial Nahuatl Publications" (Ph.D. diss., University of California, Los Angeles, 1993), p. xiii.

11. Anne Whited Normann, "Testerian Codices: Hieroglyphic Catechisms for Native Conversion in New Spain" (Ph.D. diss., Tulane University, 1985), p. 16; Palomera, *Fray Diego*, pp. 67, 308; and Donald Robertson, *Mexican Manuscript Painting of the Early Colonial Period: The Metropolitan Schools* (Norman: University of Oklahoma Press, 1994), p. 53.

12. Toribio de Motolinia, *Motolinia's History of the Indians of New Spain*, trans. Francis Borgia Steck (Washington, D.C.: Academy of American Franciscan History, 1951), p. 198.

13. Burkhart, *Slippery Earth*, pp. 21–22.

14. Lockhart, *Nahuas*, pp. 261, 263.

15. Ibid., 263.

16. Sahagún, *Florentine Codex*, vol. 3, p. 165.

17. Two wills have been found for Tenochtitlan that were apparently written in 1546 and 1548. The Nahuatl originals of both documents have been lost, and all scholars have to work with are the sixteenth-century Spanish translations. AGN, Tierras, v. 35, e. 1; AGN, Indiferente Virreinal, v. 2529, e. 1; and Lockhart, *Nahuas*, pp. 263–264. Special thanks to Ryan Crewe for sharing the Tula document with me and to James Lockhart for generous assistance with translating the document.

18. For more information on the census records, see Eike Hinz, Claudine Hartau, and Marie-Luise Heimann-Koenen, eds. and trans., *Aztekischer Zensus: Zur indianischen Wirtschaft und Gesellschaft im Marquesado um 1540* (Hannover: Verlag für Ethnologie, 1983); and S. L. Cline, *The Book of Tributes: Early Sixteenth-Century Nahuatl Censuses from Morelos* (Los Angeles: UCLA Latin American Center Publications, 1993).

19. Sell, "Friars," p. 305.

20. The Codex Valeriano, specifically, is a late sixteenth-century tribute record from the barrio of San Pablo Teopan. Its name is derived from the indigenous governor of San Juan Tenochtitlan, Antonio Valeriano. For more information, see John B. Glass, "A Census of Native Middle American Pictorial Manuscripts," in *Handbook of Middle American Indians*, vol. 14, ed. Howard F. Cline (Austin: University of Texas Press, 1975), p. 383.

21. Elizabeth Hill Boone, "Pictorial Documents and Visual Thinking in Postconquest Mexico," in *Native Traditions in the Postconquest World*, ed. Elizabeth Hill Boone and Tom Cummins (Washington, D.C.: Dumbarton Oaks, 1998), p. 193.

22. SilverMoon, "The Imperial College of Tlatelolco and the Emergence of a New Nahua Intellectual Elite in New Spain (1500–1760)" (Ph.D. diss., Duke University, 2007), p. 201.

23. *Códice Sierra*, facsimile, ed. and trans. Nicolás León (México: Editorial Innovación, 1982), p. 2.

24. Charles Dibble, "Sahagún's Historia," in *Florentine Codex: General History of the Things of New Spain*, 13 vols., eds. and trans. Arthur J. O. Anderson and Charles E. Dibble (Santa Fe: School of American Research and University of Utah, 1982), p. 10.

25. For more information on the use to which these types of documents were put, see Richard Conway, "Nahua Pictorial Documents, Testaments, and the Defense of Property in Central Mexico," in *Native Wills from the Colonial Americas: Dead Giveaways in a New World*, ed. Mark Christensen and Jonathan Truitt (Salt Lake City: University of Utah Press, 2016).

26. Sell, "Friars," pp. 305–306.

27. Alonso de Molina, *Confesionario breve, en lengua Mexicana y castellana* (México, 1565).

28. *Códice Sierra*, p. 12. The term *nenque* comes from the root *nemi* (to live). Although it does not use the more common term *tlacatl* (for person), the wording indicates people who lived or dwelt at the church. Thanks to both Kevin Terraciano and John Sullivan for their thoughts on this passage.

29. Stafford Poole, "Church Law on the Ordination of Indians and *Castas* in New Spain," *Hispanic American Historical Review* 61, no. 4 (1981), p. 637.

30. AHN, Diversos Colecciones 22, n. 13.

31. *Códice Sierra*, p. 12. "v onpuali ypan`ome pesos`omomacaque yeuantin teopannenque yuan ce mexicatl quinmahtia" (Forty-two pesos were given to those who work at the church and to a Mexica who teaches them). Over time the term *Mexicatl* came to be used in rural areas as a general term for a native Nahuatl speaker. However, the 1554 date of this entry and the use of the term *Mexicatl* in specific reference to Nahuas from Mexico Tenochtitlan elsewhere in the document support the argument that a Mexica from Tenochtitlan or Tlatelolco was instructing them.

32. Pedro de Gante, *Doctrina Christiana en lengua Mexicana,* facsimile (1553) (México: Centro de Estudios Históricos Fray Bernardino de Sahagún, 1981). Special thanks to Galen Brokaw for sharing some of his work on this source.

33. AGI, México, 168, nn. 53, 54. These letters are addressed to King Philip, though he was not officially crowned until 1558.

34. This letter was likely intended for Princess Juana, queen of Portugal, Philip II's sister. Juana acted as regent until Philip's return to Spain in 1558.

35. AGI, México, 168, nn. 108, 119. Thank to R. J. Kelly for his invaluable assistance in translating these documents.

36. AGI, México, 168, n. 120.

37. Based on handwriting, these annals were most likely written by more than one person.

38. It is likely that the Nahua parish records of Mexico City were written in Nahuatl during the sixteenth century, as suggested by the baptismal records for Santiago Tlatelolco

of 1585–1606. No corresponding records for San Josef have been uncovered for a similar time period. However, burial records at San Josef from the 1640s and 1650s appear in both Spanish and Nahuatl. AHFC, caja 21, e. 2; and AGN, Geneología, v. 431, roll 1946.

39. Gerónimo de Mendieta, *Historia eclesiástica indiana*, 2 vols. (México: Consejo Nacional para la Cultura y las Artes, 1997), vol. 2, p. 81.

40. Connell, *After Moctezuma*, pp. 70–71.

41. SilverMoon, "Imperial College," p. 49.

42. The indigenous women of Corpus Christi produced biographies of their sisters not long after 1727. It is also known that they started learning how to read and write from the nuns at San Juan de la Penetencia prior to this date. Unfortunately, no extant documents have been found. Mónica Díaz, personal correspondence, 14 February 2012.

43. Díaz, *Indigenous Writings*, p. 100; and Josefina Muriel, *Las indias caciques de Corpus Christi* (México: Universidad Nacional Autónoma de México, 2001), p. 42. Thanks to Mónica Díaz for her insightful feedback on the education of indigenous nuns.

44. Robert Stevenson, *Music in Mexico: A Historical Survey* (New York: Thomas Y. Crowell, 1952), p. 51.

45. Mendieta, *Historia eclesiástica*, vol. 2, pp. 75–76.

46. *Cartas de Indias: Facsimile of 1877 Madrid Manuel G. Hernández Edition,* 2 vols., ed. Edmundo Aviña Levy (Guadalajara, México, 1970), vol. 1, p. 56.

47. AHN, Diversos Colecciones 22, n. 13.

48. AHN, Diversos Colecciones 24, n. 35, f. 2.

49. Stevenson, *Music in Mexico,* pp. 8–13, 18–19; and Stanley Sadie, ed., *The New Grove Dictionary of Musical Instruments,* 3 vols. (London: Macmillan Press Limited, 1984), vol. 1, 91; vol. 2, 258, 816; vol 3, 567, 601.

50. Bernal Díaz del Castillo, *The Conquest of New Spain*, trans J. M. Cohen (New York: Penguin, 1963), p. 227.

51. Ibid., p. 381.

52. According to Megged, the Cuauhtinchan annal used the term *tlatzotzonaliztli* in reference to a sacrifice, and it "could mean, in Nahuatl 'the act of stringing or plucking a musical instrument.'" Amos Megged, *Social Memory in Ancient and Colonial Mesoamerica* (Cambridge: Cambridge University Press, 2014), p. 63.

53. Stevenson, *Music in Mexico*, pp. 17–19.

54. Ibid., pp. 21, 25; and Sahagún, *Florentine Codex,* vol. 3, p. 67.

55. Stevenson, *Music in Mexico*, p. 32.

56. *Códice Franciscano*, pp. 57–58.

57. *Códice Sierra*, pp. 2, 5, 10; Mendieta, *Historia*, vol. 2, 76; and Toribio de Motolinia, *Historia de los indios de la Nueva España* (Barcelona: Linkgua ediciones S.L., 2006), pp. 206–207. The Códice Sierra does not specify that trombones were created in Mexico City, as it does with trumpets and flutes. However, since Mixtecs imported these other instruments from the Mexica, who constructed all the other instruments provided in the list, it does not seem too large a leap to include trombones as well. In reference to "cornett" versus "cornet," I opt for the former, both because this spelling is found in music dictionaries and to prevent confusion with the nineteenth-century trumpet-like cornet. For more information on this instrument, see Sadie, *New Grove Dictionary*, vol. 1, 496–503; and Anthony Baines, ed., *The Oxford Companion to Musical Instruments* (Oxford: Oxford University Press, 1992), pp. 80–83.

58. Thanks to Mark Christensen for sharing photos of these documents with me. Thomas Pascual, "Choral Music Miscellany, 1635," Princeton University Garrett-Gates Mesoamerican Manuscripts Collection, Master control number 6-96-604. The Nahuatl documentation indicates a date of 1622 or 1627. Based on the Nahuatl, the music was most likely used in central Mexico and probably Mexico City. One of the named neighborhoods, San Juan Bautista, is too common a tlaxilacalli name to determine a specific altepetl,

and the other named tlaxilacalli, San Miguel Acatan, does not appear in other documentation though it could be Acaztlan—but this is only a guess.

59. *Códice Sierra*, p. 43.

60. Ibid., p. 35; and Stevenson, *Music in Mexico*, p. 33.

61. Arthur J. O. Anderson, "Introduction," in Bernardino de Sahagún, *Psalmodia christiana (Christian Psalmody),* trans. Arthur J. O. Anderson (Salt Lake City: University of Utah Press, 1993), p. xv.

62. Sahagún, *Psalmodia Christiana*, pp. 7–8.

63. These songs have been tentatively attributed to Sahagún and his aides. John Bierhorst, trans., *Cantares Mexicanos: Songs of the Aztecs* (Stanford, Calif.: Stanford University Press, 1985), pp. 7–9.

64. Ibid., pp. 179–181. The fray Pedro mentioned here was most likely fray Pedro de Gante, probably in reference to his instruction of the Nahuas in European verse.

65. Ibid., pp. 179–183.

66. Ibid., pp. 182–185.

67. For an example of this song, see Bierhorst, *Cantares*, pp. 277–287.

68. Chimalpahin, *Annals*, p. 45. The song was also performed in 1566, although on this occasion it was at Tepeyacac. Bautista, *¿Cómo te confundes?*, p. 151. It is possible that there were multiple michcuicatl and that instead of being a specific song it was actually a genre. Chimalpahin, *Annals*, p. 45n5.

69. Sahagún, *Florentine Codex*, pp. 28–29.

70. Eloy Cruz, "De cómo una letra hace la diferencia: Las obras en Náhuatl atribuidas a don Hernando Franco," *Estudios de Cultura Náhuatl* 32 (2001), pp. 257–259. Cruz also provides a facsimile and translation of the sheet music.

71. Ibid., pp. 273–274.

72. AGN, Indiferente Virreinal, caja 3873, e. 7. The hexachord was one of the basic tools of musical instruction. Girolamo Diruta, *The Transylvanian (Il Transilvano)*, 2 vols., ed. Murray C. Bradshaw and Edward J. Soehnlen (Ottawa: Institute of Mediæval Music, 1984), vol. 1 (1593), p. 43.

73. NL, Ayer Collection, MS 1481, B(3)1.

74. Teresa Rojas Rabiela, Elsa Leticia Rea López, and Constantino Medina Lima, eds., *Vidas y bienes olvidados: Testamentos indígenas novohispanos*, 5 vols. (Mexico City: Centro de Investigaciones y Estudios Superiores en Antropología Social, 1999), vol. 1, p. 112. The earliest evidence for image ownership in Mexico City is from 1570; see BNF, Fondo Mexicains, 112.

75. Chimalpahin, *Annals*, pp. 29, 37, 157.

76. Sadie, *New Grove Dictionary*, vol. 1, p. 501.

77. *Códice Sierra*, p. 2.

78. Bautista, *¿Cómo te confundes?*, pp. 196–197; Chimalpahin, *Annals*, pp. 156–157; and Lockhart, *Nahuas*, p. 285. These were by no means the only instruments in use during the colonial period. Spaniards and Nahuas also played fifes, drums, and harps, to name a few.

79. Chimalpahin, *Annals*, p. 45.

80. Linda Curcio-Nagy, *The Great Festivals of Colonial Mexico City: Performing Power and Identity* (Albuquerque: University of New Mexico Press, 2004), pp. 15–16, 19, 44.

81. Motolinia, *Historia*, p. 207; and Ricard, *Spiritual Conquest*, pp. 178–179.

82. AGN, Tierras, v. 35, e. 1; AGN, Tierras, v. 22 pt. 1, e. 5; BNF, Fondo Mexicains, 112; AGN, Tierras, v. 42, e. 5; AGN, Tierras, v. 48, e. 4; AGN, Tierras, v. 49, e. 5; NL, Ayer Collection, MS 1481, B(1)a; AGN, Tierras, v. 54, e. 5; AGN, Tierras, v. 1774, e. 10; AGN, Tierras, v. 59, e. 3; AGN, Tierras, v. 70, e. 4; AGN, Bienes Nacionales, v. 965, e. 6; AGN, Tierras, v. 1595, e. 4; AGN, Tierras, v. 3663, e. 3; AGN, Tierras, v. 101, e. 2; BNF, Fondo Mexicains, 255; AGN, Bienes Nacionales, v. 387, e. 1; NL, Ayer Collection, MS 1481, F5; AGN, Bienes Nacionales, v. 70, e. 3; AGN, Bienes Nacionales, v. 1766, e. 7; NL,

Ayer Collection, MS 1481, B(3)a; UNAM, FRAF, caja 96, e. 1413; NL, Ayer Collection, MS 1481, B(3)e; AGN, Bienes Nacionales, v. 1096, e. 8; NL, Ayer Collection, MS 1481, B(3)F; AGN, Tierras, v. 163, e. 2; AGN, Civil, v. 1763, e. 2; AGN, Civil, v. 1828, e. 5; AGN, Civil, v. 592, e. 1; NL, Ayer Collection, MS 1481, B(3)1; AGN, Tierras, 20 pt. 1, e. 3; AGN, Tierras, v. 38, e. 2; AGN, Bienes Nacionales, v. 293, e. 1; AGN, Tierras; e. 5; AGN, Tierras, v. 95, pt. 2, e. 8; AGN, Tierras, v. 157, e. 7; AGN, Tierras, v. 3711, e. 2; AGN, Tierras, v. 1720, e. 7; AGN, Bienes Nacionales, v. 339, e. 6; AGN, Tierras, v. 109, e. 4; AGN, Bienes Nacionales, v. 489, e. 2; NL, Ayer Collection, MS 1481, B(3)b; AGN, Tierras, v. 2776, pt. 1, e. 18; NL, Ayer Collection, MS 1481, B(3)d; INAH, Colegio de San Gregorio, v. 119; AGN, Civil, v. 592, e. 1; AGN, Tierras, v. 155, e. 9; and S. L. Cline and Miguel Leon-Portilla, *Testaments of Culhuacan* (Los Angeles: UCLA Latin American Center Publications and University of California Press, 1984), documents 14, 50, 92, 95. It is likely that the drums being sold in these testaments were heirlooms from precontact times.

83. Lockhart, *Nahuas,* p. 188.

84. AGN, Hospital de Jesús, leg. 210, e. 4.

85. NL, Ayer Collection, MS 1481, B(3)e and B(3)a.

86. AGN, Historía, v. 413, e. 1.

87. Ilona Katzew, *Casta Painting: Images of Race in Eighteenth-Century Mexico* (New Haven, Conn.: Yale University Press, 2004), p. 176. Thanks to Sarah Cline for sharing this image with me.

88. AGN, Bienes Nacionales, v. 387, e. 1, f. 15. Special thanks to James Lockhart and Susan Schroeder for providing assistance on this document and others.

89. Sahagún, *Florentine Codex*, vol. 11, image 43.

90. For more information on the Códice Valdés, see Cruz, "De cómo una letra."

91. Stevenson, *Music in Aztec*, pp. 171–172.

92. For information on dramas in Quechua, see Margot Beyersdorff, *Historia y drama ritual en los andes bolivianos (XVI–XX)*, 2nd ed. (La Paz, Bolivia: Universidad Mayor de San Andrés, 1993). Special thanks to Louise Burkhart for directing me to this source.

93. Sell and Burkhart, *Nahuatl Theater,* vol. 1, p. ix.

94. Louise M. Burkhart, *Holy Wednesday: A Nahua Drama from Early Colonial Mexico* (Philadelphia: University of Pennsylvania Press, 1996).

95. Vetancurt, *Teatro*, pt. 1, p. 66, and pt. 2, p. 59.

96. AGN, Bienes Nacionales, v. 1076, exp. 9; AGN, Bienes Nacionales, v. 990, exp. 10.

97. Louise M. Burkhart, "Pageantry, Passion, and Punishment: Eighteenth-Century Nahuatl Community Theater," in *Nahuatl Theater,* Vol. 4: *Nahua Christianity in Performance*, ed. and trans. Barry D. Sell and Louise M. Burkhart (Norman: University of Oklahoma Press, 2009), p. 3.

98. AGN, Bienes Nacionales, v. 990, exp. 10; Sell and Burkhart, *Nahuatl Theater,* vol. 4.

99. Chimalpahin, *Las ocho*, vol. 2, p. 187; Fernando Horcasitas, *El teatro Nahuatl: Épocas novohispana y moderna* (México: Universidad Nacional Autónoma de México, 1974), pp. 76–79; Burkhart, *Holy Wednesday,* pp. 81–86; and Vetancurt, *Teatro mexicano*, pt. 4, p. 42.

100. Ricard, *Spiritual Conquest*, 195; and Las Casas, *Apologética*, vol. 1, p. 334.

101. It is not known if this play was performed, although the script was likely written during the 1590s. Burkhart, *Holy Wednesday*, pp. 82–83.

102. Chimalpahin, *Annals*, p. 67.

103. See Sell and Burkhart, *Nahuatl Theater,* vol. 1; Barry D. Sell, Louise M. Burkhart, and Elizabeth R. Wright, *Nahuatl Theater,* vol. 3: *Spanish Golden Age Drama in Mexican Translation* (Norman: University of Oklahoma Press, 2008), pp. xvii–xviii; and

Bartolomé de Alva, *A Guide to Confession Large and Small in the Mexican Language, 1634*, ed. Barry D. Sell and John Frederick Schwaller with Lu Ann Homza (Norman: University of Oklahoma Press, 1999).

104. Sell, Burkhart, and Wright, *Nahuatl Theater*, vol. 3, pp. 90–91.

105. Ibid., pp. 82–83.

106. Only one cue in the *Sacrifice of Isaac* called for a named song, specifically, the Misericordia. Sell and Burkhart, *Nahuatl Theater*, vol. 1, p. 159.

107. See script in Sell and Burkhart, *Nahuatl Theater*, vol. 1.

108. Burkhart, *Holy Wednesday*, p. 46.

109. AGN, Bienes Nacionales, v. 1076, exp. 9.

110. AGN, Bienes Nacionales, v. 990, exp. 10; and Vetancurt, *Teatro*, pt. 4, p. 42.

111. Louise M. Burkhart, "Nahuatl Baroque: How Alva Mexicanized the Spanish Dramas," in Sell, Burkhart, and Wright, *Nahuatl Theater*, vol. 3, p. 35.

112. AGN, Bienes Nacionales, v. 990, exp. 10.

113. Ibid. The Iztapalapa Passion play is performed every year on Good Friday and is quite possibly the largest performance of this play in Mexico. Other Passion plays are enacted in small towns across the Mexican countryside as well. For information on the Iztapalapa Passion play, see Richard C. Trexler, *Reliving Golgotha: The Passion Play of Iztapalapa* (Cambridge, Mass.: Harvard University Press, 2003).

114. Burkhart, "Pageantry"; and Sell and Burkhart, *Nahuatl Theater*, vol. 4.

115. Megged, *Social Memory*, p. 2.

116. Ibid., p. 3.

117. Lourdes Turrent, *La conquista musical de México* (México: Fondo de Cultura Económica, 1993), p. 153.

Chapter 3
Cornerstones of Catholicism: Nahua Women and Religion in Mexico Tenochtitlan

During the colonial period that followed the Spanish conquest of the Aztec Empire, indigenous women witnessed a decline in their traditional positions of authority. Yet, as scholars have found, this did not diminish their individual or group agency vis-à-vis their families or local communities. In 1979, William B. Taylor found that women in colonial southern Mexico were highly visible in episodes of community violence and that, "in at least one-fourth of the cases, women led the attacks and were visibly more aggressive, insulting, and rebellious in their behavior toward outside authorities."[1] Since 1979 research on indigenous women's positions in their communities has continued. Louise M. Burkhart, comparing precontact societal and cultural understanding of women's responsibilities and men's duties, found parallels between many gendered tasks and events. For example, a woman's death in childbirth was equal to that of a man's death on the battlefield. Susan Kellogg, studying how indigenous women adjusted to Spanish colonial patriarchy, found that in the public realms of politics, law, and religion women suffered a decline in their traditional authority.[2]

Stephanie Wood, in her article "Gender and Town Guardianship in Mesoamerica," highlights Taylor's findings and the roles that women played as leaders in the rebellions he studied and presents two questions: Might women have held positions of authority in their towns that were less official than those of men but equally important? Might both men and women have held equal responsibility for the "protection and preservation" of their communities and culture? Wood focuses her research predominantly on the precontact period with the intent to establish a pattern of women's leadership that could have led to their positions as "community co-defender[s]."[3]

Both Wood's and Taylor's work suggest that women held leadership positions that existed somewhere between the traditional dichotomy of public and private.[4] Indigenous women's roles within colonial Christianity functioned in a space between the traditional public roles associated with men and the private household roles assigned to women. While performing their duties for the

Church (caring for convents and friaries, aiding the sick, and looking after religious brotherhoods, to name a few), Nahua women were neither in their homes nor holding any officially (Spanish) sanctioned positions of authority. Yet their responsibilities continued to place them in a position of power. Using Nahuatl and Spanish-language sources, this chapter examines the relationship Nahua women had with their community and Spanish Catholicism and identifies ways in which they both shared responsibility for preserving their communities and aided in the establishment of Catholicism in Mexico Tenochtitlan.

As early as 1552, Nahua women had leadership positions within indigenous cofradías. Evidence of these roles in the religious community becomes visible in a 1552 Nahuatl constitution of a cofradía attached to the indigenous chapel of San Josef de los Naturales. It mentions four women appointees, *cihuatepixque* (women in charge of people), corresponding to the appointment of four male deputies.[5] Although their responsibilities were most likely separate from the men's, they were probably of equal importance.[6]

Despite their early participation in cofradías, Nahua women were prohibited from professing as nuns until 1724. Thus, their presence in convents was largely the result of their work as servants. Their duties in the nunneries were potentially similar to some of their roles in precontact temples. Nahua religion prior to 1519 focused on the dichotomies of order and chaos, or cleanliness and filth; acts of cleaning such as sweeping and caring for religious symbols were ritualized. The very act of removing *tlazolli* (filth) created order.[7] Conversely, many of the responsibilities of Nahua women servants in a convent would have been different from precontact traditions. A distinct change between the two was that women in the precontact period could become priestesses, although others were servants; during the colonial period, Nahua women in convents primarily labored as servants. Nevertheless, within one hundred years of the defeat of Tenochtitlan, a few individuals who had gained something of an elevated status during the sixteenth and early seventeenth centuries were buried in the convents where they worked.[8]

As discussed in chapter 2, by the late 1600s Nahua women had shaken off earlier restrictions in the theater and begun taking to the stage to play female roles in local religious dramas. It appears that in doing so they defied the wishes of some Spanish religious leaders. But in many other regards they worked in accordance with their mendicant spiritual advisors. Many of their actions favored both their families and their community. Although an occasional individual stands out in the historical record, such as an actress or a woman occupying a cofradía leadership position, more often they appear as part of their community and not as individuals, suggesting a degree of solidarity among the Nahua community and women in general.

Women's testaments, especially, act as a type of covenant with the Catholic Church (see appendix 4). In these sources women demonstrate their dedication to family, community, and the Church. They show that women were not silent and submissive but rather actively engaged in religious life and commerce, even though being written out of the legal records and other sources. They expected, and enjoyed, a certain level of reciprocity with the men in their lives—the Nahua and *casta* (individuals of multiple ethnicities) politicians, Spanish friars, and their fathers, brothers, husbands, and sons. If some men went against the women in the community, there was another group of men there to defend and argue for the wishes of the women in their lives. Nahua women were by no means passive if something they or the community valued was threatened.

In the sixteenth and seventeenth centuries, Nahua women participated in the religious life of the Nahua community. During this period they adjusted to some of the Catholic Church's demands, and Catholicism changed to meet some of their requests. By the 1620s some Nahua women had become *donadas* (devout but lay cloistered women with lesser vows) and others taught catechism, prepared people for the sacraments, cared for the sick and dying, helped with church upkeep, cared for their own personal shrines, and wove habits for the friars, among many other tasks. At the end of the seventeenth century they took part in religious dramas, and by 1724 they had their own convent.[9] Conversely, in the 1770s Nahua men were officially denied their decades-long petition for their own seminary.[10] Clearly, indigenous women participated in the life of their communities. Though their authority in legal spheres declined, as Kellogg argues, I suggest that they were actively involved in shaping their communities and Nahua interaction with the divine and making certain to secure important roles for themselves. Although the secular Church authorities may not have formally recognized their contributions, that does not mean that women were inactive in religious and community life. After the defeat of Tenochtitlan, they eventually secured leadership positions in cofradías and continued their crucial domestic duties and responsibilities.[11] They pursued opportunities enjoyed by Spanish women by first becoming donadas and then nuns. Nahua women's response to the conquest of Tenochtitlan was not to sit and watch their traditional roles be taken away. Rather, they sought to secure their place in colonial society.[12]

Precontact and Iberian Background

Before the arrival of the Spaniards in 1521, the Nahuas possessed a mostly parallel-gender social system. Both men and women had responsibilities that were essential for the proper functioning of the household, community, government, and religious world. Women generally did not hold the reigns of power in the political realm; on the other hand, the second in command to the tlatoani, the *cihuacoatl* (woman serpent), held by a man, was said to represent the female other. After the death of a ruler, the cihuacoatl did not inherit the position of tlatoani but could serve in his stead.[13] Unlike the cihuacoatl, however, women did occasionally inherit the reigns of power. Lori Diel has found that women in precontact Aztec society held four main roles in the sociopolitical system: founding queen, Toltec ennobler, marriage alliance facilitator, and regent. She discovered that women were essential in the initial establishment of many "up-start and secondary communities." Their bloodlines, it was believed, could tie a newly developing altepetl, such as Tenochtitlan, to the noble Toltec lineage, thereby establishing a legitimate ruling dynasty. Moreover, Susan Schroeder has found that Nahua women served as full-fledged queens. The Nahuatl term to describe this dynastic office was *cihuatlatoani* (woman ruler).[14]

Although women did not typically serve as rulers, they did continue to operate in ways parallel to men. They worked as merchants (in markets), midwives, artisans, and priests, and they endlessly continued to weave the essential cloth for tribute, focusing much of their attention on household responsibilities. Nahua knowledge of the cosmos was based on an understanding of opposites and the need to balance them. They did not subscribe to the Christian dichotomy of good versus evil; rather, their universe operated on a perceived tension between order and chaos. At the same time, their worldview was not essentially moralistic. Whereas Christianity argued for the banishment of evil, in the Nahua cosmos one sought to strike a balance between chaos and order.[15] Their understanding of the importance of order versus chaos influenced many aspects of their lives. Accordingly, Tenochtitlan was the center (where there was more order), and the farther away from the center people traveled the closer they came to chaos and to the less sedentary indigenous groups.

Nevertheless, the center did not remain orderly without constant attention. When men went to fight far away, many women stayed at home, and it is believed that staying at home was no less important than the responsibilities of the men away fighting; rather, both responsibilities were essential. As Louise Burkhart argues, "Domestic space was, quite literally, a 'home front,' and women were its army." The women performed similar domestic tasks for the temples in the city. The female priests in these temples cleaned, cooked, and made clothing for the deities. After the defeat of Tenochtitlan, women continued to perform many of these same functions at their indigenous chapels and for the friars and nuns who came to settle in their midst. The friars began to preach against the Nahuas' religion while capitalizing on the women and their labor.[16]

When considering the positions held by indigenous women during the colonial period, it is important to understand the Iberian background of the colonizers. Many Spanish traditions and beliefs transferred to the viceroyalties on the other side of the Atlantic. In the case of Nahua women, their instruction in Iberian culture developed variously. What did the friars and nuns (who tried to teach Nahua women to be like good Spanish women) consider the ideal role for women? Mary Elizabeth Perry argues that the Spanish belief that women needed to be protectively enclosed was encouraged by the increase in European wars and colonization. However, the wars and colonization served to place more women in jobs traditionally held by men because the men were off fighting.[17] So, although the idealized situation for women was enclosure, both friars and nuns in the Iberian kingdoms and New Spain were also aware of women's ongoing presence in very public spaces.

Alongside what the friars and nuns taught is what Spanish women actually did within sight of Nahua women. In his study of the social history of Spanish Peru, James Lockhart found that a large enough number of female Spanish colonists existed by the middle of the sixteenth century to "keep Spanish Peru from being truly a womanless society." They appear to have been present in a ratio of about one out of ten Spanish men. Lockhart argues that, although indigenous influence played a role, even in the first generation enough Spanish women were present to prevent the loss of important Spanish cultural traditions.[18] Although the ratio was no doubt different, a similar situation likely existed for Spanish women in Mexico City. Spanish women started arriving in New Spain by 1521,[19] and they were important in the adaptation and stabilization of Spanish culture in the Americas. Their behavior served as examples for evangelizing priests and indigenous women. This is not to say that the Nahua population of Mexico City wanted to emulate Spanish women or even "become Spanish." Although some women may have embraced Hispanic customs, others likely fought harder to maintain their own traditions. What is important is that Nahua women were able to hear what the friars and nuns taught and then have something with which to compare it; they heard the ideal and saw the real. They could then presumably determine how they would participate in the new religion.

The Spanish ideal in New Spain was that women would be in the home or cloistered; in practice their lives were not that simple. Spanish women continued to be involved in lawsuits and active in marketplaces and religious life in New Spain, much as they had been in Spain. Additionally, it is probable that artisan wives assisted their husbands in their trades, as was done in Spain.[20] This likely encouraged Nahua women to continue working as merchants in the marketplaces of Mexico City, locales where they played important roles as vendors, land owners, and consumers.

If Nahua women sought to emulate aspects of the public lives of Spanish women, they may have done similarly in their religious lives. This is not to say that indigenous women did not wish to act independently of Spanish women. Nahua and Spanish women's traditional public and private roles were different socially and culturally. The way they understood their duties and activities varied based on their own cultural background. However, Spanish nuns and *beatas* (uncloistered religious women) were supposed to educate Nahua women, and they all heard mass from Spanish clergy. As early as 1529, through the efforts of the first bishop of Mexico City, fray Juan de Zumárraga (r. 1528–1548), a school for Indian girls was established in Tetzcoco. This school and others that followed in Mexico Tenochtitlan and elsewhere were similar to the boys' schools in their purpose to both Christianize and hispanize the students. In the case of the girls, the classes focused on turning them into good Spanish-style wives. The first such school established in Mexico Tenochtitlan was aimed at having the girls marry boys who attended the colegio at San Josef de los Naturales. According to fray Toribio de Motolinia, many of these women went "out to teach, both in the patios of the churches and in the houses of the upper classes." The first Franciscan school for girls lasted approximately ten years but failed through lack of interest on the part of Spaniards and resistance to Spanish training on the part of many indigenous families. On occasion, indigenous women were allowed to take classes with Spanish girls; however, this was generally a rare opportunity.[21]

By 1552, if not earlier, Nahua women had positions of leadership within indigenous cofradías, which were recognized as leadership positions by their community, if not by the friars as well. Yet, though they enjoyed positions in cofradías, they were still denied the opportunity to profess as nuns. It appears that during the sixteenth and seventeenth centuries only one indigenous woman was able to take the vows of a nun (in 1607), and that was because her father established the convent.[22]

Ann Miriam Gallagher convincingly argues that much of the reason for Nahua women's inability to profess came from the Spaniards' racial system of *limpieza de sangre* (pure [Spanish] blood). They believed that castas, Indians, and Africans could not be as good Christians as people with pure Spanish ancestry.[23] Moreover, natives had the additional difficulty of being new to the faith.[24] Yet these obstacles did not prevent Nahua women from being active in the Church and in Spanish convents. Their activity in the Church, and that of other indigenous women, was rewarded much later, in 1724, when the convent of Corpus Christi, established by Viceroy don Baltasar de Zúñiga y Guzmán Sotomayor y Mendoza (marqués de Valero Ayamonte y Alenquer [r. 1716–1722] prior to his departure for Spain), opened for high-ranking indigenous women. One of the statutes for entering Corpus Christi was limpieza de sangre.[25] Their cause was aided by knowledge of the life of an Iroquois woman of the Mohawk tribe, Catherine Tekakwitha. Her hagiography reports that as a young girl she renounced sex and marriage, joined a Jesuit mission, and sought spiritual perfection. After her good death she appeared as an apparition and cured several individuals, providing her with a quasi-saintly status, although she was not canonized until 2012 by Pope Benedict XVI. Her life and postmortem story were translated into Spanish and published in Mexico City in 1724 as an argument for the establishment of Corpus Christi. By this time, Nahua women had two hundred years of apprenticeship as donadas, members of church congregations, and servants of nuns. Moreover, Spaniards in favor of the establishment of their convent argued that the women were "better" than native men, citing devotion and modesty among their chief attributes.[26]

At the End of Their Lives: Women's Testaments and Religious Requests

Fray Gerónimo de Mendieta, a Franciscan friar writing at the end of the sixteenth century, credited Nahua women with convincing the indigenous community to accept and eventually adopt cofradías. Indeed, he went as far as to compare their religious behavior to that of Spanish beatas.[27] His estimation of their religiosity appears to be reflected in women's wills. In an examination of ninety testaments from sixteenth- and seventeenth-century Mexico City (forty by men and fifty by women), women requested masses or assistance for their souls and loved ones more frequently than men, and generally in greater number. Of fifty wills, forty-six women (92 percent) made a request for masses or aid for their souls; in contrast, only twenty-eight of forty men (70 percent) made a similar request. The women who did not specifically request aid for their souls died in 1609, 1616, 1678, and 1725, so the absence of the requests cannot be attributed to the newness of the religion; they were likely conscious choices. In one case, care for the soul was considered; the testatrix requested burial at the feet of San Juan Bautista. In the 1678 case, Juana Petrona requested aid for the souls of her parents, but nothing for herself. In the case of the men, two of them specified where they would like to be buried, but none of the others provided anything indicating care for their souls.[28] In all cases it may be that the testators in question had someone who predeceased them request prayers on their behalf.

The earliest testament I have encountered is a Spanish translation of an original written in Nahuatl in 1546. In this will Angelina Poqui stated that Martín Tentli owed her money. When, or if, the money was paid back she wanted it to go to her children, and if the children wished they could request something for her soul—probably masses but the testament does not specify.[29] By 1554 any confusion as to what form that spiritual aid might take was seemingly clarified, for don Hernando de Tapia requested approximately ninety masses (the majority for his soul, but others for the souls in purgatory) in his will. As a noble with close ties to Spaniards living in Mexico City, Tapia was concerned with emulating Spaniards whenever possible; indeed, in his will he requested that his children marry Spaniards.[30]

Even if the trend of requesting masses had not reached the general population of Nahuas by the 1550s, it surely had by the 1560s when María Tiacapan requested the purchase of masses for her soul.[31] Indeed, the majority of female testaments after this time specify a desire for masses. Though a request for masses may have been based on wealth, the four women who failed to request masses were not the poorest of the testators. As is suggested in their testaments, requesting masses or even aid for one's soul appears to have been a personal choice. A selection of men's wills from Mexico Tenochtitlan available for examination corroborates this finding, since twelve of them do not request prayers or aid for their soul. The possibility exists that requesting aid for one's soul was a notarial convention; this clearly seems to be the case with the eighteenth-century testaments from Toluca.[32] For Mexico Tenochtitlan, unfortunately, there is not a consistency in style across notaries and there are not enough testaments by a single notary to be able to evaluate whether omission of aid was based on notarial convention or testator desire. From the extant documents available, testaments suggest that the decision to omit a request for aid resided with the individual testators. Another explanation for the difference is that women were considered the heirs of last resort and were disposing of the accumulated wealth of their family at the time of their death, but the testaments do not bear this out. In some cases where the women had no children, such as those of Clara López and Petronila María, they did distribute an accumulated wealth, but in a majority of the testaments consulted children or other relatives were alive to inherit. What becomes clear is that, although Nahua women may have been prevented from serving in religion as they had during the precontact period, the opportunities available to them must have been somewhat appealing since they spent so much time, money, and effort to participate.

During the sixteenth and seventeenth centuries, more women than men consistently focused on religious-oriented bequests in their testaments. The men tended to concentrate more on their descendants. In religious requests regarding images and cofradías, both of which were significant in the lives of Nahuas, women and men were similarly balanced. Of the fifty testaments for women, twenty-two mention religious images of some sort, but only sixteen men mentioned them specifically. Though the numbers are similar, women typically passed on more images than did men. In reference to cofradías, four men mentioned their brotherhoods, whereas eight women spoke of theirs.

Women's testaments specifically differed from men's in two areas: their charitable donations to religious institutions, people, and activities (e.g., chapels, schools, convents, hospitals, friars, and feast day celebrations); and their special requests concerning their burial. In an examination of charitable donations made in wills, eleven women and four men specified donations of goods, property, and money to specific institutions and organizations (see table 4). Those who donated these goods had surplus incomes that allowed

TABLE 4. Mexico City Charitable Donations Bequeathed in Nahua Testaments, 1570–1700

Name	*Date*	*Donations/Recipients*	*Source*
Beatriz Papan	1570	5 pesos(?): Colegio of San Juan de Letrán[a]	BNP, Mexicain, 112
Angelina Martina	1580	Proceeds from house sale: ¼ masses for her soul, ¼ for the cofradía of the Santisímo Sacramento, ¼ to sustain the Franciscans in the friary at Santiago Tlatelolco, ¼ for her burial Proceeds from sale of cloth to the Holy Trinity at the altar for merchants Retablo of the Transfiguración: Franciscan friary in Santiago Tlatelolco	AGN, Tierras, v. 49, e. 5
María Salomén	1605	20 pesos: Sick priests in Hospital at San Francisco 20 pesos: To buy something for Nuestra Señora de la Soledad (chapel? cofradía? image?) 5 pesos: school (San Juan de Letrán?)[b] 5 pesos: Cathedral for a mass to be performed by the cofradía dedicated to the souls of purgatory	AGN, Bienes Nacionales, v. 965, e. 6
India (no name)	1613	9 pesos: Cofradía of Nuestra Señora del Rosario	ANM, José Rodriguez #555, v. 3839, yrs. 1612–1616
Petronila María	1619	10 pesos: Cofradía of San Nicolas de Tolentino (at Hospital de Indios) 10 pesos: Chapel and cofradía of Nuestra Señora de la Caridad (at Hospital de Indios) 2 tomines: To each nun of a certain order (order not specified) Image of St. Ignatius in the round with its clothing (40 pesos worth of embroidery) left to the care of a Jesuit cofradía at the chapel of San Gregorio	ANM, Hernando de Arauz #4, v. 7, yrs. 1619–1622, fs. 7–12v
Magdalena María	1625	154 pesos: Friary of Santo Domingo 31 pesos: Santisimo Sacramento (likely the cofradía of the Santisimo Sacramento) 2 Huehue(tl): Teopantlaca (church people)	AGN, Hospital de Jesús, leg. 210, e. 4

(*continued on next page*)

TABLE 4 (*continued*)

Name	*Date*	*Donations/Recipients*	*Source*
Clara López	1640	50 pesos: Chapel of San Josef for necessary items 5 pesos: Each of her four cofradías 5 pesos: Colegio of San Juan de Letrán 10 pesos: Ermita of Nuestra Señora de Belén 5 pesos: Hospital of San Lázaro Houses (unknown quantity): Convent of Nuestra Señora de Regina Celi (happens after the death of her executor don Juan de Aguilar) Copper: For the celebration of the Santisímo Sacramento at San Josef 600 pesos: For festival of Santisímo Sacramento (300 specifically for silversmith)	AGN, Bienes Nacionales, v. 387, e. 1
Juana María	1645	150+ pesos: Projects for the convent of Señora Santa Isabel de las Descalças (where she was buried) 10 pesos: Sor María de San Bernardino for a habit 4 pesos: Fiesta del Nombre de Jesús 2 pesos: María de San Josef (slave) at convent 1 peso: Magdalena de Christo (servant) 3 pesos: Ana María de la Encarnación (servant) 1 peso: Each professed nun in the convent	AGN, Bienes Nacionales, v. 70, e. 3
Micaela Angelina	1677	50+ pesos: Chapel of Santa María	NL, Ayer, MS 1481, B(3)e
Melchora de Santiago	1699	20 pesos (each year from her cacicazgo lands): Feast day of the Purificación (cover expenses for one high mass and a priest) 4 reales: Cantores for the feast day of the Purificación 2 reales: Responsory prayer for feast day of the Purificación	NL, Ayer, MS 1481, B(3)1
doña Juana Bravo de Mendoza Moctezuma[c]	1700	2 reales: Per Carmelite nun (at the convent where she wishes to be buried) 2 reales: for the canonization of Gregorio López 2 reales: for redemption of captives in war against Islam 2 reales: For the holy places of Jerusalem	AGN, Tierras, v. 1593, e. 2, cuad. 3

(*continued on next page*)

TABLE 4 (*continued*)

Name	*Date*	*Donations/Recipients*	*Source*
Martín Jacobo	1577	20 pesos: 5 to the chapel of Santa María (in tlaxilacalli of Quauhtepeque), 5 to the chapel of Santa María de la Asuncion, 5 to chapel of San Josef, 5 to the *iglesia mayor* (principal church, presumably the Franciscan church of San Francisco in the friary)	AGN, Tierras, v. 39, pt. 2, e. 1
Juan Matías	1618	10 *chiquiuhtzinli* (Small baskets): To his sister-in-law for Easter celebrations	AGN, Tierras, v. 157, e. 7
Francisco Juárez	1644	Multiple items sold, proceeds to go to chapel of San Josef	UNAM FRAF, caja 96, exp. 1413
don Juan de Aguilar[d]	1655	Money (unspecified amount): Help Nahuas of San Juan meet tribute Houses: Convent of Nuestra Señora de Regina Celi (at behest of Clara López's testament)	AGN, Bienes Nacionales, v. 489, e. 2

a. Testament asks for the customary amount to be spent. In other testaments, as well as other sources, the amount was typically five pesos.

b. This is presumed to be the Colegio de San Juan de Letrán based on the amount of the donation and other similar donations. This is the only colegio that I have seen as the recipient of testamentary donations.

c. She is the only doña to have provided donations, and in this case the "donations" seem to be tied specifically to her desire to be buried with the Carmelite nuns. Most of her money is tied up in a legal battle over her cacicazgo, and she leaves it there to support her claims even after her death.

d. Note that he is the only *don* in this selection of wills. In all of the ninety extant wills from Mexico City examined, thirteen individuals carry the *don* or *doña* title; only three are women. Seven were from Tlatelolco and six from Tenochtitlan. With only nineteen of the total testaments from Tlatelolco, they have an overrepresentation of the total population of the highest-ranking members of indigenous society in the total collection of documents.

them to do so. Even so, there were others who clearly had the money and opted against a wide distribution of donations outside their family and friends.

Donations to charitable causes presumably began for both women and men by the 1570s. Women, however, gave to a more diverse range of organizations. Men tended to focus on chapels and annual feast day celebrations. For women, the list also includes schools, friaries, convents, hospitals, money for servants in convents, and the cathedral among other destinations. Three women followed a Spanish trend in donating money to the mestizo school of San Juan de Letrán (in 1570, 1605, and 1640). In most cases individuals who donated to San Juan de Letrán received prayers for their soul by the students who attended the school. Additionally, the students walked in the burial processions of dignitaries, as in the case of Archbishop Viceroy don fray García Guerra.[33]

Only two people donated money specifically to hospitals. One donation occurred in 1605 and went to the Franciscan hospital at the friary of San Francisco in Mexico Tenochtitlan, where infirm friars were treated.[34] The timing of this donation is intriguingly near the time that mixed Nahua-Spanish cofradías were initiated in Mexico Tenochtitlan. In 1613 two cofradías were established at hospitals.[35] A second hospital donation occurred in 1640, and this testator was also a member of a mixed Nahua-Spanish hospital cofradía. Fray Juan de Torquemada, writing at the beginning of the seventeenth century, also mentioned a woman who donated money to the Franciscan infirmary, although he did not provide a date.[36] A third woman specifically bequeathed pesos to two cofradías located at the Hospital of de Indios. Although the donations did not go specifically to the hospital, their proceeds helped brotherhoods that supported the hospital. It is likely these four women believed they would receive a shorter stay in purgatory for their bequests, but there also appears to be a trend, possibly limited, of supporting institutions not solely dedicated to the Nahua community. Similar nonindigenous recipients of support include convents and the cathedral. Again, women made more of these types of donations. Only one man in this collection of wills, don Juan de Aguilar, governor of Mexico Tenochtitlan, made a donation to a convent, in 1655—and that was to carry out the testamentary directions of Clara López. None of the men in the sample of testaments made a donation to a hospital.

The amount of money bequeathed in each of these wills is especially noteworthy. Only two people carried the honorary of *don/doña*, yet the quantity of wealth donated suggests (in many cases) a good deal of money, especially on the part of the women. Only one of the women carried the *doña* title, but among the group were high-ranking principalas of some distinction, including Melchora de Santiago, Petronila María, and Clara López. In fact, of the donations made by women, that of doña Juana Bravo de Mendoza Moctezuma is tiny in comparison to most of the rest.

The donations of the Nahuas of Mexico City are even more outstanding when compared with sixty-five sixteenth-century wills from Culhuacan (table 5).[37] In the area of special burial requests are specified desires for shrouds, burial in a religious order's habit, burial outside of an indigenous chapel, and requests for specific types of burial, such as those performed alongside a high mass. In the Mexico City wills fourteen women and six men made requests along these lines. Two men and three women made simple requests regarding shrouds, and another two women requested burial in a Franciscan habit. Of the nine women and four men remaining in the sample, two women requested interment in a convent (which they received); another woman, in 1576, requested an *entierro oracíon* (burial with, presumably, a high mass). Another four women and one man requested burial masses in the presence of the

TABLE 5. Culhuacan Charitable Donations Bequeathed in Nahua Testaments, Sixteenth Century

Name	*Date*	*Donations/Recipients*	*Document No.*
Widow of Miguel Sánchez	n.d.	5 pesos to church (indigenous church?) in Culhuacan	doc. 12
Miguel García	1580	6 pesos to buy wood for the church of the Transfiguration in Culhuacan (he fulfilled the request of Magdalena, whom he borrowed the money from at her death)	doc. 31
Ana Tlaco	1581	Half the sale price of a horse (or mule) to the church of San Juan Evangelista in Culhuacan. Original price of the animal in question was 15 pesos. Candles for the church	doc. 52
Juana Martina	1587	Land to the church of Our Mother Santa María Magdalena	doc. 74
Doña María Juárez	1577	Proceeds from a land sale (15 pesos, potentially more) belong to someone who has disappeared; in his absence the proceeds were to provide needed goods to the church; if anything was left over it was to be donated to the poor and the hospital	doc. 71
Tomás de Aquino	N.D.	6 pesos to church (indigenous church?) in Culhuacan	doc. 20
Pablo Quechol	1580	Proceeds from the sale of baskets (chiquihuites) and mortars (molcajetes) provided to the sick	doc. 28
Andrés de San Miguel	1581	One *teponaztli* (log drum) for community celebrations One *huehuetl* (upright drum) for community celebrations	doc. 59
Gregorio de San Agustín	n.d.	Boat with a broken bottom to Juan and Domingo Pobre (or poor)	doc. 75
Marcos Hernández	1599	Two *chinampas* to Santisimo (seems to be a local district saint)	doc. 82

Source: Cline and León-Portilla, *Testaments.*

deceased. The burial mass in the presence of the deceased was typically an extravagant occasion, attended by priests, deacons, and subdeacons, with a vigil and high masses among other requests. The remainder had very specific burial requests, for example, outside the Spanish church of San Francisco next to the door that leads to the chapel of San Josef or under a fruit tree at San Josef.[38] Both women and men appear to have been concerned with the afterlife, or at least observant of the tenets of the Catholic faith at the moment of death. But on the basis of the testaments consulted, women provided more money for overtly religious purposes than their male counterparts. This conclusion gives even more strength to fray Gerónimo de Mendieta's statement that women were responsible for the early success of the cofradías and possibly other aspects of Spanish Catholicism as well.

Of the fifty women whose testaments I examined, forty-seven owned their own houses. Of those who did not, one had likely owned one but sold it before she entered a convent (she had quite a bit of money at the time of her death), another married a Spaniard, and a third had placed a down payment, in the form of printed Rouen cloth with lace, on a house but had not finished paying it off at the time of her death.[39] Some of the women owned additional pieces of land and others multiple houses. Four of the women, Elena Angelina (1581), María Salomén (1605), Petronila María (1619), and María Alonso (1623), all owned their own tiendas as well. Some had inherited their property; others purchased it, either on their own or jointly with their spouses.

Women do appear to become more land poor toward the end of the seventeenth century. The first woman on table 4 who did not own a house at the time of her death is María Juana (1645); she lived in a convent. The second is Juana Francisca, who died in 1652. That said, some of the women, such as a Melchora de Santiago (1699), still maintained a *cacicazgo* (privileges and rights relating to the title of cacique, in this case over a specified land area).[40] At least half left a house to their children or grandchildren. The rest either bequeathed a house to their husbands, sold it for masses, or gave it to an unrelated individual. Some of these women, such as María Salomén, appear to have been the main money earners in their family. In Salomén's case it is a bit more evident, and she was angry with her husband at the time of her death: "Second, I say when the house has been sold, 60 pesos is to come out of it and be given to my spouse Lucas Juárez, only 60 pesos are to belong to him because I suffered greatly when he served as tepixqui. I paid much of the tribute for him when he was detained in jail. It was I who was making good the tribute. That is the statement that I am making."[41]

All fifty women owned something at the time of their death and usually passed it along to either friends or family. Many of these items were women's goods, such as their clothing, either *huipiles* or *mantas* of various designs. In the situations where their family had predeceased them, they purchased masses for the souls of dead family members (as did those who passed materials along to the living). Clearly, many Nahua women looked to the care of their families and communities, both living and dead.

Noteworthy in the Eyes of Chroniclers: Nahua Women Admired for Their Religiosity

During the sixteenth and seventeenth centuries in Mexico City, Nahua women with exceptional spiritual attributes appeared in the writings of colonial chroniclers. Many of these chroniclers were Franciscans, but others such as Chimalpahin and don Carlos de Sigüenza y Góngora (1645–1700) also recorded activities of indigenous women of religious accomplishment. Although each chronicler had his own particular focus and bias, the fact that many of them knew of Nahua women who exemplified Christianity speaks to a genuine interest on the part of Nahua women to accept the Church.

In *Monarquía Indiana*, published in 1615, fray Juan de Torquemada speaks of two young Nahua girls who attended the Nahua chapel of San Josef (prior to 1572) to whom angels spoke. In this account, the two sisters went to fray Alonso de Escalona, on separate days, to confess their sins, for they had been told that they were going to die the same night of their confession. He asked the first sister to come back another day, since he was busy at the time. She told him that her guardian angel told her she would die that evening, and fray Alonso decided to hear her confession, just in case. The next day she was found dead. On the day of her death, her younger sister arrived, also predicting her demise later that day. Because of their ability to predict their deaths, they were buried next to the altar of San Diego, in the chapel of San Josef.[42]

Torquemada furnishes other examples of pious Christian Nahua women and their alms-giving practices. Ana of Tlatelolco established a devotion to the Franciscans to provide them with habits, books, and other items. She also gave 200 pesos for the sacristy and an additional 300 pesos to the hospital of San Francisco. Torquemada adds that there were another four or five women who did manual labor for the Franciscans under the direction of their *buena Capitana* (good captain). When Ana died she was publicly mourned, and in her will she donated 200 pesos to the friary of San Francisco plus additional money to the friary of Santiago Tlatelolco, and yet more money to the Franciscan hospital.[43]

Torquemada went on to mention that at San Francisco there was a "Libro de las Memorias Antiguas dell [*sic*] Convento," in which were listed many of the things that women did for the friary and sacristy. He noted that individual indigenous women often made substantial donations, from 2,000 to 7,000 pesos, as well as donations of smaller quantities that were almost "uncountable." This assertion is supported by some of the bequests listed in table 5. He has little to say about alms donated by men.[44] This is not to say that men were not dedicated to the Franciscans; it just appears that Nahua women were characteristically inclined to be generous to the Church, more so than men.

There are additional examples of women's piety. Writing at the beginning of the seventeenth century, Nahua annalist Chimalpahin recounted a miracle performed by San Diego during the month of December of the year 1600. Chimalpahin states that a small Nahua child had died and that its mother brought the child to the church and placed its body before San Diego. "With heavy weeping she prayed to the beloved of God, San Diego. And when he had approved her prayer, the child came back to life."[45] In the year 1615, Chimalpahin recorded another miracle. This story involves a boy of one and a half years who had fallen into a well. Chimalpahin says that he was "the child of a Mexica [Nahua] commoner woman." Apparently, the child died and was "dead for two and a half hours," after which San Nicolás de Tolentino brought him back to life.[46] In his annals, Chimalpahin was careful to record many details regarding Nahua religiosity in Mexico City. In both of the miracles recounted above, the children were brought back to life precisely because of the faith of their mothers. In a narrative by Mendieta, a young girl was saved from rape because of her faith in God and Mary. Such accounts served to remind Nahua women that they would be recipients of God's divine favor and protection if they followed the tenets of the Catholic Church. The stories, or belief in them, may be why women tended to provide so much money to religious institutions.

Though Nahua women were eligible for divine favor, they still did not qualify to take the religious vows to become nuns. It was not until Viceroy don Baltasar de Zúñiga y Guzmán Sotomayor y Mendoza was convinced that Indian women could truly follow the tenets of the Christian faith, to the exclusion of any precontact beliefs, that Nahua women were given the opportunity to profess and take monastic vows.[47] Still, the denial of these benefits did not altogether prevent the Nahua women of Mexico City from entering and working in convents. As early as 1529, Nahua female nobles were exposed to the life of nuns when they went to a cloistered house in Tetzcoco for basic Christian education.[48] And by the seventeenth century Nahua women were entering convents both to work for nuns and to join them as donadas. The earliest example of a Nahua donada that I have encountered for Mexico City is from the 1620s and is mentioned by Sigüenza.[49] Generally the women who became donadas had already worked as servants in the convents where they eventually took their vows.

Writing in the second half of the seventeenth century, Sigüenza provided two brief biographies of indigenous women cloistered at the royal convent of Jesús María in Mexico City. Petronila de la Concepción was originally from the altepetl of Xochimilco. According to Sigüenza, de la Concepción left home when she was ten or twelve and took the first available canoe to Mexico City. Upon reaching the island, she went straight to the convent of Jesús María and asked the nuns to allow her to work for them. The nuns put her to work baking bread, and she apparently served them zealously. Over time, she developed a close friendship with one of the nuns. This relationship was frowned upon, not because she was a Nahua and the nun a Spaniard but because it distracted them from their devotions to Christ. De la Concepción prayed to God for the strength to abandon the friendship and while doing so was touched by Christ's hand, giving her the passion with which she lived her life.

After some years in the convent, de la Concepción faced another challenge to her faith; a cancerous tumor developed on her hand. To prevent contagion, the nuns made her leave the convent. When she recovered she tried to return, but the women at the door would not allow her to enter because they thought she might still be contagious. She prayed to the Virgin Mary to help her gain admittance to the convent. In response to her prayers the Virgin Mary, accompanied by Santa María Magdalena and Santa Catalina, told her to return to the doorkeepers and that with their divine assistance the doorkeepers would allow de la Concepción entrance. Shortly after reentering the convent, she was allowed to take the *votos simples*, the minor vows of a professed donada. While cloistered with the nuns she voluntarily performed self-imposed penances, which, according to Sigüenza, were severe. Additionally, she mimicked the behaviors of nuns by maintaining long periods of silence, fasting, and continually praying, all with devotion to God. She eventually gained the respect of the women in the convent and had regular visions of the souls in purgatory. She also reported that the Virgin Mary had spoken with her regarding the 1629 flood in Mexico City. According to de la Concepción, Mary said the flood was a lesser punishment for the sins of the city, and that originally Jesus had planned to have the city burned. During periods of intense meditation she was known to lose all sense of her surroundings and enter *celestiales empleos* (heavenly employment). Without being a Spaniard, she had become something of a mystic, as they were known in early modern Spain. De la Concepción died in 1667 after spending close to forty years in the convent.[50]

Sigüenza makes reference to a second notable indigenous servant woman in the same convent. Francisca de San Miguel was born in Mexico City, and, according to Sigüenza, she possessed the gift of prophecy and foretold the onset of the 1624 Mexico City rebellion. However, it was not the prophecy that Sigüenza found truly remarkable; rather, he focused on her other exceptional accomplishment, which arrived through prayer. Apparently, San Miguel was incredibly devoted to the image of the Passion of Christ and wanted an image of the crucified Christ for herself. But she could not afford one, he stated, because she was an Indian, secluded in a convent, and was concerned with nothing other than her own spirituality. Then early one morning there was a knock on the convent door. Standing there were three Indians dressed in white, and with very courteous words they asked the person who answered the door to deliver an exquisitely made life-size image of Christ to Francisca de San Miguel, for whom they had made it. According to Sigüenza, it was one of the most beautiful images of Christ in all of Mexico City. After delivering the image, the three Indians disappeared, leaving no trace of their identity. The gift of the image, more than the prophesy of the revolt, earned Francisca de San Miguel a place in the history of the convent.[51]

What Sigüenza made little mention of was the length of time that both Petronila de la Concepción and Francisca de San Miguel spent at the convent of Jesús María. Petronila de la Concepción was there for close to four decades, if not longer, and Francisca de San Miguel probably spent the majority of her life in the same nunnery. Additionally, he noted that the two were among many indigenous women living in the convent. Sigüenza also states that it was because of their piety that de la Concepción and San Miguel were at Jesús María. It is possible that other native women were in the nunnery for the same reason, although some surely worked solely as servants. In all likelihood, de la Concepción and San Miguel were typical of other cloistered Nahua women, but there are few sources regarding this matter for the sixteenth and seventeenth centuries.

By the 1670s indigenous women commonly worked as servants in many of the convents in Mexico City. They generally worked alongside Africans, mulatas, and mestizas. For the period 1670–1675, there were at least eighteen requests either by nuns for indigenous servants or by parents for the release of their daughters from service at a convent.[52] Doubtless, the number of such requests was much higher, and it is likely that Nahua women served in nunneries for most of the seventeenth century, if not the sixteenth century as well. The age range of the Nahua girls entering the convents was twelve to twenty years, with most age twelve to fourteen. This is consistent with Sigüenza's estimate of Petronila de la Concepción's age when she entered the convent as between ten and twelve years.

Although it was the girls who entered convents, the agreement about their services appears to have been arranged between the nunnery and their parents. This is seen in the multiple requests for permission to retrieve the girls from the convents. In each of the petitions by parents, the parents presented reasons why the girl should be released; the two most common were that the girl was needed at home to help tend an ailing relative, and that the girl was being detained in the convent against her wishes. Yet it presumably was their families who had placed them in the convent in the first place. It is not known how much money, if any, the girls earned for their work in the convents. Outside the convent the young women could have earned money through any number of activities, including selling goods. So why were Nahua girls continuing to enter the convents? Did the convents pay more for the girls' labors than they could earn in the marketplace, or did the Nahuas see some benefit to the arrangement—either in the Christian upbringing they received or in the perceived spiritual rewards? As early as the 1590s, Nahuas were donating land and buildings to nuns for convents. The community perceived some benefit in establishing religious women in their communities, and they likely anticipated some benefit in placing their daughters in them.

Convents typically were a semiautonomous world for Spanish women throughout the sixteenth and seventeenth centuries. Yet Nahua women were also a constant presence in them. At different times indigenous women entered the convents as students or servants, and some eventually took the vows of a donada. They were not permitted to profess as nuns, but some at least achieved prestige within their convents. Some possibly entered convents to support themselves, and it is likely that certain convents provided shelter, food, and clothing, as they did for orphans. Even so, occasionally some servants opted to leave while others stayed. Additionally, families continued to send their daughters to work in convents. Nahuas may have had an understanding that sending women to the nunneries helped the community spiritually, socially, and economically, and for this reason many spent their lives cloistered.[53] In the early years after the Spanish invasion, the desire to have Nahua women from the community within these religious houses may have had some precedents with young women serving the community as priestesses in local temples.

Women Parishioners

An examination of a corpus of Nahuatl testaments for Mexico Tenochtitlan confirms that Nahua women in Mexico City were actively engaged in a great variety of Church activities by the end of the sixteenth century. In addition to the examples of piety noted above, it is evident that they, like men, attended Sunday mass, feast day celebrations, and cofradía meetings; worked in hospitals; most likely helped with the care of religious buildings and ornaments; and eventually, during the second half of the seventeenth century, acted in religious dramas. The sources tend to be more general but are nevertheless revealing of women's involvement with their communities' religious affairs.

In the course of writing about the life of fray Pedro de Gante, both fray Gerónimo de Mendieta and fray Pedro Oroz recounted the story of a Nahua woman who made the donation of habits to friars her devotion.[54] This unnamed woman went to speak with fray Melchior de Benavente, the chaplain of San Josef, about her devotion. She told Benavente that she was going to make six habits for brothers at the friary of San Francisco. One was specifically for Benavente, another for the deceased fray Pedro de Gante. Benavente asked the woman if she knew that Gante was dead. She replied that she knew of his death but wanted to make one for him anyway. She told Benavente he was welcome to give the habit to whomever he chose.[55] This must have transpired after fray Pedro de Gante's death in 1572 and before Oroz completed his book in 1586. This story reveals that women may have had specific devotions assigned to them, or that they had devotional preferences by the 1580s, or even earlier. In his discussion of Ana of Tlatelolco mentioned above, Torquemada states that she provided habits, books, and other items to the Franciscans.[56] Though it is difficult to be certain what other devotions women might have carried out, one can surmise that they assisted the Franciscans with a variety of tasks in the friary. In these two instances, women provided the necessary material and labor needed for the habits that clothed the friars as well as some of their books.

Another instance where female parishioners make an appearance in the historical record is in the annals of Chimalpahin. Two women, María López (a chocolate seller) and María Constanza, along with the sacristan of the chapel of San Josef, reported fray Gerónimo de Zárate to the Royal Audiencia for abuses against his parishioners. Although the sacristan, as an official of the chapel, seems the likely one of the three to initiate the suit, it was, according to Chimalpahin, María López who started it, and María Constanza and the sacristan supported her arguments and registered their own complaints. María López issued her complaint in support of her husband, whom Zárate had whipped and thrown in jail for allegedly dissipating cofradía funds. Zárate had punished her husband, Juan Pérez, even though he was very ill. Zárate had also punished the sacristan, Josef Gómez, for talking back to him, and María Constanza for missing mass. All three, Juan Pérez, Josef Gómez, and María Constanza, were stripped, tied to a pillar, flogged, and then humiliated during mass.[57] Chimalpahin does not state why María Constanza missed mass, nor does he provide any information as to why María López was not present when her husband was whipped. What is evident in Chimalpahin's annals is that both female parishioners, one in defense of her husband and the other in spite of her punishment for missing mass, took their chaplain to court.[58] As recorded by Chimalpahin, Nahua women parishioners in Mexico Tenochtitlan were far from passive participants in the daily affairs of their chapel and community. In fact, Chimalpahin goes on to praise María López in his discussion of the suit against Zárate, saying:

> The Mexica were angry about our father because he treated them like this, they had patience with him, they kept it inside, no one dared to make it public and make complaint to the Royal Audiencia, if it hadn't been for the said María López, who was so bold as to accuse him before the lords judges of the Audiencia. She did all the things aforementioned; she entered a petition when the court was in deliberation, and in her petition announced to the judges all the different things that he did at the chapel of San Josef to mistreat everyone. The lords heard and found

> out about all of it, and saw it as a very frightful thing, so that right away the judges ordered that someone go and notify fray Gerónimo de Zárate today on the said Saturday at the chapel of San Josef that his duty would no longer be at the chapel.[59]

Based on Chimalpahin's account, it appears that María López acted in defense of both her husband and the community as a whole when she reported Zárate. It seems that without her the Nahua parishioners at the chapel of San Josef may have continued to be mistreated by Zárate for an even longer period of time.

Although often nameless, other women appear in lawsuits about Nahua religious sites in Mexico Tenochtitlan. In 1613 the location of a cross, near the ermita of San Antón Chiquito, became the reason for a lawsuit between some Spanish citizens and the Nahua community of San Antón Acatlan, in southeastern Mexico City. This case appears to have been initiated over the construction of an ermita where only a cross previously stood. The cross was near the home of Diego de Senete and his wife, Mariana Rodríguez. Between their house and the cross was a piece of land that both parties believed they owned. The Nahuas' plans for their ermita included building part of the structure on this contested property. The ownership of the land, and the planned construction of an ermita on the site, was probably what brought Senete, Rodríguez, and the Nahuas of Acatlan into contention. In the lawsuit, male leaders of the Nahua community are mentioned by name. Women also make an appearance, unnamed but noted in passing as part of the larger group. The fact that the women are mentioned only as part of a large group supports Kellogg's arguments for the decline in women's legal standing. However, there is clearly more going on here. The presence of the women in the case indicates a willingness on their part to be present at the proceedings. In the lawsuit, it was the Nahua community against the two Spaniards, one male and one female.[60]

The Nahua women and men of San Antón Acatlan must have believed some advantage could be gained by having the entire community involved in the case. The image of the Nahua community appearing in court with only two Spaniards and their lawyer on the other side of the room is appealing indeed. What was the role of the Nahua women in this case? Were they there for numerical strength, or did they have another function? Was it the women who encouraged their husbands, sons, and fathers to bring the suit in the first place? Were they quite as quiet as the legal documents indicate, or did the notary impose that silence on them? Based on the above examples of individual Nahua women, I find it unlikely that these Nahua women were silent about their feelings, activities, and actions regarding what transpired in Acatlan. Their very presence probably spoke loudly.

Gonzalo Gómez de Cervantes, a Spanish alcalde mayor writing at the end of the sixteenth century, would have found their silence surprising. Documenting the participation of women in legal disputes, he stated that, when a suit was brought forward by an important and capable indigenous male, the man did not make an appearance without his wife. Gómez de Cervantes reported that when responding to questions the men either looked to their wives to lead or the women simply answered for their husbands, including when the question was as simple as asking for the man's name.[61] Still, any inference regarding what the women's actions in this particular case may have been is pure speculation. All that is known is that the women of San Antón Acatlan felt that their presence was needed in the lawsuit, and so they appeared as a group.

Nahua women had the support of their community leaders when it came to certain legal disputes against other Nahuas; they appear to have received community support against the established religious hierarchy as well. As discussed earlier, within ten years of their arrival on the shores of New Spain, Franciscan friars introduced religious dramas as a way to teach Christianity. In the seventeenth century, Nahuas did much of the translating and script writing on their own. And by the end of the century, when some of these performances began to be questioned by priests, such as fray Miguel Camacho Villavicencio, Nahua women had already begun performing on stage. Their participation in theater productions needed the support of their male counterparts, which was perceived by the friars to be part of the problem.[62]

Melveena McKendrick, writing on Spanish theater of the period 1490–1700, found that by the end of the sixteenth century women were regularly permitted to perform on stage, provided that they were married and did not dress as men. The same decree that allowed women on stage forbade young boys from dressing as women. Female performers were seen as the lesser of two evils.[63] It is difficult to know if Nahua women ever saw European actresses on stage, and it is doubtful that Spanish actresses performed within the Franciscans' religious compounds. However, by 1638 a stage was constructed as part of the Royal Hospital of San Josef de los Naturales to help cover the expenses of its operations. The actors and directors of the performances were predominantly, if not entirely, European.[64] Nevertheless, Nahua women, as part of their cofradía responsibilities, were most likely one of the main contingent of caregivers at indigenous hospitals. Through this exposure, as well as general contact in the marketplaces, Nahua women likely knew of the roles Spanish actresses performed in Spanish plays.

Another, possible area of exposure to female thespians can be found in the convents where many indigenous women worked. By the end of the sixteenth century Spanish nuns had started requesting musical performances within their cloisters, and by the middle of the seventeenth century some nunneries paid female singers to perform for them. Around this same time Philip

III ordered Archbishop Juan Pérez de la Cerna to prohibit nuns from taking on the role of actress in convent performances. Although it is difficult to ascertain if nuns did perform in conventual theater, based on decrees against such performances it is probable.[65]

It is hard to know if seeing other female actresses encouraged Nahua women to take part in religious theater, but by the end of the seventeenth century they were on stage, and during the eighteenth century, if not earlier, some Nahua women started caring for the scripts.[66] By becoming thespians these women may have become religious role models for the community. They played roles as wives, daughters, and saints.[67] Their performances would not have been beyond the watchful eyes of their religious caretakers; on the contrary, they were directly in front of them and within the Franciscan compounds. Because of the location of the performances, the Franciscans must have initially sanctioned, or simply relented to, female actresses. Then, at the end of the seventeenth century, Franciscan Miguel Camacho Villavicencio mentioned their roles in the annual Passion and Epiphany dramas held at the Nahua chapel at Santiago Tlatelolco as one of the reasons, among others, for the cessation of the performances. His opposition to the dramas, and women's parts in them, does not appear to have prevented their participation, though; Nahua women continued to play female characters in Nahuatl dramas well into the eighteenth century.[68]

Women as Leaders

The leadership position for Nahua women was the *cihuatepixqui* (pl. *cihuatepixque*, women in charge of people).[69] A male equivalent also existed, the *tepixqui* (the one in charge of people). It has been, and continues to be, difficult to find details about either position. Lockhart has encountered cihuatepixque predominantly in sixteenth-century documents, with only one occurrence for the seventeenth century.[70] In the course of my research I have come upon only two sources from Mexico City that use the term. One is in the 1552 cofradía constitution for the Nahua chapel of San Josef. The other is in the 1581 will of Elena Angelina.[71] It is likely that Torquemada's abovementioned Ana from Tlatelolco was another cihuatepixqui, for he refers to her as the *buena Capitana* of the women at Tlatelolco, indicating that she was a woman in charge, most likely of people.[72] The 1648 will of Nicolasa Juana provides a brief glimpse of another female community leader and one of her responsibilities. In this testament, Nicolasa Juana states that a woman named Ana held her parents' testaments, as well as other papers. Juana believed Ana lived in the barrio of San Pablo and was the *tenantzin* (mother of people or people's mother) of her neighborhood.[73] Her responsibilities and title suggest that she was another woman in charge.

Given the paucity of documentation on this subject, I consulted sources from areas outside Mexico City to develop a more complete understanding of the position. The genre of documents where the term is seen most frequently is cofradía constitutions and wills. In sixty-five wills from Culhuacan, for example, the position appears six times and is represented by four different women. One of them was married, another widowed, and the other two were of unknown marital status.[74] The position is, then, mentioned in wills, though there are still too few occurrences. The cofradía constitution for San Josef is also largely quiet about the responsibilities of cihuatepixque in Mexico Tenochtitlan. In Tula, however, the centrality of female positions in the religious community is much more evident; although the term is not used directly, the cihuatepixque are suggested by the leadership positions held by women. The constitution for the cofradía of the Santísimo Sacramento, unlike other cofradía constitutions, does not list women among the official positions in the initial constitution. However, women were actively involved in this cofradía from the beginning, and membership roles from the early 1570s indicate that over half the membership was in fact female. Many of the female members were single, whereas the men were frequently there with their wives. Lockhart states that female pressure may have been what brought the men to join in the first place, and generally single men joined rarely, and then usually at the time of death.[75]

By 1604, however, women in the cofradía of the Santísimo Sacremento had begun to take on leadership responsibilities. In this year "four old women" were selected to make certain that proper respect was paid to the sacraments, to approve expenditures of finances and use of goods, and to monitor behavior. The use of the number four is typical of Nahua organizational thought, follows standard altepetl structure, and is the basis for the organization of the cofradía constitution of San Josef in Mexico Tenochtitlan. Apparently, by 1631 the cofradía had fallen into a disgraceful state, members were out of wax, bread, and money, and officers were not being elected on a regular basis. To solve the problem, elections were called; the "four old women" made another appearance and were instructed to act as "four mothers of people in holy matters," take care of the cofradía, encourage people who were not members to join, and take care of the sick and orphans. The choice of term used to refer to the four women, *tenantzitzinhuan*, is telling, for it is the plural reverential of *tenantzin*, which was used sixteen years later in Nicolasa Juana's Mexico City testament mentioned above.[76] Could the tenantzin Ana have been performing a similar job to the four women in Tula, and vice-versa? In 1632 the "four old women" in Tula were officially recognized as *diputadas* (female deputies)—apparently a Spanish, not Nahua, category. In 1640 the women's leadership numbers increased to six, and in 1683 when sixty people were appointed as deputies, approximately fourteen were women.[77] The fact that the women were called diputadas rather than cihuatepixque is intriguing and may reflect a change in terminology rather than the creation of a different position. This is suggested in the cofradía constitution of San Josef, where there were four cihuatepixque and four male deputies; the cihuatepixque may have been viewed as similar to the male deputies but did not have an official Spanish title to accompany their responsibilities.

Comparing the titles and responsibilities of the Tula cofradía women with the cihuatepixque found in testaments, it is worth considering whether the women in the wills might have been fulfilling some of their responsibilities as cofradía members. Though the information from wills is limited, it suggests that age or marital status may have helped determine who could be a cihuatepixqui. This idea is supported to some extent by the Tula cofradía's reference to "four old women." Additionally, if the cihuatepixque of other areas performed duties similar to the women deputies of Tula, it follows that the main corpus of documentary evidence they appear in is related to religion. Testaments, strictly speaking, are not religious documents but legal ones, and they were generally written when individuals were morbidly ill and in bed with people gathered around them. The women of Tula and the cofradía members at the chapel of San Josef were all instructed to care for the sick. These same women may have been the ones who sent for the notary and additional witnesses when the person they were treating was near death. The evidence is more than suggestive that women were responsible for a wide range of activities in their respective altepetl.

During the sixteenth and seventeenth centuries, women were frequently found alongside the bed of ailing family and friends. In an examination of ninety wills from Mexico City (see appendix 4), women appear in fifty-five, generally under the title *cihua* (the women) or *cihuatzitzintin* (the women, in the reverential form). Women appear more frequently in the wills of other women, and they are in greater numbers from the end of the sixteenth century to around the middle of the seventeenth century in Mexico City. These trends are also evident in wills of Culhuacan and Toluca. In the sixteenth-century testaments of Culhuacan, women appear in forty-six of sixty-five wills, and in the ninety-eight testaments examined from Toluca only two wills had female witnesses, though an additional two testaments had female executors.[78] Although a familial relationship is evident in many of the instances where women appear as witnesses, there are also many women who have no specified relationship with the testator. It is possible that some women held the position of cihuatepixqui and the notary failed to mention it. It is also entirely possible that the positions of cihuatepixque in testaments disappeared, only to be replaced by "women," since they were at the bedside of ailing friends and family. Or, perhaps, the cihuatepixque directed their attention to the hospitals. It would explain their absence in the wills, which were written mostly in the homes of the sick and dying. This is a topic warranting continued research.

Women's roles and duties may have shifted from precontact to colonial times, but it does not appear that Nahua women were any less active than they had been. Rather, it seems that some Nahua women actively chose to court the colonial divine and create opportunities for themselves and other women. It is true that they were most likely encouraged in these pursuits by their mendicant preachers, the nuns they served, and even their families and other community members. They may have even thought of their roles in many of these pursuits, for a while, as keeping the Nahua universe's order. Many of their responsibilities in Christian facilities, such as the chapels, friaries, convents, and hospitals, included precontact ritual tasks such as sweeping and cleaning, that is, helping to maintain order within religious facilities. Moreover, many women may have, rather quickly, decided to embrace Catholicism in many of its forms, even when the religious were not supportive of them, as in the case of actresses. Their great agency is evident in their households, communities, and religious practices through much of the sixteenth and seventeenth centuries.

Focusing on sources from Mexico Tenochtitlan, it appears that the sociopolitical status of women diminished during the seventeenth century, especially if one considers their activities as witnesses in wills and other legal documents. By the end of the seventeenth century, the cihuatzitzintin had all but disappeared from the record. Yet, again and again, women as spiritual role models appear in Franciscan reports; they entered convents as servants and became donadas, and they continued to give large sums of money to religious institutions, eventually receiving their own nunnery in the eighteenth century. Although their activities seem to have been slowly written out of the political record by both Spanish and Nahua notaries, it does not appear that the Nahua women of Mexico Tenochtitlan were less active in their colonial religious community. Rather, they appear to have created a space for women somewhere between the officially sanctioned positions of the male hierarchy and the simple parishioners. Moreover, if women's Church activities are any indication of their participation in society, we must also begin to look in other areas where indigenous women traditionally worked, such as the marketplace. There, women continued to produce and manufacture goods to sell in the marketplace (and were even accused of increasing tortilla prices just before the 1692 riot).[79] Moreover, as chapter 5 suggests, women's marketplace activities were also crucial in supporting the development of Catholicism institutionally as well as culturally within New Spain.

It is evident that early in the colonial period Nahua women acted of their own accord and at the behest of others to embrace Catholicism. To facilitate their catechism, they heard mass weekly and received their spiritual education from nuns, beatas, and the example of Spanish women. They converted to Christianity but did not disassociate themselves from their communities in the process. Rather, their ancestry, class, and gender later became fundamental for Nahua women wishing to take the veil. These Nahua women celebrated their ethnicity and mandated that all women who entered the convent of Corpus Christi had to prove their own "limpieza de sangre"—their noble indigenous blood. In doing so, they turned one of the rules that for centuries had blocked their entry into convents as nuns to their favor. It is clear that Nahua women lost influence in some social and political spheres in the colonial period, but in other areas they made advances. The majority of these women continued to be dedicated to family, community, and the divine, and they strove to expand their influence in the areas that mattered most to them.

Notes

Sections of this chapter were published previously as Jonathan Truitt, "Courting Catholicism: Nahua Women and the Catholic Church in Colonial Mexico City" *Ethnohistory* 57, no. 3 (Summer 2010): pp. 415–444. Copyright 2010, the American Society for Ethnohistory. All rights reserved. Republished, with revisions, by permission of Duke University Press.

1. William B. Taylor, *Drinking, Homicide, and Rebellion in Colonial Mexican Villages* (Stanford, Calif.: Stanford University Press, 1979), p. 116.

2. See especially Kellogg, *Law;* Susan Kellogg, "From Parallel and Equivalent to Separate but Unequal: Tenochca Mexica Women, 1500–1700," in *Indian Women of Early Mexico*, ed. Susan Schroeder, Stephanie Wood, and Robert Haskett (Norman: University of Oklahoma Press, 1997); Susan Kellogg, "Aztec Inheritance in Sixteenth-Century Mexico City: Colonial Patterns, Prehispanic Influences," *Ethnohistory* 33, no. 3 (Summer 1986): pp. 313–330; Susan Kellogg, "The Woman's Room: Some Aspects of Gender Relations in Tenochtitlan in the Late Pre-Hispanic Period," *Ethnohistory* 42, no. 4 (Autumn 1995): pp. 563–576; Susan Kellogg, "Households in Late Prehispanic and Early Colonial Mexico City: Their Structure and Its Implications for the Study of Historical Demography," *Americas* 44, no. 4 (April 1988): pp. 483–494; and Louise M. Burkhart, "Mexica Women on the Home Front: Housework and Religion in Aztec Mexico," in *Indian Women of Early Mexico*, ed. Susan Schroeder, Stephanie Wood, and Robert Haskett (Norman: University of Oklahoma Press, 1997), p. 25.

3. Stephanie Wood, "Gender and Town Guardianship in Mesoamerica: Directions for Future Research," *Journal de la Société des Américanistes* 84, no. 2 (1998): pp. 243–276.

4. Taylor posits that women would have been less active in rebellions had the men in the communities not been working outside of their villages. Taylor, *Drinking*, p. 116; and Wood, "Gender," p. 244; and Karen Vieira Powers, *Women in the Crucible of Conquest: The Gendered Genesis of Spanish American Society, 1500–1600* (Albuquerque: University of New Mexico Press, 2005), see chap. 7 especially. Powers suggests that women were able to reshape the Spanish patriarchal system from within. The Nahua women of Mexico City appear to have done just that to some degree. Additional sources examining the lives of indigenous women in Latin America are Susan Kellogg, *Weaving the Past: A History of Latin America's Indigenous Women from the Prehispanic Period to the Present* (Oxford: Oxford University Press, 2005); Susan Schroeder, Stephanie Wood, and Robert Haskett, eds., *Indian Women of Early Mexico* (Norman: University of Oklahoma Press, 1997); and Karen B. Graubart, *With Our Labor and Sweat: Indigenous Women and the Formation of Colonial*

Society in Peru, 1550–1700 (Stanford, Calif.: Stanford University Press, 2007). Though Kellogg's monograph is of a more general nature, focused on all of Latin America, its chapter 3 provides a good overview for the multiple ways indigenous women across the Spanish Americas functioned within colonial society. Schroeder, Wood, and Haskett's edited volume brought a needed emphasis to the role of specifically indigenous women in colonial and precolonial society. Graubart's work examines indigenous women in colonial Peru. Her work was essential in directing me to, as she calls it, the "ambiguous spaces" where gender and ethnic identities were figured out in the formation of colonial society. Susan Migden Socolow's *The Women of Colonial Latin America* (Cambridge: Cambridge University Press, 2000) is also an invaluable resource. As a comparative history of women across race and social class, it demonstrates that women identified more with their race and class than with their gender. This appears to be the case with indigenous women in Mexico City as well.

5. AHFZ Constitution (see chapter 1, note 55, above).

6. For a discussion of the equivalency of precontact responsibilities, see Kellogg, "From Parallel," pp. 125–133.

7. Burkhart, *Slippery Earth*, pp. 35, 117.

8. AGN, Bienes Nacionales, v. 70, e. 3.

9. Ann Miriam Gallagher, "The Indian Nuns of Mexico City's *Monasterio* of Corpus Christi, 1724–1821," in *Latin American Women: Historical Perspectives*, ed. Asunción Lavrin (Westport, Conn.: Greenwood Press, 1978), p. 151.

10. AGI México, v. 1937. Fray Bernardino de Sahagún notes that during the sixteenth century the Franciscans allowed two Nahua men to take the habit of San Francisco. Shortly after, though, it was decided that they were not up to the calling. One Francisco Faustino Quetzalmaçatzin from Amaquemecan showed that Nahua men were allowed to become lay brothers during the seventeenth century, if not earlier. Sahagún, *Florentine Codex*, vol. 1, p. 76; and Chimalpahin, *Annals*, p. 187.

11. Louise Burkart effectively argues that in Mexica (Aztec) culture women's responsibilities at home were no less important than the responsibilities of the men away fighting during a time of war; rather, both responsibilities were essential. Burkhart, "Mexica Women," pp. 26.

12. Ideally research along these lines would not examine women as a single group but rather would consider changes along class lines, thereby distinguishing between high-ranking indigenous women and those of lower status. In this way we could see if precontact class distinctions and responsibilities had a bearing on similar colonial duties. Unfortunately, the documentation does not allow for such distinctions. One of the traditional ways of differentiating women of high status is with the Spanish title *doña*. However, very few of the documents I have seen involving indigenous women list their names with that title. That said, there are clearly wealthy Nahua women without the *doña* title included among my samples, but any consistent social distinction I could make for the Nahua women of Mexico Tenochtitlan would be based on an artificially constructed demarcation. Because of this I treat them as a group. Future research may rectify this situation.

13. Kellogg, "From Parallel and Equivalent," pp. 130–131.

14. Lori Boornazian Diel, "Women and Political Power: The Inclusion and Exclusion of Noblewomen in Aztec Pictorial Histories," *Res* 47 (Spring 2005), p. 83; and Susan Schroeder, "The Noblewomen of Chalco," *Estudios de Cultura Náhuatl* 22 (1992): pp. 45–86.

15. Burkhart, *Slippery Earth*, pp. 34–39; and Burkhart, "Mexica Women," p. 25.

16. Burkhart, "Mexica Women," pp. 26, 32, 38.

17. Mary Elizabeth Perry, *Gender and Disorder in Early Modern Seville* (Princeton, N.J.: Princeton University Press, 1990), p. 9.

18. James Lockhart, *Spanish Peru, 1532–1560: A Social History*, 2nd ed. (Madison: University of Wisconsin Press, 1994), p. 169.

19. Socolow, *Women*, p. 53.

20. Marta V. Vicente, "Images and Realities of Work: Women and Guilds in Early Modern Barcelona," in *Spanish Women in the Golden Age: Images and Realities*, ed. Magdalena S. Sánchez and Alain Saint-Saëns (Westport, Conn.: Greenwood Press, 1996), p. 129.

21. Motolinia, *Motolinia's History*, pp. 312–313; Gallagher, "Indian Nuns," pp. 150–151; and Asunción Lavrin, "Indian Brides of Christ: Creating New Spaces for Indigenous Women in New Spain," *Mexican Studies/Estudios Mexicanos* 15, no. 2 (Summer 1999), p. 228.

22. Gallagher, "Indian Nuns," p. 152.

23. Some mestizas were allowed to become nuns. Muriel, *Las indias*, p. 41.

24. Ibid., p. 152.

25. Gallagher, "Indian Nuns," pp. 152–154; and Muriel, *Las indias*, p. 41; For additional information on the convent, see Mónica Díaz, "Indigenous Nuns of Corpus Christi: Race and Spirituality," in *Religion in New Spain*, ed. Susan Schroeder and Stafford Poole (Albuquerque: University of New Mexico Press, 2007), pp. 179–192.

26. Allan Greer, "Iroquois Virgin: The Story of Catherine Tekakwitha in New France and New Spain," in *Colonial Saints: Discovering the Holy in the Americas*, ed. Allan Greer and Jodi Bilinkoff (New York: Routledge, 2003), pp. 235–239.

27. Mendieta, *Historia*, vol. 2, pp. 85–86.

28. AGN, Tierras, vol. 101, e. 2, f. 8; AGN, Tierras, v. 128 pt. 2, e. 2; AGN, Indiferente Virreinal, caja 6493, e. 8; AGN, Indiferente Virreinal, 6471, e. 11; and see appendix 4.

29. AGN, Tierras, v. 35, e. 1.

30. AGN, Tierras, v. 37, e. 2, fs. 69v–83v.

31. AGN, Tierras, v. 22, pt. 1, e. 5.

32. Caterina Pizzigoni, *Testaments of Toluca* (Stanford, Calif.: Stanford University Press, 2006).

33. Chimalpahin, *Annals*, p. 203.

34. The sources have not provided a specific name for this hospital.

35. AGN, Indios, v. 34, e. 37, f. 40; Chimalpahin, *Annals*, p. 217; Vetancurt, *Teatro*, pt. 4, p. 111; and Chimalpahin, *Annals*, p. 243.

36. Torquemada, *Monarquía*, vol. 3, pp. 217–218.

37. To further extend the research in this area, I also compared the ninety-eight wills from Caternia Pizzigoni's volume *Testaments of Toluca*. The donations in the Toluca wills were more frequent than those in either the Mexico City or Culhuacan wills. However, some of these donations, such as those to "Holy Jerusalem," appear to have been a standard procedure during the eighteenth century. Pizzigoni found that fifty-nine of the ninety-eight wills made donations to the Jerusalem fund, the majority coming after 1700 (Pizzigoni, *Testaments*, p. 17). Aside from standardized donations there was also a marked increase in donations to saints and cofradías. The financial wealth in most donations was still less than that found in the Mexico City wills, but the difference in the types of donations made in the Toluca wills in contrast to the Mexico City and Culhuacan testaments makes it difficult to establish an effective comparison here. To add to potential research, men appear to have started making more donations during this period than they did in the sixteenth and seventeenth centuries. Because of these and other factors, an effective comparison and compilation of all three collections is outside of the parameters of this volume.

38. AGN, Hospital de Jesús, leg. 210, e. 4; ANM, Hernando de Arauz #4, v. 7, yrs. 1619–1622, fs. 7–12v; and AGN, Tierras, v. 1458, e. 11.

39. AGN, Bienes Nacionales, v. 70, e. 3; AGN, Bienes Nacionales, v. 1096, e. 8; and NL, Ayer Collection, MS 1481, B(3)F.

40. Though her father used the title *don*, it is surprisingly absent from any reference to Melchora de Santiago. This is especially surprising since she inherited the cacicazgo.

41. AGN, Bienes Nacionales, v. 965, e. 6. "ynic . ii . niquitohua . yn iquac tla omonamacac . ỳ caltzintli . oncan quiçaz . yepohualli pesos . macoz . ỳ nonamictzin lucas Xuarez . ytech pohuiz . ynic zan epoualli p°s . ytech nicpouhtiuh . ypāpa . cēca onitlaihiyohui . ynic omotlatequipanilhui ypā tepixcayotl . miec yn ipā oniquixtlauh tlacalaquilli . yn iquac ylpilo yn carçel . nevatl onicpatiaya in tequitl . yuh niquitohua . ỳ notlatol."

42. Torquemada, *Monarquía*, vol. 3, p. 245.

43. Despite the large sums of money Ana donated to the Franciscans and her title of *buena Capitana*, Torquemada does not refer to her as a doña. This is perhaps oversight on his part. Unfortunately, his is the only work that I am aware of that mentions her. Ibid., vol. 3, pp. 217–218.

44. Ibid., vol. 3, pp. 217–220.

45. Chimalpahin, *Annals*, p. 69.

46. Ibid., p. 305.

47. Ibid., p. 231.

48. Ibid., p. 227.

49. Carlos de Sigüenza y Góngora, *Paraíso occidental* (México: Cien de México, 2003), pp. 282–283. Asunción Lavrin also discusses this account in *Brides of Christ,* pp. 250–252.

50. De la Concepción was most likely never recognized as a mystic; she probably lacked the necessary connections. Sigüenza, *Paraíso*, pp. 283–286. For more information on Spanish mystics, see Stephen Haliczer, *Between Exaltation and Infamy: Female Mystics in the Golden Age of Spain* (New York: Oxford University Press, 2002); and Nora E. Jaffery, *False Mystics: Deviant Orthodoxy in Colonial Mexico* (Lincoln: University of Nebraska Press, 2005).

51. Sigüenza, *Paraíso*, pp. 286–287; and Lavrin, "Indian Brides," pp. 235–236.

52. AGN, Bienes Nacionales, leg. 45, e. 30; AGN, Bienes Nacionales, v. 181, e. 2; and AGN, Bienes Nacionales, leg. 859, e. 1.

53. AGI, México, v. 1937; and Lavrin, "Indian Brides," p. 240.

54. Oroz, *Oroz Codex*, p. 84.

55 It is probable that both Oroz and Mendieta took this story from the same source or that one copied it from the other. Ibid.; and Mendieta, *Historia Eclesiástica*, vol. 2, p. 312.

56. Torquemada, *Monarquía*, vol. 3, pp. 217–218.

57. Flogging appears to have been a regular punishment for missing mass. For another example, see AGN, Bienes Nacionales, leg. 732, e. 1.

58. Chimalpahin, *Annals*, p. 195.

59. Ibid., pp. 196–197.

60. AGN, Tierras, v. 95 pt. 2, e. 8. This case is discussed in more detail in chapter 1. Nahua women appear in a similar manner in a case of a cross and alley near the indigenous chapel of San Josef. Again they are not mentioned by name but rather appear as part of a larger group. AGN, Tierras, v. 103, pt. 1, pt. 2, e. 6.

61. Gonzalo Gómez de Cervantes, *La vida económica y social de la Nueva España al finalizar del siglo XVI* (México: Antigua Librería Robredo de J. Porrúa e Hijos, 1944), p. 135.

62. AGN, Bienes Nacionales, v. 990, exp. 10; Burkhart, "Pageantry."

63. Melveena McKendrick, *Theatre in Spain, 1490–1700* (Cambridge: Cambridge University Press, 1989), p. 49.

64. AGN, Historias, v. 467, e. 1.

65. Lavrin, *Brides of Christ,* pp. 327–328.

66. Burkhart, "Pageantry."

67. Horcasitas, *Teatro Náhuatl*; and Sell and Burkhart, *Nahuatl Theater*, all volumes.

68. AGN, Bienes Nacionales, v. 990, exp. 10; and Burkhart, "Pageantry."

69. S. L. Cline and Miguel Leon-Portilla, eds. and trans., *The Testaments of Culhuacan* (Los Angeles: UCLA Latin American Center Publications and the University of California Press, 1984).

70. Lockhart, *Nahuas,* p. 139.

71. AHFZ Constitution; and NL, Ayer Collection, MS 1481, B(1)a.

72. Torquemada, *Monarquía*, vol. 3, pp. 217–218.

73. AGN, Bienes Nacionales, v. 1766, e. 7. For more information on this case and a transcription and translation of the will, see Truitt, "Revelations," pp. 55–67.

74. Cline and León-Portilla, *Testaments*, docs. 34, 38, 41, 64, 65, 74.

75. Lockhart, *Nahuas*, pp. 226–227.

76. Ibid., p. 227 (and p. 542n93 for the Nahuatl transcription of the quote); and AGN, Bienes Nacionales, v. 1766, e. 7.

77. Lockhart, *Nahuas*, pp. 227–229; and Barry D. Sell, "The Molina Confraternity Rules of 1552," in *Nahua Confraternities in Early Colonial Mexico: The 1552 Nahuatl Ordinances of Fray Alonso de Molina*, ed. and trans. Barry D. Sell (Berkeley: Academy of American Franciscan History), pp. 60–61.

78. Cline and León-Portilla, *Testaments*; and Pizzigoni, *Testaments.*

79. R. Douglas Cope, *The Limits of Racial Domination: Plebeian Society in Colonial Mexico City, 1660–1720* (Madison: University of Wisconsin Press, 1994), p. 127; and Kellogg, *Law*, pp. 118–119.

Chapter 4
Cofradías and the Nahua Community

Cofradías were one of the most dynamic of sanctioned indigenous forms of religious expression in New Spain. Cofradías associated with indigenous chapels in Mexico City were initiated, encouraged, sanctioned, overseen, but not controlled entirely by the regular orders or the secular Church. Nahua women and men organized and directed their sodalities and fought to participate in the city's religious rituals even when friars tried to exclude them. In Mexico City, the processions and festivities of cofradías acted as some of the most vibrant of all visible aspects of indigenous cultural, social, and religious life.[1] In addition to rituals, specific leadership positions for men and women developed in these sodalities by the 1550s, if not earlier. Finally, the Nahuas used them to directly influence the development of colonial society in Mexico City. From within the relative safety of the cofradías Nahuas shaped life in Mexico City, by establishing leadership positions for women, supporting mixed Spanish-Nahua brotherhoods for work at the hospitals, and, on occasion, defying the orders of their mendicant spiritual leaders.

Spaniards developed sodalities for non-Spanish populations in Europe as early as the 1400s.[2] By the time they arrived in New Spain, conditions for the organization of cofradías for non-Christian societies had been established. Though the friars now dealt with a completely foreign culture, the procedures were familiar. The community-based nature of the cofradías made their introduction to the community-focused societies of New Spain that much easier.

Historians have shown that indigenous cofradías across New Spain helped shape group identity among the differing social classes over the course of the sixteenth and seventeenth centuries.[3] Some friars believed that they assisted with the conversion of the native people. Other religious thought that the Nahuas had a natural inclination to the brotherhoods because of their diligent participation in devotional ceremonies and religious exercises.[4] Charles Gibson argues that "cofradías offered their members a spiritual security and a sense of collective identity otherwise lacking in seventeenth-century native life." He adds that they became especially important to towns that suffered population loss and Spanish immigration.[5]

This case is probably true for Mexico City as well, where death from disease was common and Spanish immigration was greater than most other areas in New Spain. In addition to arriving Spaniards, the Nahuas of Mexico City had to contend with an influx of Africans, Asians, and other non-Nahuatl-speaking groups. Lay sodalities offered the opportunity for individuals to come together with family, friends, and neighbors to affirm their place in the changing social and cultural atmosphere of the viceregal capital.

The Nahuas effectively altered the institution of the Spanish cofradía to fit their religious and social needs; they made them their own cultural entities and frequently fought off attempts at clerical control.[6] The popularity of the cofradías is visible in their rapid and continued growth during the Hapsburg period. Additionally, the importance of the institution can be seen in the incorporation of the term *cofradía* into the Nahuatl language as a loanword. Instead of forming a new word, as they did for bellows (*ehuatlepitzaloni*),[7] for example, the Nahuas adopted *cofradía*, as early as 1566, and added their own suffix.[8] James Lockhart argues that the use of Spanish loanwords by Nahuas demonstrated their desire to espouse that part of Spanish society to fit their own needs.[9]

Thus far most scholarly research on indigenous cofradías in the Americas has focused on rural areas, and few historians have specifically examined the brotherhoods in the confines of an exclusively urban setting. This chapter explores Nahua sodalities within Mexico Tenochtitlan. Although similar in many regards to rural cofradías, circumstances in the capital of New Spain, such as population size and the frequent interactions with Spaniards, Africans, and Asians, created an environment that was different from that in most other altepetl, where foreign populations were much smaller and at times virtually nonexistent. In the context of the urban environment, cofradías actively preserved a distinct Nahua identity in the capital city during the sixteenth and seventeenth centuries. The Nahuas' early adoption and then continued expansion of the cofradías demonstrate their desire to manage as much of their religious and social life as possible.

Cofradías were the most readily accessible communal religious organizations available to Nahuas. Though the Nahuas of New Spain could technically join the priesthood and religious orders, in the sixteenth and seventeenth centuries it was generally with great difficulty.[10] The adoption and popularity of the brotherhoods in central Mexico placed Nahuas in a position of strength when negotiating between the religious orders' approval of certain cultural traditions (e.g., dancing and singing in church) and Nahua acceptance of other aspects of Christian instruction.[11] Although cofradías were not the only institution through which Nahuas maintained their society and identity, they were one of the most important, and they persevered well into the eighteenth century.

What made the cofradía popular for conversion, in the minds of the mendicants, and what made the cofradía popular for participation, in the view of the Nahuas, was likely the same thing—namely, a set of rules for performing Christianity. Cofradías allowed Nahuas to take part in Christianity. Regardless of their belief in Catholicism, cofrades engaged the adopted religion much as did Nahua thespians and musicians (see chapter 2). The mendicant supervisors also benefitted from the display of the cofrades' performance, since the processions acted as a public display of the friars' success in bringing new converts to the faith. So long as the cofradías' outward appearance adhered to the guidelines applied in their constitutions, there was no problem. It was harder to question the Nahuas' inner faith if their outward appearance and actions were seen to be accurate and appropriate.

Directives of the Colonial Nahua Cofradía

The constitutions of indigenous sodalities, like their European counterparts, provided regulations regarding financial support (through alms, donations, membership fees, and fines) and leadership elections. The process of selecting leaders and successfully meeting the cofradía's spiritual, social, and financial obligations relied on widespread community support and acceptance. When Nahuas selected their leaders and pooled their money to cover the expenses of the organizations, they were determining how they would support each other. Though some Nahua cofradía constitutions included a broad swathe of the Nahua community, the constitutions themselves should not be relied on exclusively as proof of membership or activity. Cofradía constitutions, like other legal documents, were formulaic in nature. Just as fray Alonso de Molina created a "model testament" in 1569, so he also wrote a set of ideal ordinances in 1552 to assist in establishing legal constitutions for Nahua cofradías.[12]

The earliest extant cofradía constitution for Tenochtitlan is based on Molina's model ordinances to such an extent that he is credited with drafting it.[13] Its ordinances are a utopian model for an ideal indigenous cofradía, but the mendicants probably realized that each constitution had to differ based on local circumstances, and this was especially the case in New Spain. Cofradías in an urban environment, for example, could be deliberately exclusionary or segregationist in the sixteenth century, unlike their rural counterparts. Similarly, a small sodality likely required fewer leadership positions than did a large one. Molina's understanding of the need for this flexibility is evident in the San Josef constitution. The differences between the model ordinances and the actual constitution are largely about leadership. The author dropped certain religious content when he wrote the constitution, but he did not add any new or controversial information either.

In the area of leadership, the constitution of San Josef and Molina's ordinances parallel each other at many points. Molina wrote his ordinances as a template for the Nahuas to use in their constitutions. The San Josef constitution was designed to fit the needs of its cofrades. If, as the document claims, the author was Molina, then by penning the constitution in the same year as his ordinances he demonstrated that cofradía constitutions should be adapted to fit local circumstances. Discrepancies between the model and the actual constitutions reveal how the earliest Nahua cofradías functioned. For example, the constitution belonging to San Josef stated that members who desired to take on positions of leadership had to be adults as well as parents. Neither Molina's ordinances nor any Spanish cofradía constitution that I have examined has any stipulation about age or parental status. Additionally, indigenous cofradías created the position of cihuatepixqui (see chapter 3). The cihuatepixque were the Nahuas' greatest deviance from European cofradía norms and demonstrate indigenous women's importance in the community and religion.[14]

Leaders of the cofradía were elected to their offices on the first day of the year, the feast day of the Circuncisión. For the San Josef cofradía constitution, on this day members elected a *prioste* (leader of the cofradía), four deputies "who will look after all the members of the cofradía in the various tlaxilacalli," a mayordomo to "guard" the property of the sodality, and a notary to record everything. It is likely that the cihuatepixque were also selected at this time.[15] The prominence in the constitution of leadership duties and elections (including a missing page that explains at least some of the deputies' duties and possibly those of the cihuatepixque) demonstrates the importance of the positions for the mendicant orders as well as Nahua society.

Offices conveyed prestige and conferred respect outside the brotherhood. In wills and other documents, some witnesses were identified by their leadership title. Both mayordomos and cihuatepixque make appearances in wills and other documents.[16] Lockhart has found that some of the positions came to be held by the same person for multiple years and were occasionally passed from one generation to the next. At times, cofradía leaders also held positions simultaneously in the Nahua government.[17] Additionally, the number of positions available within a cofradía was determined by the needs, or desires, of each group. When fray Alonso de Molina discusses specific roles in his cofradía ordinances, he does it briefly and states that there should be two deputies and two mayordomos.[18] The cofrades of the San Josef constitution elected four of each of the deputies, mayordomos, and cihuatepixque for the "various tlaxilacalli," matching the number of barrios that made up Mexico Tenochtitlan.[19] Because of the number of roles, I believe that this particular document derives from one of the earliest Nahua cofradías established in Mexico Tenochtitlan. Other sodalities established at the visita chapels and at San Josef most likely had a different number of leadership positions based on the neighborhoods they served. In other Nahua communities, cofradías elected different numbers of people to fulfill the various responsibilities, depending on local needs. In the case of a brotherhood in the altepetl of San Miguel Coyotlan, they elected an actor, mayordomos, two deputies, a *bitor* (cheerleader), a prioste, and cihuatepixque capitanas.[20]

The organization of the cofradía in the 1550s demonstrates ways in which precontact culture and colonial institutions came together during the first century of Spanish rule. The fact that the cofradía of San Josef opted for four deputies to assist the prioste as well as four cihuatepixque suggests that it had people assigned to each of the four subdistricts of Mexico Tenochtitlan.[21] Having representatives from each barrio drew on precontact traditions of noble leadership for each of the major subdistricts of the larger altepetl. The Nahuas of Mexico Tenochtitlan modeled the institution of the European lay sodality to fit their social and religious interests. They used the organization of the cofradía and its leadership to unite the community by means of practices with which they were accustomed.

The election process of Nahua cofradías demonstrates the use of both precontact and Catholic cultural traditions. For example, natives began their election day by ritually sweeping the meeting area in the early hours of the morning. Franciscans saw this as an act of devotion and a dedication to cleanliness, but sweeping was ritualized in precontact religious traditions and represented the process of removing filth to maintain order and balance.[22] The San Josef constitution describes how the "home of" San Josef was to be prepared for the elections after its early morning sweeping. Cofradía members were instructed to drape flowers and "shake reeds and grasses" in the chapel. The use of reeds and grasses is again reminiscent of ancient practice, although the friars may have thought it a suitable substitute for incense. The election process also contained many European Catholic elements, such as the ringing of church bells, the recitation of the "Veni Creatur Spiritus" and the "Te Deum Laudumus Te Dominum," and the lighting and placement of a Spanish-style candle on the altar.[23] The ritualized detail is very reminiscent of Spanish Catholic practice at the time. The nature of the ceremony was probably also familiar to the Nahuas of central New Spain. The election procedures had specific directions for gaining divine favor, just as did precontact religious rites. As a ritualized religious procedure, the ceremony to install officers was an aspect of spiritual life that the Nahuas could control and perform correctly or incorrectly. Though a friar may have been present at the elections, it was the Nahuas who ran the electoral process (as they did for their Spanish-styled *cabildos*, or town councils).[24] Their procedural decisions demonstrate a desire to maintain important precontact traditions alongside the newer Hispanic ones.

The San Josef constitution identified the duties of the cofradía's officers. The prioste was the leader, the mayordomos were to watch over the sodality's property, and the notary recorded all of the property in a book. The deputies also had a book for recording some aspect of the activities of cofradía members. Unfortunately, that information is contained on the one page that is missing from the constitution. The Nahuas were strangely silent on the duties of the cihuatepixque. At other points in the constitution additional responsibilities relating to the position of the prioste are mentioned. As the leader of the cofradía, it was the prioste's duty, along with "those who govern," to determine the number of lashes to be given to an individual who had committed five mortal sins (and been informed of their four previous transgressions) and then expel him or her from the cofradía. The constitution also states that it was the responsibility of the prioste and the notary to "go to the sick so that they will make a testament for him."[25] It is probable that some of the other leaders, both male and female, accompanied the notary instead of the prioste, for they acted as witnesses for some wills and testaments.[26] Additionally, it was the parallel responsibility of the prioste and the Nahua governor of Mexico Tenochtitlan to report the abuses, or neglect, committed by the friary guardian (or other friars) to his superiors. Another of the duties of the mayordomo was to collect the fines, and the notary was charged with recording them.

The process of electing both men and women to positions of leadership surely enhanced the members' sense of community. The duties of the officers further demonstrate a concern with controlling the social conduct of the indigenous society. By acting as their own supervisory force, Nahuas could extend some influence over religious practices and make decisions regarding which native and Spanish customs they employed.

As communal organizations, cofradías helped their members meet religious obligations while they were alive and after they died. Expenses accrued on behalf of their members included fees associated with specific masses, feast days, processions, times of economic difficulty (such as periods of illness), care for the sick, marriages, and burials. To cover the costs associated with these duties, Nahua religious brotherhoods solicited donations of money, goods, and labor from their members. Additionally, to help with expenses and as a deterrent against bad behavior, constitutions listed fines that members faced for improper behavior or neglect of duty. The process of collecting donations and fines served a communal effort to maintain moral actions deemed important by the community. The revenue went to their political and spiritual leaders. When money was collected, it was typically placed in a community chest owned by the general membership of the sodality.

As stipulated by its constitution, all members of the cofradía of San Josef performed labor obligations. Unlike tribute labor (required of them by Spaniards and their precontact rulers), the cofrades were instructed to participate in all cofradía duties and labor voluntarily, no matter how humbling. All members belonging to the cofradía of San Josef—be they of noble, middling, or commoner status—were to take part in the "disposal of urine, the throwing out of feces, washing the faces and feet of others, and serving food to people." They were not to "regard it as hateful tribute work, you will not make the food for the sick as tribute duty."[27] Fray Pedro de Gante wrote to Charles V in 1552 to request that he reduce the amount of tribute labor to allow the natives more time to work for the salvation of their souls.[28] The chores performed for the chapel and its associated hospital, as instructed by the constitution, were seen as humbling and to be performed in imitation of Christ. By being humble and providing voluntary labor for the hospital, cofrades could obtain the "pardon of sin for those in purgatory."[29]

A mid-1560s bigamy case suggests that Nahua women were, at the very least, performing jobs assigned to them by the cofradía. The case involved the head of the Hospital Real de los Naturales, Juan Bravo Acre, and two indigenous women. Over the course of the case it becomes evident that other indigenous women, married and unmarried alike, worked at the hospital. Several witnesses point to Bravo Acre's attempted rape of women, regardless of marital status, and that his actions kept women from working in the hospital.[30] Though information in the case does not link these women to a cofradía, the sodalities' ties to hospitals and Nahua women's involvement in the brotherhoods suggest the connection.

The provisioning of supplies and equipment was just as important as voluntary labor to the sodalities. Fray Pedro Oroz and Chimalpahin mention some of the materials that cofradías and their members had to pay for: banners, candles, candleholders, crosses, fireworks, platforms for images, torches, and vestments. In addition to these items, brotherhoods generally paid for a specific feast day and for certain goods necessary for weekly mass. A feast day celebration in 1679 cost five pesos for the friars to say mass and one peso for the cantores. The cost of a friar on the occasion of a special mass or sermon could range from three to six pesos. Through any given year, the total cost of all processions might exceed 156 pesos, which was greater than the annual income of many indigenous people.[31] All of the expenses were associated with the community's religious celebrations. For this reason, members of the cofradía necessarily provided the funding to cover the outlay.

Alms were another means to cover financial expenditures. Cofrades had to receive permission from the bishop before soliciting alms. In Tlaxcala, Nahua cofradías accepted almost any type of alms, monetary or otherwise: blankets, chilies, dogs, sheep, and shirts are just a few examples of the donations they received. At San Josef, members of the cofradía were "greatly obligated to make offerings" whenever they celebrated a feast day at the Hospital Real de los Naturales. After a burial, cofrades were encouraged to make an offering on behalf of the deceased.[32] Alms also went to care for the religious images of the brotherhoods. The Archdiocese of Mexico encouraged the collection of these alms initially, and both Nahua men and women took part in their collection. By the end of the eighteenth century, though, the ecclesiastical hierarchy sought to regulate it.[33]

Most likely the offerings made by the cofrades at San Josef took many forms, as seen by those accepted by the Tlaxcala brotherhood mentioned above. The variety and type of donations provided by Nahuas to their cofradía differed, in some ways, from the aid Spaniards provided to their sodalities. Donations by Spaniards tended to be monetary. In contrast to the monetary offerings made by Europeans in the sixteenth century, the contributions Nahuas provided their brotherhoods had a more directed impact on individual lives within their communities. Spanish cofradías generally dedicated their donations to charitable institutions, whereas Nahuas focused specifically on the community and the individuals who were part of it. Over time, as hard currency became more common, it is likely that Nahuas shifted to currency-based donations. The money and other donations helped cover the social and cultural needs of the Nahuas.

Obligations of and Licensing for Cofradías

The one surviving Nahua cofradía constitution belonging to San Josef de los Naturales lists "five firm obligations" which "absolutely no one [who is a member] will trespass against." The list includes leadership duties, the organization of mass and public gatherings, prayer responsibilities, care for the sick and dying, and the cofrades' public deportment.[34] The lay sodality's "obligations" influenced numerous aspects of people's daily lives and served to tie the Nahuas of Mexico Tenochtitlan together, distinguishing them from Spaniards and other indigenous groups such as the Mixtec and Zapotec immigrants from south-central New Spain. By agreeing to support the obligations, the cofradía was apparently able to preserve some aspects of indigenous culture while insulating its society against the imposition of other European cultural mores.

To receive official recognition of their cofradía, the cofrades needed a license issued by a bishop and a constitution approved by the Council of the Indies and the king. The brotherhood had to be associated with a local chapel and meet only in the presence of the chaplain and a royal representative. Admittance to the sodalities was supposed to happen only after baptism.[35] It is impossible to prove that all members had received baptism, but it is known that many cofradías started operating prior to approval and others never received official sanction for social, cultural, and economic reasons.[36] The majority of native brotherhoods tended to be inclusive and did not typically organize based on marital status, age, or gender, though all such factors could help determine the leadership of a sodality. The leadership of the groups was predominantly male, though positions developed for women as early as 1552, a situation distinct from European mixed-sex sodalities.[37] Only one known group (the Cofradía del Santísimo Trinidad de los Sastres, tailors), established at San Josef, was trade specific, though this was an atypical case.[38] Documents suggest that Nahuas could move between communities and parishes within Mexico Tenochtitlan. Even emigrants could join cofradías and, by extension, the community.

The popularity of the groups can be seen in the Third Mexican Council's estimate that three hundred Indian cofradías existed in New Spain in 1585.[39] One year before the report, the Audiencia of New Spain sent a letter to King Philip II stating that Viceroy don Martin Enríquez was interfering with the archbishop's responsibility to oversee indigenous cofradías.[40] The conflict probably developed over the growing dispute surrounding secular Church authority and the rights of the regular orders who were responsible for the establishment of the cofradías.[41]

Arguments not related to the secular Church and regular orders' struggle for power also developed around cofradías. The concerns do not appear to be doctrinally based. Rather, there seem to have been two big points of contention. For one, brotherhoods called for the established organization and mass congregation of large groups of people. They set leadership for the group, allowed them ample time to organize at their regular meetings, and the festivals where they all came together provided the perfect opportunity for a widespread revolt. Indeed, this very fear hampered Holy Week celebrations across the sixteenth century in Tenochtitlan.[42]

The second difficulty to arise between the mendicant supervisors and the cofrades appears to have been competition for finances. Just as indigenous craftsmen were heralded for their skill by ecclesiastics and victimized for it by Spanish competitors, so it seems indigenous dedication to their sodalities had a similar consequence.[43] Ecclesiastics singled out cofradías as a problem in two areas. One was illegal brotherhoods. These were established ad hoc, lacked a constitution, and were complained about at various levels within the Church hierarchy. Since they did not have a constitution, it was impossible for the Church to make sure they were orthodox in their practices. Just as unwelcome as their illegality, these groups could take prospective members and their money and good works from sanctioned sodalities.

The competitive aspect becomes more apparent when two brotherhoods of the same devotion were established within close proximity to each other. This happened in 1612 when a Nahua woodcarver by the name of Diego López successfully petitioned Rome for the establishment of a cofradía at San Francisco in Tlatelolco with two devotions, Niño Jesús Perdido and Santa María del Rosario. The Jesuits helped him obtain the requisite licenses from the pope. When the dual brotherhood was finally allowed to march in procession in 1613, its members were prevented from taking its image of Santa María del Rosario with them by the Dominicans, who had an indigenous sodality of the same dedication located at their friary of Santo Domingo in Mexico Tenochtitlan.[44]

Competition did not halt the expansion of sodalities. By the end of the sixteenth century, six sodalities had been organized at San Josef, two at the chapel of San Sebastián, and potentially one at the friary of Santo Domingo.[45] Friars Agustín de Vetancurt, Pedro Oroz, and Juan de Torquemada credit the establishment (or at least official recognition) of the first four cofradías to fray Pedro de Gante.[46] Chimalpahin records the foundation of the Cofradía de la Soledad de la Virgen in 1591, although the process for establishing the cofradía started in July 1590. Nahuas and Franciscans established the brotherhood, but its membership was specifically for Nahuas.[47] Chimalpahin also notes that by 1612 each of the four barrios of Mexico Tenochtitlan had its own cofradía.[48] By the close of the seventeenth century at least twenty-nine officially sanctioned brotherhoods of indigenous membership had received licenses to operate in Mexico Tenochtitlan (see appendix 1).[49] Eleven, just over one-third, of the brotherhoods had been established at the chapel of San Josef de los Naturales.[50] The appeal the institutions had to the Nahuas can be seen in a viceregal census, 1790–1794. By this time, in the archdiocese alone there were 951 cofradías.[51]

Social Importance of Cofradías

Cofradías in the Americas were involved in their members' lives in many ways. They provided more than spiritual assistance. They acted as a mutually supportive society dedicated to the well-being of their members during times of illness and financial stress and enhanced communal identity and solidarity through participation in festivities and processions. Information on these activities provides a glimpse into the cohesiveness of the Nahua community in Mexico Tenochtitlan during the sixteenth and seventeenth centuries.

Asunción Lavrin argues that cofradías provided social order in the community to which their members belonged. With a person's acceptance into the brotherhood came an agreement to adhere to the rules of membership. The constitution of San Josef had two stipulations for belonging to its cofradía: only people belonging to the chapel of San Josef de los Naturales could be members; and no one would prevent a person from the altepetl (Mexico Tenochtitlan) from being listed on the membership roll.[52] The leadership of the brotherhoods explicitly stipulated which kinds of behavior were considered appropriate to a member and ultimately decided who could be removed from the sodality for transgressions.[53] Thus membership itself functioned as a means to promote community cohesion and identity.

Cofrades, as well as officials appointed by the indigenous governor, were to take a count at each mass to make certain that all members capable of attending did so.[54] Anyone failing to appear without a legitimate reason received a fine. The regulations regarding confession also discuss social life: "Here is declared how they will live in public so that they preserve their reputations and are prudent, and so that no one will take a bad example from them."[55] Although the Nahuas did not always understand the dictates and mysteries of Catholicism, the community was dedicated to trying to meet most of the standards of religious and social conduct expected of them by the Franciscans.

In an attempt to maintain a high social standard, the cofradía constitution specified expected behavior and how members who complied could receive assistance for marriage. Members who wished to marry, young men or women or widows and widowers, were to make their intentions known so that cofrades could determine how they might provide assistance. Additionally, two members (of very good standing) were elected to collect donations. If such donations could not be collected, cofrades were to provide what they could for the couple. A couple that failed to announce their marriage plans was not assisted with alms. The reward for good behavior was probably a strong incentive for at least the poorer members of the society. The cost to perform an indigenous marriage for cofrades in 1679 was eleven pesos for the priest and cantores alone.[56] The act of gathering alms for a local marriage helped to reaffirm the group's support of its individual members. Moreover, the guidelines went beyond marriage to include suggested family practices. For example, if children did not obey their parents (or spouses, male or female, did not listen to their marriage partner), the offending party was to be "admonished two or three times" in the presence of the other cofrades. If the offending party still refused to curb his or her ways, he or she was then reported to a priest.

Cofradías also provided the means for conflict resolution in the neighborhoods. On feast days cofrades were required to settle all grievances with each other. If they did not, other members of the brotherhood were to intervene to avoid offending the saint.

In preparation for feast day processions, Nahuas decorated banners, arches, the chapel of San Josef, the friary of San Francisco, as well as many of the streets. Whenever there was a procession, everyone—men, women, and children—was to be present. If the sacrament was taken in procession, they rang the main church bell four times at five different intervals to call everyone to the chapel; at San Josef, the sacrament was taken in procession at least four times a year. For the procession, participants dressed in their scapularies and other religious attire associated with their position and cofradía. They lined up in order, from the lowest-ranking cofradía to the highest. Before leaving the chapel, they lit torches and candles, the number varying from one procession to another.[57] Upon reaching the streets, the natives joined with the cofradías of Spaniards, castas, and Afro-Mexicans. Children threw olive branches onto the procession from treetops. The sights and sounds of tolling bells, dancers, drums, fireworks, and singing accompanied many of the processions. In addition, terraces, patios, and rooftops were lit with candles, fires, and torches.[58] These events indeed acted as a means to express religious, community, and ethnic solidarity. And the Nahuas were very proud of their involvement.

As reported by Chimalpahin, the Nahuas were dedicated to observing saints' feast days, no matter the weather or danger. He records that on 17 April 1612 soldiers secured the roads into and out of Mexico City in anticipation of a slave revolt. Chimalpahin states that the Nahuas had no concern but rather laughed at how the Spaniards' fear tore them apart. Because of their fear the Spaniards ordered all churches closed prior to Good Friday, and they could not open again until the following dawn, which prevented the Good Friday celebrations. There were only two places where the Stations of the Cross were performed: one was at the friary of San Francisco in Mexico Tenochtitlan, the other at Santiago Tlatelolco.[59] The Spaniards did not allow anyone to go in procession in the city streets, but this did not stop the Nahuas from coming together in celebration of Good Friday and parading around the grounds of the friary. Based on the accounts of Chimalpahin, it seems that Nahua cofradías went in procession on certain feast days no matter what, even when Spaniards did not. The Nahuas of Mexico Tenochtitlan sought to meet their religious obligations even when Spanish authorities limited them to the immediate vicinity of the Franciscan friary; their chaplains probably encouraged such zeal.

The Nahuas were especially proud of their place in religious processions. Their pride is evident in Chimalpahin's description of when fray Gerónimo de Zárate prevented the Nahuas at the chapel of San Josef de los Naturales from going through the streets in procession with other cofradías on Maundy Thursday in 1613. The Nahuas of San Josef had fashioned two new statues two days before the celebration. Zárate, the chaplain at San Josef, was initially unaware of the construction of the two images. When he learned of their existence, he encouraged the indigenous governor of Mexico to help block them from going in procession. In turn, the Nahuas convinced a judge of the Audiencia to oppose the governor. But Chimalpahin accuses Zárate of bribing the judge, since the judge changed his mind. The story of the Nahuas' frustration at being unable to take their new images in procession reveals their initiative in civil and religious life. Also, as chaplain at San Josef, it is surprising that Zárate did not know of the carving, sculpting, construction, or design of the new statues, and this may be evidence of the independence with which the

Nahua cofradías gathered and prepared themselves for religious days and processions. It suggests that they took care of their own religious obligations. It also demonstrates that, when denied a chance to take part in processions, they could and occasionally did take legal action. Eventually, the cofradía received permission to take its images in procession in the immediate vicinity of San Francisco. Another group facing opposition to taking their image in procession sneaked out and paraded its image through the streets during the darkness of night.[60] The tenacity with which the Nahuas fought for their right to go in processions demonstrates that their enthusiasm went beyond Franciscan expectations.

Processions occurred frequently through the year. On average more than one took place every fortnight. Easter Week saw the most processions, generally at least one a day, and Corpus Christi held the honor of being the largest and most expensive festival held in the city. Hundreds of people from across the city, including representatives of all the parishes, cofradías, religious orders, government institutions, and ethnic groups, participated.[61] Table 6 lists the many religious festivals that may have occurred in any given year.

The feast days provided a time and an opportunity for the Nahuas to gather as a community. They relished the chance to participate as spectators, participants, and laborers in the celebrations. Special commemorative occasions for processions included the beatification or canonization of an individual, supernatural events such as miracles, and deaths. Chimalpahin mentions festival occasions for each.[62] Natural disasters were another occasion to come together. Epidemic disease was common during the sixteenth century and then tapered off for a while in the early seventeenth. Already susceptible to floods because of its location in the middle of Lake Tetzcoco, Mexico Tenochtitlan faced even greater risk with the continued deforestation and ensuing erosion of the mountainsides surrounding the basin. Often, in an attempt to stop an epidemic, flood, or drought, Nahuas, friars, and others went in procession carrying crosses and images of the Virgin or saints between churches while flagellating themselves.[63] Residents of Mexico Tenochtitlan seem to have believed that the intercession of the saints was the best help for such tribulations.[64] Nahuas took the images in procession in hope of assistance, and they covered the religious symbols with cloth to help protect them. Efforts to halt the spread of epidemics and natural disasters were often a community endeavor. The Catholic Church encouraged large processions of parishioners (of all ethnic groups) during times of great disaster to plead for the saints' assistance; still, each group organized and paraded according to its ethnicity, helping to reinforce distinct ethnic identities.

TABLE 6. Selected Catholic Feast Days with Processions

January	*February*	*March*	*April*	*May*
1 Circuncisión	**2 Nuestra Madre de la Purificación de Candelaria**	1 Ángel Custodio[a]	25 San Marco Evangelista	3 Santa Veracruz (feast of the invention of the True Cross)
6 Día de los Reyes	3 San Blas	7 Santo Tomás Aquino[b]	29 San Pedro Mártir	26 Espíritu Santo
7 Encarnación de la Palabra Divina	24 San Matías Apóstol	**19 San Josef**		27 San Luis Beltrán
20 San Sebastián		25 Anunciación de Santa María		28 Ascención
23 San Ildefonso				
25 Conversión de San Pablo				
June	*July*	*August*	*September*	*October*
11 San Bernabé	2 Visitación	1 San Pedro de Víncula	5 Vírgen de Remedios	3 Nuestra Señora de la Soledad
24 San Juan Bautista	20 San Elías	4 Santo Domingo	10 San Nicolás Tolentino	**4 San Francisco**
29 San Pablo y San Pedro Apóstoles	22 Santa María Magdalena	5 Santa María de las Nieves	13 Santa Veracruz (feast of the Exaltation of the True Cross)	5 Santa Teresa de Jesús[c]
	25 Santiago	6 Transfiguración	**15 Nuestra Señora de la Natividad**	28 San Simón and San Judas Tadeo Apóstoles
	26 Santa Ana	15 Nuestra Señora de la Asunción	21 San Mateo Apóstol	
	31 San Ignacio de Loyola[d]	16 San Roque		29 San Miguel Arcángel

(continued on next page)

TABLE 6. (*continued*)

June	*July*	*August*	*September*	*October*
		24 San Bartolomé	30 San Gerónimo	
		28 San Agustín		
November	*December*	*Lent*	*Easter*	*Pentecost*
1 Día de los Santos	8 Concepción Inmaculada	**Palm Sunday**	Holy Monday	**First day of Pentecost**
2 Día de las Ánimas (or Día de los Muertos)	**14 Epifanía**		Holy Tuesday	**Trinity Sunday**
12 San Diego	**25 Christmas**		Holy Wednesday	**Corpus Christi**
17 San Gregorio Taumaturgo	**26 San Esteban**		**Maundy Thursday**	Corazón Sagrado
30 San Andrés Apóstol	**27 San Juan Evangelista and San Juan Apóstol**		**Good Friday**	Corazón Inmaculado de Santa María
	28 Santo Inocentes		**Holy Saturday**	
			Easter Sunday and two following days	

Note: Feast days in bold were required by the Third Mexican Provincial Council. All other feast days are indicated in the sources as occasions when celebrations were held, although they may not have been as grand as those required by the Third Provincial Council and were not necessarily annual celebrations. The numbers refer to the dates of the corresponding month. The festivals listed under Lent, Easter, or Pentecost moved according to the lunar cycle and thus are not assigned to a specific month. This list was developed based on information found in *Concilio III provincial mexicano*, pp. 142–143; Chimalpahin, *Annals*; and AHFZ Sumario.

a. Ángel Custodio was celebrated for the first time in Mexico in 1614. Chimalpahin, *Annals*, p. 273.

b. According to Chimalpahin, this feast day was held for the first time in 1594 by order of the pope and was to be "observed in grand style." Chimalpahin, *Annals*, pp. 47–49.

c. Chimalpahin notes that Santa Teresa de Jesús was not yet canonized in 1614, when they first celebrated a feast day in her name. Chimalpahin, *Annals*, p. 289.

d. This feast day was celebrated for the first time in 1610. Chimalpahin, *Annals*, p. 165.

Beginnings and Changes in Nahua Cofradías

During the Reformation, Martin Luther attacked cofradías, with the result that these sodalities came under increased scrutiny and control by the Catholic Church. To assist in the process, large umbrella groups, or archcofradías, were established in Rome starting in the 1530s. As part of their promotion they gained additional status, prestige, and papal indulgences. Other sodalities across the Catholic world of a similar devotion became tied to them and shared their rules, devotion, dress, and access to indulgences.[65] This period of greater control of European brotherhoods and the development of archcofradías paralleled the development of indigenous sodalities in New Spain. Though not all Nahua cofradías tied themselves to an archcofradía, at least two, and likely more, possessed such a connection. The earliest evidence for such a connection comes from fray Alonso de Molina's 1568 Nahuatl translation of the summary of indulgences for the cofradía of the Santísimo Sacramento. The second sodality with a known connection is Santa María del Rosario, whose summary of indulgences was also translated by Molina to Nahuatl, in 1572. For Nahuas, connection to an archcofradía could grant the same things it did Spaniards, namely, prestige, status, and indulgences. It is probable, at least initially, that the link was encouraged or fostered by the mendicants.[66]

My research suggests that Mexico Tenochtitlan's native cofradías developed in four phases: (1) establishment cofradías (based at San Josef de los Naturales), (2) visita cofradías, developing after the doctrina of San Josef began to split into separate parishes, (3) ethnically mixed cofradías, and (4) more inclusive cofradías. The establishment phase started with the founding of the first Nahua cofradía. The earliest documentary evidence that we possess for Mexico Tenochtitlan indigenous cofradías comes from fray Toribio de Motolinia's *Memoriales*. In it he reports on the proceedings of the "cofrades de la cruz de Cristo." The account is dated either 1536 or 1537. Presumably these cofrades belonged to the cofradía of La Veracruz, which was active in the second half of the sixteenth century.[67]

There is some evidence that the period was fraught with tension between the indigenous and Spanish cofradías. In a letter to Philip II in 1572, Viceroy don Martin Enríquez remarked that Spaniards had almost constantly feared an indigenous revolt during the Maundy Thursday processions for the previous thirty years.[68] Based on Chimalpahin's account of the cessation of Easter Week festivities in 1612, the Spaniards had shifted the focus of their fear to African slaves, although Chimalpahin may have refrained from mentioning any fear of an indigenous revolt.[69]

The cofradías became an expression of Nahua social and political desire within the surrounding communities. The specific rules and obligations to which Nahua cofrades were expected to adhere allowed them to express their own style of religious veneration of their saints, perform charitable works for "heavenly awards," and benefit their community. Larissa Taylor has noted that fray Alonso de Molina encouraged indigenous brotherhoods to participate in two types of devotion, *laudesi,* based on praise or veneration, and *disciplinati,* based on penitence.[70] Mexico Tenochtitlan's Nahuas were active in both types of devotion by 1538.[71]

The first Nahua cofradías in Mexico Tenochtitlan were based at the chapel of San Josef de los Naturales. According to Lockhart, the first sodality in a given area tended to be the cofradía of the Santísimo Sacramento. It was generally succeeded by the cofradías of Ánimas, Rosario, Veracruz, and Santa Comunión.[72] The Nahuas of San Josef may have followed a similar pattern. They definitely established three of the brotherhoods listed by Lockhart: Santísimo Sacramento, Ánimas, and Veracruz. Fray Agustín de Vetancurt, writing at the end of the seventeenth century, states that one of the cofradías established during this period was dedicated to the Santísimo Sacramento. Additionally, Molina's 1568 sumario was most likely written for a brotherhood located in Mexico City.[73] Corroborating Motolinia's information about a sodality dedicated to La Veracruz is don Hernando de Tapia's 1554 testament, in which he is established as a member of La Veracruz.[74] Based on established patterns, Ánimas was probably one of the first four as well.[75] The three brotherhoods plus one other were active by 1564.[76] Furthermore, the only extant documents from any of the cofradías are Molina's summary of indulgences and a 1552 constitution for an unnamed cofradía based at San Josef. Unfortunately, it is uncertain as to which brotherhood the constitution belonged. Based on the similarity of the constitution with fray Alonso de Molina's 1552 cofradía ordinances, it is probable that other early constitutions were of similar content. Finally, there is also evidence for the existence of the cofradía of the Rosario by 1572, but it was likely housed in the Dominican friary.

The second, visita, phase of Nahua cofradía development occurred sometime between 1562 and 1576. It appears that the earlier tensions between Spanish and Nahua cofradías had diminished by this point. This period is marked by the formation of sodalities at the four main visita chapels in Mexico Tenochtitlan, and the trend probably extended to additional visita areas on and off the island.[77] The brotherhoods at the Nahua chapels in Mexico City during the sixteenth century probably maintained a purely indigenous membership. This differs from what could be found on the mainland, where mixed Spanish-Nahua cofradías developed as early as 1570.[78] The establishment of visita-specific sodalities may have accelerated in 1562 with the separation of the visita of San Pablo Teopan from the jurisdiction of San Josef. During the next half-century San Josef was split into four indigenous parishes.[79] By 1612 each of the four had multiple cofradías representing them.[80]

Also in this phase were the foundings of the Nahua congregations of Nuestra Señora de la Anunciata (c. 1584) and de la Circuncisión (c. 1598) at the Jesuit Colegio de San Gregorio.[81] The Jesuits stated that the congregations were different from the more group-centered mendicant cofradías in that they focused first on the individual. Members were to concentrate initially on "personal spiritual perfection." Their exercises were similar to the Jesuits' religious exercises. After achieving this spiritual goal, they reached out to others in the brotherhood. Although the focus was on the individual, cofrades still gathered in groups and possessed a hierarchical leadership similar to the regular cofradías and were fully supported by the parish community.[82] Thanks to cofrade records from a 1710 Jesuit congregation, we know that membership in the congregations spanned parish lines. The Jesuits, unlike the Franciscans, Augustinians, and eventually Dominicans, did not possess a specific parish based on geography or indigenous ethnicity. Instead, it appears that membership in their congregations derived from the students attending their Nuestra Señora de Loreto church at San Gregorio, who were high-ranking Nahuas from in and around the city and viceroyalty.

The third, ethnically mixed, phase in Nahua cofradía participation started around 1612. The year was marked by the foundation of a mixed Nahua-Spanish cofradía at the Poor Clares convent of San Juan de la Penetencia.[83] This brotherhood was unique in its mixed membership and establishment away from a Nahua chapel. It is the earliest known instance of Nahua participation in a Mexico Tenochtitlan cofradía outside one of their chapels.[84] The sodality was followed in 1613 by the establishment of the non-Mexica indigenous cofradía of San Roque at the Hospital de San Lázaro and the cofradía of Santa María de la Caridad at the Hospital Real de Nuestra Señora de la Caridad, which comprised natives from Michoacan and Mexico City. In 1614 neighboring Mexico Tlatelolco saw the establishment of its first mixed Nahua-Spanish brotherhood in the parish of Veracruz.[85] The development of brotherhoods away from the mendicant church compounds indicates a level of increased religious trust between the friars and their indigenous parishioners. Their mixed nature demonstrates a willingness of the population of Mexico City to interact socially, culturally, and spiritually on a larger scale than may have occurred previously.

The formation of the brotherhoods also demonstrates an increased level of hispanization among Nahuas living in Mexico Tenochtitlan. Even though the membership rosters of the groups were mixed, the cofradías seem to have gone in procession along distinct ethnic lines, at least in the case of Nahua-Spanish brotherhoods.[86] Nahuas who joined the sodalities may have been more inclined to embrace Spanish customs than other natives in the city, but they also maintained memberships in their Nahua-only cofradías and were involved in their local leadership and community. Given the multiethnic nature of the city, indigenous communities constantly found themselves interacting with people of different cultural backgrounds, be they European, African, Asian, or one of a number of migrants from a diversity of indigenous groups—the Purapechas, Mixtecs, or Zapotecs, to name a few.

The final phase of development of indigenous cofradías came at the end of the seventeenth century and saw the establishment of brotherhoods that were more inclusive in their overall membership. In 1694 a mixed Nahua-Filipino cofradía was founded at the Nahua chapel of San Sebastián. This is the only known mixed brotherhood to have been established at any of the principally Nahua chapels. There are three possible reasons for its organization. One is that the Asian population had been present and established in Mexico City long enough for the Nahuas of the parish of San Sebastián to invite the Filipinos into their chapel. Another is that it reflected the changing status of *chinos* (Asians) in the eyes of the Catholic Church and Spanish government from that of slaves to indigenous people. As of 1672 they were no longer legally allowed to be enslaved.[87] A third possibility is that the parish of San Sebastián was undergoing a loss of population (from migration, miscegenation, or any number of other reasons), and the Augustinians encouraged the acceptance and incorporation of the "naturales de las islas felipinas" to make up for decreasing chapel attendance.[88] Nothing similar appears to have occurred at San Josef while it remained an indigenous chapel.[89] The parish of Mixtecos possessed another mixed sodality that included Filipinos. When it started including Filipinos in its membership is not known, but they were included as parishioners by the end of the 1660s.[90]

This phase also saw an addition to the Jesuit congregations. In 1710 the congregation of the Buena Muerte, or Good Death, started performing its devotions and exercises. Two years later, official papal bulls arrived granting the congregants a license and access to indulgences. Unlike the two previous congregations, Buena Muerte accepted membership from all levels of Nahua society and apparently was not based on students and alumni.[91] The open enrollment for membership in Buena Muerte and the establishment of the Nahua-Filipino cofradía at San Sebastián show the possible opening of previously exclusive class and ethnic barriers in Mexico City society. The increased inclusivity was further echoed in 1757 when fray Antonio Claudio de Villegas commented on the Spanish third-order Dominicans' removal of a wall separating their devotional space from that of the indigenous cofradía de Indios Extravagantes (Migrant Indians).[92]

Over the course of the Hapsburg period, it seems that only two licensed sodalities ceased functioning. One was the Jesuit congregation of Nuestra Señora de la Anunciata in 1676, replaced by a congregation dedicated to Señor San Josef in 1701.[93] The second was La Veracruz at the chapel of San Josef.[94] Based on the information available, it seems that once a Nahua cofradía was licensed it continued to be active for an extensive period of time.

Death and Remembrance

Burial processions and the tolling bells associated with them acted as constant reminders of the frequency of death in New Spain. Many cofradía constitutions promised a burial procession for each member.[95] At San Josef when someone was about to die the ordinances instructed cofrades to visit the sick and maintain a vigil. When the person died, prayers were said and all the members of the brotherhood received lit candles and congregated to reminisce about the departed. The coming together of the community for each member's burial served as a fitting memorial for the deceased cofrade. During the period of mourning, the neighborhood also assisted with the more immediate emotional and financial needs of the surviving family.

The San Josef constitution mentions that church bells should be rung after the death of a cofrade but does not specify the number of times. In her 1625 testament, Magdalena María left ten tomines to have the bells rung at five separate chapels.[96] A constitution from a Tula sodality provides an even greater sense of the amount of bell ringing that may have occurred at San Josef at the time of a cofradía member's death, stating that the bell should be rung three times at five separate intervals. If cofrades observed the rule, then one person received fifteen tolls at death.[97] Toward the end of the sixteenth century, each town's church bells were most likely ringing with the sound of death. The bells tolled so frequently for the deceased during this period that Nahuas came to associate them with death more than anything else, including feast days. Tellingly, the Nahuas' initial term for bells was *miccatepuztli* (dead-person metal).[98] The Nahuas' awareness of their own mortality may have helped to remind community members of the need to support widows and orphans, especially since the next family to suffer could be their own.

Funerary processions were central in the eulogy of the deceased. By examining the documents related to the 1640 death of Clara López, an *india principala* (Spanish term for an indigenous female of high rank) of San Juan Moyotlan, in conjunction with the funeral proceedings of Archbishop don fray García Guerra, it is possible to reconstruct aspects of some Nahua burial processions.[99] The interment provides insight into the roles of Nahua sodalities and the increasing hispanization of the Nahuas of Mexico Tenochtitlan during the seventeenth century.

After Archbishop don fray García Guerra died on 22 February 1612, his body lay in state for four days. During this time the people of Mexico City passed by his body to pay their respects and all of the religious orders took it in turn to say a responsory prayer for him. A *catafalque* (wooden shrine used to display the deceased) was built for him in the cathedral. The procession for Guerra was led by all of the "Mexica" sodalities from San Juan, San Pablo, San Sebastián, Santa María, and Santiago Tlatelolco. In the procession, the mestizo students of the Colegio de San Juan de Letrán followed the Nahua cofradías.[100]

It is unlikely that a structure similar to a catafalque was constructed for Clara López, but her will specifically requests a high mass in the presence of her corpse.[101] Documents included with her will show her executor, don Juan de Aguilar, carrying out her wish.[102] Doubtless, her body was on display for at least the length of the mass. Additionally, her body was attended to by twenty-four Franciscans and was probably accompanied by the four cofradías to which she belonged.[103] Beyond the Franciscans and cofrades, it is likely the boys of San Juan de Letrán accompanied her body, for she donated five pesos worth of alms to them, which was the same amount given to her cofradías. She also paid for ten high masses to be said at the chapel belonging to San Juan de Letrán (the same number she requested held at San Josef).[104]

Clara López showed her dedication to the Nahua cantores at San Josef when she asked for their presence at her burial. The Nahua choir's agreement to attend the burial and provide polyphonic music provides another facet of some similarity between Spanish and indigenous burial practices in Mexico Tenochtitlan.[105] It is probable, then, that the twenty-four Franciscans, who were paid 130 pesos to perform the mass, also went in procession with her body and most likely walked at the end of the line, which was the position of most respect.

Clara López was among the most affluent Nahuas in Mexico Tenochtitlan. At the time of her death she possessed greater financial wealth than her executor, Governor don Juan de Aguilar. Because of her wealth she was able to afford a burial that may have approximated those of the colony's well-to-do Spaniards. Even in her burial proceedings she demonstrated a dedication to the indigenous community. She chose to have her cofradías and the Nahua choir of San Josef present. Additionally, she wanted to be buried at the Nahua chapel of San Josef. Had she wished, she probably could have picked a different location at which to be interred, as did the "india" Juana María when she chose to be buried at the convent of Santa Isabel.[106] Clara López's burial proceedings demonstrate her preference, and that of other Nahuas, to have religious ceremonies that were similar to Spaniards'. Most likely less affluent Nahuas had simpler burials. In both Guerra's and López's interment ceremonies, Nahua cofradías were visibly active. Based on the cofradía constitution, they probably treated even their poorest members in a similar fashion.[107]

Nahuas were concerned about the afterlife during the sixteenth and seventeenth centuries. Although the cost of López's burial was above and beyond (at least 135 pesos) what most Nahuas would have expected to pay, the cost of death was significant at most levels of society. In 1679 a cofradía burial for an adult cost three pesos, a candle, and four reales, and that for a child cost two pesos, a candle, and one-fourth of a real. A 1691 report on indigenous contributions to the Franciscan friary in the barrio of Santa María has the Nahuas paying fourteen pesos per burial.[108] The prices did not include the cost of masses for their souls or the expense of the funeral procession, although they did include the cost for singers. To make certain that members' souls received salvation, both Molina's ordinances and the constitution of San Josef urged the creation of wills to stipulate how their estates should be distributed between heirs and the Church (to cover the cost of prayers for their soul). If the individual did not provide a will, Molina's ordinances state that the cofradía would seize their property (as was done with Spaniards) and that the property then belonged to an indigenous hospital. The San Josef constitution also mandated the seizure of property if the deceased had no spouse, children, older brothers, or neighbors, in which case the local hospital received the property. As can be seen, there is a distinct difference between what the Nahuas believed should be done and what Molina's ordinances proposed. The ideal ordinances focused on the maintenance of the Franciscan friary and institutions connected to it. The San Josef constitution is less concerned with the maintenance of institutions specifically associated with the Church; rather, it focuses more on making sure the community had what it needed.

Hospitals

Writing between 1533 and 1569, the author of the Códice Franciscano noted that one of the most important duties of the indigenous cofradías was their care for the sick and went on to state that hospitals came to act as the meeting ground for the cofradía members.[109] His statements find support in the cofradía constitution of San Josef and fray Alonso de Molina's cofradía ordinances. Both documents begin by mentioning the performance of service at a hospital.

> [Molina:] yn aquiq̃ z yncenyolocacopa, yn teoyotica yn moneltolitique yn motlayecoltia yn ichantzĩco yn elhuicac vey Cihuapilli tlacnopilhuiani, Sancta Maria. y nican Ospital ontlamantli. ynic moyeyecoltia.
>
> Likewise it is necessary that those who spiritually vowed with all their hearts to serve in the home of the great noblewoman of heaven, the blessed Saint Mary, will thank her. Here in the hospital there are two ways of performing service.
>
> [San Josef constitution:] yn aquique yn motlayecoltia yn ichantzinco yn ilvicac vey çiuapili tlacnopilhuiani . . . Sancta Ma[a] y nicã ospital ontlamanti yc motlayecoltilia . . .
>
> Likewise it is necessary that those who serve here in the home of the heavenly great noblewoman, she who is blessed, will give thanks to her

> . . . Saint Mary. Here in the hospital there are two ways of performing service.[110]

The term *ospital* appears in the San Josef constitution on twenty-six occasions (excluding the missing sheet) in twenty pages, and it makes thirty-one appearances in the forty-one pages of Molina's 1552 ordinances. And the term is used fifty-eight times in his revised 1575 copy.[111] These numbers suggest how closely interwoven hospitals and cofradías were during the early colonial period.

Based on the information above, it is evident that the hospitals were involved in the lives of the cofrades of San Josef. Although a similar institution may have existed prior to European contact, the use of the Spanish loanword *ospital* in the 1552 Molina ordinances suggests that a parallel word in Nahuatl did not fit Molina's idea (or that of the Nahuas with whom he worked) of what a hospital was designed to be. Fray Alonso de Molina was one of the greatest Nahua interpreters in sixteenth-century New Spain. His 1555 dictionary remains one of the best sources for scholars working with early Nahuatl. Molina's decision to use the term *ospital* was no doubt influenced by the Nahuas' understanding of the Spanish term. Because of his position as a friar and his familiarity with Nahuatl, Molina knew which Spanish concepts had been introduced to the Nahuas (by the friars) through the use of words containing a definition similar to a Spanish term, such as the friars' use of *mictlan* (land of the dead) for the Christian concept of hell. Molina's use of *ospital* suggests that the idea of a hospital was both new and useful to the Nahuas and had no precontact equivalent.

Historian Robert Ricard credits the construction of the first indigenous hospital to fray Pedro de Gante. And it was Gante who, writing in 1552, urged Charles V to reestablish a hospital that had been turned into a school.[112] By writing the ordinances the way he did, Molina may have been trying to tie the Nahua cofradías to this European institution in a more official capacity than it had been prior to the 1550s.[113] It made sense for cofradías and hospitals to be associated because of the number of epidemics that affected the Nahuas during the sixteenth and seventeenth centuries and the sodalities' obligations to care for their members. It is probably because of the epidemics and the societal responsibilities of the brotherhoods that the hospital was emphasized within the constitution.

The need to dedicate even more people and resources to hospital expenses seems to have developed toward the end of the sixteenth century. In 1595, Chimalpahin recorded the viceregal declaration for the Nahuas of Mexico Tenochtitlan to start paying tribute (a sum of 7,400 chickens) directly to six different hospitals (San Hipólito, Los Desamparados, Hospital Real, Huitzillan, Contaduría, and the Hospital de las Bubas). In 1600 the mayordomo of the Hospital de Nuestra Señora de la Concepción complained that the Nahuas were not adhering to their assigned tribute payment of 954 chickens for this additional hospital, as had been ordered in 1599.[114] Although the tribute payments were a type of obligatory support, Nahuas provided additional voluntary funding in the form of hospital cofradías. In 1613 natives of Michoacan and the Nahuas of Mexico City formed a cofradía dedicated to the Hospital Real de Nuestra Señora de la Caridad, a hospital for natives.[115] Additionally, a cofradía in devotion to the Tránsito de Nuestra Señora was established at the Hospital de los Desamparados prior to 1640.[116] Furthermore, multiple testators left money in direct support of hospitals and hospital cofradías.[117] Perhaps because of the organization of hospital cofradías, brotherhoods established later, such as the mixed Nahua-Filipino cofradía of Nuestra Señora de los Dolores y Soledad, opted not to have hospital duties included in their constitutions.[118]

Nahua sodalities associated with hospitals were also charged with determining who was allowed to practice medicine. This aspect of their duties was so important that both the Molina and the San Josef constitutions dedicated the first couple of "obligations" to them. In her examination of the European nature of fray Alonso de Molina's ordinances, Larissa Taylor briefly focuses on the obligations related to preventing "deceiving enchanters, devils and their leaders, those who lie, the fortune-telling medical practitioners" from plying their trade in cofradía-sponsored hospitals. Taylor and Barry Sell believe that the inspiration for this section is in Exodus 22:18, which states, "You will not permit witches to live." Taylor argues that the discussion took place because of a contemporary European fear of sorcery. She points out that Molina made an exception for healers who used beneficial "grass medicines" but added that the cofrades should still be wary of "deceiving enchanters."[119] This section of the constitution was influenced by the European fear of witchcraft and probably by mendicants' encounters with indigenous healers. Both Molina and the author of the constitution believed that good healers did exist and that they needed to practice their skills at the hospitals. However, it seems that, in writing at least, the Nahuas were comfortable following the European definition of good medical practice. By applying European rules to local, respected, indigenous healers, Nahuas could have their own medicinal specialists tend the sick instead of being dependent on European doctors. These indigenous healers were respected to such a degree that a Spanish nun requested one during a time of illness.[120] Furthermore, three of them were called on as witnesses in the Bravo Acre case mentioned earlier in this chapter.[121]

As is true with the Molina ordinances and the San Josef constitution, many of the areas Molina discusses in his Nahuatl consititution are also apparent in the San Josef constitution. In the sixth "obligation," however, there is a variation. It is at this point that Molina continues to discuss the hospital, whereas the San Josef constitution provides details of the cofradia's leadership responsibilities. The constitution considers the duties of cofrades to the hospital and mentions that "each year all those who take care of things here in the hospital will go switching off among themselves."[122] The constitution continues the discussion on hospitals as well as care for the sick, but it still differs from the instructions provided by Molina.

Both Molina and the Nahuas of Mexico Tenochtitlan were concerned about caring for ill residents of the Nahua community. But it seems, based on the constitution of San Josef, that the Nahuas, not the Franciscans, decided how they took care of the sick. The Nahuas provided some medical care and support staff to hospitals as one of the duties of cofradía membership. But they organized things in their own way. In addition to caring for the physically sick, the hospital seems to have performed a function similar to a church in the minds of the Nahuas. Independent of Molina's ordinances, the San Josef constitution states that the Nahuas will not permit an officer of the secular government to remove a repenting sinner from the hospital. This seems to indicate support for the idea of being pardoned for one's crimes through penitential activity and demonstrates Nahua dedication to protecting their own.

The cofradías were essential to the functioning of hospitals. Their duties included reviewing the medical practitioners, verifying the authenticity of the medicine, cleaning rooms, preparing food for the sick, looking to spiritual duties (such as the organization of the church service), and providing companionship for the ill.[123] Though the cofrades performed the most menial of hospital tasks, the hospitals could not have functioned without them. Most of the labor was free and not considered tribute duty.

Souls of the Living and Departed

Care for the sick and dying occupied the natives. What is not known is how much they understood about the Catholic concept of purgatory. It seems that a degree of belief in purgatory did develop, for they continued to purchase prayers for their souls in wills and took part in processions dedicated to the salvation of souls in purgatory. During the sixteenth and seventeenth centuries, the Franciscans encouraged the Nahuas of San Josef to aid souls trapped in purgatory. By 1552, fray Pedro de Gante requested that Holy Roman Emperor Charles V "order that some indulgences from His Holiness be sent for the said [indigenous] chapel of Saint Joseph, and permission for some kind of special celebration there."[124] Gante's request appears to have been successful; in 1554, Pope Julius III provided a ten-year grant of a jubilee (each jubilee is a one-year indulgence) to the parish of San Josef.[125]

More fascinating is that the fear of purgatory could, apparently, encourage cooperation among secular and regular branches of the Church during the 1550s and 1560s, a period of heightened religious infighting between the archbishopric and the mendicant orders. The cooperation is evident in Archbishop Montúfar's request that Franciscan fray Alonso de Molina translate into Nahuatl two summaries of the indulgences granted to the cofradías of the Santísimo Sacramento and the Rosario by several popes. Prior to 1568, Montúfar had Molina's bilingual Nahuatl-Spanish dictionary (among other works) censored.[126] Purgatory and the pursuit of indulgences influenced the lives of cofrades. The Franciscan approach to explaining purgatory and indulgences in the early years of the colonial enterprise and how the Nahuas came to interact with these two ideas are important to an understanding of the function of the colonial cofradía. Though belief in indulgences and purgatory cannot be proved, attempts to obtain indulgences and avoid purgatory suggest that the Nahuas were engaged in the Catholic Church's pursuit of the salvation of souls.

Purgatory and the indulgences were probably introduced to the indigenous population shortly after 1524, with the arrival of the so-called apostolic twelve (Franciscans). In the 1571 edition of his dictionary, fray Alonso de Molina translates *purgatorio* as *nechipaualoyan* (place where people become purified) or *neyectiloyan* (place where people become good).[127] Molina's 1552 ordinances and the San Josef constitution have *purgatorio* in use as a loanword.[128] The term "indulgence" appears to go through a similar process. In his dictionary Molina translates *Yndulgencia perdon* (Indulgence pardon) as *tlayhiyouilizcaxaualiztli* (kept from things that torment), *tetlapopolhuiliztli* (to pardon people for things), and *tetlaocoliliztli* (mercy). Similarly, *indulgencia* was in use as a loanword by Molina in his Nahuatl ordinances from 1552 and in the two cofradía summaries of indulgences from 1568 and 1572. Chimalpahin also uses the term *indulgencia*, though he pairs it with *tetlapopolhuiliztli*.[129] The translation of the ideas of purgatory and indulgence and the subsequent adoption of both loanwords into Nahuatl suggest that these two ideas in Nahua culture developed in parallel fashion, which makes sense given that one necessarily brought to mind the other.

Mundane documents written in Nahuatl included *purgatorio* as a loanword by the early 1560s.[130] Molina's use of the word in 1552 suggests that the Franciscans and the Nahuas with whom they worked most closely, such as the fiscales of the chapels, understood that a comparable concept to purgatory did not exist in Nahua culture. Thus, they started using the term prior to 1552, and it had became part of standard Nahua vocabulary by 1560. The concept of purgatory was new to the Nahuas; in their understanding of the afterlife, there was nowhere a person could go to await transfer to a different spiritual dimension. Although the terms Molina used in his dictionary to define purgatory are descriptive, and indeed Chimalpahin pairs *nechipaualoyan* with *purgatorio* on occasion, the words do not explain the length of time a soul stayed there or what needed to happen for a soul to achieve release.[131]

That explanation was left to other material, such as fray Bernardino de Sahagún's 1562 Sermonario: "On account of each mortal sin he or she will do penance for seven years. . . . On account of all of his or her sins, perhaps it will be 400 years. But to the Holy Church, by God's order, belongs Indulgence. Indulgence derives from the Passion, the suffering of our lord, which is the foundation stone of the Holy Church."[132]

The term used to designate four hundred years is *centzonxihuitizque*, the root of which, *centzontli,* means a large number or a multitude.[133] Literally translated, it is in reference to a "head full of hair."[134] Sahagún, one of the foremost experts of his time in Nahuatl, probably chose *centzontli* to refer to a multitude of years rather than four hundred, which seems small in comparison to years of forgiveness granted by the summaries of indulgences Molina translated. Additionally, Sahagún was not unfamiliar with such summaries. He coauthored the prologue to the 1568 sumario. This prologue contains a description and justification of purgatory, information absent from the 1572 sumario: "We also need to know that although through the sacrament of penance we are pardoned from eternal suffering, nevertheless it is necessary that we suffer for some time here on earth. If we do not want to do penance and suffer here on earth, we need to do penance and suffer in purgatory, but the suffering there is much greater, more fearful, and more excruciating."[135]

Both Sahagún and Molina explained purgatory and why indulgences were so important to members of the faith. An understanding, and preferably a fear, of purgatory was likely viewed as necessary by the friars if they were going to convince Nahuas to strive for indulgences and forgiveness of their souls and all the other souls in purgatory.

Following the prologue in Molina's 1568 sumario is a list of important Church events beginning with Advent, continuing to Lent, and ending shortly after Easter. Most likely the document continued through the rest of that year, as does a 1642 Spanish copy created for a sodality in Puebla, though the portion following Easter is lost.[136] The sumario details specific days when cofrades were to perform ceremonial activities such as fasting and self-flagellation. Most of their actions gained them plenary indulgences, although on specified days, with the correct actions, they had the ability to free a soul from purgatory. What the Nahua cofrades of the Santísimo Sacramento received for their efforts appears excessive, especially when compared to the 1572 sumario. For example, the largest amount of forgiveness granted to the cofradía del Rosario at any given point was 1,800 years, and this was given only once. In contrast the cofradía of the Santísimo Sacramento was regularly granted 28,000 years. The difference between the two sumarios could speak to a hierarchy in the cofradías, for the sodality dedicated to the Santísimo Sacramento was usually the first established in a given location, and the brotherhood dedicated to the Rosario generally developed later.[137]

To obtain their indulgences and pardons, the cofrades of the Santísimo Sacramento were appointed to say the Our Father and Ave Maria five times each and to show respect for the Santísimo Sacramento. If they carried these out, the rewards could be great. For example, on the first Sunday of Advent (St. Andrew's feast day) the Nahuas attained 28,000 years of forgiveness for their sins and those Nahuas who fasted for a period of forty days, or a "quarantine," received forty days of individual forgiveness and had their sins destroyed. Likewise, on the second Sunday in Advent they could obtain another 28,000 years of forgiveness and their sins would be destroyed by receipt of a plenary indulgence. Over the course of Advent alone cofrades could receive in excess of 451,000 years of forgiveness and thirty plenary indulgences. As the document and religious calendar progressed, the rewards became ever greater, including the freeing of souls from purgatory. Between Septuagesima (the third Sunday before Lent) and the first full week after Easter, the Nahuas, if they had done everything necessary, would have freed seven souls from purgatory. Over the course of an entire year they could free as many as ten.[138] Although the amounts listed appear excessive, and may have been, there are European examples of greater excess. In Flanders a person could gain 80,000 years of pardon for reciting an Our Father and a Hail Mary in front of a painting, and in England a sinner could receive 33,000 years for reciting multiple creeds, Our Fathers, and Hail Marys in front of a depiction of "Christ as Man of Sorrows." Historian R. N. Swanson suggests that these were "unauthorised" pardons.[139] Molina's sumario, on the other hand, appears to have been sanctioned by the pope.

Whether or not the Nahuas understood the Catholic concept of purgatory, they knew that the pope and the Franciscans had granted them, as cofrades, access to indulgences, which were a central tenet of the Catholic faith. From the accounts of Franciscan and indigenous chroniclers (e.g., fray Gerónimo de Mendieta and Chimalpahin), it seems that the Nahuas of Mexico City desired them. Chimalpahin demonstrates that by the early seventeenth century some Nahuas pursued indulgences eagerly:

> And in the second procession on the said Holy Tuesday the Mexica of Santiago Tlatelolco were to come out for the first time, the children of our precious revered mother Santa María del Rosario, also called the children of Niño Jesús Perdido. The Holy Father Paul V granted very many pardons, indulgences, for the occasion of the procession. As to how this could be done, it was through the sending and petitioning of my beloved friend Diego López . . . who is the true founder of the said confraternity; [some of] our precious fathers the religious of the Company of Jesus who were going to Rome got the Bulls for him.[140]

Unfortunately for the cofrades, all Holy Week processions were canceled that year.[141] Chimalpahin was so impressed by his friend's accomplishment at both establishing the double cofradía (it had two dedications) and receiving indulgences from the pope that he made sure to record when cofrades received the indulgences one year later: "And also the said Holy Tuesday in the afternoon was when at last also the members of the confraternity . . . were able to come out and go in procession once. . . . Those who went on this procession voluntarily . . . earned thereby very many pardons, indulgences." The two other occasions when Chimalpahin mentions indulgences pertained to Spaniards. One was with the establishment of a new Spanish cofradía whose members could obtain a jubilee indulgence. The other dealt with a Jesuit named Pedro de Morales who had received permission to issue jubilees in the name of the pope.[142]

It is difficult to know how quickly the Nahuas took to the ideas of purgatory and indulgences. The 1546 testament of Angelina Poqui states ambiguously that her children could, if they wished, use some of the money she bequeathed them to request something for her soul. Poqui's uncertainty about her soul's fate is absent from Nahuatl wills of the 1560s (see chapter 3). A 1564 letter by Nahua Juan de San Antonio supports an engagement with the idea of purgatory if not a belief in it. In his letter he uses the term *purgatorio* in reference to where his brother was likely residing at the time ("if it is in vain that he lives in Purgatory, aid him"), and he requests that his older brother say masses for the souls of their deceased siblings and thereby show his Christianity.[143] Further evidence of the Franciscans' desire to encourage belief in purgatory, and potentially the Nahuas' belief in it, was the establishment, circa 1564, of the Nahua cofradía dedicated to souls in purgatory. In 1605 testatrix María Salomen demonstrated her support for the sodality by bequeathing five pesos to the cathedral's cofradía of the Souls of Purgatory to perform a mass, presumably on behalf of the souls of purgatory.[144] By the end of the sixteenth century Nahuas were supporting the Church's notion of purgatory, and as Chimalpahin demonstrates they sought indulgences by the beginning of the seventeenth century.

As a destination in the afterlife, purgatory exists between heaven and hell. Mendicant friars first had to explain heaven and hell, then purgatory. Unlike heaven and hell, purgatory is not a permanent destination, and souls in purgatory can receive succor from the living population. Thus, the goal of the mendicants was not only to convince the Nahuas of the existence of purgatory but also to get them to strive for the salvation of the souls of people they never knew. This was made doubly difficult given that the Christian concept of a soul was also fairly new. That friars were able to get the terms *purgatorio* and *indulgencia* adopted by Nahuas speaks to some of their success. Though Nahua use of the terms and rituals does not guarantee their belief in purgatory or indulgences, the pursuit of indulgences from the pope, as carried out by Chimalpahin's friend, demonstrates at the very least the Nahuas' appreciation of the prestige attached to papal indulgences. Furthermore, Nahua efforts saved souls from purgatory. In the eyes of the Catholic Church, this must have been seen as a victory for the souls in purgatory as much as it was a strike against the heresies of Protestants like Martin Luther.

As the political center of the Viceroyalty of New Spain, Mexico City was a focal point of interaction between Nahuas and Europeans. More than most other facilities, the indigenous chapels of Mexico City, especially San Josef, acted as an arena for social, cultural, and religious interaction. Though Nahuas were continually in contact with friars, the chapels and the institution of the cofradía created a buffer against some of the forces that might otherwise have induced the disintegration of indigenous society. During the middle years of the sixteenth century, Nahuas elected both men and women as cofradía leaders in each of the constituent parts of the altepetl. With time and the partitioning of the Franciscan parish of San Josef, the allocation of leadership positions in each cofradía probably changed to reflect the needs of the smaller communities with which the brotherhoods were associated. However, each sodality established a procedure for obtaining fines, alms, and membership fees to cover financial expenditures. Most expenses could be met in a manner comparable to tribute obligations, although the Franciscan friars and Nahua leadership were quick to state that they were not to be considered as "hateful" tribute requirements. The institution of the cofradía operated in ways similar to the European cofradías, but it was a more inclusive, communal organization in which culture (or ethnicity) trumped gender, class, and trade.

Mendicants employed cofradías as a tool in their conversion efforts. The sodalities brought Nahuas together and engaged them in the central tenets of the faith. The brotherhoods' contributions to introducing, explaining, and supporting ideas of purgatory and indulgences and to assisting tormented souls were central aspects around which the sodalities met. They were spiritually affirming institutions that the friars believed would assist them in instructing the dogma of the Catholic faith to the indigenous populations. And in many ways the brotherhoods helped to teach Nahuas the ideas essential to the faith, even if those ideas failed to reach the substance of the religion.

More than a religious institution, Nahua cofradías provided community leadership, financial and medical assistance, religious festivities, and funerals. They also defined and proscribed unacceptable behavior and voluntarily built, staffed, and funded their own hospitals. The institution of the hospital was emphasized in cofradía constitutions and in the lives of the natives of Mexico

City. Franciscans introduced both institutions to the natives of Mexico Tenochtitlan. Yet, even with their close proximity to the friars, it is apparent that the Nahuas maintained significant control over how their societies functioned and how they handled their religious obligations.

By the early seventeenth century, Nahuas were joining brotherhoods with mixed memberships. The addition of these particular sodalities demonstrates a willingness by Spaniards and natives to work together for spiritual enrichment. It shows the creation and expansion of the existing spiritual community of Mexico Tenochtitlan. Unlike other areas in New Spain where mixed cofradías started earlier and were the rule, the new mixed sodalities mostly developed beyond the friaries, and they seem to have been created willingly by both participating ethnicities.

The creation of the mixed brotherhoods did not, however, disrupt the popularity of the exclusively Nahua cofradías. Their continued operation and growth demonstrates a desire by the Nahuas to cultivate critical spheres of religious influence inside their discrete communities. The exclusive Nahua brotherhoods acted as a buffer between Nahua and European society. As a group, the cofrades of Mexico Tenochtitlan could tailor aspects of the Spanish culture as it was being introduced, determining which religious obligations they would meet and which elements of their precontact culture they might maintain. The Christian sodality was a unique organization adopted by the Nahuas of Mexico Tenochtitlan to support and maintain their society and way of life. And, as we see in chaper 5, its effect on the culture and society of the Nahuas was felt not only in their religious life but also in their nonreligious daily activities, including those involving a market for Catholic paraphernalia in the indigenous marketplace. The desire to supply the sodalities with the trappings of the faith facilitated a trade in the goods necessary for the celebration of the divine in colonial Mexico City.

Notes

1. An interesting comparison to Nahua religious brotherhoods is Maureen Flynn's work on cofradías in Zamora, Spain, from the fifteenth through the eighteenth century. She found that "the confraternities institutionalized popular religious beliefs and brought diverse local strains of piety into contact with official Catholicism. They standardized popular religion by creating a network of common devotional exercises among members." Maureen Flynn, *Sacred Charity: Confraternities and Social Welfare in Spain, 1400–1700* (Ithaca, N.Y.: Cornell University Press, 1989), p. 5.

2. Nicole von Germeten, *Black Blood Brothers: Confraternities and Social Mobility for Afro-Mexicans* (Gainesville: University Press of Florida, 2006), p. 2.

3. Asunción Lavrin, "Confraternities in Colonial Spanish America," in *Nahua Confraternities in Early Colonial Mexico: The 1552 Nahuatl Ordinances of Fray Alonso de Molina, OFM,* ed. Barry D. Sell (Washington, D.C.: Academy of American Franciscan History, 2002), p. 23; Amos Megged, "The Religious Context of an "'Unholy Marriage': Elite Alienation and Popular Unrest in the Indigenous Communities of Chiapas, 1570–1680,"

Ethnohistory 46, no. 1 (Winter 1999), pp. 149, 154; and Adriaan C. Van Oss, *Catholic Colonialism: A Parish History of Guatemala, 1524–1821* (Cambridge: Cambridge University Press, 1986), p. 109.

4. *Códice franciscano,* pp. 68, 90–91.

5. Gibson, *Aztecs,* pp. 127, 132.

6. Lavrin, "Confraternities," p. 32.

7. Literally, "hide instrument to blow on a fire." Lockhart, *Nahuas,* p. 266.

8. Bautista, *¿Cómo te confundes?,* pp. 275, 309; and Schroeder "Jesuits, Nahuas, and the Good Death Society in Mexico City, 1710–1767," *Hispanic American Historical Review* 80, no. 1 (2000), p. 49. Although the date of the cofradía constitution of San Josef is earlier (1552), we do not know how much of the document was written by Franciscan friars. Thus, I go with a slightly later use of the term, 1566, but one that was definitely written by a Nahua.

9. Lockhart, *Nahuas,* p. 285.

10. Poole, "Church Law," pp. 637–650. See discussion in chapter 2.

11. Charles Gibson notes that fray Pedro de Gante specifically sought to fuse the Nahuas' love of song and dance with Christianity. Gibson, *Aztecs,* p. 133.

12. For the model testament, see Sarah Cline, "Fray Alonso de Molina's Model Testament and Antecedents to Indigenous Wills in Spanish America," in *Dead Giveaways: Indigenous Testaments of Colonial Mesoamerica and the Andes,* ed. Susan Kellogg and Matthew Restall (Salt Lake City: University of Utah Press, 1998), pp. 13–33. For the ordinances, see Sell, *Nahua Confraternities.*

13. AHFZ Constitution. Molina is credited with the authorship of the document referred to here as the San Josef constitution (not be confused with the 1701 Jesuit congregation of Señor San Josef), but many others from the same time period were produced by indigenous assistants. It is not known if assistants helped him with this piece, but it is clear that the constitution reflects the needs of the local situation, suggesting either Nahua influence or participation in the creation of the document. The dating of this document also presents an interesting dilemma. Its first couple of pages are in a different hand than the rest. The only date that could be related to the age of the document (18 September 1552) is on the opening page. The problem is that the ordinances prepared by Franciscan fray Alonso de Molina contain an almost identical statement:

> [Molina] nican motenehua Axcan ya caxtolli ypan yei tonalli ypan metztli Setiembre. Auh in xihuitl yc motlacatilli yn totlaçotemaquixticatzin. Jesuchristo De 1552 anos. (Sell, *Nahua Confraternities,* pp. 82–83)
>
> Here it is said on the 18th of the month of September in the year since the birth of our precious savior 1552.
>
> [San Josef constitution] nicā moteneva axcā ya castolomej ylvitl ypā metztli Septiembre auh ỹ xivitl ~~ypā metztli~~ yc motlacatili ỹ ttyo totlasotemaquizticatzin Jesu xpõ de. 1552. años
>
> Here it is said on the 18th day of the month of September in the year since the birth of our precious savior 1552.

Some of the spellings and choices of words suggest that the San Josef document is a late sixteenth-century copy of an earlier document. However, if it is a copy of an earlier document, one wonders which was written first, the Molina ordinances or the San Josef constitution. Documents dealing with the Hospital Real de los Indios as well as its relocation from the friary of San Francisco to a location nearby, but outside of the Franciscan compound, around this same time lead us to believe that the original San Josef constitution was written near the same time as the Molina ordinances and was most likely a copy of those ordinances. Either way, it is likely that one of the documents was a template for the other. The translations provided above differ stylistically from the Molina ordinance published by Barry Sell but are essentially the same in meaning.

14. Before the Reformation, England saw the development of all-women's groups within some parishes. The cihuatepixque held positions of leadership within mixed-sex sodalities, whereas the women in England appear to have still been segregated by their gender. For more information on the all-women's groups in England, see Katherine L. French, *The Good Women of the Parish: Gender and Religion after the Black Death* (Philadelphia: University of Pennsylvania Press, 2008), chap. 4. As with indigenous women, Afro-Mexican women in New Spain assumed leadership roles in mixed-sex cofradías. For information on Afro-Mexican women's roles in their sodalities, see von Germeten, *Black Blood Brothers*, chap. 2.

15. AHFZ Constitution. The constitution's use of *tlaxilacalli* seems to be a reference to the four barrios, or subdistricts, of Mexico Tenochtitlan and differs from the way I use the term. In a majority of the Nahuatl documents, *tlaxilacalli* appears in reference to the smaller communities in a given barrio.

16. NL, Ayer Collection, MS 1481, B(1)a; NL, Ayer Collection, MS 1481, B(3)1; INAH, Colegio de San Gregorio, v. 119, fs. 32–32v; AGN, Tierras, v. 1720, e. 7, f. 4; AGN, Bienes Nacionales, v. 1766, e. 7, fs. 5v, 6v; and AGN, Bienes Nacionales, v. 339, e. 6, f. 88v. Included in the sources are some listing *cihuatzitzintin*. To date there is not enough evidence to prove that the women were cihuatepixque. Although they are generally listed in groups, they are also at times listed individually, indicating some level of prominence. My suspicion is that the cihuatzitzintin are also the cihuatepixque. See chapter 3 for more information. Note that the second document cited here may be a seventeenth-century forgery of a request for masses for the soul. Nevertheless, it shows that the people forging the document thought it important to list the mayordomo of the cofradía as a witness.

17. Lockhart, *Nahuas*, pp. 218–225. Lockhart believes that the prioste and the deputies of Nahua cofradías were assistants to the mayordomo. William Taylor has found that the term *prioste* was sometimes in reference to the mayordomo and at other times to lower positions of leadership. As relates to the cofradía of San Josef, the prioste was the head of the sodality; however, the mayordomo was in charge of protecting the cofradía's property. It is probable that lay sodalities chose positions of leadership based on local circumstances. Taylor, *Magistrates*, p. 302.

18. Sell, *Nahua Confraternities*, p. 101; and AHFZ Constitution.

19. Lockhart, *Nahuas*, p. 25.

20. Barry D. Sell, "Our Lady of Solitude of San Miguel Coyotlan, 1619: A Rare Set of Cofradía Rules in Nahuatl," *Estudios de Cultura Náhuatl* 31 (2000), pp. 343, 353. Page 343 is the Nahuatl transcription from which Sell's translation comes. It is necessary to look at both, since Sell's excellent translation has a small accidental omission. His English translation reads "As to how it will be done: there will be one 'actor' and a 'monitor' (that is to say, a 'prioste'), and women in charge of people, [i.e.,] female captains." The Nahuatl is as follows: "Auh oncan mopepenasque: cofradiasme: yn quenen mochihuas oyes ce Actor: yhuan mayordomos yhuan ome depotados yhuan bitor yhuan monitor quitosneque freoste: yhuan Cihuatipixque: capitana[.]" But it should read "As to how it will be done: there will be one 'actor' and mayordomos and two deputies and bitor and monitor (that is to say, a 'prioste') and a woman in charge of people, [i.e.,] a female captain." At this time I have not been able to find an appropriate English translation for the position *bitor*. However, I am led to believe that the duties of the bitor, or victor, was to lead in celebratory praises.

21. If the leadership did come from the four separate subdistricts of Mexico Tenochtitlan and continued to be thus maintained through the seventeenth century, the cofradía could have been a Nahua archcofradía or head cofradía.

22. See discussion in chapter 3.

23. AHFZ Constitution.

24. For more information on cabildo elections, see Connell, *After Moctezuma*, pp. 18–20 and elsewhere.

25. AHFZ Constitution.

26. Thus far I have not found a single reference to a prioste in the wills of sixteenth- and seventeenth-century Nahuas from Mexico City. In contrast to the prioste, both mayordomos and cihuatepixque are noted.

27. AHFZ Constitution.

28. AHN, Diversos Colecciones, v. 23, n. 59.

29. AHFZ Constitution.

30. Maher Memarzadeh, "Medical Practitioners in Early Colonial Mexico" (Ph.D. diss., University of California, Los Angeles, 2005), pp. 264–268.

31. UNAM, FRAF, caja 106, e. 1461, f. 10.

32. AHFZ Constitution; Sell, "Our Lady," p. 354; and Sell, "Molina Confraternity," p. 59.

33. Edward W. Osowski, *Indigenous Miracles: Nahua Authority in Colonial Mexico* (Tucson: University of Arizona Press, 2010), pp. 86–87.

34. AHFZ Constitution.

35. *Recopilación*, libro 1, titulo 4, ley 25; Lockhart, *Nahuas*, p. 219; Sell, "Molina," p. 53; and Taylor, *Magistrates*, p. 301.

36. Serge Gruzinski, "Indian Confraternities, Brotherhoods and Mayordomías in Central New Spain: A List of Questions for the Historian and the Anthropologist," in *The Indian Community of Colonial Mexico: Fifteen Essays on Land Tenure, Corporate Organizations, Ideology and Village Politics*, ed. Arij Ouweneel and Simon Miller (Amsterdam: CEDLA, 1990), pp. 208–209. Van Oss has found that in Guatemala Episcopal and royal approval generally did not matter. Van Oss, *Catholic Colonialism*, p. 109.

37. Lockhart, *Nahuas*, p. 139; John Frederick Schwaller, ed. and trans., "Constitution of the Cofradía del Santíssimo Sacramento of Tula, Hidalgo, 1570," *Estudios de Cultura Náhuatl* 19 (1989), p. 238; Sell, "Our Lady," p. 353; Sell, "Molina Confraternity," pp. 53–54, 60; and Van Oss, *Catholic Colonialism,* pp. 109–110.

38. INAH, Fondo Franciscano, v. 145, fs. 268–274; Vetancurt, *Teatro*, pt. 4, pp. 41–42; and Gibson, *Aztecs,* p. 399.

39. Gruzinski, "Indian Confraternities," p. 207.

40. AGN, Reales Cédulas Duplicadas, v. 2, e. 39, f. 18v.

41. For more information regarding the secular-regular dispute, see Roberto Moreno de los Arcos, "Los territories parroquiales de la ciudad arzobispal," *Gaceta del arzobispado: Sancta metropolitan ecclesia mexicana* 22, nos. 9–10 (September–October 1982), pp. 163–167; Gibson, *Aztecs*, pp. 372–376; and Ricard, "Documents," pp. 216–235.

42. *Cartas de Indias*, vol. 1, pp. 283–284.

43. For information on conflicts between Spanish guilds and Nahua craftsman, see Gibson, *Aztecs*, pp. 399–402.

44. Chimalpahin, *Annals*, pp. 217, 243. Some of the conflict may have been in how one defined Mexico City. To Spaniards it was one city, but to Nahuas it was two altepetl, so having two cofradías to the same dedication would not have seemed significant.

45. Louise Burkhart found a 1572 summary of indulgences translated to Nahuatl by fray Alonso de Molina for the cofradía of Santa María del Rosario. The earliest known Nahua cofradía with a dedication to the Rosary was established at the friary of Santo Domingo. Other than the 1572 summary, the earliest extant information on the sodality we have is from 1610. Based on the Dominicans' strong support and influence over brotherhoods dedicated to the Rosary, it seems that this document indicates an early founding date for this sodality, or at least early plans for it. Thanks to Louise Burkhart for sharing

both her transcription and translation of this document with me. The original can be found, as [Dogmas of the Church and Devotional Materials in Nahuatl], in the Indigenous Languange Collection, John Carter Brown Library, Brown University, Providence, R.I., https://archive.org/details/dogmasofchurchde00unkn.

46. Fray Pedro de Gante arrived in New Spain in 1523 and was a teacher of the Nahuas at San Josef until his death in 1572. AGN, Tierras, v. 48, e. 4, fs. 7–9v; Bautista, *¿Cómo te confundes?*, p. 275; Chimalpahin, *Annals*, pp. 35, 57; Juan de Grijalva, *Crónica de la orden de N.P.S. Agustín en las provincias de la Nueva España: En cuatro edades desde el año de 1533 hasta el de 1592* (México: Editorial Porrúa, 1985), pp. 161–162; Oroz, *Oroz Codex*, p. 83; Vetancurt, *Teatro*, pt. 4, pp. 41–42; and Torquemada, *Monarquía*, vol. 3, p. 428.

47. Chimalpahin, *Ocho relaciones*, vol. 2, pp. 267–269.

48. Chimalpahin, *Annals*, pp. 201–203.

49. One of the cofradías, which was based in Santa María, seems to have been a double cofradía. My understanding is that double cofradías possessed two devotions instead of one. The only other reference I have seen to a double cofradía comes from Chimalpahin, *Annals*, p. 243, where he talks about his friend Diego López establishing a double cofradía, Niño Jesús Perdido and Santa María del Rosario in Tlatelolco. For the cofradía in Santa María, see UNAM, FRAF, caja 64, e. 1209, f. 7.

50. Four of the cofradías listed in the group of twenty-nine possessed a mixed membership; two were Nahua-Spanish, one Nahuas and natives from Michoacan, and one Nahua-Filipino. NL, Ayer Collection, MS 1481, B(3)a and B(3)c; AGN, Tierras, v. 48, e. 4, fs. 7–9v; AGN, Bienes Nacionales, v. 1028, e. 28; AGN, Bienes Nacionales, v. 387, e. 1; AGN, Cofradías y Archicofradías, v. 188, e. 3; Chimalpahin, *Annals*, pp. 215, 217, 243, 245, 277; Mendieta, *Historia*, vol. 2, pp. 104–105; Motolinia, *Memoriales*, p. 93; Vetancurt, *Teatro*, pt. 4, pp. 41–42; and Moreno de los Arcos, "Los terriotorios," p. 167.

51. Alicia Bazarte Martínez, *Las cofradías de españoles en la ciudad de México, 1526–1869* (México: Universidad Autónoma Metropolitana, 1989), p. 46.

52. This condition supports dating the constitution before the 1560s, when Archbishop Montúfar began removing the various subdistricts of Mexico Tenochtitlan from the control of San Josef. Once San Pablo was separated from the doctrina of San Josef, this condition was irrelevant, since some Nahuas still lived in Tenochtitlan but no longer belonged to San Josef.

53. Lavrin, "Confraternities," p. 29.

54. AGN, Indios, v. 9, e. 300, fs. 147–147v.

55. AHFZ Constitution. The Nahuatl reads "ynic macuillamantli. nican. mitoz yn quenin. teyxpan. nemizque. ynic momalhuizque. mimatizque. ynic ayac. yntech miçaviz."

56. UNAM, FRAF, caja 106, e. 1461, f. 10. This interesting document provides a listing of differing expenses based on ethnicity and, it seems, membership. In regard to "indios," it lists them in two groups: those of the pueblo, or town, and "Indios de Quadrilla." The indios de quadrilla were members of work gangs who stayed in a location more temporarily.

57. Mendieta, *Historia,* vol. 2, pp. 97–99; Thomas F. Reese, "The Structure of Colonial Devotional Space in the Andes," paper presented at Princeton University (3 April 2002), p. 13; Schwaller, "Constitution," pp. 227, 230–231; and Sell, "Our Lady," pp. 350–351.

58. Mendieta, *Historia*, vol. 2, pp. 104–105; Chimalpahin, *Annals*, pp. 85–89; and Motolinia, *Motolinia's History,* pp. 141–143.

59. Chimalpahin, *Annals*, p. 217–219.

60. Ibid., p. 245.

61. Curcio-Nagy, *Great Festivals*, p. 28; and Vetancurt, *Teatro*, pt. 4, pp. 41–42.

62. Chimalpahin, *Annals*, pp. 163–167, 287–289.

63. Ibid., pp. 81–83; and Motolinia, *Motolinia's History*, p. 144.

64. Sixteenth-century Spaniards had a tradition of requesting assistance from saints during periods of crisis. Similar practices seem to have crossed the Atlantic with them. For more information on sixteenth-century Spanish local religion, see William A. Christian Jr., *Local Religion in Sixteenth-Century Spain* (Princeton, N.J.: Princeton University Press, 1981).

65. Christopher F. Black, *Italian Confraternities in the Sixteenth Century* (Cambridge: Cambridge University Press, 1989), pp. 72–73.

66. At this time there is not enough documentation available to uncover the functional differences between a nonaffiliated cofradía and one tied to an archcofradía, so I treat them together.

67. The problem with the dating is Motolinia's "en este año" (in this year). The only reference preceding this citation is on page 85, where he marks the year as 1536. The next notation of a year comes on page 99, and it is 1538. Presumably he continued a chronological approach to his work. Aside from La Veracruz, the next earliest known indigenous cofradía in central Mexico comes from the Tlaxcala region and dates from 1539. Motolinia suggests a sense of permanence regarding the activities of both the brotherhoods he discusses, which could indicate an even earlier founding date. Toribio de Motolinia, *Memoriales; o, Libro de las cosas de la Nueva España y de los naturales de ella*, ed. Edmundo O'Gorman (México: Universidad Nacional Autónoma de México, 1971), p. 93; Motolinia, *Historia*, pp. 85–86; and Burkhart, *Holy Wednesday*, p. 82.

68. *Cartas de Indias*, vol. 1, pp. 283–284.

69. Chimalpahin, *Annals*, pp. 217–219.

70. Larissa Taylor, "Molina 1552: A European Perspective," in Sell, *Nahua Confraternities*, pp. 14, 18.

71. Motolinia, *Memoriales*, p. 93.

72. Lockhart, *Nahuas*, p. 219.

73. The sumario mentioned here [hereafter AHFZ Sumario] is a detailed listing of indulgences granted from the pope to an indigenous cofradía of the Holy Sacrament in 1568. The document, though incomplete, is seven folios in length. Although this document was found in Zapopan, I believe that it belonged to either Tlatelolco or Tenochtitlan, since both fray Alonso de Molina's and fray Bernardino de Sahagún's names are included in the document, and both friars were present in Tenochtitlan and Tlatelolco at this time. Additionally, the possibility that it did not originally belong to Zapopan is supported by evidence from the cofradía constitution found there, which almost certainly belongs to the chapel of San Josef in Mexico Tenochtitlan. It also seems likely, because of the rivalry between Tenochtitlan and Tlatelolco, that a cofradía dedicated to the Santisimo Sacramento existed in Tenochtitlan, since one had been established in Tlatelolco by 1576 when Juana de Santa Ana recorded her testament. AGN, Tierras, v. 56, e. 8.

74. Motolinia does not provide the name of the chapel to which these cofrades belonged in either his *Historia* or *Memoriales*. The most likely place is San Josef. See Motolinia, *Memoriales*, p. 93; Motolinia, *Historia*, p. 74; and AGN, Tierras, v. 37. e. 2, fs. 69v–83v.

75. The possibilities for the other cofradía established at San Josef during this time include de la Cuerda, Santo Entierro, Santísima Trinidad de los Sastres, San Juan Bautista, and Tránsito de la Vírgen.

76. Bautista, *¿Cómo te confundes?*, p. 275. By 1576 a list was created for what seem to be the Spanish cofradías in Mexico City at the time, with eighteen brotherhoods included on this list. Although the Nahuas did not have as many, they were not that far behind either. AGI, México, 317.

77. AGN, Tierras, vol. 48, e. 4, fs. 7–9v.

78. Schwaller, "Constitution," pp. 217–244, provides a transcription and translation

of this document. The original can be found at the Lilly Library, Indiana University, in the Latin American Manuscripts collection.

79. Moreno de los Arcos, "Los territorios," p. 165; and Torquemada, *Monarquia*, vol. 3, p. 228.

80. Chimalpahin, *Annals*, p. 201. The one exception to this was the visita chapel of San Juan de la Penetencia. This chapel was established for the Nahua community of San Juan Moyotlan, who gave their chapel to the Poor Clares (for their convent) in 1592. Part of the agreement was that the Nahuas would be allowed to hold some celebrations there (e.g., feast days of San Juan Bautista and San Juan Evangelista). Other than these occasional celebrations, the Nahuas of San Juan seemed to have fully appropriated San Josef as their main chapel after this point. AGN, Indios, v. 6, e. 344, fs. 92–92v.

81. INAH, Colegio de San Gregorio, v. 119, f. 19r; and Schroeder, "Jesuits," p. 47n15. The dating of the second congregation, "de la Circuncisión," comes from the date of the document, 1632 minus thirty-four years based on a statement in the source indicating that the congregations of Circuncisión and Nuestra Señora de la Anunciata were established more than thirty-four years before.

82. Schroeder, "Jesuits," pp. 46–47.

83. Chimalpahin does not provide a specific name in reference to this cofradía. Instead he refers to its members as the "Niños de San Juan." Vetancurt also mentions a cofradía dedicated to San Juan at the convent of the Poor Clares, which he refers to as the "cofradía de San Juan." In appendix 1 the cofradía is listed as San Juan. Vetancurt records an additional cofradía at this convent dedicated to Nuestra Señora de Guadalupe but does not state who the members are, and for this reason I do not include it in the cofradía table. Chimalpahin, *Annals*, p. 217; and Vetancurt, *Teatro*, pt. 4, p. 111.

84. San Juan de la Penetencia was an ideal location for the first mixed Spanish-Nahua cofradía since this convent had previously been the Nahua chapel of San Juan. For more information, see chapter 1. It is likely that by the end of the seventeenth century this cofradía was no longer mixed. In a document from 1692 there is reference to the cofradía de San Juan de los Naturales. AGN, Indios, v. 34, e. 37, f. 40.

85. Chimalpahin, *Annals*, pp. 241, 241n4, 243, 277.

86. Ibid., p. 277.

87. Tatiana Seijas, *Asian Slaves in Colonial Mexico: From Chinos to Indians* (Cambridge: Cambridge University Press, 2014), p. 202.

88. AGN, Bienes Nacionales, v. 1028, e. 28.

89. The cofradías at San Josef may have become mixed after the chapel's secularization in the 1770s, though this is not known at this time.

90. O'Hara, *Flock*, p. 3, 239n4; and Seijas, *Asian Slaves*, 207–208.

91. Schroeder, "Jesuits," p. 50.

92. O'Hara, *Flock*, p. 1. The cofradía de Indio Extravagantes is the only religious brotherhood that I have heard of named in terms of its membership rather than its devotion. It seems likely that this is a name applied to the indigenous cofradía de Nuestra Señora del Rosario, also located at Santo Domingo, by fray Antonio Claudio de Villegas, rather than being the actual name of the sodality.

93. Ibid., p. 47 and n15.

94. The closure of the sodality of La Veracruz is based on documentary omission. La Veracruz was clearly established during the sixteenth century. However, two of the best known seventeenth-century historians, Chimalpahin and Vetancurt, do not mention it in their otherwise detailed accounts. It is possible that Chimalpahin failed to mention it in his *Annals* simply because he did not know of its exact year of establishment and assumed that since it was one of the first established it would continue to be there. Vetancurt is a bit more problematic. In his *Teatro Mexicana* he specifically provides a list of sodalities still operating at the chapel of San Josef at the end of the seventeenth century (*Teatro*, pt. 4,

pp. 41–42). He states that there were eight, then provides a list of nine. The cofradía of La Veracruz is not mentioned on the list, so either it ceased functioning or Vetancurt accidentally omitted it.

Another possibility is that it was replaced by a different cofradía. Information about the establishment and closure of Nahua cofradías in Mexico Tenochtitlan is far from complete, and sources about the parishes of San Pablo, San Sebastián, Santa María, Santa Cruz, and Mixtecos are largely lacking. Another cofradía developed at San Josef during Vetancurt's tenure as guardian of San Francisco, two years after he finished writing his book. This is the cofradía of Nuestra Señora de la Candelaria. AGN, Cofradías y Archicofradías, v. 188, e. 3. A published facsimile of this document is available in Alicia Bazarte Martínez and Clara García Aluardo, *Los costos de la salvación: Las cofradías y la ciudad de México (Siglos XVI al XIX)* (México: Centro de Investigación y Docencia Económicas, 2001), p. 315.

95. E.g., AHFZ Constitution; Molina, *Nahua Confraternities*, p. 121; and Schwaller, "Constitution," p. 229.

96. AGN, Hospital de Jesús, leg. 210, e. 4.

97. Schwaller, "Constitution," p. 230.

98. By the early seventeenth century, the Nahua annalist Chimalpahin regularly used the Spanish loan word *campana* instead of *miccatepuztli* in his reference to bells.

99. It does not state in the documents surrounding her death that she had a procession. However, based on the San Josef cofradía constitution, the Molina ordinances, and other cofradía constitutions it is likely that the four cofradías to which she belonged promised a burial procession upon her death. Neither the San Josef constitution nor Molina specifically use the term "procession." The idea, however, is there:

> [Molina] çan mochintin yn macehualtin yn cihuatzitzintin anoço pipiltotontin ympampa mocentlalizque yn Confrariasme ynic quimotoquilitihui yn teopan Auh yn yquac tetocatihui motecpantiazque cenpantiazqyn oquichtin yhuan yn Cihua
>
> For the sake of all the commoners, women, or little children, the members of the cofradía will gather together in order to go bury him in the church. When they go to bury people, the men and the women will line up and go together.
>
> [San Josef document] yn macevaltin. yn çivatzitzintin. anoço. pipiltotontin. ynpanpa. moçētlalizque. yn cofrades. ynic quimotoquilitivi. yn teopa. auh yn iquac. tetocativi. motecpantiazque. yn oquichtin. yhuan. yn çiva.
>
> Because of all the commoners, women, or little children, the members of the confraternity will gather together in order to go bury him in the church. When they go to bury people the men and the women will go in orderly lines.

Also of interest is that, though referred to as an *india principala,* Clara López was never referred to as *doña* in the documentation. AGN, Bienes Nacionales, v. 387, e. 1; AHFZ Constitution; and Molina, *Nahua Confraternities*, pp. 120–121.

100. Chimalpahin, *Annals*, pp. 201, 207, 211.

101. AGN, Bienes Nacionales, v. 387, e. 1, f. 7. "por mi alma; una misa de cuerpo presente cantada." In 1572, Philip II excluded anyone from outside of the royal family being laid in a catafalque, but the law tended to be ignored by the wealthiest citizens. Carlos M. N. Eire, *From Madrid to Purgatory: The Art and Craft of Dying in Sixteenth-Century Spain* (Cambridge: Cambridge University Press, 1995), p. 155.

102. Don Juan de Aguilar became governor of Mexico Tenochtitlan sometime between 1640 and his death in 1654. He is mentioned as governor once in the documents dealing with Clara López. Otherwise, he is referred to as don Juan de Aguilar. He also acted as the executor for Clara's sister, Martina. AGN, Bienes Nacionales, v. 387, e. 1; and AGN, Bienes Nacionales, v. 489, e. 2.

103. The accompaniment of brotherhoods in her burial procession is based on the cofradía constitution of San Josef, wills, and receipts of payment. In three of four wills that mention an individual's membership in a cofradía, there seems to be an assumed responsibility on behalf of the brotherhood toward the cofrade. In the fourth will, that of Micaela Angelina, there is a direct statement:

> yhuan nicpie noCofradia , intla ytla nechtlaoculizque mochi missas ic nichihuililoz nehualt, yhuan in notatzin nonantzin ihuan in achtopa nonamictzin omoetzticatca mochi moçeçeloz [probably moxexeloz] qualyotica.
>
> And I have a cofradía, and if they favor me with something, masses are to be performed with all of it for me, my father and mother, and my late first spouse; it is all to be properly distributed.

The receipts of payment are found with Clara López's will and demonstrate don Juan de Aguilar's payment of five pesos to each of her cofradías. AGN, Bienes Nacionales, v. 387, e. 1; AGN, Bienes Nacionales, v. 489, e. 2; AGN, Tierras, v. 48, e. 4, fs. 7–9v; and NL, Ayer Collection, MS 1481, B(3)e.

104. Lopéz's will does not stipulate that the orphans of San Juan accompany her body, but it seems likely that they did. In comparison to her will is that of doctor Francisco Cervantes in 1575. After his death the boys of San Juan Letrán received ten pesos and four tomines for their part in his burial. The five pesos López paid suggests a similar activity, for she paid separately for masses, as did Salazar; he bequeathed twenty pesos for forty masses (whether low or high was unstated). Cervantes de Salazar, *Crónica*, vol. 1, p. 32.

105. Chimalpahin, *Annals*, pp. 207, 211; and AGN, Bienes Nacionales, v. 387, e. 1, f. 15. Intriguingly, this is the only page in this 113-page document that is written in Nahuatl. It is also the only case that I have found that deals solely with the singers of San Josef. For a translation and transcription of the Nahuatl, see appendix 2.

106. AGN, Bienes Nacionales, v. 70, e. 3.

107. It also seems that Governor don Antonio Valeriano's 1605 funeral had even more pomp than that of Clara López. Torquemada reports that Valeriano was interred at the chapel of San Josef to the accompaniment of a multitude of Spaniards and Nahuas. His body was carried to the courtyard by "religiosos," presumably Franciscans, and placed in a sepulcher. Torquemada, *Monarquía*, vol. 3, pp. 114–115.

108. UNAM, FRAF, caja 106, exp. 1461, f. 10. There are two prices listed for the expenses incurred by natives regarding burial, one for "Indios de Pueblo" and one for "Indios de Quadrilla." UNAM, FRAF, caja 64, exp 1209, f. 7.

109. *Códice Franciscano*, pp. 68–69.

110. Sell, *Nahua Confraternities*, pp. 82–83; and AHFZ Constitution. A possible alternative translation of the San Josef constitution is "Here in the hospital [of] St. Mary. There are two ways of performing service." Also, see note 115, below.

111. Special thanks to Barry Sell for verifying my numbers with searches of his electronic copies.

112. AHN, Diversos Colecciones, v. 23, n. 59; and Ricard, *Spiritual Conquest*, p. 157.

113. It is also possible that Molina was trying to generate revenue for the hospitals via membership dues, but there is not certain evidence to support this within Mexico Tenochtitlan at this time.

114. The payment in chickens may have been in turkeys, since the Nahuatl term *totolin* and the Spanish *gallina* were used interchangeably for both types of fowl. AGN, General de Parte, v. 5, e. 1140, fs. 244–244v; and Chimalpahin, *Annals*, p. 53, 53n5.

115. I am not certain if the cofradía constitution of San Josef refers to the same hospital. At the beginning of the document it states, "Sancta Maa y nicã ospital ontlamanti yc motlayecoltilia," which can be translated as either "Saint Mary. Here in the hospital there

are two ways of performing service," or "Here in the hospital [of] Saint Mary there are two ways of performing service." Chimalpahin's account of the establishment of a cofradía at the Hospital Real de Nuestra Señora de la Caridad, "where we commoners [Nahuas] are treated," lends support to the idea that the cofradía of San Josef supported the Hospital de la Caridad. To add confusion, at the very end of the cofradía constitution the hospital is referred to as "Auh yntla aca. momiquilli nican. ospital. sc. Joseph" (If someone has died here in the hospital of San Josef). However, Pedro Quadrado, official contador of the Church in New Spain from 1550 to 1568, refers to the hospital as "El hospital Real de los yndios Llamado Sant Joseph en esta ciudad de mexico" (The royal hospital of the Indians called San Josef in Mexico City). Quadrado credits the establishment of this hospital, around 1529, to fray Pedro de Gante. Based on a 1583 list of hospitals in Mexico City, the cofradía was probably dedicated to the Hospital Real de San Josef, which had a chaplain assigned to it who spoke Nahuatl. If, as I assert, this cofradía was dedicated to the Hospital Real de San Josef and not to the Hospital Santa María, it increases the chance that the San Josef cofradía constitution was written after Molina's ordinances. Most likely, the hospital and cofradía that Chimalpahin discusses came later. AGI, México, v. 336a, ramo 2, doc 104 (7), f. 7v; AGI, México, v. 287; AGI, México, v. 317; AGI, Patronato, v. 183, n.1, r. 8, digital image 3; and Chimalpahin, *Annals*, p. 243. On the Hospital Real de San Josef de los Naturales, see also Josefina Muriel, *Hospitales de la Nueva España*, 2 vols. (México: Universidad Nacional Autónoma de México, Cruz Roja Mexicana, 1990), vol. 1, p. 172; and Antonio Zedillo Castillo, *Historia de un hospital: El hospital real de naturales* (México: Instituto Mexicano del Seguro Social, 1984), p. 13.

116. In 1613, Chimalpahin also mentioned the establishment of the cofradía of San Nicolás de Tolentino at the Hospital Real de Nuestra Señora de la Caridad. I am not certain if this sodality was of indigenous membership. Additionally, a cofradía of migrant natives dedicated to San Roque was formed at the Hospital de San Lázaro in the same year. Although she was not a member of this cofradía, Clara López bequeathed some money to this hospital in her 1640 will. AGN, Bienes Nacionales, v. 387, e. 1, fs. 7v, 24; and Chimalpahin, *Annals*, pp. 241, 243.

117. ANM, Hernando de Arauz #4, v. 7 yrs. 1619–1622, fs. 7–12v; AGN, Tierras, v. 37, e. 2, fs. 69v–83v; and AGN, Hospital de Jesús, leg. 210, e. 4.

118. AGN, Bienes Nacionales, v. 1028, e. 28.

119. Taylor, "Molina 1552," p. 17; and Sell, *Nahua Confraternities*, p. 85.

120. AGN, Bienes Nacionales, v. 78, e. 38.

121. Memarzadeh, "Medical Practitioners," pp. 264–268.

122. AHFZ Constitution. The Nahuatl is "çeçexiuhtica. mopapatlatiazque. yn ixquichtin. yn tlamocitlavia. nican. ospital. yntla h^{ve}cucahuazque."

123. Sell, *Nahua Confraternities*, pp. 77–79.

124. The translation comes from Pedro de Gante, "Gante's Letter to Charles V," in Mills, Taylor, and Graham, *Colonial Latin America*, p. 111.

125. The process of granting jubilees and altars for the salvation of souls and the attainment of indulgences continued during the sixteenth and early seventeenth centuries. UNAM, FRAF, caja 143, e. 1743–1747; and Gante, "Gante's Letter to Charles V," p. 111.

126. Martin Austin Nesvig, *Ideology and Inquisition: The World of the Censors in Early Mexico* (New Haven, Conn.: Yale University Press, 2009), pp. 122, 233.

127. Alonso de Molina, *Vocabulario en lengua Castellana/Mexicana Mexicana/Castellana* (Ciudad de México: Editorial Porrúa, 2008), f. 100r.

128. Sell, *Nahua Confraternities*, pp. 81–82.

129. Molina, *Vocabulario*, f. 75r; Sell, *Nahua Confraternities*, pp. 108–109; Chimalpahin, *Annals*, pp. 216–217.

130. Burkhart, *Slippery Earth*, p. 53.

131. Chimalpahin, *Annals*, p. 241.

132. Burkhart, "Death and the Colonial Nahua," in Sell and Burkhart, *Nahuatl Theater,* vol. 1, p. 35.

133. Ibid., vol. 1, p. 35n5; and Bernardino de Sahagún, *Sermonario de dominicas y de sanctos en lengua mexicana* (Mexico, 1563), copy in NL, Ayer Collection, MS 1485, 52r. Thanks to John Montes for digitizing sections of the manuscript for me.

134. James Lockhart, *Nahuatl as Written: Lessons in Older Written Nahuatl, with Copious Examples and Texts* (Stanford, Calif.: Stanford University Press and UCLA Latin American Center, 2001), p. 50.

135. Dogmas of the Church and Devotional Materials in Nahuatl, John Carter Brown Library; see note 45, above. Thanks to Jim Lockhart for his help with this translation.

136. There is a facsimile edition of the summary created for the Puebla sodality: *Sumario de las indulgencias y perdones, concedidas a los cofrades del Santísimo Sacramento visitando la iglesia donde está instituida la dicha cofradía son las siguientes* (México: Edición Facsimilar, 1992).

137. Ibid.; and Dogmas of the Church and Devotional Materials in Nahuatl, John Carter Brown Library.

138. AHFZ Sumario; and *Sumario de las indulgencias.*

139. R. N. Swanson, *Indulgences in Late Medieval England: Passports to Paradise?* (Cambridge: Cambridge University Press, 2007), pp. 20–21.

140. Chimalpahin, *Annals,* p. 217.

141. Ibid.

142. Ibid., pp. 273, 285.

143. Chimalpahin, *Codex Chimalpahin,* vol. 2, p. 239.

144. AGN, Bienes Nacionales, v. 965, e. 6.

Chapter 5
Nahuas, Religious Goods, and the Veneration of Saints in Colonial Mexico City

Catholicism was introduced to the native peoples of Mesoamerica by Spaniards and propagated by the mendicant orders, but it was the Mesoamericans themselves who proved crucial to fostering the faith. In Mexico City the Nahuas provided both the labor and goods needed for the spread of the gospel by their mendicant spiritual leaders. Moreover, their sustenance of the colonial divine went beyond providing for the religious; they also created a market for personal Christian goods in the local economy. Christianity was introduced during the first half of the 1500s; by 1600 (due in large part to the growth of Nahua cofradías) a market for Catholic paraphernalia had developed in the indigenous community. And by the middle of the seventeenth century the demand for such items had increased exponentially.

The market for items dedicated to the Catholic divine began as soon as Nahuas came to know and appreciate the trappings of the Church. The initial outlet for ornate indigenous religious handiwork, beyond that of the physical labor needed to construct buildings, was the mendicant orders, and possibly the secular Church and other lay Spaniards. This chapter examines indigenous training in some of these essential crafts at the Colegio de San Josef de los Naturales and the artisans' efforts to meet the local demand for accessories for the colonial divine. In the course of Franciscan efforts to train Nahua artisans for their personal religious needs, the friars also trained them to assist indigenous communities in the construction and maintenance of their ermitas and cofradía banners and the manufacture of their statues, among other items. Moreover, these skills allowed the Nahuas to bring their talents and beliefs to the smallest of social units, the family. The development of a market for saintly images and other paraphernalia to support and decorate their paintings and statues was well under way by the 1560s and became fashionable during the seventeenth century. Aside from examining Nahua artisanal training, the chapter also explores how that training made it feasible for Nahuas to embrace particular aspects of Christianity, especially the veneration of the saints, in the most personal of spaces, their own homes.

Although scholarship exists on Nahua celebration of the saints, the *tianguiz* (marketplace), and indigenous education, little has been done to bring the three together.[1] There is information on the goods sold in indigenous markets, for example, but there is little mention of religious items such as saints' images. Similarly, work has been done on religion and education that explores instruction in the creation of religious paraphernalia and veneration of the saints, but it says little about how the physical aspect of that veneration—that is, the images—came to be. By examining the market, native education, and Nahua involvement in the generation of ecclesiastical accoutrements together, it is possible to see the Nahua response to Christianity on a new level. Such a study reveals a changing and expanding area of commerce in the tianguiz of Mexico City, one that is pervasive in many marketplaces there today.

During the colonial period there were three main marketplaces in Mexico City: one in Santiago Tlatelolco, another in the tlaxilacalli of San Juan Bautista de Xihuitongo in the barrio of San Juan Moyotlan, and the marketplace of San Hipólito, likely in the tlaxilacalli of San Diego de Amanalco, also in San Juan Moyotlan.[2] The San Hipólito marketplace was created for the convenience of Spaniards in 1545. Both the Tlatelolco and Xihuitongo tianguiz existed during the precontact period.[3]

The tianguiz was important for the sale of finished goods, but raw materials for manufacturing items in the home such as cloth, wood, and paint could also be purchased there.[4] These goods, as well as various finished products, had a place in the market involving Catholic paraphernalia.

Artisan Training and the Accoutrements of Christianity

The Nahuas were principally responsible for supplying and adorning the Nahua chapels of Mexico Tenochtitlan, their ermitas, and, on occasion, the friaries. Part of the cost for these endeavors came out of labor drafts assigned to the Nahuas by the crown. By the beginning of the 1560s, the Augustinians, Dominicans, and Franciscans had indigenous peoples from across central Mexico helping with the construction and repair of their friaries.[5] In addition to the labor received through these drafts, the mendicants needed assistance in the form of supplies. An array of materials went to the friaries, indigenous chapels, and Spanish churches.

San Josef was obviously the largest and most important of the indigenous chapels, since it is mentioned repeatedly in sources regarding Franciscan budgetary needs. The Franciscans listed their friaries and the chapel of San Josef, the number of friars assigned to each, and the quantity and types of supplies needed to sustain and operate their facilities. Yet the only chapel that regularly made an appearance on the lists was the chapel of San Josef de los Naturales. The supply requests for this chapel and the number of friars who officially served it were as large as those of some of the large rural friaries. Additionally, San Josef was kept separate from the friary of San Francisco, although it was still a part of the same Franciscan compound. In contrast, generally all of the other indigenous chapels' requirements were included in the estimates for the friaries with which they were associated.[6] The alms, donations, and labor of the Nahuas of San Juan Tenochtitlan helped to supply the needs of San Francisco and San Josef. Their labor went toward chapel and friary repairs, clothing, and ornate artisan crafts.[7]

Although Nahuas were essential in helping with the reconstruction of Mexico Tenochtitlan, and they provided the main labor force for much of the Basin of Mexico, they were not initially familiar with European building styles. The very newness of Spanish architectural forms is evident in their reaction to the vaulted construction of the church of San Francisco. For Nahuas, this was likely the first vaulted architectural work they had witnessed, and many, apparently, initially refused to walk under the arches and vaulted ceilings of the church.[8] Their surprise at European architectural styles was matched by Franciscan curiosity at the range of materials with which the Nahuas could work, especially such mediums as flint, jasper, and alabaster.[9]

The combination of Iberian architecture and Nahua skill with native stone made the construction of many of the friaries, chapels, and churches of Mexico City possible. The initial training many Nahuas received in European building techniques occurred at the Colegio de San Josef. Natives from areas surrounding the Basin of Mexico and within Mexico City were sent to the colegio specifically for such instruction; both children and adults learned techniques of construction, ornamentation, and how to furnish religious buildings. Moreover, they were taught to use metal tools, such as picks and chisels, and how to build arches, Spanish-style doorways, windows, columns, and pilasters.[10] Writing during the 1530s, fray Toribio de Motolinia expressed his amazement at how quickly the natives learned Spanish trades and how very adept at them they became. He claimed that, wherever a friary was located, indigenous artisans produced both their own crafts and those learned from Spaniards, improving upon them each year. He was especially impressed that they could observe a task and then copy it without necessarily training under a master artisan.[11]

The culmination of their indigenous and European training was visible in religious buildings, such as the chapel of San Josef. Although rebuilt on different occasions in both the sixteenth and seventeenth centuries, the chapel of San Josef was mostly constructed by indigenous laborers and contained ornate stonework. Writing at the end of the seventeenth century, fray Agustín de Vetancurt mentioned that the chapel of San Josef contained a mirror made of *tlalchinol*, an indigenous stone, which he said was more beautiful than either jasper or alabaster.[12] Moreover, he described fountains, baptismal fonts, pillars, and doorways as being constructed of jasper and alabaster. Other religious works by Nahua artisans included pulpits, priest and deacon vestments, statues, tapestries, and doorknobs, to name a few. Nahua silversmiths crafted other doorknobs, doorjambs, and the crucifix in the chapel out of silver. Speaking of a fountain in one of the cloisters in the friary of San Francisco, Vetancurt said it was made of white jasper, contained two basins, and included a carved image of San Diego. Artisans also created many of the smaller images of saints in silver and gold for home and chapel use.[13] Though some of the labor and materials supplied for the work was delivered as part of native tribute, much of it came as donations.

Because the friary was on the old aviary grounds and Nahuas could enter and leave it easily, the community had ready access to supplies necessary for traditional indigenous trades such as featherwork. Vetancurt spoke of the innumerable flocks of birds of all shapes and sizes that nested and flew about the friary. The birds provided feathers for the featherwork that natives held in high esteem. In the precontact era, they used feathers to decorate their shields, spears, capes, and tapestries. After the defeat of Tenochtitlan, Nahuas still made tapestries and clothing decorated with feathers. Examples include mitres, the ornamental chasuble, a sleeveless outer garment worn by an officiating priest at mass, and dalmatics, the outer vestment worn by deacons (fig. 19). Nahuas made buttons for the dalmatics out of silver, and the chasuble probably had something similar, although Vetancurt does not mention it.[14] Additionally, female artisans, as discussed in chapter 3, supplied the friars with their habits, providing them as part of their devotional activities and probably part of their tribute obligations.[15]

There was also a large garden containing a great variety of plants in the Franciscan compound. Natives went there to collect the substances and materials they used for medicine and craftwork. For example, the *tianquizpepetla* (of the amaranth family) had multiple uses. Nahuas frequently wove the large green leaves from this plant into multicolored birthing mats. They also used their skill with these leaves, and those of other flora, to create images of saints, animals, and birds in their tapestries. They then hung the artwork in their chapels for feast day celebrations.[16]

Although friaries and chapels provided the earliest and most obvious outlet for much of their religious craftwork, another market, at the community level, soon developed. With the introduction of cofradías and feast day processions came a need for likenesses of the saints and other religious imagery. But the need for these items went beyond the parading of cofradías to include groups of organized indigenous laborers, such as the painters, tailors, tradespeople, and blacksmiths. As mentioned in chapter 4, only one of these groups, the tailors, is known to have formed a cofradía. Nevertheless, lack of an official cofradía or guild brotherhood did not prevent specialist artisans from gathering together in celebration.

FIGURE 19. Sixteenth-century bishop's mitre decorated with indigenous featherwork. Mitre de Plumas de México, © Patrimonial Nacional, Spain.

Many craftspeople had lived, and likely continued to live, in particular designated tlaxilacalli. During the precontact era, the tlaxilacalli of Amantlan in Tlatelolco was specifically known for its feather workers. Similarly, as late as 1580 *pochteca* (merchants) were known to reside in the tlaxilacalli of Tlatelolco Telpochcaltitlan.[17] Members of the various crafts cared for and manufactured their own images. As early as 1564, groups of Nahuas associated by skill, such as the weavers, began to display their own images. Then, on 4 October 1566, for the feast day of San Francisco the tradespeople of Mexico

City displayed an image of San Francisco in a habit. Additionally, carpenters carved a San Josef, and a Niño Jesús in a metal house also made an appearance.[18] On festivities associated with the procession of the Holy Sacrament in June 1593, Chimalpahin relates that in the courtyard of San Francisco "all the different tradespeople set up a platform each. There they carried out their activities, and the merchants, blacksmiths, church attendants [musicians], and carpenters celebrated and danced on the wooden platforms." Earlier that same week, a group of Nahuas carried banners and two litters with statues of San Francisco and San Diego. Indigenous artisans were surely responsible for the carving and painting of the statues and the creation of the banners. Moreover, other artisans, such as tailors and yarn spinners, were also involved, for both images were clothed in woolen garments. Additionally, at the conclusion of the procession more of the Nahuas' labor was dedicated to repairing the two statues, which had been damaged when the litters collapsed.[19] Fray Gerónimo de Mendieta mentions a Good Friday procession that took place during the 1590s in which the Nahuas paraded with a remarkable 230 images of Christ, Mary, and other saints all gilded and brightly colored.[20] The quantity of images in this procession alone is suggestive of the burgeoning market for community-produced Catholic goods.

Nahua Painters and Religious Images

Although painters performed much the same as the other participating craftspeople mentioned above, I treat them separately here because of their unique position in precontact and colonial society. With the arrival of Europeans, they became fixtures in the creation of religious images.[21] The change in their vocational duties—from those of a record keeper as well as an artist to that of an artist alone—likely affected their position and prestige in colonial society. Painters' duties during the precontact period included providing beautiful works of art and recording essential information in pictorial codices. Some of what is known about early Mesoamerica today can be found in the surviving codices. Information has been uncovered through readings of pictorial manuscripts by both modern scholars and colonial authors such as Sahagún and Chimalpahin.[22]

It is likely that some of the precontact painters were priests or were directed by priests, especially in the case of the *tonalamatl*, the book of astrology.[23] But other author/painters were dynastic nobles who passed their books to an appropriate next of kin, always attempting to keep the records in the family.[24] They were responsible for recording royal lineages, histories, and possibly tribute transactions, among other duties.[25] When, in the 1560s, Bernal Díaz del Castillo recorded his recollections of Cortés's meeting with Moctezuma's ambassadors, he said that they brought with them "skilled painters . . . and that he gave them instructions to make realistic full-length portraits of Cortes and all his captains and soldiers, also to draw the ships, sails, and horses, Doña Marina and Aguilar, and even the two greyhounds. The cannon and cannon-balls, and indeed the whole of our army, were faithfully portrayed, and the drawings were taken to Montezuma."[26] He mentioned that, not only did Moctezuma send an ambassador to meet with Cortés and report back to him, but he also sent additional people to record the information so he could both see and hear of the meeting and its surroundings.

Precontact painters held an important position in their society as artists and recorders of information. The two tasks were so intertwined that it is not known if they distinguished between the two functions. The Nahuatl term for painter, *tlacuilo*, meant both painter and writer.[27] During the colonial period, however, their responsibilities eventually divided as the Franciscans' introduced writing in the Roman alphabet and the Nahua community adopted it. Because of the new alphabetic writing, the act of recording information and painting became two separate functions. Although it was possible to perform both duties, their tasks began to separate. Chimalpahin is a good example of this separation. For a time, he had in his possession the history and royal genealogy of his home altepetl, Tzaqualtitlan Tenanco. Though he clearly knew how to read and interpret pictorial codices, he chose to record his own books in alphabetic script.[28] Chimalpahin also understood well that, for both present and future purposes, Nahuatl alphabetic writing best served his fellow Nahuas. This deviation in record-keeping practices likely led to a slight downturn in painter prestige, hinted at in the naming patterns of fifty-six indigenous painters from sixteenth- and seventeenth-century Mexico City, provided in table 7.

Of the painters listed, thirty-three were active during the sixteenth century and another eleven from 1601 to 1605. The difficulty in locating additional "painters" from the seventeenth century is telling in its own way. However, of those identified individuals, none used the cherished title *don*. During the sixteenth century, when the title was not awarded as readily, it is likely that individuals who also held posts in the indigenous government may have received it had they lived during the seventeenth century. However, known painters in the seventeenth century held no such title.

Painters were important to the colonial political hierarchy of the sixteenth century because of their abilities to recreate precontact record-keeping forms and assist in their interpretation. Their status during the seventeenth century likely differed, relating more to their artwork than to the information they portrayed in their artistic renderings. Nevertheless, in the Nahua community they continued to be important as the painters of religious iconography in the chapel and the home. Their positions as the creators of saints' images was a significant element of their maintenance in Nahua society.

Table 7. Mexico City Painters, Sixteenth through Seventeenth Century

Name	*Barrio*	*Year Recorded*	*Source*
Juan Yaotlaloc	San Juan	1564	Bautista, *¿Cómo te confundes?*, p. 199
Mateo Xaman	San Juan	1564	Bautista, *¿Cómo te confundes?*, pp. 199, 283, 291
Miguel Tepotzitolloc	San Juan	1564	Bautista, *¿Cómo te confundes?*, p. 199
Pedro Chimalatl	San Juan	1564	Bautista, *¿Cómo te confundes?*, pp. 199, 283
Francisco Canpolihuiz	San Juan	1564	Bautista, *¿Cómo te confundes?*, p. 199
Antonio Hueton	San Juan	1564	Bautista, *¿Cómo te confundes?*, p. 199
Martín Yaotlapan	San Juan	1564	Bautista, *¿Cómo te confundes?*, p. 199
Miguel Teyol	San Juan	1564	Bautista, *¿Cómo te confundes?*, p. 199
Martín Cocho	San Juan	1564	Bautista, *¿Cómo te confundes?*, pp. 199, 291
Miguel Xochitl	San Juan	1564	Bautista, *¿Cómo te confundes?*, p. 199
Miguel Matlalaca	San Juan	1564	Bautista, *¿Cómo te confundes?*, pp. 199, 313
Francisco Xinmamal (tepixqui in 1564)	San Juan	1564	Bautista, *¿Cómo te confundes?*, pp. 199, 251, 275, 283, 291
Josef Xochihua	San Juan	1564	Bautista, *¿Cómo te confundes?*, p. 199
Cristóbal Quauhtli	San Juan	1564	Bautista, *¿Cómo te confundes?*, p. 199
Marcos Çipac	San Juan	1564	Bautista, *¿Cómo te confundes?*, pp. 199, 275
Pedro Cocolin	San Juan	1564	Bautista, *¿Cómo te confundes?*, pp. 275, 283
Martín Miztli	San Juan	1564	Bautista, *¿Cómo te confundes?*, pp. 283, 291
Juan Cocohua	San Juan	1564	Bautista, *¿Cómo te confundes?*, p. 291
Hernando Çolli	San Juan Atiçapan	1569	Bautista, *¿Cómo te confundes?*, p. 183
Pedro Xochmitl	San Juan Atiçapan	1569	Bautista, *¿Cómo te confundes?*, p. 183
Baltesar (no surname given)	San Juan Tlatilco	1619	ANM, Hernando de Arauz #4, v. 7, yrs. 1619–1622, fs. 7–12v
Lorenzo Martin	San Juan Tlatilco	1619	ANM, Hernando de Arauz #4, v. 7, yrs. 1619–1622, fs. 7–12v
Gaspar San Hernandez (possibly a Spaniard)	San Juan Tlatilco	1619	ANM, Hernando de Arauz #4, v. 7, yrs. 1619–1622, fs. 7–12v

(continued on next page)

Table 7. (*continued*)

Name	*Barrio*	*Year Recorded*	*Source*
Gerónimo de Mendoza	San Juan	1692	AGN, Historía, v. 413, e. 1
Martín Mixcohuatl (Alguacil as well)	San Pablo	1564	Bautista, *¿Cómo te confundes?*, pp. 199, 251, 275
Hernando Tlacacochi	San Pablo Teocaltitlan	1565	Bautista, *¿Cómo te confundes?*, p. 305
Juan Ycnotzin (*Tlacuillocan capitán*, Captain of the painters)	San Pablo	1568	Bautista, *¿Cómo te confundes?*, p. 181
Marcus Diego	San Pablo	1646	AGN, Tierras, v. 109, e. 4
Martín Momauhti	San Sebastián	1564	Bautista, *¿Cómo te confundes?*, p. 183
Toribio (No surname provided)	Santa María	1564	Bautista, *¿Cómo te confundes?*, p. 251
Bartolomé (No surname provided)	Santa María	1691	AGN, Historía, v. 413, e. 1, f. 53
Felipe de Santiago	Santa María	1691	AGN, Historía, v. 413, e. 1, f. 54v
Mateo Cornelio	Santiago Tlatelolco/ San Martin Telpuchcal-titlan Pochtla	1580	AGN, Tierras, v. 49, e. 5
Juan Rodríguez	Tlatelolco: San Martín	1601–1605	AGN, Bienes Nacionales, v. 732, e. 1
Domingo Maçario	Tlatelolco: San Martín	1601–1605	AGN, Bienes Nacionales, v. 732, e. 1
Francisco de la Cruz	Tlatelolco: San Martín	1601–1605	AGN, Bienes Nacionales, v. 732, e. 1
Miguel de la Cruz	Tlatelolco: San Martín	1601–1605	AGN, Bienes Nacionales, v. 732, e. 1
Lorenzo Martín	Tlatelolco: San Martín	1601–1605	AGN, Bienes Nacionales, v. 732, e. 1
Francisco Días	Tlatelolco: San Martín	1601–1605	AGN, Bienes Nacionales, v. 732, e. 1
Sebastián Francisco	Tlatelolco: San Martín	1601–1605	AGN, Bienes Nacionales, v. 732, e. 1
Juan de Cebedeo	Tlatelolco: San Martín	1601–1605	AGN, Bienes Nacionales, v. 732, e. 1
Pedro de Cebedeo	Tlatelolco: San Martín	1601–1605	AGN, Bienes Nacionales, v. 732, e. 1

(continued on next page)

Table 7. (*continued*)

Name	*Barrio*	*Year Recorded*	*Source*
Baltazar Gerónimo	Tlatelolco: San Martín	1601–1605	AGN, Bienes Nacionales, v. 732, e. 1
Agustín García (Head of the painters)[a]	Tlatelolco: San Martín	1601–1605	AGN, Bienes Nacionales, v. 732, e. 1
Diego de los Santos	Tlatelolco: Santa Ana Ocolco (lived in San Juan Tomatlan)	1691	AGN, Historia, v. 413, e. 1, f. 56
Nicolás de los Angeles	Tlatelolco: Santa Ana Ocolco	1691	AGN, Historia, v. 413, e. 1, f. 56
Juan Gerónimo	Tlatelolco	1691	AGN, Historia, v. 413, e. 1, f. 60
Martín Tochmaçatl	Mexico City	1564	Bautista, *¿Cómo te confundes?*, p. 279
Juan Ahuach	Mexico City	1564	Bautista, *¿Cómo te confundes?*, p. 279
Juan Mateo	Mexico City	1564	Bautista, *¿Cómo te confundes?*, pp. 251, 283
Miguel Cihuaten	Mexico City	1565	Bautista, *¿Cómo te confundes?*, p. 313
Juan Ytzcuin	Mexico City	1565	Bautista, *¿Cómo te confundes?*, p. 313
Pedro Quauhtli	Mexico City	1566	Bautista, *¿Cómo te confundes?*, p. 147
Miguel Toxochicuic	Mexico City	1566	Bautista, *¿Cómo te confundes?*, p. 147
Luis Xochitototl	Mexico City	1566	Bautista, *¿Cómo te confundes?*, p. 147
Miguel Yohualauach	Mexico City	1566	Bautista, *¿Cómo te confundes?*, p. 147

a. This document is available only in Spanish, so the title listed here differs from that of Juan Ycnotzin.

As was the case with music (see chapter 2), a specific school, or class, was developed at the Colegio de San Josef for the instruction of artists. Fray Diego Valadés states that fray Pedro de Gante taught indigenous artists how to draw and paint in the courtyard of San Francisco. Moreover, fray Juan de Torquemada states that students at San Josef learned painting in addition to other trades such as sculpture, embroidery, and how to make shoes and jewelry.[29] As part of their instruction, students learned to draw and paint by copying pictures owned by the Franciscans.[30] Such work helped instruct them in European artistic styles and likely familiarized them with Catholic images they could appropriate for community and household religious devotion. Barbara Mundy argues that this type of lesson would have been well received by native artists, for it was similar to the way they learned in the precontact period, through a representative model rather than direct observation.[31] Although the Nahua artists learned European artistic forms, they may have included some precontact artistic iconography in their renderings of the saints' images, as they did with some religious murals.[32] The quantity of precontact imagery in each painting probably depended on the amount of training in European forms each artist received.

The annals of Juan Bautista suggest that Nahua painters from Mexico Tenochtitlan were already actively creating religious images by 1560. The annalist mentions that a fray Çintos went in that year to San Francisco to obtain some small images that had been painted there to take them to Zacatecas.[33] The annals do not provide specific details as to who the painters were, but they were most likely Nahuas; whether students or previously trained artisans is not known. It is revealing that a friar working as far away as Zacatecas obtained his images from the Franciscan compound in Mexico Tenochtitlan. It suggests that in the 1560s some areas outside the city lacked sufficiently trained artists.

By 1564, if not earlier, painters had organized enough to have a designated tepixqui and their own building, a *tlacuilolcalli* (house of painting). The house appears to have been used as a location where people, such as fray Alonso de Molina, could meet with them as a group and where they could work on their craft. In 1568 a captain of the painters represented them in discussion with indigenous government officials.[34] It is probable that both the tlacuilolcalli and the positions of leadership had existed prior to the Spaniards' arrival and continued to be maintained by the painters as a group. Other luxury trade workers, such as lapidaries and feather workers, had organized similarly during the precontact period.[35] During the 1560s the painters' responsibilities as record keepers had changed radically, as evidenced by the creation of bills of sale and possession for land and other legal documents written in Nahuatl. It should be noted, however, that some imagery, such as property drawings, continued to be employed.[36] The change is evident in fray Bernardino de Sahagún's Primeros Memoriales. Sahagún began collecting information in the 1560s. Art historian Eloise Quiñones Keber argues that the Nahua scribes and artists working with Sahagún on this project differed.[37] However, traces of precontact ways of recording information were also evident during the 1560s and 1570s. In 1565, Nahuas in charge of recording tribute donation did so through painting. And again in 1574 the tribute for the barrio of San Pablo was recorded using both pictorial images and the Roman alphabet.[38] By the seventeenth century, however, these modes, as official forms of record keeping, appear to have faded.[39]

The organization of painters as a group does not appear to have waned initially with the separation of duties. In 1601 ten painters from Tlatelolco initiated a complaint on behalf of all of the painters of Tlatelolco against the guardian of the Franciscan friary of Santiago Tlatelolco, fray Juan de Torquemada. They accused Torquemada of stripping their foreman and then using his belt of knotted rope to whip him about the head until he bled and came close to death. The painters reported that the reason for the punishment was missing mass, but they emphasized, in their defense, that they were in Xochimilco painting a mural for the Franciscans. They had attended mass in Xochimilco.[40]

Based on the annals of Juan Bautista, it appears that the Nahua painters of Mexico City were in great demand, in their altepetl of Mexico Tenochtitlan and Mexico Tlatelolco but also in other polities. Was this group of painters popular because of the ability of the religious orders and others to claim the work of indigenous painters as tribute labor (making them less expensive than their Spanish counterparts), because of their skill, or both? Franciscans such as fray Miguel de Navarro praised the painters, saying that they surpassed Spaniards in many of their abilities. If the skill of Mexico City painters was indeed as good as he said, it could explain why they went to work in Xochimilco in 1564.[41] By the 1570s and 1580s, Nahua artists were being trained in European artistic styles at other mendicant friaries, yet as mentioned above in the case of Xochimilco the Nahua painters from Mexico City were still traveling to other altepetl at the beginning of the seventeenth century.[42] During the seventeenth century, Nahua painters' responsibilities focused less on the creation of pictorial codices, which had mostly ceased by the end of the sixteenth century, and more on the creation of secular and religious art. They employed their skills in the houses of Spaniards, in religious and government buildings, and in painting artistic pieces for special occasions.

In explaining how the Nahuas created large paintings or images, Vetancurt stated that ten skilled workers divided an image into parts. Each artisan then took his portion home to work on it without seeing the work of his fellow craftsmen. When everyone was finished, they joined the images together to create the final product.[43] An example of the process can be seen in an image created in 1593 to decorate the chapel of San Josef. In stages, the Nahuas placed an image of San Francisco riding an eagle on a prickly pear cactus with clouds on either side on the roof of San Josef. First, they situated the center image of San Francisco sitting on an eagle perched on a cactus, and then they placed clouds on either side of the central picture. Four months later, they placed a sculpture of San Francisco on the eagle at the base of the cross in the courtyard of the friary.[44] A similar process of decoration occurred in 1598. The occasion was the arrival of the relics of the Discalced Franciscans, who had died in Japan. Under the direction of fray Francisco de Gamboa, Nahua painters created a lienzo of four cloths depicting the scene of the Discalceds' martyrdom and hung them on the walls of San Josef.[45]

Despite training in Christian iconographic styles, Nahua painters working during the sixteenth century continued to incorporate aspects of both their surroundings and their precontact traditions in many of their colonial murals. In the frescoes of the Augustinian religious compound in Malinalco, butterflies and bees drink from flowers, a precontact image said to indicate happiness in the afterlife among deserving individuals. The Nahuas who painted the frescoes of Malinalco incorporated both indigenous and European styles. The artists with greater skill in European artistic tradition worked on the central sections, leaving apprentices to work on embellishments, and these areas especially exhibit a greater precontact technique. The existence of both styles suggests that Spaniards eventually left the Nahuas to their own devices when it came to the creation of murals and frescoes.[46] It is difficult to know if similar work occurred at the chapel of San Josef in Mexico Tenochtitlan, since it was destroyed toward the end of the nineteenth century. But considering the use of the image of San Francisco riding an eagle perched on a prickly pear cactus, it seems likely that both European and indigenous styles were intertwined at San Josef as well.

Inasmuch as the Nahuas were able to incorporate precontact images and ideas into the works of art executed at religious compounds, it is probable that a similar mix of styles existed in the saints' images they produced in the confines of their own homes and shops. Also, as demonstrated by the work at Malinalco, the amount of European or indigenous style present in each image likely depended on the training of the artist creating the image. Moreover, because many of the images were intended for private households, it is likely that they underwent less ecclesiastical scrutiny than did images for a chapel, church, or other religious building.

As in the case of other artisans, much of the painters' initial religious duties related to the decoration of friaries, convents, churches, and chapels. But, as the Nahua community adopted aspects of Christianity, the market for Nahua painters who knew how to create European religious images grew. A local market for the images may have begun as early as 1536 or 1537, with the initiation of the first known Nahua cofradía. However, there would have been an exigency placed on trained Nahua artists during this time for their work in religious buildings specifically. By 1564 there was most likely a marked increase in community demand, with at least four cofradías active in Mexico Tenochtitlan by then.[47] The additional activities of trade groups at feast day celebrations, as discussed above, would have only served to increase the interest in religious paraphernalia.

Growth and Development of the Veneration of Saints in Colonial Mexico City

Whereas a market developed for Christian ceremonial items at the community level, the evidence for the start of another, even more particular market, that of the family and individual, appeared by 1564, though it may have been in place earlier.[48] Traces of this market were visible in the sixteenth century, but the period of greatest growth and expansion for household sacred works was in the seventeenth century. The desire for images in the domestic sphere likely spurred an increase in the production of Catholic goods to meet the rise in demand. The growth of the veneration of saints (and items, such as the vestments, needed for their adoration) in households is suggestive of changes affecting the goods sold in the marketplaces of Mexico City.

In early modern Spain, saints were seen as intercessors between humans and God. Communities made vows to saints they believed would intercede with God on their behalf to help prevent natural disasters and other calamities. Saints typically were thought to have a responsibility to the people of a particular town, and the townspeople had reciprocal duties they needed to perform for the saint. Failure to fulfill one's responsibilities to the saints could lead to fines, public shaming, or other punishments, for angering a town's saint(s) could bring harm to the entire community.[49] A town's request for aid from a saint was not necessarily an act of faith. During periods of need, local citizens could shift from saint to saint until the desired outcome was achieved. The realization of their goal did not necessarily serve as confirmation of their religious views; rather, as William Christian observes, it served "as proof of the intercession of a particular saint."[50]

Belief in the intercession of saints went deeper than vows at the community level. It was also thought that saints acted on behalf of individuals. Perhaps an extreme example is that of Philip II. In preparation for his death, he constructed the royal residence of San Lorenzo del Escorial, designed in the shape of the grill on which San Lorenzo was martyred. The structure also served as a royal mausoleum and retreat, and it contained a monastery, library, and shrine holding over 7,500 saintly relics. It was consecrated on the feast day of its patron saint, San Lorenzo. Philip began searching for relics for the Escorial as early as 1563 and received a tooth of San Lorenzo's in 1564. Soon relics, some fought for and others delivered as gifts, began to arrive from all over Europe. He was especially pleased with a collection that he saved from destruction by Protestants in Germany and the Low Countries. Many people believed in the curative power of relics, and it is likely that Philip did as well. As his health worsened, he had relics from his collection placed on his mouth, eyes, head, and hands. His belief in their curative powers can be seen in his request that the relic of the entire knee of Saint Sebastian, containing the skin and the bone, be brought to him before having his own knee lanced.[51]

At the time of his death, Philip, like so many testators before him, asked the saints to intercede on his behalf. His list of saints, though—nineteen named plus "all the angels in heaven"—came close to matching the list of saints invoked by all of Madrid's testators from the period. Although Philip was the king of Spain, he did not stand at the pinnacle of Spanish Catholic society. That was the place of the saints; the king could not extend his power beyond earth and mortality. A case in point comes from Francisco de Quevedo's 1628 revelation that Santa Teresa de Ávila, a contemporary of Philip who predeceased him, managed to secure Philip's release from purgatory in eight days. In the end, it was not the masses for the king's soul that saved him but the intercession of a single saint. It was believed that Santa Teresa had rescued him from a long and deserved stay in purgatory. This action by Santa Teresa demonstrates the saints' powers over the most illustrious of mortal personages and their ability to intercede with God, presumably, on behalf of even the most grievous sinners.[52]

Shortly after the Franciscans arrived in Mexico City, they introduced the saints to the Nahuas in a variety of ways—giving individuals a Christian name upon baptism, adding the name of a saint to the names of all major polities, and through church names. Franciscans gave a saint's name to the altepetl, the barrios, and the tlaxilacalli. Mexico Tenochtitlan and Mexico Tlatelolco became San Juan Tenochtitlan and Santiago Tlatelolco, respectively. As discussed briefly in chapter 1, each of the four barrios of Tenochtitlan received a saint's name. It is uncertain who provided the individual tlaxilacalli with their Christian identities. Of the known eighty-seven tlaxilacalli for Mexico Tenochtitlan, fewer than half of their Catholic names have been uncovered (see table 1). Of those thirty-six, twenty-one were named after male saints, three after female saints, four after Mary, four after Christ, and two each for the cross and the Holy Spirit.

Upon baptism, a Nahua received a Christian name. Initially, the names were chosen from the Spaniards in New Spain. Names such as Juan, Pedro, Miguel, María, Magdalena, and Ana all became common among the Nahuas. During the early sixteenth century, the indigenous name was frequently retained with the Christian one, but by the 1550s Nahua surnames started to change. The new names frequently matched the name of the mendicant performing the baptism or the saint's day of the event. Though many friars kept their original surnames, others opted to take a religious surname at the time of their vows, such as fray Gerónimo de San Martín. For the Nahuas, however, James Lockhart argues that the "de San" became so redundant that it was eventually dropped from indigenous names on more informal occasions. This, however, did not change the fact that individuals still possessed the "de San" portion of their name, and they would employ it for more formal occasions.[53] It likely served as a reminder that they, too, were named after the saints, just as the friar who named them may have been.

Along with the application of saints' names to sundry people and places, the mendicants encouraged the Nahuas to hold Catholic saints in awe, as did the Spaniards in New Spain and Iberia. Emulating practices of Castilians in sixteenth-century Spain, Mexico City Nahuas turned to their saints to halt bad weather, epidemics, and other natural disasters. In December 1595 the people of Mexico City—Nahuas, Spaniards, Africans, and castas—sought the Virgin Mary's aid through a procession in an attempt to end a measles epidemic. Chimalpahin reports that in 1604 Nahuas and Spaniards went in procession to stop the rain. They carried with them images of Christ, the saints, and a relic of the True Cross.[54]

Although the Franciscans of Mexico City possessed nowhere near the collection of relics that Philip II did, their collection by the end of the sixteenth century was impressive nonetheless. According to fray Pedro de Oroz, the friary of San Francisco contained the following relics, among many others: a bone from the Eleven Thousand Virgins, two bones from the heads of some of the Eleven Thousand Virgins, a bone of San Martín Obispo, part of the veil of Santa Lucía, an arm bone of Santa Anastasía, a bone from the Santo Inocentes, a bone of San Cristóbal, a portion of the vesture of San Sebastián, a bone of San Alexander, a bone from one of the Ten Thousand Martyrs, a bone of San Pacratius, and two bones of Santa Theban. It is not known how familiar with the relics the Nahuas were, but they did understand that they held religious importance. When the 200-foot-tall cross in the courtyard of San Francisco was taken down because of rot in 1601, indigenous parishioners apparently kept pieces of it as if they were relics. In a case noted by Chimalpahin, mentioned above, in 1604 a relic of the True Cross was sent in procession in Mexico City.[55] Their treatment of their own cross and Chimalpahin's mention of the relic of the True Cross suggest that the Nahuas were familiar with Christian relics and their spiritual powers.

Although Nahuas and Spaniards in New Spain sought assistance from the saints, it seems, based on the accounts of Chimalpahin, that they also believed that failure to do one's duties to the saints or God could adversely affect a community. Chimalpahin reports that "a very strong earthquake such as had never happened before" struck Mexico City during the early morning hours of 26 August 1611, damaging the city and surrounding altepetl and even setting parts of the lakes boiling. Severe aftershocks struck later that same afternoon. Chimalpahin and, he says, Spaniards and religious alike blamed Viceroy Archbishop don fray García Guerra for his failure, as leader of the viceroyalty, to initiate prayers, processions, and penance to halt the aftershocks. It was because of a miracle performed by San Nicolás de Tolentino on behalf of a woman and her children during the quake that San Nicolás became the patron saint of the city.[56] Chimalpahin's report of the miracle suggests that he, and likely other Nahuas, believed in the intercession of the saints. No doubt the Church encouraged this belief, as seen with fray Agustín de Vetancurt's account of an image of Santa Verónica, housed at the chapel of San Josef de los Naturales, producing copious tears over a period of four months in 1635.[57] Serge Gruzinski argues that many natives believed that their saintly images could move, cry, sweat, and bleed like humans.[58]

Saints continued to be important to indigenous peoples on both community and individual levels. Images begin to appear to native peoples in the forests, hills, fields, caves, and lakes in the countryside in a pattern similar to one in sixteenth-century Spain. The individuals who discovered the images, and then their communities, believed in a direct connection between themselves and the saint portrayed in the image.[59] The initial acceptance of veneration of the saints in New Spain may have been aided by similarities to aspects of precontact religious expression.[60] Indeed, Lockhart suggests that if someone whose experience with indigenous religion came primarily from "reading mundane Nahuatl documentation" were asked about the nature of native colonial religion, they would "inevitably answer that religion was about saints." They are pervasive in wills, bills of sale, annals, and "almost everything the Nahuas wrote without supervision and primarily for their own eyes."[61]

During the precontact period, Nahuas worshiped images of their gods and believed in the deification of certain religious objects.[62] Priests dedicated to the deities cared for their images, their accoutrements, and their religious space by cleaning, making repairs, keeping fires lit, and performing the necessary rituals.[63] Much of indigenous religious belief was organized around a central religious calendar that was also important for keeping track of the passage of time. The feast day calendar of the Catholic Church, with its multitude of religious celebrations, may have served as a replacement. Initially, some Franciscans even tried to merge the liturgical calendar with the indigenous one.[64] This endeavor was eventually halted, but the calendar, as well as the similarities regarding the ritual treatment of precontact deities and colonial Christian icons (e.g., sweeping and cleaning important religious paraphernalia), likely encouraged Nahuas to adopt the saints. Friars also promoted interest in the saints by writing hagiographic texts in the native languages.[65] Although the sixteenth century clearly witnessed the beginning of Nahuas venerating the saints, the middle to end of the seventeenth century was when it truly flourished.

As early as 1564, Nahuas in Mexico City were building houses dedicated to the saints.[66] Similarly, a 1580 will from the altepetl of Culhuacan requested the construction of a stone house for an image of "our Lord."[67] These structures may have been erected even earlier, for ecclesiastical authorities expressed their concern in 1539 regarding potential continuities of precontact traditions in the plethora of small chapels constructed by natives.[68] In the 1570s, the Dominican friar Diego Durán noted the existence of family altars in indigenous houses.[69] Writing during the first quarter of the seventeenth century, Augustinian fray Juan de Grijalva stated that natives had "clean and decent" oratories in their homes. Each personal chapel had many images, according to the wealth of the individual, colorful rugs, flowers, and perfumes. It was not uncommon for some privately owned images to be taken in procession on behalf of the neighborhood in which one resided. Even the saints not taken in procession were set outside their homes with candles and other adornments to watch as religious processions passed by. Grijalva goes on to say that competitions and lawsuits among natives could develop over the images.[70]

It is uncertain how common a practice it was in Mexico Tenochtitlan to build private shrines or altars to the saints. It is known that houses, tables, chairs, and other goods continued to be bequeathed to the images of saints during the sixteenth and seventeenth centuries.[71] Of fifty-two Mexico City wills from the seventeenth century, six individuals left an altar or a house to their saint(s). It is possible that this number is higher, but the wording in some of the testaments instructs the heirs to care for the images and fails to mention where and how their saints were displayed.[72] Moreover, dedication to the saints was clearly demonstrated in indigenous annals and wills during the sixteenth and seventeenth centuries. In 1598 a proclamation was issued by the Holy Office of the Inquisition banning the sale of "clay candle holders in the shape of angels and the leaded censers in the form of a male or female saint and the tobacco that they put in them . . . on pain of excommunication."[73] Lockhart argues that such items were banned for the use of "preconquest magical substances like tobacco." Despite the proclamation, it is probable that the items did not altogether disappear, especially considering the growing popularity of the saints' images.[74] Grijalva reported that an indigenous person who refused to spend two reales on food or clothing would easily spend one thousand reales on a single image; moreover, one who had only one building in which to live, sleep, and cook might well build a large structure specifically for saints.[75] Although doubtless an exaggeration, Grijalva's statement suggests a growth in the popularity of the saints by the beginning of the 1600s.

An examination of Nahua wills from Mexico City suggests that the saints started to become important enough for some Nahuas to bequeath images in their testaments as early as the 1570s in Mexico Tenochtitlan, ten years earlier than has been found for other areas of New Spain.[76] The first occurrence is from the 1570 Spanish translation (the Nahuatl having been lost) of Beatriz Papan's testament from the barrio of San Juan, in which she states that she has an image of "Nuestra Señora." The second, and the first in a surviving Nahuatl will, is from the 1576 testament of Juana Francisca from the barrio of San Sebastián. She leaves a crucifix and two Santa Marías to her daughters.[77] The 1625 testament of Magdalena María directly ties the *pochteca* to the sale and procurement of saints' images, though their trade in saints' images likely started before then.[78] Individual veneration of the saints continued, increased, and diversified in Mexico Tenochtitlan until at least the end of the seventeenth century, with the most significant growth occurring between the 1640s and 1700. A similar increase in popularity also transpired in Toluca by 1675, if not earlier.[79] During the sixteenth and seventeenth centuries the number of individuals and the number of images each individual owned increased in Mexico City.[80] Moreover, although the trend purportedly began with women, men's ownership of images increased too. Women, however, owned images more frequently than men and in greater quantities. Of the forty-two women's testaments examined from the sixteenth and seventeenth centuries, twenty-three (54.7 percent) mention images. In contrast, only sixteen of the thirty-six men's testaments (44.4 percent) bequeathed images. My findings differ from Stephanie Wood's research on late seventeenth- and eighteenth-century Toluca, in which men owned more images than women.[81] When early eighteenth-century wills are included in the sample, indigenous men's and women's ownership of images in Mexico City over the two centuries becomes roughly equal, at 54 percent.

These Mexico City testators usually identified each individual image by name, but the care they took in listing each image also increased during the latter half of the seventeenth century. Between 1651 and 1700 only one individual bequeathing his images failed to name them, coinciding with a period of more substantial image ownership. In contrast, from 1546 to 1650 thirteen people did not list the names of their images, and among them eleven images of the Virgin Mary did not have a specific representation (e.g., Candelaria) listed for her. Images of Mary, followed by Christ, made the most appearances, sixty-three and thirty-four, respectively. Of their various representations, Nuestra Señora de la Asunción and Niño Jesús were the most popular. Of the named saints, the most popular was an Augustinian saint, San Nicolás de Tolentino, whose earliest known appearance is in a 1592 Nahua testament.

San Nicolás's popularity seems to have increased in the 1640s and later. Chimalpahin credits him with saving a Spanish woman and her children from a collapsed roof in the 1611 earthquake mentioned above. In 1615, San Nicolás helped his Mexico City faithful again, only this time it was a Nahua woman and her child. Though Nahuas from the Augustinian parish of San Pablo mention him first and most frequently in their testaments, Nahuas in the Franciscan parishes of San Josef and Santa María also owned images of him, probably because of his elevation to patron saint of the city.[82]

During the sixteenth and seventeenth centuries, the images of saints appeared in three varieties: lienzos, *imagenes de bulto* (images in the round), and *retablos* (altarpieces). Retablos appeared in two wills in reference to three images. In both cases, the term itself was used in the Spanish translation of the original Nahuatl document. The Nahua notaries opted for the Nahuatl *teixiptla* (image) or the seventeenth-century Spanish loanword *imagen*. The first appearance of an image specified as a lienzo was in 1580, though the saint itself was not identified.[83] In the sixteenth-century testaments from Culhuacan, the Nahuas also preferred the term *teixiptla*.[84] Images in the round appear in testaments from Mexico City as early as 1592, but the only two references are in Spanish-language wills that are missing the original Nahuatl.[85]

By 1600, however, lienzos and images in the round had become common enough among Mexico City Nahuas for both *lienzo* and *de bulto* to be adopted as loanwords.[86] Many seventeenth-century testators mention the design of some of their images, but a signficant number went unclassified. Of 136 images bequeathed during the 1600s, lienzos are mentioned thirty-two times, images in the round thirty-seven times, retablos twice, and sixty-five were not identified.[87] It is not possible to discover the types of the sixty-five unknown images since testators of these wills owned multiple styles of images but failed to provide specific information related to all of the images mentioned in their wills.

Only twenty-six of the testators examined listed the types of images they owned. Of them, nine women and three men owned at least one of each. If an individual owned only one type of image, it was generally an image in the round. Though lienzos appear less frequently than images in the round, they are still an obvious presence in many of the testaments. Of note, there are fewer appearances of lienzos in the later Toluca wills. More than one hundred Toluca testators mention images, some 63 percent. Of these, only two mention lienzos, and one of them owned three, the other one.[88] In contrast, twenty of ninety testators from Mexico City mention ownership of a lienzo, with an average of two apiece. The differences between the findings for the two areas and time periods suggest a regional difference, a shift away from lienzos in the eighteenth century (the time period of many of the Toluca testaments), or both. The very limited corpus of early eighteenth-century testaments examined for this research supports a regional difference; of the eleven eighteenth-century wills, seven testators owned images, and of those five mentioned the specific design of some of their images. All five of these testators owned at least one lienzo, though two owned three and one four, and four of them owned one or more images in the round.[89]

Fray Juan de Grijalva's claim that the Nahuas would impoverish themselves for their images portrays their popularity at the beginning of the seventeenth century. The 1642 testament of Josef Melchor provides a sense of how much money Nahuas were able to spend on images. In his will, he states the amount he owes to a group of people for his saints. Unfortunately, he does not specify whether the images were in the round or lienzos. He owned seven different images, valued from six tomines to sixteen pesos, and owed a total of thirty-one pesos and eight tomines for his collection of images. All other debts listed in his will combined came to two pesos and six tomines, suggesting that Grijalva's statement was not an exaggeration.[90]

Images held a unique place in testaments. Whereas land, houses, and clothing or other moveable goods were frequently bequeathed to individuals or sold to pay for debts or masses, saints' images and, more important, their care, were passed on to friends, family members, or religious orders. Of the more than 136 images accounted for in ninety testaments, only two were sold. In both cases, neither image was in the possession of the testator at the time of death. One image was being refinished; the other had been paid for but was still being made.[91] Only one testatrix, Nicolasa Juana, destroyed some of her images. Based on the reverence and care Nahuas took with their saints, her destruction of them is a bit surprising. However, a closer reading of her testament suggests that her disposal of them, through fire, may have been appropriate. The images were cheap woodcuts that had aged and faded with time. Nicolasa bequeathed her other images to friends and family. Included among those passed on was an image of Santa María used in an unspecified benediction ceremony. Her possession of such an important image suggests that she knew what she was doing when she ordered the others burned. The use of fire reflects precontact ideas of death and rebirth, reinforcing the idea that the Nahuas viewed saints' images as vessels that could be inhabited by those they represented.[92] A lawsuit from the annals of Juan Bautista, discussed below, suggests that Spaniards also supported the disposal of images through fire.

A good example in wills of Nahua care for their images can be seen in the 1699 testament of Melchora de Santiago. Santiago bequeathed the care of her saints' images to her adopted daughter. She also left a small fortune's worth of items to the image of Nuestra Señora de la Purificación:

> yhuan niquitohua ca in totlazonantzin Purificacion tictopielia nicnocahuililia çe corona teocuitla sobredorado , yhuan ce tozcatl corales ome hilo neliuhtica aljofar , oc ce tozcatl corales çan mixcahua ome hilo yhuan oc ce hilo corales , yhuan yei bara yhuan tlaco Raso ayamo mitzoma, imantotzin mochihuaz intotlazonantzin Purificacion

> And I say that to our beloved precious mother of the Purification that we have I leave a gilded crown [of silver] and a necklace of two strands of coral and small pearls, another necklace of two strands of corals only, and another strand of coral and three and a half varas of satin, not yet sewn; it is to become a cloak for our precious mother of the Purification.[93]

The image had been passed on to Santiago by her father, don Juan de Santiago, when he died a few years earlier. Don Juan requested that "a high mass with a priest" be said for the image on its feast day.[94] The care some Nahuas took with their saints may be explained by the belief that saints could and sometimes did aid people in need, as occurred with the miraculous examples of San Nicolás mentioned above and with the resurrection of a child by San Diego in 1600.

Although Melchora de Santiago's testament was written more than one hundred years after the origin of saints' images in the marketplace, it (and other indigenous wills) demonstrates that the Nahuas' dedication to the saints and their way of expressing their devotion endured in Mexico City, at least until the end of the seventeenth century. As Lockhart convincingly argues, it seems that Nahuas such as Melchora de Santiago continued to perceive the physical representation of the saint and the tangible religious entity as one and the same being. He found that "the saints seem to have symbolized household identity and continuity." Entire houses were frequently given to saints with the hope that members of the household would continue to take care of them.[95] In Melchora's will, she also expressed the desire that "if God gives her [Melchora's daughter] life, perhaps she will become his sweeper for the images."[96] The act of sweeping was a carryover from precontact times, as were some of the other duties assigned to a saint's caregiver. Such responsibilities were also associated with the care of precontact temples and later colonial chapels. The continuation of specific religious responsibilities in homes, such as the devotion to saints' images, suggests a similar tie between precontact and colonial personal shrines. The range of the Nahuas' devotion to their religious duties appears to extend from the larger entity of the altepetl inward, in incremental levels, to the barrio, tlaxilacalli, family, and, then, individual. The Nahuas' relationship with their saints was both a personal and a community manifestation of their religiosity.

Saints and the Marketplace

It is probable that the shift from supplying offerings to the idols of precontact deities to providing for the saints was not a difficult one to make. As mentioned above, some of the Nahuas cared for their saints in ways comparable to precontact traditions. Moreover, some items bequeathed to saints, and sold in marketplaces, may have been used for a similar function during the precontact period. Frances Berdan found that one of the responsibilities of precontact feather workers was to adorn the Nahua god Huitzilopochtli with a feathered cloak.[97] Colonial testators also made gifts to their saints' images. Many of these items probably adorned their saint prior to their death; others may have been granted from the deathbed. Two individuals from Mexico City provided one of their saints with either a cape or satin fabric to be made into a cloak.[98] A third testatrix paid an indigenous embroiderer forty pesos to dress her image of St. Ignatius of Loyola.[99] It is difficult to tell how common a trend dressing one's images was during the sixteenth and seventeenth centuries, but the dates of these three wills (1619, 1623 and 1699) suggest that it was not a one-time occurrence.[100] Other items bequeathed to saints include a table, box, mantas, chairs, pedestals, silver halo, land, houses, silver crown, and necklaces.[101]

The items listed above, as well as the images themselves, indicate the wide range of artisanal crafts employed specifically for devotion to the saints. The tables, box, and chairs were most likely made out of wood and may have required a carpenter in their manufacture. The pedestals may have been of stone or wood and gilded, likely in silver or gold. The crown and halo had to have been fashioned by silversmiths, and a jeweler probably made the necklaces, which contained coral and pearls. A necklace alone engaged trade from pearl and coral divers (probably along the Pacific coast), to mule drivers transporting the goods, to merchants selling the raw materials in Mexico City, to jewelers making the necklace.[102]

Though many of the images were one-dimensional lienzos or sculpted carvings, other trades were also involved. In the 1677 testament of Micaela Angelina, it appears that she employed blacksmiths to create an image of Christ: "And I say again that the craftsmen who are blacksmiths are not to demand anything concerning the [image of] Christ, for I already provided it with its silver halo."[103] The employment of blacksmiths to create an image demonstrates that the manufacture of images went beyond painters and carvers of wood and stone and had the potential to impact a wide range of Nahua artisans in many areas of the marketplace. Images from two separate 1721 testaments demonstrate that goldsmiths and silversmiths were involved with more than the accoutrements of the images. One, a Virgin of Guadalupe, possessed golden arms, and the second, a San Francisco, was made entirely out of silver.[104]

The market for saints' images in Mexico City seems to have developed by 1564 and was apparently a somewhat contested area. According to Bautista, on 22 September of this year a group of painters from the four barrios of Mexico Tenochtitlan went to speak with an unnamed official, likely a representative of Archbishop Montúfar. The meeting involved the sale of images in the marketplaces of Mexico Tenochtitlan. Apparently people from both Tetzcoco and Tlatelolco were selling their images at the tianguiz of San Juan Tenochtitlan. The agreement the Nahua painters reached with the official was that they would produce some of their own images and present them to the official and archbishop. Once they presented their images, the official promised to ban images from Tetzcoco (which they said were poorly made) and Tlatelolco, stating that anyone who ignored the order would have his images burned.[105] This edict virtually granted a monopoly of the sale of saints' images within Mexico Tenochtitlan to artisans who lived there. It is not known how successful the ban was, if at all.

Because many of the images were passed from one generation to the next, artisans were responsible not only for their manufacture and supply but also for their maintenance. As early as 1580, Nahuas took their images to specialists for repair and restoration. The 1606 testament of Magdalena Ramírez from San Sebastián Cuitlahuactonco states that her images were left to her by her grandfather and had been renovated by him as well.[106] Although the skill levels of artisans undoubtedly varied, both Nahuas and Spaniards considered some natives exemplary in their craft. Fray Juan de Torquemada claimed at the beginning of the seventeenth century that one indigenous sculptor in the parish of Tlatelolco was better than some of his Spanish counterparts.[107] Similarly, don Carlos Sigüenza y Góngora relates the story of an indigenous woman, Francisca de San Miguel, who prayed for an image of the crucified Christ. Three indigenous men dressed in white were credited with its delivery, and probably its construction, to the convent in which San Miguel was cloistered. Sigüenza refers to the image as the "most beautiful carving of Christ in Mexico [City]."[108]

The market for religious items expanded beyond simply the support of religious images to include other personal affects, such as rosaries. It is difficult to identify when a specific market for rosaries developed in Mexico City. Although the rosary was predominantly a Dominican devotion, other religious orders, including the Franciscans and Augustinians, embraced it. Dominican friar Tomás de San Juan, later known as Tomás del Rosario, is credited with the introduction of the devotion to New Spain, circa 1535.[109] The Franciscans began to teach the rosary and other bead prayers by the 1540s, and the strings of beads make appearances in works by both Sahagún and Gante. Moreover, Nahuas appear to have started selling rosary beads by as early as 1569, when Molina made reference to them in his confession manual.[110] During the late sixteenth century a cofradía dedicated to Nuestra Señora del Rosario had been established in the parish of Mixtecos.[111] By 1623, images of Nuestra Señora del Rosario were cared for in Nahua households and continued to make an appearance in testaments until at least 1700.[112]

Though none of the wills demonstrate ownership of a rosary, other evidence, such as Molina's mention of rosary vendors, suggests that Nahuas were purchasing and making rosaries during the sixteenth century. Indeed, Molina's 1552 model cofradía constitution assumes ownership of a rosary by cofrades. And though the San Josef cofradía constitution does not mention a rosary specifically, the number and type of prayers it recommends that its members recite suggest that cofrades owned rosaries for the purpose of reciting their prayers.[113]

It is uncertain whether the Nahuas possessed rosaries during the sixteenth century, but they were definitely manufacturing and selling them by the end of the seventeenth. Census-like records from 1691 and 1692 note the occupation of five men, three from the barrio of San Juan and two from Tlatelolco, as *rosarieros*, individuals who sell or make rosaries and likely do both. Inasmuch as the evidence is for Nahuas who lived with Spaniards, or outside of their parish, it is probable that there were many more rosarieros at this time.[114] As with other artisans and vendors, such as a *zapatero* (shoemaker), this was likely their principal form of employment, suggesting that enough people—Spaniards, Nahuas, and castas—purchased or had their rosaries repaired on a regular enough basis to allow them to be identified as specialists. Other individuals were listed in the documents as *peones* (manual laborers) or without any designation of specific employment.

The only rosarieros named were men, but the sale of religious paraphernalia involved both male and female vendors. Women had been active in the marketplace during the precontact period and continued to be visible in both the sixteenth and seventeenth centuries. In 1623 a female Nahua candlemaker was selling her wares in the Tlatelolco tianguiz. Doubtless, candles were sold for purposes other than religion, but it is possible that some of her profit came from sales intended for religious use. Table 8 lists known marketplace items that were sold for religious use and other purposes. Though not all of the goods listed here were intended solely for religious use, the table does demonstrate the impact that personal shrines and religion probably had on the marketplace and the economy.

Because Mexico City was the capital of the viceroyalty, its marketplaces had regular interactions with other regions of New Spain. Goods arrived in the capital to fulfill the demands of the local populace. Similarly, Mexico City produced goods that were sold to other locales, and many of these goods went to support the expansion of Christianity. The Codice Sierra, created in Oaxaca, provides a list of the expenses generated by the *ñuu* (Mixtec equivalent of altepetl) of Santa Catalina Texupan between 1550 and 1564. Included are items to be purchased from Mexico City, including silver candlesticks, candleholders, and flutes. With many of these items it is difficult or impossible to know who was making the item or selling it, but in one case we know that in 1554 they paid forty-two pesos for a Mexica to teach the *teopan nenque* (church dwellers), showing that one of the "goods" produced in Mexico City was indigenous teachers. These teachers were apparently hired out to support Catholicism within thirty years of the fall of Tenochtitlan.[115]

The development of saint veneration in Nahua households in Mexico City suggests a more personal embrace of Catholicism than is otherwise visible on the macro scale of altepetl and Church studies. Such a deep penetration of

Table 8. Goods Used for Religious Purposes Sold in Sixteenth-Century Mexico City Marketplaces

Item	*Earliest Known Date*	*Citation*
Tobacco	1540s–1550s?	Lockhart, *Nahuas*, pp. 187–188; Durand-Forest, "Cambios," pp. 121–124; Chimalpahin, *Annals*, p. 65
Paint or dyes	1540s–1550s?	Lockhart, *Nahuas*, pp. 187–188; Durand-Forest, "Cambios," pp. 121–124; Bautista, *¿Cómo te confundes?*, p. 199
Feathers[a]	1540s–1550s?	Lockhart, *Nahuas*, pp. 187–188; Durand-Forest, "Cambios," pp. 121–124; AGN, Tierras, v. 49, e. 5
Cloaks	1540s–1550s?	Lockhart, *Nahuas*, pp. 187–188; Durand-Forest, "Cambios," pp. 121–124; NL, Ayer, MS 1481, B(3)1
Mats	1540s–1550s?	Lockhart, *Nahuas*, pp. 187–188; Durand-Forest, "Cambios," pp. 121–124; Grijalva, *Crónica*, p. 162
Capes	1540s–1550s?	Lockhart, *Nahuas*, pp. 187–188; Durand-Forest, "Cambios," pp. 121–124; BNF, FM 299
Silk	1540s–1550s?	Lockhart, *Nahuas*, pp. 187–188; Durand-Forest, "Cambios," pp. 121–124; NL, Ayer, MS 1481, B(3)1
Candles[b]	1550s (Woman candlemaker in Mexico City by 1623)	Lockhart, *Nahuas*, pp. 187–188; AHFZ Constitution; Grijalva, *Crónica*, p. 162; BNF, FM 299
Saints images	1564	Bautista, *¿Cómo te confundes?*, pp. 251–253
Clay candle holders (in shape of angels)	1598	Chimalpahin, *Annals*, p. 65
Leaded censers (in shape of male or female saints)	1598	Chimalpahin, *Annals*, p. 65
Rosaries	1569?	Molina, *Confesionario*, f. 37v; AGN Historia, v. 413, e. 1

Note: The table is limited to those items that have been cited as sold in one of the Mexico City marketplaces. This list should, in all probability, be expanded. Missing from it are such items as the jewelry mentioned in the text as well as flowers and perhaps certain types of food found so frequently in offerings today. For an example of modern-day saint offerings, as well as other types of offerings, in an indigenous village, see Sandstrom, *Corn Is Our Blood*, pp. 292–293.

a. At this time, evidence for the use of feathers in personal oratories during the colonial period has not been found. However, feathers were used in the decoration of Huitzilopochtli's cloak during the precontact era and for the ornamentation of priestly garb in the colonial period. It is likely that they were still used in the home. Moreover, they are included here because there is evidence of their sale in the marketplace until at least the 1580s.

TABLE 8 (*continued*)

b. The earliest known documentary evidence for candles in the Mexico City marketplaces is in 1623 in the Tlatelolco market. The dates provided here reflect an earlier probable date. Evidence does demonstrate that candles were sold in Coyoacan as early as 1550. Additionally, the cofradía constitution of San Josef makes frequent reference to their use. It seems highly unlikely that people living in the viceregal capital would travel to Coyoacan for their candles.

Christianity required a greater availability of religious items at the marketplaces of Mexico City. As Christian worship became common, there was a complementary dynamic—altepetl-wide influence extending even to individuals and local markets to satisfy supply and demand. The needs of consumers such as friaries, indigenous chapels, convents, cofradías, trade groups, and families were met by a remarkable variety of producers, from pearl divers on coastal regions to local silversmiths, painters, and sculptors, all for the altepetl marketplace.

The training for the manufacture of religious items began in the mendicant colegios, most notably the Colegio de San Josef de los Naturales. Whether the mendicant teachers intended this training to support the sale of items for indigenous family shrines is not known. However, Nahuas who were either trained or partially schooled in European artistic genres likely met the demand for religious goods. Because use of and care for the images may have incorporated some precontact traditions, it is also probable that some of the paintings and carvings, as with the murals of Malinalco, included some precontact symbolism.

Saint veneration and home altars flourished during the sixteenth and seventeenth centuries. Such popularity would not have been possible without, at least, the initial training received at the hands of Franciscan teachers and the growth in the market for religious wares. Certain aspects of the veneration of Catholic saints may have been tied to the worship of precontact deities, such as the gifting of cloaks and sweeping, but new Christian paraphernalia appeared at the Nahua marketplaces and in homes, such as rosary beads, suggesting an embrace of, if not a partial interest in, Catholicism at a very personal level.

To gain a better understanding of Nahua Christian belief and practice during the colonial period, the fellowship of the individual in the community must be considered. Staying with the theme of the saints, it appears that by the end of the sixteenth century and beginning of the seventeenth some individuals believed in the saints' powers of intercession. Their trust may also have stimulated the acquisition and veneration of images. The belief in miracles performed by San Nicolás de Tolentino prompted Nahuas and Spaniards to designate him the patron saint of Mexico City. With his ascension to patron saint status, ownership of his image seems to have increased in Nahua homes across the city. Clearly, religious artistic training, adoration of images, and sale of religious goods were related and quite complementary.

Notes

1. On saints, see Stephanie Wood, "Adopted Saints: Christian Images in Nahua Testaments of Late Colonial Toluca," *Americas* 47 (1991): pp. 259–293; and Antonio Rubial García, "Icons of Devotion: The Appropriation and Use of Saints in New Spain," in *Local Religion in Colonial Mexico*, ed. Martin Austin Nesvig (Albuquerque: University of New Mexico Press, 2006), pp. 37–61. On markets, see Lockhart, *Nahuas*, pp. 176–198; and Hassig, *Trade*, pp. 228–240. For references to education, see chapter 2.

2. The tlaxilacalli placement of both San Juan Moyotlan marketplaces is my best estimate. It is known that the main San Juan tianguiz was located next to the visita chapel of San Juan de la Penetencia in the southeast corner of the barrio. Two tlaxilacalli within the barrio have the Christian title San Juan, but one of them, Chichimecapan, is a tlaxilacalli known to be resident to a community of Otomis and thus is an unlikely location for a Mexica marketplace, considering the latter's view of the Otomis. The other difficulty with this placement is that I have found two tlaxilacalli in San Juan with the name Xihuitongo; the existence of two of the same name within one barrio would be an anomaly. They may have been a single tlaxilacalli before the Spaniards arrived that was then split after the defeat of Tenochtitlan, but this is only a guess. The San Hipólito marketplace was located next to the ermita of San Diego in the northwestern portion of the barrio. Based on the placement of the marketplace near this ermita, it seems a safe assumption to locate it in the tlaxilacalli of San Diego de Amanalco. For more information on the tlaxilacalli and their Christian names, see table 1.

3. Hassig, *Trade*, p. 234; and Chimalpahin, *Annals*, map 1. The San Hipólito market was closed, at least for a time, in 1592, but it appears to have reopened by 1607, when it was closed again, this time because of flooding. Moreover, other smaller marketplaces may have opened in different areas in the city. Chimalpahin, *Annals*, pp. 37, 101, 137.

4. Bautista, *¿Cómo te confundes?*, p. 199; and Lockhart, *Nahuas*, pp. 187–188.

5. Gibson, *Aztecs*, p. 119.

6. UNAM, FRAF, caja 64, e. 1208, fs. 1–35; and UNAM, FRAF, caja 106, e. 1461, fs. 11–14.

7. Nahua laborers also helped with the repair and upkeep of other religious buildings. As late as 1690, indigenous workers could be found helping to repair buildings belonging to the nunnery of la Concepción near the visita of San Juan de la Penetencia. AGN, Bienes Nacionales, v. 100, e. 58.

8. Mendieta, *Historia*, vol. 1, pp. 489–491; and Kubler, *Mexican Architecture*, p. 153.

9. Vetancurt, *Teatro*, pt. 1, p. 23.

10. Mendieta, *Historia*, vol. 2, pp. 70–73; Torquemada, *Monarquía*, vol. 3, p. 211; and Kubler, *Mexican Architecture*, p. 153.

11. Motolinia, *Motolinia's History*, p. 154.

12. Vetancurt, *Teatro*, pt. 1, p. 23.

13. Ibid., pt. 1, pp. 22–23; pt. 2, pp. 59–60; pt. 4, p. 33; and Chimalpahin, *Annals*, p. 64.

14. Vetancurt, *Teatro*, pt. 1, p. 66; pt. 2, p. 59.

15. Oroz, *Oroz*, p. 84.

16. The Nahuas used a white liquid from the red leaf stems of the tianquizpepetla to reduce swelling, and these plants were available in the friary. Vetancurt mentioned the *floripundio* (angel's trumpet, genus *Brugmansia*), a small tree, which also served artistic and medicinal uses. Regarding the tianquizpepetla, Francisco Hernández in his sixteenth-century botanical history of New Spain states that it is another name for the *chalcuitlatl* plant. When tasted initially it is sweet but then has an acrid aftertaste. The Nahuas used it in food and drinks and in enemas against typhus. Additionally, Hernández believed the drink and food acted as a diuretic and could be useful against expelling stones. He does

not mention the floripundio. Intriguingly, neither the Badianus manuscript nor fray Bernardino de Sahagún in the Florentine Codex mentions either of these plants. Vetancurt, *Teatro*, pt. 1, pp. 40, 62, and pt. 2, p. 59; *The Badianus Manuscript (Codex Barberini, Latin 241) Vatican Library: An Aztec Herbal of 1552*, ed. and trans. Emily Walcott Emmart (Baltimore: Johns Hopkins University Press, 1940); Francisco Hernández, *Historia de las plantas de Nueva España*, 3 vols. (México: Imprenta Universitaria, 1946), vol. 3, p. 720; Sahagún, *Florentine Codex*, vol. 11; and Robert A. Bye Jr. and Edelmira Linares, "Mexican Market Plants of 16th Century: I. Plants Recorded in *Historia Natural de Nueva España*," *Journal of Ethnobiology* 10, no. 2 (Winter 1990), p. 162.

17. AGN, Tierras, v. 49, e. 5; and Berdan, *Aztecs*, p. 27.

18. Bautista, *¿Cómo te confundes?*, pp. 151, 271.

19. Chimalpahin, *Annals*, pp. 43–45.

20. Mendieta, *Historia*, vol. 2, p. 104.

21. Other traditional crafts that had been highly esteemed by the Nahuas in precontact times, such as featherwork, also underwent significant change. Based on the testament of Angelina Martina, it appears that featherwork was still sought as late as 1580. In her will she mentions owning a minimum of 415 feathers of differing varieties. AGN, Tierras, v. 49, e. 5. For more information on Nahua feather workers in the precontact period, see Berdan, *Aztecs*, p. 26.

22. Sahagún, *Florentine Codex*, vol. 1, p. 54.

23. Robertson, *Mexican Manuscript*, p. 27.

24. Susan Schroeder, "Writing Two Cultures: The Meaning of "Amoxtli" (Book) in Nahua New Spain," in *New World, First Nations: Native Peoples of Mesoamerica and the Andes under Colonial Rule*, ed. David Cahill and Blanca Tovías (Eastbourne, East Sussex: Sussex Academic Press, 2006), pp. 22–24.

25. Motolinia, *Memoriales*, p. 5.

26. Díaz del Castillo, *Conquest*, p. 91.

27. Lockhart, *Nahuas*, p. 326.

28. Schroeder, "Writing," pp. 20–24.

29. Torquemada, *Monarquía*, vol. 3, p. 211; and Edgerton, *Theaters*, pp. 119–120.

30. Torquemada, *Monarquia*, vol. 3, pp. 208–210.

31. Mundy, *Mapping*, p. 77.

32. Lockhart, *Nahuas*, p. 423.

33. Bautista, *¿Cómo te confundes?*, pp. 160–161, see n54.

34. Ibid., pp. 181, 251, 255, 275.

35. Berdan, *Aztecs*, pp. 27–28.

36. For more information on the continued use of pictorial land records during the colonial period, see Richard Conway, "Accessories to Inheritance: Nahua Pictorial Documents and Testaments in Early Colonial Central Mexico," in *Native Wills from the Colonial Americas: Dead Giveaways in a New World*, ed. Mark Christensen and Jonathan Truitt (Salt Lake City: University of Utah Press, 2016), chap. 5.

37. Keber notes that there has been disagreement regarding the identification of the artists of the document. Ellen T. Baird, for example, argues that the authors and artists may have been the same. However, there are only four known indigenous authors and six different artistic styles. Moreover, as Keber points out, the artists' hands do not match the handwriting of the scribes. Eloise Quiñones Keber, "An Introduction to the Images, Artists, and Physical Features of the *Primeros Memoriales*," in Bernardino de Sahagún, *Primeros Memoriales: Paleography of Nahuatl Text and English Translation*, trans. Thelma D. Sullivan, ed. H. B. Nicholson, Arthur J. O. Anderson, Charles E. Dibble, Eloise Quiñones Keber, and Wayne Ruwet (Norman: University of Oklahoma Press with Patrimonio Nacional and Real Academia de la Historia, Madrid, 1997), pp. 33–34.

38. Bautista, *¿Cómo te confundes?*, p. 311; and *Codex Valeriano*.

39. Another exception can be made, in this case with the development of the Techialoyan codices at the end of the seventeenth century. However, even these were made with the intent of demonstrating land ownership in a specific altepetl. Moreover, most, if not all, of the documents were created for regions outside of Mexico Tenochtitlan. Stephanie Wood, "The Techialoyan Codices," in *Sources and Methods for the Study of Post-conquest Mesoamerican Ethnohistory*, Provisional Version (e-book), ed. James Lockhart, Lisa Sousa, and Stephanie Wood (Eugene, Or. Wired Humanities Project, University of Oregon, 2007), http://whp.uoregon.edu/Lockhart/index.html, pp. 1–3.

40. AGN, Bienes Nacionales, v. 732, e. 1. The friar's use of his belt in this way was probably seen as doubly offensive, for the belt, in the view of Chimalpahin, at least, was supposed to be representative of the Franciscans assisting to lift souls out of purgatory. In 1613 an image belonging to the cofradía de las Ánimas in the barrio of Santa María and depicting an image of San Francisco using his belt for this purpose went in procession. Also of note is the punishment for missing mass—stripping followed by whipping. Although it is not known how common this was, a similar case occurred in 1612 at the chapel of San Josef. Chimalpahin, *Annals*, pp. 195, 241. The case of the whipping at San Josef is briefly treated in chapter 3.

41. Bautista, *¿Cómo te confundes?*, pp. 231–233.

42. AGN, Bienes Nacionales, v. 732, e. 1; and Mundy, *Mapping*, p. 76 (see especially n6).

43. Vetancurt, *Teatro*, pt. 2, p. 59. A similar division of forces for the creation of an altarpiece occurred in 1564. The piece contained images of several saints, a crucifix, and the Last Supper. The work was created in multiple parts divided among the four barrios. Bautista, *¿Cómo te confundes?*, p. 295.

44. Chimalpahin, *Annals*, pp. 47–49.

45. Ibid., p. 65.

46. Jeanette Favrot Peterson, *The Paradise Garden Murals of Malinalco: Utopia and Empire in Sixteenth-Century Mexico* (Austin: University of Texas Press, 1993), pp. 39–40, 134–135.

47. Motolinia, *Memoriales*, p. 93; and Bautista, *¿Cómo te confundes?*, p. 275. For more information on the growth of cofradías in Mexico Tenochtitlan, see chapter 4.

48. Dibble, *Historia*, p. 105; and Lockhart, *Nahuas*, p. 237.

49. Christian, *Local Religion*, pp. 31–35, 55–59.

50. Ibid., p. 65.

51. Eire, *From Madrid*, pp. 258–260, 266–267, 332.

52. Ibid., pp. 284, 284n1, 371.

53. Lockhart, *Nahuas*, pp. 121–122.

54. Chimalpahin, *Annals*, pp. 55, 81–83.

55. Oroz, *Oroz*, pp. 157–159; Chimalpahin, *Annals*, pp. 75, 81–83; and John McAndrew, *The Open Air Churches of Sixteenth-Century Mexico: Atrios, Posas, Open Chapels, and Other Studies* (Cambridge, Mass.: Harvard University Press, 1965), p. 248.

56. Chimalpahin, *Annals*, pp. 187–193.

57. Vetancurt, *Teatro mexicano*, pt. 4, p. 134.

58. Gruzinski, "Indian Confraternities," pp. 217–218.

59. Taylor, *Magistrates*, p. 268.

60. Rubial García, "Icons of Devotion," pp. 42–45.

61. Lockhart, *Nahuas*, p. 235.

62. Burkhart, *Slippery Earth*, p. 40.

63. Berdan, *Aztecs*, p. 131.

64. Burkhart, *Slippery Earth*, p. 73. In 1582, Franciscans in Mexico City received permission to print a calendar dedicated to their religious practices. AGN, Indios, v. 2, e. 188, f. 42.

65. García, "Icons of Devotion," p. 40.

66. Dibble, *Historia*, p. 105; and Lockhart, *Nahuas*, p. 237.

67. Cline and Leon-Portilla, *Testaments*, doc. 29.

68. Ricard, *Spiritual Conquest*, p. 269.

69. Diego Durán, *Book of the Gods and Rites and the Ancient Calendar*, ed. and trans. Fernando Horcasitas and Doris Heyden (Norman: University of Oklahoma Press, 1971), p. 235.

70. Grijalva, *Crónica*, p. 162.

71. Dibble, *Historia*, p. 105; and Lockhart, *Nahuas*, p. 237.

72. See appendix 4 for citations.

73. Chimalpahin, *Annals*, p. 65.

74. Lockhart, *Nahuas*, p. 237.

75. Grijalva, *Crónica*, p. 162.

76. The earliest "unambiguous" example, from a Nahuatl testament, previously came from 1580 in the Culhuacan area. Lockhart, *Nahuas*, p. 243.

77. BNF, Fondo Mexicains, 112; and AGN, Tierras, v. 48, e. 4.

78. AGN, Hospital de Jesús, leg. 210, e. 4.

79. Wood, "Adopted Saints," p. 289.

80. This information is based on ninety testaments from Mexico City. Crucifixes were included in the tally of images from these wills. A total of four were discovered, two from the sixteenth century and one each from the seventeenth and eighteenth centuries. The increase in images appears to have been widespread in New Spain. An examination of sixty-five testaments (fifty-two complete wills and thirteen fragments) from sixteenth-century Culhuacan found only three crucifixes, one image, and three unnamed altarpieces. In contrast, Stephanie Wood's study of 170 testaments from the latter half of seventeenth-century and eighteenth-century Toluca found that more than one hundred individuals, 63 percent, owned images at the time of their death. Cline and Leon-Portilla, *Testaments*; and Wood, "Adopted Saints," p. 270.

81. Wood, "Adopted Saints," p. 277.

82. Chimalpahin, *Annals*, pp. 191–193, 305; and see appendix 4.

83. AGN, Tierras, v. 49, e. 5; and BNF, Fondo Mexicains, 299.

84. Cline and León-Portilla, *Testaments*.

85. AGN, Tierras, v. 1774, e. 10; and AGN, Tierras, v. 1595, e. 4.

86. AGN, Tierras, v. 104, e. 8.

87. AGN, Tierras, v. 1595, e. 4; BNF, Fondo Mexicains, 299; AGN, Bienes Nacionales, v. 387, e. 1; NL, Ayer Collection, MS 1481, F5; AGN, Bienes Nacionales, v. 1766, e. 7; AGN, Tierras, v. 1595, e. 4; NL, Ayer Collection, MS 1481, B(3)a; NL, Ayer Collection, MS 1481, B(3)e; AGN, Bienes Nacionales, v. 1096, e. 8; NL, Ayer Collection, MS 1481, B(3)F; AGN, Tierras, v. 163, e. 2; AGN, Civil, v. 1763, e. 2, fs. 3–5; AGN, Civil, v. 1828, e. 5; NL, Ayer Collection, MS 1481, B(3)1; AGN, Tierras, v. 1720, e. 7; AGN, Bienes Nacionales, v. 339, e. 6; AGN, Tierras, v. 101, e. 2, fs. 2; AGN, Tierras, v. 109, e. 4; NL, Ayer Collection, MS 1481, B(3)b; AGN, Tierras, v. 2776 pt. 1, e. 18; AGN, Bienes Nacionales, v. 1766, e. 7; NL, Ayer Collection, MS 1481, B(3)d; AGN, Tierras, v. 163, e. 2; AGN, Civil, v. 592, e. 1; AGN, Tierras, v. 155, e. 9; AGN, Tierras, v. 128 pt. 2, e. 2; ANM, Hernando de Arauz #4, v. 7, yrs. 1619–1622, fs. 7–12v; AGN, Hospital de Jesús, leg. 210, e. 4; AGN, Tierras, v. 1586, e. 2; AGN, Hospital de Jesús, leg. 210, e. 4; and AGN, Indiferente Virreinal, caja 3873, e. 7.

88. Wood, "Adopted Saints," p. 270.

89. AGN, Tierras, v. 104, e. 8; NL, Ayer Collection, MS 1481, B(3)k; AGN, Indiferente Virreinal, caja 1124, e. 25; AGN, Tierras, v. 1458, e. 11; and AGN, Tierras, v. 581, e. 2.

90. AGN, Tierras, v. 101, e. 2, f. 2; and Grijalva, *Crónica*, p. 162.

91. Chimalpahin, *Annals*, pp. 191–193, 305; and see appendix 4. See especially, AGN, Tierras, v. 49, e. 5; and NL, Ayer Collection, MS 1481, B(3)a.

92. Truitt, "Revelations," pp. 58–59; and Susan Kellogg and Matthew Restall, "The Irreplaceable Window: Reflections on the Study of Indigenous Wills," in *Native Wills from the Colonial Americas: Dead Giveaways in a New World*, ed. Mark Christensen and Jonathan Truitt (Salt Lake City: University of Utah Press, 2016), p. 244.

93. NL, Ayer Collection, MS 1481, B(3)1. The Nahua notary of this document used a comma-like symbol where many other notaries used a period. In an effort to provide a transcription as close to the original as possible, I use the comma rather than the period.

94. Ibid.

95. Lockhart, *Nahuas*, p. 238.

96. NL, Ayer Collection, MS 1481, B(3)1. Nahuatl: "aço quimochicahuiliz in Dios, aço yehuatl ytlachpancatzin mochihuaz in tlaixiptlayotzitzintin."

97. Berdan, *Aztecs*, p. 28.

98. A possible comparison can be made between the feathers that adorned Huitzilopochtli's cloak and the satin fabric for the saint. Feathers and clothing made from them were highly valued during the precontact period. Similarly, satin was an expensive fabric during the sixteenth and seventeenth centuries. NL, Ayer Collection, MS 1481, B(3)1; and BNF, Fondo Mexicains, 299.

99. ANM, Hernando de Arauz #4, v. 7, yrs. 1619–1622, fs. 7–12v.

100. NL, Ayer Collection, MS 1481, B(3)1; BNF, Fondo Mexicains, 299; and ANM, Hernando de Arauz #4, v. 7, yrs. 1619–1622, fs. 7–12v.

101. Along with the three aforementioned wills, AGN, Bienes Nacionales, v. 339, e. 6; AGN, Tierras, 1595, e. 4; NL, Ayer Collection, MS 1481, B(3)e; AGN, Bienes Nacionales, v. 1766, e. 7; and AGN, Civil, v. 1763, e. 2.

102. Spaniards encountered indigenous pearl divers in the Baja California region in 1533. For more information on pearl diving in this area, see Peter Gerhard, "Pearl Diving in Lower California, 1533–1830," *Pacific Historical Review* 25, no. 3 (August 1956): pp. 239–249.

103. NL, Ayer Collection, MS 1481, B(3)e. "yhuan niquitohua oc çepa aoctle quitlanizque in oficiales tepotzpitzque in ipanpatzinco in christo , ca ye onicnonemactili ytlanetzin iztac teocuitlalt."

104. AGN, Tierras, v. 104, e. 8; and NL Ayer Collection, MS 1481, B(3)k.

105. Bautista, *¿Cómo te confundes?*, pp. 251–253.

106. AGN, Tierras, v. 1595, e. 4; and AGN, Tierras, v. 49, e. 5.

107. Torquemada, *Monarquía*, v. 3, p. 209.

108. Sigüenza y Góngora, *Paraíso*, pp. 286–287. This story is treated in more detail in chapter 3.

109. Louise M. Burkhart, *Before Guadalupe: The Virgin Mary in Early Colonial Nahuatl Literature* (Albany, N.Y.: Institute for Mesoamerican Studies University at Albany, 2001), pp. 121–123.

110. Molina, *Confesionario mayor*, f. 37v; and Eileen M. Mulhare and Barry D. Sell, "Bead-Prayers and the Spiritual Conquest of Nahua Mexico: Gante's 'Coronas' of 1553," *Estudios de Cultura Náhuatl* 33 (2002), p. 219.

111. Agustín Dávila Padilla, *Historia de la fundación y discurso de la provincia de Santiago de México, de la orden de predicadores, 1596–1625* (Mexico: Editorial Academia Literaria, 1955), pp. 354–360.

112. BNF, Fondo Mexicains, 299; AGN, Bienes Nacionales, v. 1766, e. 7; AGN, Civil, v. 1828, e. 5; AGN, Tierras, v. 101, e. 2; and AGN, Tierras, v. 104, e. 8.

113. AHFZ Constitution; and Molina, *Nahua Confraternities*, pp. 112–113.

114. AGN, Historía, v. 413, e. 1.

115. *Codice Sierra*, f. 12.

Conclusion: Refashioning Nahua-Divine Interactions

Though Nahuas had not experienced Christianity prior to 1519, the idea of supporting and interacting with religion was familiar to them. Much as the precontact image for military defeat, a destroyed pyramid (see fig. 1), did not represent the end of life in an altepetl, so the defeat of the Aztec Empire did not bring an end to the need for religion. Almost immediately after the fall of the capital, Nahuas started working to rebuild their altepetl. In the process they taught the Spaniards about the traditional political boundaries within their capital. Although a doctrina overlay the entirety of the altepetl initially, the construction of visitas in each of the four barrios and the erection of smaller ermitas in various tlaxilacalli served to reinforce precontact political and religious divisions. The importance of structures as a symbol of community unity is seen repeatedly in the writings of Nahua authors, in the legal battles waged by tlaxilacalli to preserve their religious sites, and in the way indigenous author/artists indicated geographic locations by using religious structures, as had been done in the precontact period (see figs. 1, 2, 7).

When in the mid-sixteenth century Archbishop Montúfar tried to secularize the doctrina of San Josef, he did it along prehispanic organizational lines, thereby demonstrating the continuation of organizational structures between the two periods. Despite his religious authority the Nahuas spoke out, through violence, to secure the spiritual leaders they wanted. Later, in 1689 when the last Hapsburg effort to secularize the indigenous parishes occurred, the ecclesiastical leadership, led by Archbishop Aguiar y Seijas y Ulloa, failed again. Over the course of the sixteenth and seventeenth centuries, then, the indigenous residents of Mexico Tenochtitlan continued to use Spanish institutions to secure their own political and religious ambitions. This was clearly the case when the parish of Santa Cruz managed to form by breaking away from both San Pablo and San Sebastián. And though this was important to the Nahuas of that parish, the change hardly influenced Spanish ecclesiastical power structures, because the Augustinians, who were in charge of both San Pablo and San Sebastián, remained in charge at Santa Cruz. Changes like this one came at the behest of Nahuas working through their own cultural understanding. The indigenous community continued to maintain and control key properties—religious and otherwise, such as the marketplace—and to leverage that real estate to their own perceived benefit, as seen with the gifting of San Juan de la Penetencia to the Poor Clares. Franciscans may have influenced that donation, but there are also clear instances of Nahuas working directly against their Franciscan spiritual advisors, as in the cases involving fray Gerónimo de Zárate.

When it came to interactions with their religion, the Nahuas often acted of their own accord. Despite having given their visita to the Poor Clares, the Nahuas cared for the chapel. This was most evident in 1692 when they requested and received a reduction in tribute so they could conduct the necessary restorations. In the process of submitting the requisite paperwork for permission to do the repairs and receive a tribute reduction, the indigenous community left evidence suggesting that they took it upon themselves to continue to care for their religious sites. Though it is clear that what the Nahuas cared for had changed over the course of the colonial period, the community still demonstrated a desire to attend to religious spaces and see that they fulfilled their obligations to the divine.

The care and organization of indigenous religious space extended to creating hierarchies of leadership within the chapels. Known as the teopantlaca, the individuals who staffed the chapels took attendance, cared for religious paraphernalia, cleaned, provided music, and watched out for the community beyond the confines of the physical grounds of the religious buildings. The prominence and importance of the leadership positions to the community grew over time and intersected with jobs in the secular government. Within the altepetl a hierarchy of chapels appeared; fiscals at ermitas did not possess the coveted title *don* that those at the more prestigious principal parishes did. Beyond the hierarchy from ermita to primary chapel, the chapel of San Josef continued to hold an elevated status among the indigenous population until the end of the seventeenth century. Interestingly, documents suggest that, despite Mexico Tenochtitlan having the largest Spanish population of any location in New Spain, its highest-ranked indigenous religious position, the fiscal, still operated with considerable autonomy when it came to negotiating disputes within the indigenous community. Though friars approved the solutions, it appears that they were comfortable following the recommendations of the fiscales.

By the beginning of the seventeenth century, some Nahuas viewed certain non-chapel spaces as religious sites. When these locations came into contention, community members gathered to protect them through the legal system. The fight for these properties makes it clear that parish identification was very important to members of the indigenous community. Beyond their association with their home parish and community leaders' desire to protect unofficial religious space, it is evident that women continued to work alongside men on behalf of the community's religious responsibilities despite the lack of official positions within the Spanish sanctioned hierarchies of the Church. Indigenous women's involvement continued to change over the course of the colonial period, but glimpses of their responsibilities and actions in testaments, lawsuits, and other sources demonstrate that many of their roles continued to differ from that of Spanish women.

While establishing the physical requirements for the regular celebration of mass, Spaniards started teaching the Nahuas of Tenochtitlan about Christianity. To assist in this process they opened schools and provided advanced training for some students at the Colegio de Santa Cruz in Tlateloloco. Despite the Europeans' growing despair about indigenous religious education, the Nahuas did learn from the priests who taught them, and they used the skills gained in a multitude of ways inside and outside ecclesiastical walls.

Mendicant friars worked to learn the indigenous languages. As they gained proficiency they started the process of shifting the record-keeping system from pictorials to the Roman alphabet. As early as the 1540s, Nahuas trained in Mexico City used alphabetic script to record information. Over time their literacy created thousands of pages of material, from religious treatises to legal cases and hymnals. By looking at some of the earliest religious works written by friars for the conversion effort and placing them alongside sources like the Codice Sierra, which shows Mexica traveling in New Spain for purposes of teaching other indigenous peoples, it can be inferred that Nahuas exported the skills they learned beyond the confines of their chapels. When we look at other educational pedagogies employed by the Franciscans, it seems likely that the Nahuas shared those skills with the members of their community and households as well.

Early in the proselytization process the Franciscans started teaching Nahuas European-style music. They introduced instruments, taught the Nahuas how to make certain instruments, instructed them in chant and polyphonic music, and taught them to read European musical notations. During the precontact period music had been important, just as record keeping was, but the processes of learning, creating, and performing music were different. Unfortunately, we do not know what role indigenous women played in music prior to 1519; with that knowledge, we might be able to look for continuities with the colonial period. Evidence suggests that women were involved as more than simple spectators during the colonial period. By the beginning of the seventeenth century, one woman was at least a caretaker of a traditional drum, and at the end of the Hapsburg period one indigenous woman had probably learned to play the harp. If she did, either it was accomplished of her own accord or someone from the community taught her.

Religious dramas were, perhaps, the most foreign of the pedagogical tools the mendicants deployed in their efforts to teach Christianity, yet still there was continuity between the religious pageantry of the prehispanic period and the neixcuitilli of the colonial era. This instructional aid combined alphabetic literacy with music in ways that were unlike those of Spanish dramas, and the encouragement of memorization of stories was familiar to pre-Columbian Nahua culture. Taken in conjunction with the seeming autonomy of the fiscales, choirmasters, and female musicians, the growth, development, and performance of neixcuitilli, despite ecclesiastical opposition, suggest that even in the viceregal capital indigenous communities negotiated many of the terms of their own religious involvement outside of the sanctioned Church hierarchies.

Europe's society and religion were patriarchal and, as they intersected with the indigenous populations of the Americas, Spaniards sought out male leaders. This does not mean that they did not make use of women, but they did not accord them anywhere near the same level of respect they did men. Because of the Spaniards' disregard for indigenous women, they did not work to create positions of responsibility for them in the new colonial society. Rather, Spaniards often ignored indigenous women and expressed surprise, or occasionally annoyance, when Nahua women continued to be active and integral members of their communities. Yet, through the lens of women's testaments and the accounts of both Spanish and Nahua chroniclers, we can see that indigenous women far outstripped men in terms of their dedication to, and interaction with, religion. In terms of charitable giving, joining religious brotherhoods, collecting saints' images, and for pure religiosity women appear to engage earlier and in greater number than their male counterparts. Indigenous men became more active at the end of the seventeenth century as women's influence appears to have waned, but in terms of establishing the religion the record strongly suggests that women were more significant.

Female Nahuas faced a veritable wall of patriarchal opposition when trying to maintain their traditional positions of leadership within the Spanish-sanctioned indigenous political hierarchy. Despite Spanish customs, they carved out spaces for themselves, with the support of their male counterparts, within the religious brotherhoods and in the community at large. Although the positions of cihuatepixqui, tenantzin, diputada, and potentially others only make the occasional appearance in the extant documentation, their continued presence, though less frequent toward the end of the seventeenth century, suggests a continuity of female leadership within the indigenous community. Spanish record-keeping traditions and male notaries, then, were responsible for women's silence in the historical record. This is not to suggest that the position of women within the wider community did not lessen over the seventeenth century. On the contrary, wills alone suggest that they were not allowed to act as witnesses to the degree they had previously. And yet their activities on stage in the neixcuitilli, and their appearance as a group within lawsuits, demonstrate their ongoing role as advocates for the larger Nahua community.

Most indigenous women were denied the opportunity to profess as nuns during the Hapsburg period, yet they entered convents as donadas. As dedicated servants, some of these women received high accolades, and their devotion to Catholicism paid off with the eventual establishment of the first convent dedicated to women of royal indigenous blood in the early eighteenth century. Conversely, there is not as much information on indigenous donados, their male counterparts—in fact, the dearth of information has left donados out of this book entirely. Some indigenous men were able to take the vows of a priest, but they were few and far between. And whereas women were eventually granted a convent, the men's effort to obtain a seminary was denied in the second half of the eighteenth century.

As neophytes to the faith, Nahuas were generally prevented from taking the vows of a priest or nun and therefore denied the opportunities to climb the religious hierarchy. Cofradías were one institution within the Catholic Church that allowed them to be more than simply parishioners within the faith. As a brotherhood and a community, cofradías provided an avenue on which Nahua men and, unlike their Spanish counterparts, women took on positions of leadership within their shared religion. As a community effort the brotherhoods supported and monitored their membership. Cofradías required cofrades to behave in certain prescribed ways while also offering certain benefits of membership. Although the initial cofradía memberships in Mexico Tenochtitlan developed along racial lines and parish membership, by the early seventeenth century they had expanded to include mixed Spanish-Nahua hospital cofradías. As the official number of brotherhoods increased, so too did the existence of unlicensed cofradías. Tracking the unlicensed ones is difficult, but their continued growth is demonstrated by the vexation of the ecclesiastical hierarchy at their very existence. The fact that the Nahuas established unofficial brotherhoods supports the supposition that even in the capital of the viceroyalty the indigenous community possessed enough autonomy in regards to their religious engagement that actions against the illicit brotherhoods were virtually left at an admonition.

As religious brotherhoods, cofradías looked to the care of the broader community. They paraded for feast days and against bad weather and epidemics, among other important occasions. Their ability to go in procession was prized to such an extent that in a few instances, when friars attempted to block them, they sneaked out to go regardless. When Spaniards were afraid of rebellion and blocked Holy Week processions, the Nahuas held theirs within the confines of the Franciscan friary and the chapel of San Josef de los Naturales. Community-building endeavors of the cofradía were especially prevalent by the end of the seventeenth century, when a Nahua-Filipino brotherhood formed. Asians had been in Mexico City for over a century by this point, but their status was mixed. The creation of this brotherhood suggests that more people in Mexico Tenochtitlan had started to view Asians as "Indians" and were open to them being more active within the religious community of the barrio of San Sebastián.

Perhaps the most visible form of daily interaction with Catholicism was the creation and sale of the paraphernalia, such as rosaries, required for the various official ceremonies and for personal devotion. Although Nahuas immediately became involved in the process of supporting the construction of religious structures through labor drafts, their role in creating materials to sustain the divine can be interpreted differently. Many indigenous parishioners were no doubt believers and interacted with the faith as part of that belief. Others were no doubt nonbelievers who saw a valuable market for selling their goods and generating an income to feed their families.

No matter their reasons for engaging in the marketplace of religious goods, Nahua men and women were essential actors in sustaining the divine. Men were the painters and performed the hard physical labor of building and repairing the religious structures. Women appear to have been a dominant force in the marketplace. Looking at land ownership next to the tianguiz as well as at tienda ownership, women outnumbered men. Women's participation in the religious marketplace increases when saints' images are taken into consideration; they were more heavily involved in the purchase, decoration, and care of saints' images during the sixteenth and seventeenth centuries than men. Beyond the cult of saints is the evidence of women's more rapid adoption of cofradías. Although we cannot be certain of how heavily involved women were in making decisions about the brotherhoods, their membership and dedication to cofradías helped them grow and their expansion supported a corresponding increase in the demand for religious paraphernalia. The Nahuas' religious superiors did not insist on their involvement with the saints and images. Rather, the individuals who bought images of saints for their household or brotherhood did so of their own accord. After the purchase of a saint's image, some individuals spent lavishly on providing clothing and other accoutrements for it as well. Just as there is a market for car purchases today that supports aftermarket upgrades, mechanical repairs, and body shops, so too there were multiple layers of support for saints' images, all with varying levels of financial expenditures tied to them.

When the Spaniards introduced Catholicism to central Mexico, they presented it to a culture that held deep religious convictions and understood that there was need to sustain the divine in all its guises. Because it was polytheistic, the precontact responsibilities and expectations of preconact religion could be shifted to support the very high needs—in terms of buildings, images, clothing, and extensive paraphernalia—of Catholicism. In fact, the needs and desires of the early colonial Church could not have been supported without the indigenous population.

Each chapter in this volume represents ways in which the indigenous people of Mexico Tenochtitlan interacted with the colonial divine, Catholicism, during the sixteenth and seventeenth centuries. Though not all of the actions can be directly tied back to pre-Columbian traditions, many of them have roots in that period. The similarities in the responsibilities expected in both religious systems allowed the indigenous parishioners to continue to perform duties that were familiar to them. When acknowledged differences in religious responsibilities were encountered between the two cultures that did not have to do with strict religious dogma, such as the role of women in community leadership, exceptions for indigenous practice were permitted that generally did not appear elsewhere in colonial practice. These adjustments to what was permitted and expected of indigenous parishioners eased the adoption of Catholicism in Mexico City. During the period under consideration change was slow, but the natives controlled that change at its most functional daily level. Although the Catholic Church directed the religious messages in Mexico City and determined what was and was not orthodox Catholicism, the physical support for its structures, the quotidian interactions with its indigenous parishioners, and the way the parishioners used and adopted its lessons, religious and otherwise, were in the hands of Nahuas. The changes they made to their own interactions with the divine built off of their immediate needs and past understandings. One thing that becomes clear is that when it came to their religious responsibilities they were active in determining what role their community took in sustaining the divine in Mexico City.

On the subject of indigenous interaction with Catholicism in Mexico Tenochtitlan, there is still much that needs to be explored in greater detail. The role of the Franciscan schools of Santa Cruz in Santiago Tlatelolco and San Josef de los Naturales is discussed here. Although the Colegio de Santa Cruz is not explored in as great a depth as San Josef, it has received treatment elsewhere. However, a third and very important school, the Mexico City Jesuit Colegio de San Gregorio for Nahuas, opened toward the end of the sixteenth century and lasted until the mid-nineteenth century. Although some work has explored aspects of that colegio, a strong understanding of its influence and benefits to indigenous society is lacking.

The role of indigenous migrants is also essential to a greater understanding of the cosmopolitan nature of Mexico City during the colonial period. Various groups of migrant natives have been mentioned here, but their activities in relation to local society are not known. How essential were they to the establishment of the parish of Mixtecos, for example? Along similar lines, more work needs to look at the establishment of the parish of Santa Cruz Contzinco. Did Mexica live there? Or was Santa Cruz Contzinco organized in response to immigrant needs? Finally, though not Native Americans, Filipinos formed a cofradía with Nahuas in the barrio of San Sebastián at the end of the seventeenth century. What other roles, if any, did they play in the parish of San Sebastián prior to the establishment of the cofradía? Who suggested a joint brotherhood—the Nahuas, the Filipinos, or their Augustinian chaplains?

Noticeably absent from most of this book is the Moctezuma family, though members of the family lived in Tlatelolco before and after the arrival of the Spaniards. There were many Moctezumas still in Mexico Tenochtitlan through the colonial period, but their presence in the community appears to have diminished by the second half of the sixteenth century. This is especially surprising, for Mexico Tenochtitlan was their traditional seat of power. Testaments and other documents suggest that the highest-ranking members of mid-sixteenth-century indigenous society in Tenochtitlan, such as the Moctezuma family and others like don Hernando de Tapia, worked to hispanize themselves and their families. They do not appear in documentation connected to indigenous chapels in Mexico Tenochtitlan. Intriguingly, Moctezuma's granddaughters were some of the only women of indigenous descent allowed to profess as nuns in a Spanish convent, suggesting that the Spanish crown saw them differently. Finally, using don Hernando Tapia's will as support, it seems as if members of the indigenous nobility actively sought to have Spaniards marry their children. By all appearances, it looks as if the highest ranks of Tenochtitlan nobility sought hispanization for their families. Why they decided to abandon their ties to the indigenous population while others reaffirmed it seems to be through a desire to tie their future to the ruling party.

Despite the seeming disassociation of the sixteenth-century Nahua nobility from the indigenous of Mexico Tenochtitlan, by the end of the seventeenth century Nahuas were actively sustaining the colonial divine. They helped define parish boundaries and constructed their own ermitas, they adopted Franciscan pedagogical tools and used them in their feast day celebrations, they utilized cofradías to strengthen community ties, they brought Christianity into their homes in the form of religious images and personal oratories, and they established roles for women as cihuatepixque in cofradías and as donadas in the Spanish convents. They had effectively refashioned interactions with the divine.

Epilogue

Since my research began with the chapel of San Josef de los Naturales, it seems fitting to conclude the project with a brief examination of its decline. By 1749 the process of secularizing the Franciscan parishes of San Joseph, Santiago Tlatelolco, and Santa María la Redonda had resumed. Efforts toward this continued until at least 1772. Archbishop Montúfar had reduced the parish of San Josef in the sixteenth century, but it still covered an impressive geographic area. A 1768 map of the parish of San Josef during the final secularization process reveals that it still enjoyed a substantial presence both on and off the island (fig. 20).

In an effort to maintain control of San Josef, the Franciscans emphasized its history as the first indigenous parish in New Spain. In the eighteenth-century petitions to the crown, they mention the accomplishments of many of their parishioners and students, such as don Antonio Valeriano (the elder). They use the works of fray Juan de Torquemada and fray Juan Bautista in arguments in defense of their ongoing ministry to the Nahuas. Ultimately, the Franciscans lost the argument, and in 1771 a secular priest became chaplain at San Josef and the chapel was opened to Nahua and nonindigenous alike.[1]

The conflict over secularization appears to have been among the Franciscans, the secular Church, and the crown, with no known involvement of the Nahua community. Still, based on one of the concessions granted to the Franciscans, the Nahuas do not appear to have been without agency in the process. For one thing, although the Franciscans lost their position as the administrators of the chapel of San Josef, they were granted the opportunity to continue ministering to the Nahuas, albeit in a different and smaller chapel. In a bit of symmetry, the chapel where they were to continue their work was the chapel of San Antonio de los Callejones in the convent of Santa Clara. Although this chapel was under a different name at this time, it appears that the Nahuas were returning either to the old visita chapel they had donated to the Poor Clares in the 1590s or, at least, to something very near it, for this chapel was part of the convent religious complex. The income the Franciscans received from the Nahuas at this location could go solely toward supporting the local chaplain and was not to be used to help the order as a whole. It was officially the new location of the sole indigenous parish of Mexico City, but the Franciscans were to minister only to Nahuas living in San Juan Moyotlan, thus limiting the number of their parishioners. This effectively provided a greater portion of ecclesiastical income to the secular

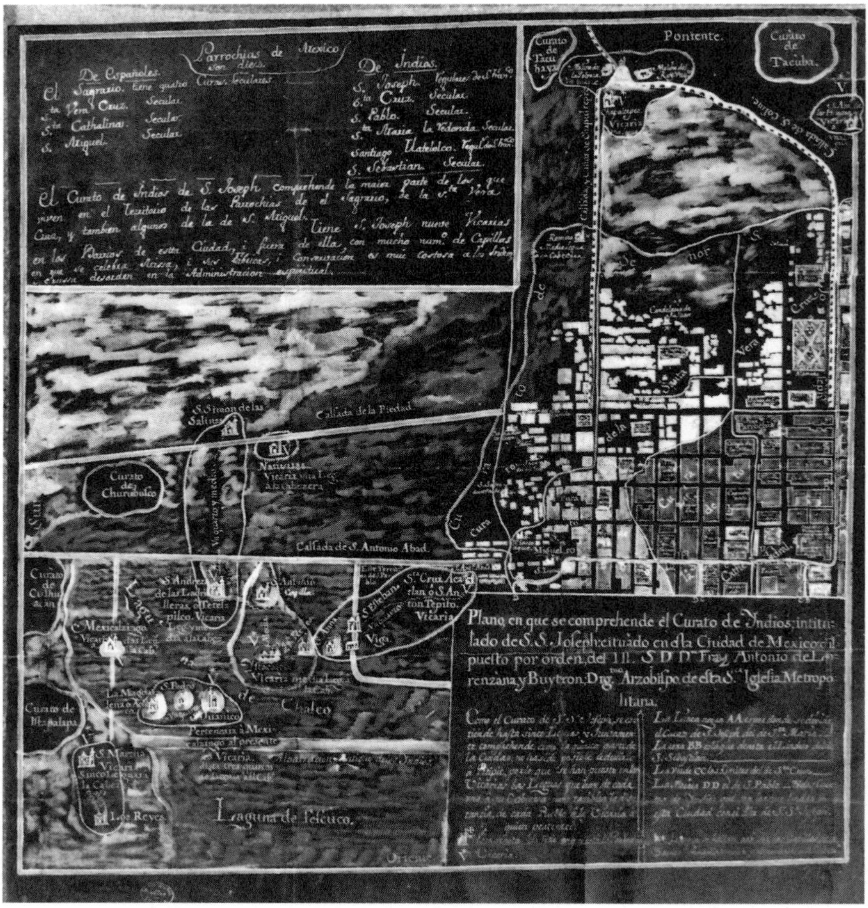

FIGURE 20. Map depicting the parish of San Josef, 1768. Spain, Ministry of Education, Culture and Sports, General Archive of the Indies, AGI, Mapas y Planos: Bulas y Breves, México 247.

Church, for Nahuas living in other parts of the altepetl had to attend mass in a secular parish.[2]

The concession granted to the Franciscans may have been at their request and without consideration of the Nahua community's wishes. The Nahuas' attention appears to have been focused elsewhere. Their shift in perspective is evident in a petition for an indigenous seminary, which received support from Nahuas in Mexico Tenochtitlan and other altepetl. Nahua involvement in the seminary project suggests that the Nahua leadership of Mexico Tenochtitlan was still active in influencing decisions relevant to indigenous religion in the altepetl and viceroyalty as well.

The petition for the seminary was started around 1754 by a Tlaxcalteca mestizo of high rank, don Julián Cirilo de Galicia y Castilla Aquiahualcateutle. He was trained in Mexico City as a presbyter, or priest, and could officiate at mass. While studying in Mexico City he made contact with other petitioners. Initially, don Julián suggested that the seminary be established in the Villa de Guadalupe. But after the expulsion of the Jesuits in 1767, don Julián suggested that the seminary be established on one of the Society of Jesus's confiscated properties, reducing the crown's cost in the project substantially. Gathering support and evidence of the possible success of such an effort, don Julián cited the history of the Colegio de Santiago Tlatelolco and some of its students as well as the recently established indigenous convent of Corpus Christi for women. He stated that the purpose of the seminary would be to train indigenous priests knowledgeable in the indigenous languages. After their training the native priests would be sent to rural areas where Christianity had not been as successfully received. He had the support of both the secular Church and mendicant orders in Mexico City, most of whom noted the need for priests conversant in native languages.[3] His argument in favor of the seminary was strikingly similar to the sixteenth- and seventeenth-century arguments made by mendicant friars to retain indigenous parishes—because of their better command of native languages. By secularizing most mendicant doctrinas, the secular Church and the crown provided the Nahuas with another strong, albeit old, argument in favor of indigenous priests, namely, language skills.

These seminary discussions occurred during a timeframe similar to that of the secularization of San Josef. Though the main person in charge of the petition was a Tlaxcalteca, Nahuas of Mexico Tenochtitlan were active in the process. It is possible that they considered the establishment of an indigenous seminary a salve on the loss of their old parish. In 1774 it was suggested that the seminary be established at the old Jesuit Colegio de San Gregorio in Mexico City, leaving its entailments in place. King Charles III officially granted the income at San Gregorio for an indigenous seminary on 27 July 1778, but their efforts were for naught; the project was soon canceled.[4]

San Josef's secularization was not the end of the chapel or the friary of San Francisco. In a series of presidential orders in the 1850s and 1860s, the friary of San Francisco was first reduced in size and then seized by the government, divided into different lots, and sold to individual bidders.[5] Little of the original friary remains today.

For tourists visiting the central plaza, the Zócalo, there is little to tell of the friary's former dominance. Walking west out of the Zócalo along Calle Madero, one comes across the remnants of San Francisco. A High-Life clothing store at the intersection of Calle Gante (a pedestrian walkway) and Calle Madero marks the northeastern corner of the friary, and the Torre Latinoamericana marks the northwestern edge. The High-Life building and restaurants sit where the chapel of San Josef de los Naturales used to stand, and only four buildings contain any of the colonial architecture that was once part of the religious compound. The Spanish church of San Francisco is now well below street level on Calle Madero and is run by the Franciscans once again (for a time it had been a Chiarini Circus and a stable).[6]

Walking down Calle Gante, one cannot help but notice the façade of a Methodist church. The chapel of this church was one of the old Franciscan cloisters. To the dismay of many in Mexico City, missionaries from the United States inaugurated the cloister as a Methodist church in 1873.[7] Continuing down the pedestrian walkway, it is nearly impossible to miss the fragrance wafting from a large *panadería* (bakery or bread store) located just around the corner. Although the treats may have appeal, the interior architecture of the panadería is worth a visit on its own. If you continue past the panadería to the corner of Eje Central and 16 de Septiembre you come to a Fondo de Cultura y Económica bookstore, the inside of which contains more of the remnants of the old friary. Aside from the pedestrian walkway, named for fray Pedro de Gante, only one memorial exists of what used to be there, a statue of Gante and one of his indigenous students at the end of the street. It was erected primarily in remembrance of the achievements of Gante and not so much for the parishioners who played such a central role in the life of the man and place. Perhaps in time a monument will exist in remembrance of them all.

Notes

1. AGI, Mexico, v. 727.
2. Ibid.
3. AGI, Mexico, v. 1937.
4. Ibid.
5. Chauvet, *San Francisco*, chap. 5.
6. Ibid., p. 76.
7. Gonzalo Baez-Camargo, *Biografía de un templo: Iglesia metodista de la Santísima Trinidad exclaustro mayor de San Francisco* (México: Sociedad de Estudios Históricos del Metodismo en México, 1973), p. 123.

Appendix 1
Documented Nahua Cofradías in Mexico Tenochtitlan, Sixteenth through Early Eighteenth Century

Cofradía	Location	Source	Notes
Santísimo Sacramento	San Josef	Vetancurt, *Teatro*, pt. 4, pp. 41–42	
De las Ánimas	San Josef	AGN, Bienes Nacionales, v. 387, e. 1; Vetancurt, *Teatro*, pt. 4, pp. 41–42; INAH FF, v. 145, #4486, fs. 268–274	
De la Cuerda	San Josef	Vetancurt, *Teatro*, pt. 4, pp. 41–42	The name of this cofradía, presumably, refers to the cord worn by the Franciscan order.
Santo Entierro	San Josef	Vetancurt, *Teatro*, pt. 4, pp. 41–42; INAH FF, v. 145, #4486, fs. 268–274	
Santísimo Trinidad de los Sastres	San Josef	Vetancurt, *Teatro*, pt. 4, pp. 41–42; INAH FF, v. 145, #4486, fs. 268–274	Only known indigenous guild cofradía for San Josef
Soledad de la Vírgen	San Josef	Chimalpahin, *Annals*, p. 35; Chimalpahin, *Ocho relaciones*, v. 2. pp. 267–269; AGN, Bienes Nacionales, v. 387, e. 1; Mendieta, *Historia Ecclesiastica*, v. 2, p. 85; Vetancurt, *Teatro*, pt. 4, pp. 41–42	Established 1591
San Juan Bautista de la República	San Josef	AGN, Bienes Nacionales, v. 387, e. 1; Vetancurt, *Teatro*, pt. 4, pp. 41–42	
Tránsito de la Vírgen	San Josef	Vetancurt, *Teatro*, pt. 4, pp. 41–42	
San Diego de Alcalá	San Josef	Chimalpahin, *Annals*, p. 57; Vetancurt, *Teatro*, pt. 4, pp. 41–42; INAH FF, v. 145, #4486 fs. 268–274	

Cofradía	Location	Source	Notes
De la Veracruz	San Josef	Mendieta, *Historia eclesiástica*, v. 2, pp. 104–105; Burkhart, *Holy Wednesday*, p. 84; Motolinia, *Memoriales*, p. 93; AGN Tierras, v. 37, e. 2, fs. 69v–83v	
Nuestra Señora de la Candelaria	San Josef	AGN, Cofradías y Archicofradías, v. 188, e. 3.	
San Josef	San Josef	Mendieta, *Historia Ecclesiastica*, v. 2, pp. 104–105	
San Juan	Convento de San Juan de la Penitencia	AGN, Indios, v. 34, e. 37, f. 40; Chimalpahin, *Annals*, p. 217; Vetancurt, *Teatro*, pt. 4, p. 111	Spanish-Nahua[a]
Jesús Nazareno[?]	Santa María la Redonda	NL, Ayer, MS 1481, B(3)a	If this was a brotherhood, it was unlicensed.
Santísimo Sacramento	Santa María la Redonda	NL, Ayer, MS 1481, B(3)c; Vetancurt, *Teatro*, pt. 2, p. 83	
Ánimas de Purgatorio & Nuestra Señora de la Assumpción	Santa María la Redonda	Chimalpahin, *Annals*, pp. 215, 241; UNAM FRAF, caja 64, e. 1209, f. 7; Vetancurt, *Teatro*, pt. 2, p. 83.	This seems to be a double cofradía.[b] Vetancurt only mentions Assumpción.
Santo Entierro	Santa María	UNAM FRAF, caja 64, e. 1209, f. 7	Unlicensed
[Nuestra Señora de la] Soledad	Santa María	UNAM FRAF, caja 64, e. 1209, f. 7	Unlicensed
Tránsito de Nuestra Señora	Santa María	UNAM FRAF, caja 64, e. 1209, f. 7	Unlicensed
San Roque	Hospital de San Lázaro, Atenantitech	Chimalpahin, *Annals*, p. 241	This was a cofradía of non-Mexica natives.
Santa María de la Concepción	San Sebastián	AGN, Tierras v. 48, e. 4, fs. 7–9v; Grijalva, *Crónica*, p. 161–162	Augustinian. Grijalva mentions that in "all" of the Augustinian convents, there were cofradías dedicated to Las Ánimas del Purgatorio and Nuestra Señora.
Nuestra Señora de los Dolores y Soledad	San Sebastián	AGN, Bienes Nacionales, v. 1028, e. 28	Nahua-Filipino

Cofradía	Location	Source	Notes
De las Ánimas del Purgatorio	San Sebastián	Grijalva, *Crónica*, pp. 161–162	Augustinian
De las Ánimas del Purgatorio	San Pablo	Grijalva, *Crónica*, pp. 161–162	Augustinian
Nuestra Señora	San Pablo	Grijalva, *Crónica*, pp. 161–162	Augustinian
Santa María de la Caridad	Hospital Real de Indios de Nuestra Señora de la Caridad	Chimalpahin, *Annals*, p. 243; ANM, Hernando de Arauz #4, v. 7, yrs. 1619–1617, fs. 7–12v	Michoacan natives and Nahuas
San Nicolás de Tolentino	Hospital Real de Indios de Nuestra Señora de la Caridad	Chimalpahin, *Annals*, p. 243; ANM, Hernando de Arauz #4, v. 7, yrs. 1619–1622, fs. 7–12v	May be a mixed brotherhood (definitely including Nahuas)
De las Ánimas de Purgatorio	Hospital Real de Indios de San Josef de los Naturales	Muriel, *Hospitales*, v. 1, p. 147	
Entierro de Nuestro Señor Dios	Santa Cruz Contzinco	Chimalpahin, *Annals*, p. 245	Augustinian
Nuestra Señora del Rosario	Capilla de Nuestra Señora del Rosario at friary of Santo Domingo	Dávila Padilla, *Historia*, pp. 354–360; "Doctrina, evangelios y epístolas en nahuatl," Codex Indianorum 7, John Carter Brown Library	This cofradía was in the parish of Mixtecos.
Tránsito de Nuestra Señora	Hospital de los Desamparados	AGN, Bienes Nacionales, v. 387, e. 1, f. 24	
Nuestra Señora de la Anunciata	Colegio de San Gregorio	Schroeder, "Jesuits," p. 47; INAH, CSG, v. 119, f. 19r	Jesuit congregation
De la Circuncisión	Colegio de San Gregorio	Schroeder, "Jesuits," p. 47; INAH, CSG, v. 119, f. 19r	Jesuit congregation
San Gregorio	Colegio de San Gregorio	ANM, Hernando de Arauz #4, v. 7, yrs. 1619–1617, fs. 7–12v	Jesuit congregation
Señor San Josef	Colegio de San Gregorio	Schroeder, "Jesuits," p. 47	Jesuit congregation
Buena Muerte	Colegio de San Gregorio	Schroeder, "Jesuits," pp. 43–76	Jesuit congregation

a. See "Growth and Change of Nahua Cofradías," chapter 4.
b. The only place I have seen reference to another double cofradía is in Chimalpahin, on one in Tlatelolco. See Chimalpahin, *Annals*, p. 243.

Appendix 2
Nahuatl Documents from the Chapel of San Josef

Receipt of Payment by the Nahua Choirmaster of San Josef from Juan de Aguilar

AGN, Bienes Nacionales, v. 387, e. 1, f. 15

Yn axcan martes a 23 d. Julio d. 1640 años otictocaque yn tehuantin cantores nican capilla San Juseph yn omomiquili yn itoca ocatca clara lopes chane tianquiztenco auh yn yehuatzin señor Juan de aguilar albasea omochiuh yehuatzin otechmotlaxtlahuili macuili pesos otechmomaquili ynicc omotocac moch ica ynicc omochiuh yn imisa cuerpo preçente mochi canto de organo huel mahuiztic ynicc otictocaque auh yni macuili pesos nehuatl nomaticca oniccuic: nicçeli yn nehuatl maestro nican capilla sanc juseph mochintin yn ixpa yn ermanos cantores auh ynic neltiliztli melahuac nican nictlalia yn notoca yhuan yn nofirma ffecho e mexico

Francisco de San Juan Maestro de la capilla.

5 pesos.

Today, Tuesday the 23rd of July of the year of 1640, we the singers [or cantors] here at the chapel of San Josef buried the deceased person who was named Clara López, citizen of Tianquiztenco. Señor Juan de Aguilar, who was made executor, paid us 5 pesos. He gave it to us for burying her, including the performance of her mass in the presence of the body, complete with part-singing. How we buried her was very splendid. And I the [choir]master here in the chapel of Josef took these 5 pesos in my hand; I received them before the brothers cantors. And [to show] that it is authentic and true I place here my name and signature. Done in Mexico [City].

Francisco de San Juan, choirmaster.

5 pesos.

Receipt of Payment of Performance of Low Mass on Behalf of Deceased

AGN, Tierras, v. 2776, e. 18, f. 213

v Axcan biernes yc chiCuey tonatiuh mani metztli agusto de 1664 años teopixcatlatohuani Nrõ P^{e} guar^{a} oquimochihuili Cen.Misa Resada yc opalehuiloc yn ianiman fran^{co} Antonio chane Candelaria yehuatl ypolito lupez de alvarado oquicalaquin huentli Cen peso nomatica onicnomaquili nrõ P^{e} gu^{a}ar oquimocelili ynic neli nican quimotlalilia ytocatzin yhuan yfirmatzin———
ypanpa tlalmatli yc oquinamacac

1P^{s}

Fr. Pedro Camacho

v Axcan Sabado yc chiucnahui tonatiuh mani meztli agusto de 1664 años teopixcatlatohuani Nrõ P^{e} gu^{a}ar. oquimochihuilin Çemisa Re~~qui~~sada yc opalehuiloc yn ianiman fran^{co} Antonio Çano yehuatl [y]polito lupez de alvarado . oquicalaqui huentli Çen peso Ça ye no ypanpa ytlalman ya quicohuilin nehuatl fiscal don pedro de San pablo nomatica onicnomaquilin Nrõ P^{e} gu^{a}ar oquimocelili ynic quimoneltililia nican quimotlalilia ytocatzin yfirmatzin——————

1P^{s}

Fr. Pedro Camacho

v Nehuatl fiscal nitlaneltilia ynic omochiuh ymisa fran^{co} Antonio ynic neli nican nictlalia notocan yhuan nofirma——————

D. Pedro + de S Pablo
fiscal de S Juseph

Today, Friday, eighth day of the month of August of 1664. The priestly ruler, our father guardian [fray Pedro Camacho], performed a low mass to aid the soul of Francisco Antonio, citizen of Candelaria. Hipólito López de Alvarado delivered the offering of 1 peso. With my hands I gave it to our father guardian myself; he accepted it. To show that it is true, he placed his name and signature here.———

For a lot[1] that he [Francisco Antonio] sold.

1 peso Fray Pedro Camacho

Today, Saturday fourth day of the month of August of 1664. The priest ruler, our father guardian [fray Pedro Camacho], performed a low mass to aid the soul of Francisco Antonio. Likewise, Hipólito López de Alvarado delivered the offering of 1 peso, also for the lot he [Hipólito López de Alvarado] already bought from him [Francisco Antonio]. With my hands, I the fiscal don Pedro de San Pablo gave it to our father guardian myself; he accepted it. To verify it, he placed his name and signature here.——————

1 peso Fray Pedro Camacho

I, the fiscal, verify that the mass for Francisco Antonio took place. To show that it is true I place my name and signature here.

don Pedro de San Pablo
fiscal de San Josef

Note

1. *Tlamantli* literally means leveled land.

Appendix 3
Nahua Fiscal's Report on an Inheritance Dispute

UNAM FRAF, caja 96, e. 1413

This set of documents records an inheritance dispute in the barrio of San Pablo Malcuitlapilco in Mexico Tenochtitlan. Included in this folder are two bills of sale from 1640, two wills (from 1644 and 1673), and two fiscal reports (for lack of a better term) from 1655 (dated 9 October and 12 October). The materials were written at the end of Lockhart's stage 2 and the beginning of stage 3. Because of the wealth of material found in them, and possibly because of the point at which they were written, the sources display some of the active processes of language change and suggest that loanword adoption did not necessarily occur as rapidly in Mexico Tenochtitlan as had been assumed.

These materials witness the continual use of Nahuatl sibling terminology until 1655. Though this ongoing usage is what is witnessed for outer-lying areas, scholars expected an earlier adoption of loanwords in Mexico City. Stage 3 of the evolutionary process had developed by 1650.[1] In the records, the term *-oquichtiuh*, derived from *oquichtli* (male person) was generally in reference to a female's older brother. But because Nahuatl kinship terms were frequently transposed for politeness, the older relative was called younger or the younger older, and it is possible the term was used in this fashion. Based on the reading of the sources, it seems more likely, however, that at this time, when Spanish kinship terminology was used more readily, the use of *oquichtli* had shifted to indicate brother in general, with no age specification. Yet in that very same source where *oquichtli* is used more generally we see precisely the use of many traditional kinship terms (understanding that the terms for people in direct line of descent, such as children and grandchildren, appear to have remained the same everywhere). Two other possible changes, ones that need additional corroboration before certainty can be established, concern the use of the term *yuctzin*, the younger sibling of either gender of a female, and *ipitzin*, older sister of a female.

In the documents considered here there are three siblings mentioned by name. In two places there exists the possibility for a fourth unnamed sibling. The notary and fiscal involved in recording the case are known to have made a mistake regarding the name of the eldest named sibling, referring to her as Juana María when she was actually named María Francisca (as discovered from other evidence present in the materials). It is thus also possible that they mistakenly added a fourth sibling to the list. The mention of the fourth sibling appears twice in close succession in the fiscal reports, but this individual is not referenced in either of the testaments. If this sibling did not exist, it is probable that the second mention of an unknown sibling reflects my misunderstanding of the defining characteristics of some of their Nahuatl terms at the time the documents were written. As seen in the case of other terms, such as *pia* (eventually, to have), it is possible that there was slight shift in the meaning of these kinship terms as well. The phrase in question is

> aocmo çenpan . mixnamictzinoz yhuan . yn ipitzin yhuan . yuctzin yhuan . yn iyoquichtiuh,
>
> there will be no more contention between her [María Francisca] and her older sister and her younger sibling and her older brother.

As discussed above, *yoquichtiuh* is generally an older brother of a female, but it appears to be consistently used in reference to a brother in general in this document. And it is fairly certain that María Francisca was older than her brother and her sister. The slight change of definition for *yoquichtiuh* is enough to throw the rest of the phrase into question.

The next term to be considered is *ipitzin* (older sister). It appears only once in these documents; the inheritance debate appears to be mainly between María Francisca and her brother, Francisco Juárez. However, based on the documentation, María Francisca seems to be an elder half-sibling to Francisco Juárez and the other, sister Ana Francisca, and she seems to be from a previous marriage of their mutual father, making her the elder of the three. Thus, *ipitzin* is either being used in reference to yet another unnamed sibling or refers to Ana Francisca and is used in a manner similar to *yoquichtiuh* and no longer refers to a specific age relationship.

The final sibling term, *yuctzin*, then becomes the next question. This word, referring to a younger sibling of either gender, could be in reference to Ana Francisca, if the possibility of a fourth unnamed sibling is allowed. By removing the existence of a fourth sibling, the word must refer to something and may, in fact, be modifying the *yoquichtiuh* that follows it or the *ipitzin* that precedes it. This would support the change that *yoquichtiuh* appears to have undergone (and *ipitzin* may have), for the word could then be modified to a younger male brother. If all of these changes happened, the translation should read

> aocmo çenpan . mixnamictzinoz yhuan . yn ipitzin yhuan . yuctzin yhuan . yn iyoquichtiuh,
>
> there will be no more contention between her [María Francisca] and her sister and her younger sibling, her brother.

This translation makes the number of siblings consistent with the rest of the documents. It is, however, still a stretch to make it fit, especially since only one of the two terms, which traditionally referenced an elder sibling, is modified. But with the onset of Lockhart's stage 3, sibling terminology undergoes one more significant alteration, the adoption of Spanish kinship terms, virtually removing the Nahuatl terminology. This appears in the latest of the documents included in appendix 3, where the word *hermana* (sister) is used in reference to Ana Francisca. Clearly, kinship terms were in flux during this period, and they were starting to emulate the Spanish terminology that did not reference age relationships. These sources show the slow process through which language modification occurred. In this case it appears to have commenced with an alteration to the definition of the traditional term before being replaced by a loanword.

A few more terms are also of note in these documents. The word *tlamantli* (leveled land) and the Spanish term *sitio* (site) appear to be used interchangeably to mean house lot, instead of the word *solar*, which was so common in Nahuatl texts. This suggests that Nahuas had entered a period of fluctuation concerning the use of property terms in the middle of the seventeenth century. The final word of note is *topilecapan* (where the topilque are). This is a title given to one of the alguaciles mayores and is a bit puzzling. It is possible that Baltasar de los Reyes, the alguacil mayor topilecapan, was in charge of the lower officials, occasionally called topiles, within the Church. Based on this reading of the term, the additional title of *topilecapan* may have indicated a differing set of duties from that of other alguaciles mayores at the chapel of San Josef. Although the positions of alguacil mayor and topile make occasional appearances in other documents from Mexico City, and elsewhere, this is the only time that I have encountered an alguacil mayor topilecapan, suggesting that change in ecclesiastical terms and positions may have occurred locally.

Nahuatl Transcription

[f. 29]

v Axcan lunes . a 12 de otobre de 1655 años . ypanpa yn itoca Fran^{co} Juarez ynic oquimotilitzinoco yehuatzin . teopixcatlatohuani $\overline{\text{nro}}$ P^{e} Pruvicial P^{e} Mansu . ynic oquimoztlacahuilico . yn itocan Fran^{co} Juarez . ynn oquiton . hi ye quinamacaznequi yn ihermana yn itocan Juana maría huel yhueltihuatzin Ça centatli yhuan Ça çe nantli huell iyaxca huel ytlatquin . huel quinemac~~tt~~titiuh yn itatzin . Auh yehuatl . Ça quinequi quiÇuiliz . yn iucton . yn omoteneuh Fran^{co} Juarez Auh ytla huell iyaxca ytlatquin . quenin . quiÇuiliznequin . ytla huel ypā teneuhtican . yn testamento . yn iuhuqui [*sic*] oquitotia yntatzin . amo huel monamacaz . ypanpa Ca oncaten ypilhuan . quincahuilitiaz auh yn iquac . oquimocaquiltin yehuatzin . yn tobicario P^{e} fr P^{o} Camacho . yhuan yehuatzin totlaçotatzin P^{e} fr Sebastian de olibares temachtiani . oquimopohuiliquen . y testamento yn oquitlalilian yntatzin . Auh niman . onechmonochiliquen . nehuatl fiscal onechmolhuiliquen . ma xicmotilin ynin testamento . onechmotitlanilili . otechmolhuili . ma hamehuantzitzin xicomotilican ynhuan xicmonemililican yn quenin huel mochihuaz . huel hiyomatzinco $\overline{\text{nro}}$ P^{e} Prouincial . auh ma tehuatzin fiscal xicmotili yhuan xicmonemilili . yn quenin huel mochihuaz . auh ymomextintzitzin oniquinonanquilili . oniquinolhuili . notlaçotatzinen Ca ye nicmaticatqui ynontzin testamento yn quenin catqui yn quenin . oquixexelhuitian yn intatzin . ynic onquinenemactitian . ytla oncaten ynpilhuan . auh oniquinolhuiliqui . ytlacamon ye mocehuizquen moxeloz quin [*sic*] . ypanpa . Ca ça netech Çaliuhtica . ytlacamon . moxeloz . aocmo Çenpa yc mixnamiquizquen yni yoquichtiuh . Ca çecni Catquin yn tleyn . ynemac . Ca hamon . ytech açin . auh oquimitalhuiq̄ ymomextintzitzin . y P^{e} guar̄ yhuan temachtianin . ma yuhqui mochihuan . ma ximohuican . ma xicmontilin . yhuan . ma xicmoxelhuin yPanpa . amon quimitalhuiz . yn teopixcatlatohuanin . aço camon tictotlacamachiltian yn tley techmonahuatilia . oniquinolhuili . notlaÇontatzinen . Ca nicneltiliz yn amoteopixcatlatoltzin . Ca lunes hopa niyaz . niquitatiuh . auh axcan [Lu]nes . onihuala . y nican . ypan tlaxilacalli nr̄a S^{ra} de la candelaria . malCuitlapilco . onictemon hi yehuatl yxpantzincon . omoteylhuicon . teupixcatlatohuani Prouinçial yn itocā Fran^{co} Juarez . onictlatlanin . yn ihermana . oniquilhuin . Catlin y moquichtiuh . onechilhuin . Ca hayac . Ca ça niman . hoya yn Sabado . oqualantian . Ca noço quinequin Çan iuhqui nechÇuiliznequi . oniquilhuia hamo huel mitzCuiliz ypanpa Ca maxcan Ca motlatquin . Axcan . motamachihuaz . auh niman . omotamachiuh tlalmantli Çition . tonatiuh ycalaquianpahuic Caxtoli yhuan Çenbaras . auh ynoc centlapal . otlicapan yc omotamachiuh matlactloCenbara . auh ynic patlahuac Çanon yxquich . matlactlocenbaras . auh yn chinamitl [29v] yc omotamachiuh nauhtetl . Cenpohuali yhuan chiÇuey baras . yhua Centetl Caltontli antle quipien Puerta . tonati ycalaquianpa ynic on[mo]tamachiuh nahui bara yhuan tlacon ynic huiyac yey baras yhuan tl[a]Con ynic patlahuac . auh yn tleyn . hiyaxca . angustin butello on[e]chititin[2] . y canpa tlantican . hiyaxcan . mochin . onicahuili yhuan y[. . .]tli . Canpa . oquiquetzcan xacalin . quixitiniz . yn onicmacato . posses[ion] quiquetzaz . yn ontlin yn itocan . Juana Maria yhuan ynamic y[n]tocan thomas P^{o} yhuan ypilhuan .. omentin hi yacapantli A[na] de Stiago Caxtolxihuitl quipien ynic ome Maria de la Çruz mat[lac]tlonahui xihuitl . Auh ynin . huel omopacanonotzinoquen. yn ih[ue]poltzin yhuan . yhuepoltz [*sic*] yometzin . aocmo çenpan . mixnamictzinoz yhuan . yn ipitzin yhuan . yuctzin yhuan . yn iyoquichtiuh . auh axca ye quali yc omoxelon yn tlalli . aocmo quemanian . Çenpa tleyn . ic mixnamiquizquen . auh yn aquin Cenpa quipehualtiz tlatoli . aço y[e]huatl . yn ipitzin noço yuctzin . quixtlahuazque pena Cenpohuali [pesos?] yc mocohuaz . açeyten ytetzinco pohuiz y S^{mo} Sacramento . auh [ne]huatl . fiscal . onicchiuh . yhuan . onicneltili ynic onechhualmihuali totlaçotatzin P^{e} vicario fr P^{o} Camacho . onicneltilicon ymixpan[tzin]co tlaxilacalequen testigos ynic çe tlacatl . Sebastian de Stiago fiscal pasado . yhuan . yhuan . [*sic*] Miguel geronimo . yhuan . diego luis fiscal ca[nde]laria . yhuan Juseph de aquinon yhuan grauiel de la cruz yehuatin . testigos omochiuhquen . auh nehuatl fiscal . onictamachihuato ynic nicneltilia . nican . nictlalia notocan yhuan . nofirma fecha.

\+ \+
D martin Alunso pedro de S pablo
fiscal S Juseph alhuaçil mayor

\+
baltasar de los reyes
alhuacil mayor pil[?]
topilecapan

NixPan . omochiuh
\+
Sebastian BonifaCio
Es^{o} de la yglesia

Carta de venta Candelaria malcuitlapilco[3]

[f. 30]
v Ma moçenquizcayectenehua yn itocatzin dios tetatzin yhuan . dios tepiltzin yhuan dios Spū Santo ma yuh mochihua . Axcan . a 28 de Enero de 1644 años nicchihua notestamento nehuatl . Fran^{co} Juarez nican . notlaxilicallian . Candelaria malCuitlapilco ypanpa notech quimotlalilia yJusticiatzin dios . ytla nechpopolhuiz nican tlalticpac Ca yc ninomaquixtia yxpantzinco dios —

v ynic centlamantli niquitohua notlatol nehuatl Fran^{co} Juarez . yn itechcopa Caltzitzintin . tepitoton . ytla nechmopolhuiz dios niquincahuilitiuh . y nopilhuan . yhuan . nonamic María geronima Centetl Canlin . tonatiuh yquiÇayanpa ytzticac . ontequiztimanin . ymomextin . niquincahuilitiuh y nopilhuan yhuan y nonamictzin y notelpoch . ytocan Fran^{co} Juarez . yhuan . nochpoch . Ana Fran^{ca} auh ynin Calin . onicteneuh yhuan ythualo tlamelahua yhuan ytlalmayo yhuan yetetl chinamitl . tepitoto yhuicalo auh ytla moztla huiptla quimopolhuiz dios nonamictzin . amo huel monamaCaz yn calin Ça quincahuilitiaz y nopilhuan . auh yehuatl quimatin . haçon missa quimitlanilitiaz yc palehuiloz yn ianimantzin . auh y nopiltzin Fran^{co} Jua̅z̅ nicmacatiuh Centetl telar freçada . auh niquitlanilitiuh ome missas Cantadas yc palehuiloz y nanimantzin . amon huel aquin . quitlacoz y notlatol neltiz mochihuaz yn iuhqui niquitotiuh —

v[4] ynic ontlamantli niquitohua . notlatol y nochpoch ana fran^{ca} yhuan . y nonamictzin . niquimitlanilitiuh ÇeÇentetl Misa Cantada yc palehuiloz y nanimantzin yn oncan tocapilla S Juseph ÇeÇentetl Misa totech pohuiz Çe nehuatl yhuan Cen ytech pohuiz yn achtopa nonamictzin Catca Çeçilia dominica . auh y nomōtzin thomas . P^{o} Ca ye onicmacac yn inemac . tlalmantli yhuan chiquaçentetl chinamitl . yhuicalon . ayc tleyn . netequipacholi quimacaz y nonamictzin yhuan y nopilhuan . auh niquitlanilitiuh Çen . misa Cantada yc palehuiloz y nanimatzin . amon ytlacahuiz y notlatol neltiz mochihuaz —

v ynic yetlamantli niquitohua . notlatol . hocan . notzotzoma Çentetl tzomitl noCalçones . yhuan . Çe notzomitilma yhuan . oc çen Çanon tzomitl . notilma . monamacaz y tleyn ypatiuh mochihuaz Calaquiz yn toteopan S Juseph . amon ytlacahuiz y notlatol neltiz mochihuaz —

v̲ Ca ye yxquich ynic nictzonquixtia notestamento ymixpantzinco testigos tlaxilacalequen . nican . motocayotizquen — +

Migl̄ de la Cruz	Ju^{o} geronimo	miguel Geronimo
te^{o}s	testigo	testigo
v̲ Çihuatzintzintin	dō nicolas de medina	Nixpan
v̲ Fran^{ca} Juana te^{o}s	fiscal S Juseph	Sebastian BonifaCio
v̲ Mariana testigo	D martin Alunso	Es^{o} de la yglesiano
v̲ Ana X̄pina testigo	fiscal y Sindico	

[f. 30v]

v̲ Axcan Sabado . a 9 de otubre de 1655 años . nehuatl nicnoCuitlahuia Sta yglesia fiscal . oniquilhui. yn EsCriuano xiquixtlapana ynin testamento . yn itestamento yn quenin Can ynenanahuatil micatzintli huel yuhqui xictlalin . ypanpa quicactiez yni tei[ch]poch . ypanpa . amo quitoz . amon . oniquitac yn quenin . omix[tla]pan . ytestamento . ymomextin . yxpan yn inamic . auh ytla o[ti]quixtlapan . tiquinpohuiliz . quicactiezquen . auh yn itech can Carta de pago . ticmacaz quihuicaz . ypanpa . ytla quemania . oc cenpa mixnamiquizquen . monenehuiliz ynin testamento . auh nehua EsCriuano . oniquinpohuili . oquicacque . niman . oniquinmacac . oquihuicaquen . auh nehuatl . fiscal ynic notencopa . omochiuh nican . nicneltilia notocan yhuan . nofirma ffecho —

+		
D martin Alunso	onicneltili	Fran^{co} Juarez chanen
fiscal S Josef	+	malCuitlapilco
ytestamento		
Pedro de S Pablo	Sebastian BonifaCio	ypan de 1644 años[5]
alhuacil Mayor	Es^{o} de la yglesia	

Señor don Joseph de lan[s?]o[. . .]Gorta Mealesa [?] Mealesa [?]

[f. 31]

Jesus maria i Jocep

Ma moCenquisCayectenehua yn itlaSomahuisteotoCatzi yn Dios tetatzin yn Dios tepiltzi in Dios espi Sto ma yn mochihua Ca yCenmatzinco noContlalia y noyolia yn nanimantzi y noteotzi notlatoCatzi Ca ytlamaquixtiltzi Ca ytlachihualtzi ma quimohuiquilis yn ichantzinCo yn iquac quitlalCahuis y notlalo ỹ noSoquio ynic yhuantzinCo motlamachtis

—

nicpehualtia nomemoria yn nehuatl notoCa maria fran^{Ca}

Ynic Centlamatli niquitohua y nehuatl notoCa maria fran^{Ca} nicmaCatiuh ỹ noConeuh ontetl metlatl Ce huey Ce tepito Conanas ytoCa ana de Santiago neltis mochihuas yn notlatol

Ynic ontlamantli niquitohua notlatol yn nehua notoCa maria fran^{Ca} nicmaCatiuh y noxhuiuhtzi ytoCa Roq̄[?] de Santa maria Sentetl huipili yanCuic ystac mimicho yhuan centetl metlatl nechihuilis miSa tepitzin Centetl ypalehuiloCa mochihuas yn nanimantzi neltis mochihuas y notlatol

Ynic yetlamatli niquitohua [n]otlatol ỹ nehuatl notoCa maria fran^{Ca} nicmaCatiuh y noxhuiuhtzi ytoCa mechiora de los reYes nicmaCatiuh Centetl huipili tlamacho ystac yhuan centetl metlatl auh Centetl misa tePitzi niquitlantiuh yc nechpalehuilis nanimantzi neltis mochihuas ỹ notlatol
Ynic nauhtlamatli niquitohua nehuatl notoCa maria fran^{Ca} y noxhuiuh ytoCa maria Bauhtista nicmaCatiuh Centetl huipili yhuan Centetl Cueytl Ce Sotl morado Ce Sotl berde yhua Centetl metlatl auh Ce misa tepitzi nechtepotzitoctis ypalehuiloCa mochihuas y nanimantzi neltis mochihuas yn notlatol
Ynic maCuillamantli niquitohua y nehuatl notoCa maria fran^{Ca} nicpie noermana ytoCa ana franÇisCa nicmaCatiuh Çe tl[a]panCaltontli y Caltitlan iCac ytech Saliuhti Ca yni Calio ynic huiac nahui bara yhuan cemistitl ynic patlahuac yei bara auh Ce miSa tepitzi nechtepotztoctis ypalehuiloCa mochihuas y nanimantzi neltis mochihuas ỹ notlatol .

[31v]
Axca onicchiuh nomemoria nehuatl notoCa maria fran^{Ca} ymixpan tlaxilaCaleq̃ testigos niquinochihuiliq̃ Ju^{a}n Luys fisCal ytechCaCopatzinCo noestra S^{ra} de la Candelaria

niColas agostin
Ju^{a} P^{o} domingo Lassaro
diego miguel Ju^{a}n niColas
Ju^{a}n ypolito Çihuatzitzinti Beronica martina
onictlali ynin memoria ypan xihuitl 1673 as a 21 de Jolio e^{o}s Ju^{a}n de la Croz.

[f. 32]
v axca lunes a 30 de abril de 164[0] años niquitohua nehuatl Juan diego niquinamaquiltia notlalma ca notlatqui noyollo yca ye niquinamaquillitia ytoca thomas pe^{o} yn inamic maria fran^{ca} nahui yn ichinayo ymixpantzinco tlaxillacaleque y niquimaca
v desticos ynic ce miguel de la cros regidor —
v ynic ome Juan geronimo rexidor —
v ynic ey grabiel augostin —
v ynic nahui Juseph thi aquino —
v ynic macuilin Juan pe^{o} —
v yhuan ce sihuatzintli Juana Jusepina —
v Nehuatl Escribano Juan Diego
v axca llones a 30 de abril de 1640 años —
quinamaca ytlalma Juseph di aquino yn quinamaquiltia ytoca thomas p^{o}e yn inamic maria francisca auh ynic patlahuac namatl yhua ce yollotli auh nic [*sic*] huiyac chiquace matl auh yn ichinayo macuiltetl ypatiuh 3 p^{o}s ypatiuh mochihua ymipantzinco [*sic*] tlaxillacalleque —
v ynic se Juan geronimo
v ynic ome miguel de la cros

v 3 grabiel augostin
v 4 Juan p^{o}e
v nehuatl Escrivano Juan diego

[f. 33v]
v mallcuitlapilco tlaxallacallin

Translation

[f. 29]
v Today, Monday the 12th of October of the year 1655, concerning the person named Francisco Juárez, about how he came to see the priestly ruler our father the provincial head Father Mansu, about how the one named Francisco Juárez deceived him. What [Father Mansu] said was this: "[Francisco Juárez] wants to sell something that is fully the property of his full older sister, with one [the same] father and one [the same] mother, named Juana María, and that her father made fully her inheritance at death.[6] But her younger sibling, the said Francisco Juárez, wants to take it from her. But if it is fully her property, how is it that he wants to take it from her if it is clearly mentioned in the testament that their father declared at death? It cannot be sold because she has children to whom she will leave it at death." And when our vicar Father Pedro Camacho and our precious father the Father fray Sebastián de Olivares, preacher, heard it, they read the testament that their father issued, and then they called me, the fiscal, and said to me, "Look at this testament that our father the provincial head personally sent me. He told us, 'May you [pl.] look at it and consider what is to be done.' And may you the fiscal look at it and consider what can be done." And I answered both of them and told them, "My precious father,[7] I already know about that testament and how it is and how their father distributed things at death, how he made the various bequests to them and if they have children." And I said to them, "If they aren't placated [come to agreement], it should be divided, because it [the inherited property] is attached to each other, if it isn't divided, [and then] she and her brother would no longer contend over it, because what she has inherited will be separate and he will not touch it." The two of them, the father guardian and the preacher, said, "Let it be done so; go, inspect it, divide it, so that the priestly ruler will not say that we do not obey him in what he orders us to do." I said to them, "My precious father, I will carry out your [pl.] priestly statement. I will go there on Monday to look at it." And today, Monday, I came here into the tlaxilacalli of Nuestra Señora de la Candelaria Malcuitlapilco. I sought the person who came to make complaint before the priestly ruler, the provincial head, named Francisco Juárez. I questioned his sister; I said to her, "Where is your brother?" She said, "He is absent. He just left on Saturday; he went in anger because he wants to take it from me just that way [without further formalities]." I told her, "He can't take it from you because it is your property." And then the leveled land and site[8] were measured at 16 varas toward the west, and on the other side, on the road, 11 varas, and the same

amount in width, and the four chinampas [f. 29v] were measured at 28 varas, and a little house that has no door, toward the west, was measured at 4½ varas in length and 3½ varas in width. As to what is the property of Agustín [Botero?], he showed me where his property ends. I left it all to him, and [. . .] where he had built a thatch hut [jacal] he is to demolish it. [Juana María? Agustín Botero?] is to build a passageway. I went to give possession to the person named Juana María and her spouse named Tomás Pedro and [his? her?] two children, the eldest A[na] de Santiago, who is 15 years old, and second María de la Cruz, 14 years [old]. And she and her brother-in-law and her brother-in-law who is [the brother of the first?][9] came to a very happy agreement; there will be no more contention between her and her older sister[10] and her younger sibling and her brother. Today the land was well divided; they are never to contend again over anything. And whoever should ever begin a suit, whether it be her older sister or her younger sibling, they are to pay a fine of 20 pesos to buy olive oil to belong to the holy Sacrament. And I the fiscal did it and carried out what our precious father the father vicar fray Pedro Camacho sent me about. I came to carry it out in the presence of the tlaxilacalli heads as witnesses: first Sebastián de Santiago, former fiscal; Miguel Gerónimo; Diego Luis, fiscal at Candelaria; Josef de Aquino; Gabriel de la Cruz. They became the witnesses. And I the fiscal went to measure it; to verify it I place here my name and signature. Date [above].

Don Martín Alonso, fiscal of San Josef. Pedro de San Pablo, alguacil mayor. Baltasar de los Reyes, alguacil mayor topilecapan. It was done before me, Sebastián Bonifacio, notary of the church.
Bill of Sale, Candelaria Malcuitlapilco[11]

[f. 30]
v̲ Be entirely praised the name of God the father, God the child, and God the Holy Spirit. May it be done. Today, the 28th of January of the year 1644 I Francisco Juárez make my testament here in my tlaxilicalli of Candelaria Malcuitlapilco because God has placed his justice on me [made me ill]. If he makes me disappear from here on earth, with it [the testament] I redeem myself before God.
v̲ First, I Francisco Juárez make a statement concerning the small houses; if God removes me I am leaving them to my children and my spouse María Gerónima. I am leaving a house facing east, divided into two buildings, to both my children, my son named Francisco Juárez and my daughter Ana Francisca, along with my spouse. As to this house I have mentioned and its patio [that goes straight to it?] and the leveled land and three small chinampas that go along with it, if in the future God removes my spouse, it cannot be sold. She is to leave it at death to my children. It is up to her whether she requests a mass [i.e., from the children in return for the property] to help her soul. And I am giving to my child Francisco Juárez a mechanical loom [for blankets?][12] and I am requesting from him two high masses to help my soul. No one can go against my statement; it is to be carried out and executed as I am saying.

v Second, I make the statement that I am asking my daughter Ana Francisca and my spouse for a high mass each at our chapel of San Josef to help my soul. Each mass is to belong to us, one to me, and one is to belong to my first spouse Cecilia Dominica, deceased. To my son-in-law Tomás Pedro[13] I have already given his inheritance, leveled land and six chinampas that go with it. He is never to give my spouse and children any grief. And I am requesting from him a high mass to help my soul. My statement is not to be violated; it is to be carried out and executed.
v Third, I make a statement that I have clothing, a pair of trousers of wool, a woolen cloak, and another cloak likewise of wool, that are to be sold. Whatever their value turns out to be is to be delivered to our church of San Josef. My statement is not to be violated; it is to be carried out and executed.
v That is all, with which I conclude my testament. [Done] before witnesses who are citizens of the tlaxilacalli, who are named here: Miguel de la Cruz, witness; Juan Gerónimo, witness; Miguel Gerónimo, witness; don Nicolas de Medina, fiscal of San Josef; don Martin Alonso, fiscal and syndic. The women: Francisca Juana, witness; Maríana, witness; Ana Cristina, witness. [Done] before me, Sebastián Bonifacio, notary of the church.

[f. 30v]
v Today, Saturday the 9th of October of 1655, I the fiscal who takes care of the holy church told the notary, "Make a copy of this testament, of how the deceased's testament and his various orders are; put it down exactly as it is, so that the daughter will hear it and will not say, 'I did not see how the testament was copied before both of them,[14] her and her spouse.' When you have copied it you are to read it to them and they are to hear it [or listen to it]; and the receipt [letter of payment] is attached to it. You are to give it to her; she is to take it so that if they ever argue again, it can be compared [with] this testament." I the notary read it to them and they heard it; then I gave [the testament and bill of sale] to them, and they took it. It was done by order of me the fiscal; here I verify it with my name and signature. Date [above].

Don Martín Alonso, fiscal of San Josef; Pedro de San Pablo, alguacil mayor. I verified it, Sebastián Bonifacio, notary of the church.
Señor don Josef de lan Gorta mealesa[?][15]
Testament of Francisco Juárez, citizen of Malcuitlapilco, in the year of 1644.[16]

[f. 31]
Jesús, María, and Josef
Be entirely praised the precious revered divine name of God the father, God the child, and God the Holy Spirit. May it be done. I place my spirit and soul entirely in the hands of my deity and ruler, for it is something redeemed by him and his creature. May he take it to his home [heaven] when it abandons my earthly body in order to be happy with him.
I named María Francisca begin my memorandum [of testament].

First, I named María Francisca say that I am giving my child named Ana de Santiago two metates [grinding stones], a big one and a small one; she is to take them. My statement is to be carried out and executed.
Second, I named María Francisca make a statement that I am giving my grandchild named Ro . . . ?] de Santa María a new white huipil in the Mimicho style.[17] and a metate. She is to have a low mass performed for me to become the aid to my soul. My statement is to be carried out and executed.
Third, I named María Francisca make a statement that I am giving my grandchild named Melchora de los Reyes a white embroidered huipil and a metate. I am requesting a low mass with which she is to help my soul for me. My statement is to be carried out and executed.
Fourth, I named María Francisca make a statement that I am giving my grandchild María Bautista a huipil, a skirt with one length purple and one length green, and a metate. She is to have arranged a low mass for me to become the aid of my soul. My statement is to be carried out and executed.
Fifth, I named María Francisca say that I have a sister named Ana Francisca. I am giving to her a small house with a flat roof. This house is attached to the [main] house. It is 4 varas long plus a span by 3 varas wide. She is to have arranged a low mass for me to become the aid of my soul. My statement is to be carried out and executed.

[f. 31v]
Today I named María Francisca made my memorandum [of testament] before those whom I made witnesses who are citizens [or leaders] of the tlaxilacalli: Juan Luis, fiscal for Nuestra Señora de la Candelaria; Nicolás Agustín; Juan Pedro; Domingo Lázaro; Diego Miguel; Juan Nicolás; Juan Hipólito. Women: Verónica Martina.

I the notary Juan de la Cruz set down this memorandum in the year 1673 on the 21st of July.

[f. 32]
v Today, Monday the 30th of April of 164[0] I Juan Diego state that I am selling my leveled land that is my property voluntarily; I sell it and its four chinampas to Tomás Pedro and his spouse María Francisca. I give it to them before the tlaxilacalli leaders.
v witnesses; First, Miguel de la Cruz, regidor.
v Second, Juan Gerónimo, regidor.
v Third, Gabriel Agustín
v Fourth, Josef de Aquino
v Fifth, Juan Pedro
v and one woman, Juana Josefina
v I the notary Juan Diego
v Today, Monday the 30th of April of the year 1640

Josef de Aquino is selling his leveled land. He sells it to the person named Tomás Pedro and his spouse Mariá Francisca. It is four matl and one yollotli wide and six matl long, and it has five chinampas. The price that it brings is 3 pesos. Before the tlaxillacalli leaders.
v First, Juan Gerónimo
v Second, Miguel de la Cruz
v 3rd Gabriel Agustín
v 4th Juan Pedro
v I the notary Juan Diego
[f. 33v]
Tlaxilacalli Malcuitlapilco

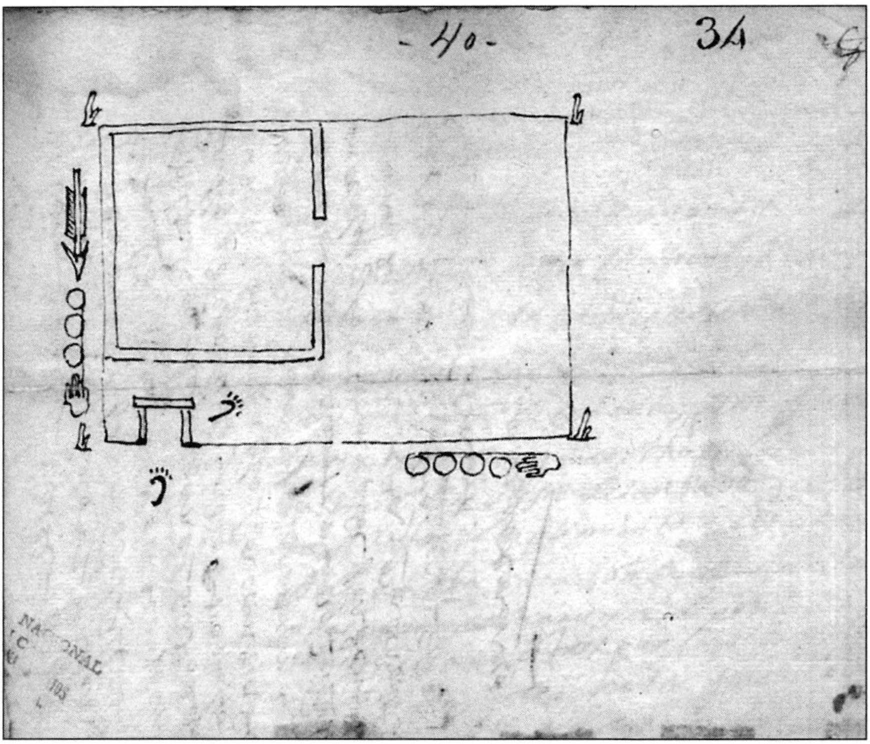

Notes

1. Lockhart, *Nahuas*, pp. 284–306.

2. For *onechittiti*.

3. Label on left side of the page.

4. On the left margin and in the binding:
[t?]e oqui[c]hiuh yn [m]isa
mo qui[ch]iuhquī misa yno im itla[...]litia mi[?]tzintli[?]n intatzin [i]xpan [fis?]cal omo[ch]iuh misa [?]ctlalia [n]ofirma martin [A]lunso fiscal
This note seems to report that the requested masses were performed and witnessed by fiscal don Martín Alonso.

5. Label on the right side of the page.

6. Based on the grammar used, it is also possible that it is Juana María/María Francisca who wants to sell her own property. However, from the context it seems more likely that it is Francisco Juárez who wants to sell the property.

7. Although it should be plural to match the previous statement, the notary uses the term in the singular, here and once again below.

8. Both *tlalmantli* and *sitio* are used in a sense approaching the definition of a house lot.

9. ih[ue]poltzin yhuan . yhuepoltz [sic] yometzin. This seems to assert that Juana María/María Francisca has two brother-in-laws, indicating there was another sibling otherwise unmentioned in the documentation. The apparent second brother-in-law of the woman is called the *-ome* of the first, which would mean that two brothers had married two sisters of the woman. Since two sisters of Juana María/María Francisca cannot be identified, the passage remains extremely puzzling. Additionally, one of the sisters might be JM/MF herself.

10. *Ipitzin* is in reference to the older sister of a female. This is followed by *yuctzin*, the younger sibling of either gender of a female, and *yoquichtiuh*, generally an older brother of a female, though in this document it appears to be used in reference to a brother in general. Again the document makes mention of a third, unnamed female sibling. The otherwise silent presence of this elder sibling is especially odd, since neither she nor her husband is mentioned by the father in his will.

11. Label on left side of the page. The label does not match either of the surrounding documents, suggesting that a bill of sale may be missing from the collection or that the bills of sale at the end of the source were bound out of their original order.

12. This could also conceivably be a blanket of the type made on a mechanical loom.

13. Tomás Pedro is married to Francisco Juárez's (the father) eldest daughter, María Francisca. Note that María Francisca is not mentioned by name in the will. On folio 32, two bills of sale are recorded. In them are notes that María Francisca is the wife of Tomás Pedro as early as 1640.

14. One of these wills is most likely Francisco Juárez's (the father). It is not known to whom the other belongs.

15. Thus far we have been unable to discover who this individual is or his position in the proceedings. The "M" of the last part of his name may, in fact, be two letters.

16. This label is on the right side of the page.

17. Mimicho appears to be its own style of huipil. This is based on the use of *mimicho* in the Spanish translation of Magdalena Ramírez's 1606 testament, where it states that she has a "guepil gayado de algodón y lana, que llaman mimicho" (a huipil with cotton and wool in separate strips, that they call mimicho). AGN, Tierras, v. 1595, e. 4.

Appendix 4
Indigenous Testaments by Sex, from Mexico City, in Nahuatl or Spanish, 1546–1725

Women

Name	Barrio	Year	Source
1. Angelina Poqui	San Sebastián Cotolco	1546	AGN, Tierras, v. 35, e. 1
2. Magdalena Tiacapan	San Pablo (may be San Juan) Tlachquac	1561	AGN, Tierras, v. 22, pt. 1, e. 5
3. María Tiacapan	Santiago Tlatelolco	1561	AGN, Tierras, v. 2729, e. 20
4. Beatriz Papan	San Juan	1570	BNF, FM 112
5. Juana Hernandez	Santiago Tlatelolco: Santa Ana Huitzila	1574	AGN, Tierras, v. 56, e. 8
6. Francisca Tlaco	San Pablo	1576	AGN, Tierras, v. 42, e. 5
7. Juana Francisca	San Sebastián Atzacualco	1576	AGN, Tierras, v. 48, e. 4
8. Juana de Santa Ana	Santiago Tlatelolco: Huitzalan	1576	AGN, Tierras, v. 56, e. 8
9. Angelina Martina	Santiago Tlatelolco/ San Martin telpuchcaltitlan pochtla	1580	AGN, Tierras, v. 49, e. 5
10. Elena Angelina	Tlatelolco: San Martin Atezcapan	1581	NL, Ayer, MS 1481, B(1)a
11. Isabel Ana	San Juan Tlatilco	1587	AGN, Tierras, v. 54, e. 5
12. María Gerónima	San Pablo Ateponasco	1592	AGN, Tierras, v. 1774, e. 10
13. Juana Antonia	San Juan Necaltitlan	1595	AGN, Tierras, v. 59, e. 3
14. Juana Mocel	San Juan Ayoticpac (Cihuatlan)	1596	AGN, Tierras, v. 70, e. 4
15. María Salomén	San Juan Xalcalpan	1605	AGN, Bienes Nacionales, v. 965, e. 6
16. Ana María	San Pablo	1606	ANM, José Rodriguez #555, v. 3836, yrs. 1602–1608, f. 1092
17. Magdalena Ramírez	San Sebastián Cuitlahuactonco	1606	AGN, Tierras, v. 1595, e. 4

Name	Barrio	Year	Source
18. Juana Agustina	Santiago Tlatelolco: San Juan Huitznahuac	1609	AGN, Tierras v. 128, pt. 2, e. 2
19. India (name unknown)	Santiago Tlatelolco: Santa Catarina Martir	1613	ANM, José Rodriguez, #555, v. 3839, yrs. 1612–1616
20. María Ana	San Sebastián Cuitlahuactonco	1615	AGN, Tierras, v. 3663, e. 3
21. Juana María	San Juan Tepetitlan	1616	AGN, Tierras, v. 101, e. 2, f. 8
22. Petronila María	San Juan Tlatilco	1619	ANM, Hernando de Arauz #4, v. 7, yrs. 1619–1622, fs. 7–12v
23. María Alonso	Santiago Tlatelolco	1623	BNF, FM 299
24. Magdalena María	??	1625	AGN, Hospital de Jesús, leg. 210, e. 4
25. Clara López	San Juan Tianquiztenco (Ayoticpac – Cihuatlan)	1640	AGN, Bienes Nacionales, v. 387, e. 1
26. Ana Melchora	San Juan Tecpancaltitlan	1642	NL, Ayer, MS 1481, F5
27. María Juana	San Juan in the convent of Santa Isabel de los Descalsos	1645	AGN, Bienes Nacionales, v. 70, e. 3
28. Nicolasa Juana	San Pablo Xihuitongo (parishioner of Mixtecos)	1648	AGN, Bienes Nacionales, v. 1766, e. 7
29. Juana Francisca	Santa María Colhuatonco	1652	AGN, Tierras, v. 1595, e. 4
30. Gerónima Verónica	Santa María Teocaltitlan	1657	NL, Ayer, MS 1481, B(3)a
31. María Francisca	San Pablo Malcuiltlapilco	1673	UNAM FRAF, caja 96, e. 1413
32. Micaela Angelina	Santa María Iztacalecan	1677	NL, Ayer, MS 1481, B(3)e
33. María Geronima (Son is don Pedro Felipe #36)	Santiago Tlatelolco: Santa Ana Tequixquipan	1677	AGN, Indiferente Virreinal, caja 3873, e. 7
34. Juana Petrona	San Juan Tepetitlan	1678	AGN, Indiferente Virreinal, caja 6493, e. 8
35. Nicolasa de los Angeles	Santa María, near convento de Santo Domingo	1679	AGN, Bienes Nacionales, v. 1096, e. 8
36. Diega Nicolasa	Santa María Copolco	1683	NL, Ayer, MS 1481, B(3)F
37. doña Angelina María	San Pablo Teocaltitlan	1686	AGN, Bienes Nacionales, v. 1766, e. 7
38. Ana Santiago	San Antón	1688	AGN, Tierras, v. 163, e. 2

Name	Barrio	Year	Source
39. Juana de los Angeles	San Juan Huehuecalco	1693	AGN, Civil, v. 1763, e. 2, fs. 3–5
40. Ana María	Mexico City, no barrio given	1693	AGN, Civil, v. 1828, e. 5
41. Teresa de Jesús	San Pablo Teocaltitlan	1695	AGN, Civil, v. 592, e. 1
42. Melchora de Santiago (Father is don Juan de Santiago #35)	Santa María Copolco	1699	NL, Ayer, MS 1481, B(3)1
43. Juana María	Purificación[a]	17th cen?	AGN, Hospital de Jesús, leg. 210, e. 4
44. doña Juana Bravo de Mendoza Moctezuma	Santiago Tlatelolco	1700	AGN, Tierras, v. 1593, e. 2, cuad. 3[b]
45. Ana María (Daughter is María de la O #47 Grand-daughter is doña Juana y Laria de los Santos #48)	Santiago Tlatelolco: Santa Ana Apahuazca	1700	AGN, Tierras, v. 104, e. 8
46. Maria de la Trinidad	Tenochtitlan: San Phelipe Teocaltitlan	1701	AGN, Tierras, v. 396, e. 6
47. María de la O (Mother is Ana María #45 Daughter is doña Juana y Laria de los Santos #48)	Santiago Tlatelolco: Santa Ana Apahuazca	1712	AGN, Tierras, v. 104, e. 8
48. doña Juana y Laria de los Santos (Grand-mother is Ana María #45 Mother is María de la O #47)	Santiago Tlatelolco: San Francisco Tepito	1721	AGN, Tierras, v. 104, e. 8
49. Rosa Gertrudis	Santa María la Redonda Colhuacotonco	1721	NL, Ayer, MS 1481, B(3)k
50. Pascuala Zarate	San Juan or San Pablo (unclear which) in the tlaxilacalli of Candelaria	1725	AGN, Indiferente Virreinal, caja 6471, e. 11

Men

Name	Barrio	Year	Source
1. Juan Tehuitzil	San Sebastián Cotolco	1548	AGN, Tierras, v. 35, e. 1
2. Martin Lázaro Pantecatl	San Juan	1551	AGN, Tierras, v. 20 pt. 1, e. 3
3. don Hernando de Tapia[c]	San Pablo Tucanitlan	1554	AGN, Tierras, v. 37, e. 2[d]
4. Diego Tlacochcalcatl	San Sebastián Cotolco	1566	AGN, Tierras, v. 48, e. 4
5. Antonio Quauitencatl	San Sebastián Cuitlahuactonco	1569	AGN, Tierras, v. 1595, e. 4
6. Francisco Hernández Quahuicequi	San Juan Xihuitonco	1576	AGN, Tierras, v. 38, e. 2
7. Francisco Xochpanecatl	Santa María Apanohuayan	1576	AGN, Bienes Nacionales, v. 293, e. 1
8. Martín Jacobo	Santa María Cuepopan	1577	AGN, Tierras, v. 39 pt. 2, e. 1
9. Pedro Tozan	Santa María Tezcatzonco	1587	AGN, Tierras, v. 442, e. 5
10. Pedro Jacobo	San Juan Necaltitlan	1588	AGN, Tierras, v. 59, e. 3
11. don Gaspar de Buena Ventura	Santiago Tlatelolco	1590	Tulane Latin American Library, Gates, 758A, box 1, folder 21[e]
12. Josef Ramxirez Mahuitoca	San Sebastián Cuitlahuactonco	1591	AGN, Tierras, v. 1595, e. 4
13. Martín Xochitl	San Juan Huehuecalco	1604	AGN, Bienes Nacionales, v. 1455, pt. 2, e. 5
14. Antón Jacobo	San Antón Acatlan	1607	AGN, Tierras, v. 95, pt. 2, e. 8
15. Juan Matías	Santa María Analpan	1618	AGN, Tierras, v. 157, e. 7
16. don Melchor de Mendoza (Son is Gaspar de Mendoza #18)	Santiago Tlatelolco: Los Reyes Capoltitlan	1618	AGN, Tierras, v. 1586, e. 2
17. Gregorio Hernández	San Juan (San Hipólito)	1624	AGN, Tierras, v. 3711, e. 2
18. Gaspar de Mendoza (Father is don Melchor de Mendoza #16)	Santiago Tlatelolco: Los Reyes Capoltitlan	1630	AGN, Tierras, v. 1593, e. 1 cuad 3
19. Melchor Jacobo	Mexico City: Santa María Nativitas[f]	1631	AGN, Hospital de Jesús, leg. 210, e. 4

Name	Barrio	Year	Source
20. Sebastián Francisco	San Juan Almanalco	1634	AGN, Tierras, v. 1720, e. 7
21. Baltazar Bautista	San Pablo	1639	AGN, Bienes Nacionales, v. 339, e. 6
22. Josef Melchor	San Juan Tepetitlan	1642	AGN, Tierras, v. 101, e. 2, f. 2
23. Francisco Juárez	San Pablo Malcuiltlapilco	1644	UNAM FRAF, caja 96, e. 1413
24. Simón Gaspar	San Pablo Ateponasco	1649	AGN, Tierras, v. 109, e. 4
25. don Juan de Aguilar	San Juan	1655	AGN, Bienes Nacionales, v. 489, e. 2[g]
26. Matías Juárez	Santa María Copolco	1659	NL, Ayer, MS 1481, B(3)b
27. Josef Francisco	San Pablo(?) Nuestra Señora de la Candelaria Macuiltlapilco	1661	AGN, Hospital de Jesus, leg. 210, e. 4
28. Francisco Antonio	San Pablo Malcuitlapilco/ San Antón Acatlan	1662	AGN, Tierras, v. 2776, pt. 1, e. 18
29. Juan Gaspar	San Pablo Teocaltitlan	1675	AGN, Bienes Nacionales, v. 1766, e. 7
29a. Juan Gaspar	San Pablo Teocaltitlan	1675	AGN, Bienes Nacionales, v. 1766, e. 7
30. Juan de la Cruz	Santa María Analpan	1679	NL, Ayer, MS 1481, B(3)d
31. Miguel de la Cruz	San Sebastián Xocotlan[h]	1691	INAH, CSG, v. 119
32. Francisco Agustín	San Pablo Atenponasco	1691	AGN, Tierras, v. 163, e. 2
33. Francisco de San Pedro	San Pablo Teocaltitlan	1692	AGN, Civil, v. 592, e. 1
34. don Felipe de la Cruz	Santa Cruz Contzinco	1692	AGN, Tierras, v. 155, e. 9
34a. don Felipe de la Cruz	Santa Cruz Contzinco	1692	AGN, Tierras, v. 155, e. 9
34b. don Felipe de la Cruz	Santa Cruz Contzinco	1692	AGN, Tierras, v. 155, e. 9
35. don Juan de Santiago (Daughter is Melchora de Santiago #42)	Santa María Copolco	1693	NL, Ayer, MS 1481, B(3)1
36. don Pedro Felipe (Mother is María Geronima #33)	Santiago Tlatelolco: Santa Ana Tequixquipan (?)[i]	1697	AGN, Indiferente Virreinal, caja 3873, e. 7
37. don Baltasar Gonzales	San Juan Teocaltitlan	1703	AGN, Tierras, v. 396, e. 6

Name	Barrio	Year	Source
38. Josef de Santiago	San Sebastían Atzacualco Zacatlan	1712	AGN, Indiferente Virreinal, caja 1124, e. 25
39. don Josef Nicolas	Santiago Tlatelolco: San Miguel Atlanpa	1713	AGN, Tierras, v. 1458, e. 11
40. don Pascual Francisco	Santiago Tlatelolco: San Martin Sacatlaco	1714	AGN, Tierras, v. 581, e. 2

a. This one is difficult to place, though it appears to be located within Mexico City. Whether it is in Tlatelolco or Tenochtitlan is not known.

b. Thanks to Margarita Ochoa for sharing her images of this testament.

c. Though don Hernando de Tapía was clearly wealthy and of noble lineage, his testament did not use the title *don* with his name. Inasmuch as the extant will is a translation that was included as part of a later lawsuit, it is entirely possible that the title was dropped out of neglect on the part of the translator/notary assigned to the 1576 legal case. Either way, I have restored the title he was identified with in a 1552 document related to don Baltasar de Mendoza Austria Calnauacatl Moctezuma. AGN, Tierras, v. 1593, e. 1, cuad. 3.

d. Thanks to Bill Connell for sharing his transcription of this document with me.

e. Thanks to Margarita Vargas Betancurt for telling me about this testament.

f. This one is difficult to place, though it appears to be located within Mexico City. Whether it is in Tlatelolco or Tenochtitlan is not known.

g. This is a summary of the will, not the will itself.

h. See table 1, tlaxilacalli entry on San Sebastián Xocotlan.

i. The altepetl and tlaxilacalli are not mentioned in this will, but the rest of the documents in this folder come from Santiago Tlatelolco: Santa Ana Tequixquipan which is also where his mother was located.

Bibliography

Archives

American Museum of Natural History
    Division of Anthropology
Archivo General de la Nación, Mexico City
    Bienes Nacionales
    Civil
    Cofradías y Archicofradías
    Geneología
    General de Parte
    Historia
    Hospital de Jesús
    Indiferente Virreinal
    Indios
    Reales Cédulas Duplicadas
    Tierras
Archivo General de Notarías de la Ciudad de México
Archivo General de Indias, Seville, Spain
    Mapas y Planos: Bulas y Breves
    México
    Patronato
Archivo Histórico de la Basílica de Guadalupe, México
    Antiguedad de Guadalupe
Archivo Histórico José María Basagoiti Noriega del Colegio de las Vizcaínas, Mexico City
Archivo Histórico Franciscano de Coyoacan, Mexico
Archivo Histórico Franciscano de Zapopan, Mexico
Archivo Histórico Nacional, Madrid
    Diversos Colecciones
Biblioteca Nacional de España, Madrid
Bibliothèque Nationale de France
    Fondo Mexicains
Bodleian Library, University of Oxford, England
British Library
Instituto Nacional de Antropología e Historia, Archivo Histórico, Mexico City
    Colegio de San Gregorio
    Fondo Franciscano

John Carter Brown Library, Brown University, Providence, Rhode Island
Latin American Library, Tulane University, New Orleans, Louisiana
Lily Library, Indiana University
Monasterio de San Lorezo de El Escorial
Nationaal Archief, Den Haag, Netherlands
Nettie Lee Benson Latin American Collection, University of Texas, Austin
Newberry Library, Chicago
    Ayer Collection
New York Public Library
    Astor, Lenox, and Tilden Foundations
Princeton University
    Garrett-Gates Mesoamerican Manuscripts Collection
Universidad Nacional Autónoma de México, Biblioteca Nacional
    Fondo Reservado: Archivo Franciscano

Published Sources and Dissertations

Alva, Bartolomé de. *A Guide to Confession Large and Small in the Mexican Language, 1634.* Ed. Barry D. Sell and John Frederick Schwaller with Lu Ann Homza. Norman: University of Oklahoma Press, 1999.

The Badianus Manuscript (Codex Barberini, Latin 241) Vatican Library: An Aztec Herbal of 1552. Ed. and trans. Emily Walcott Emmart. Baltimore, Md.: Johns Hopkins University Press, 1940.

Baez-Camargo. Gonzalo. *Biografía de un templo: Iglesia metodista de la Santísima Trinidad exclaustro mayor de San Francisco.* México: Sociedad de Estudios Históricos del Metodismo en Mexico, 1973.

Baines, Anthony, ed. *The Oxford Companion to Musical Instruments.* Oxford: Oxford University Press, 1992.

Bautista, Juan. *¿Cómo te confundes? ¿Acaso no somos conquistados? Anales de Juan Bautista.* Ed. and trans. Luis Reyes García. México: Centro de Investigaciones y Estudios Superiores en Antropología Social, Biblioteca Lorenzo Boturini Insigne y Nacional Basílica de Guadalupe, 2001.

Bazarte Martínez, Alicia. *Las cofradías de españoles en la ciudad de México, 1526–1869.* México: Universidad Autónoma Metropolitana, 1989.

Bazarte Martínez, Alicia, and Clara García Aluardo. *Los costos de la salvación: Las cofradías y la ciudad de México (Siglos XVI al XIX).* México: Centro de Investigación y Docencia Económicas, 2001.

Berdan, Frances F. *The Aztecs of Central Mexico: An Imperial Society.* New York: Harcourt Brace College, 1982.

Beyersdorff, Margot. *Historia y drama ritual en los andes bolivianos (XVI–XX).* 2nd ed. La Paz, Bolivia: Universidad Mayor de San Andrés, 1993.

Bierhorst, John. *Cantares Mexicanos: Songs of the Aztecs.* Stanford, Calif.: Stanford University Press, 1985.

Black, Christopher F. *Italian Confraternities in the Sixteenth Century.* Cambridge: Cambridge University Press, 1989.

Boone, Elizabeth Hill. "Pictorial Documents and Visual Thinking in Postconquest Mexico." In *Native Traditions in the Postconquest World*, ed. Elizabeth Hill Boone and Tom Cummins, pp. 149–193. Washington, D.C.: Dumbarton Oaks, 1998.

Burkhart, Louise M. *Before Guadalupe: The Virgin Mary in Early Colonial Nahuatl Literature.* Albany, N.Y.: Institute for Mesoamerican Studies University at Albany, 2001.

———. "Death and the Colonial Nahua." In *Nahuatl Theater*, Vol. 1: *Death and Life in Colonial Nahua Mexico.* Ed. and trans. Barry D. Sell and Louise M. Burkhart, pp. 29–54. Norman: University of Oklahoma Press, 2004.

———. *Holy Wednesday: A Nahua Drama from Early Colonial Mexico.* Philadelphia: University of Pennsylvania Press, 1996.

———. "Mexica Women on the Home Front: Housework and Religion in Aztec Mexico." In *Indian Women of Early Mexico*, ed. Susan Schroeder, Stephanie Wood, and Robert Haskett, pp. 25–54. Norman: University of Oklahoma Press, 1997.

———. "Nahuatl Baroque: How Alva Mexicanized the Spanish Dramas." In *Nahuatl Theater*, Vol. 3: *Spanish Golden Age Drama in Mexican Translation.* Ed. and trans. Barry D. Sell, Louise M. Burkhart, and Elizabeth R. Wright, pp. 35–49. Norman: University of Oklahoma Press, 2008.

———. "Pageantry, Passion, and Punishment: Eighteenth-Century Nahuatl Community Theater." In *Nahuatl Theater*, Vol. 4: *Nahua Christianity in Performance.* Ed. and trans. Barry D. Sell and Louise M. Burkhart. Norman: University of Oklahoma Press, 2009.

———. *The Slippery Earth: Nahua-Christian Moral Dialogue in Sixteenth-Century Mexico.* Tucson: University of Arizona Press, 1989.

Burland, C.A. "The Map as a Vehicle of Mexican History." *Imago Mundi* 15 (1960): pp. 11–18.

Bye, Jr., Robert A., and Edelmira Linares. "Mexican Market Plants of 16th Century: I. Plants Recorded in *Historia Natural de Nueva España.*" *Journal of Ethnobiology* 10, no. 2 (Winter 1990): pp. 151–168.

Canons and Decrees of the Sacred and Ecumenical Council of Trent: Celebrated under the Sovereign Pontiffs, Paul III, Julius III and Pius IV. Ed. and trans. J. Waterworth. Facsimile. Chicago: Christian Symbolic Publication Society, 1848.

Cartas de Indias: Facsimile of 1877 Madrid Manuel G. Hernández Edition. 2 vols. Ed. Edmundo Aviña Levy. Guadalajara, México, 1970.

Caso, Alfonso. *Los barrios antiguos de Tenochtitlan y Tlatelolco.* México, D.F.: Imprenta Aldina, 1956.

Castañeda de la Paz, María. *Conflictos y alianzas en tiempos de cambio: Azcapotzalco, Tlacopan, Tenochtitlan y Tlatelolco (siglos XII–XVI).* México: Universidad Nacional Autónoma de México y Instituto de Investigaciones Antropológicas.

Cervantes de Salazar, Francisco. *Crónica de la Nueva España.* 2 vols. Ed. Manuel Magallón. Madrid: Ediciones Atlas, 1971.

———. *México en 1554 y túmulo imperial.* Ed. Edmundo O'Gorman. México: Editorial Porrúa, 1963.

Chauvet, Fidel de Jesús. *San Francisco de México.* México: Editorial Tradición, 2006.

Chimalpahin Quauhtlehuanitzin, Domingo de San Antón Muñón. *Annals of His Time.* Ed. and trans. James Lockhart, Susan Schroeder, and Doris Namala. Stanford, Calif.: Stanford University Press, 2006.

———. *Codex Chimalpahin: Society and Politics in Mexico Tenochtitlan, Tlatelolco, Texcoco, Culhuacan, and Other Nahua Altepetl in Central Mexico.* 2 vols. Ed. and trans. Arthur J. O. Anderson and Susan Schroeder. Norman: University of Oklahoma Press, 1997.

———. *Las ocho relaciones y el memorial de Colhuacan.* 2 vols. Trans. Rafael Tena. México: Consejo Nacional para la Cultura y las Artes, 1998.

Christensen, Mark Z. *Nahua and Maya Catholicisms: Texts and Religion in Colonial Central Mexico and Yucatan.* Stanford, Calif.: Stanford University Press and Academy of American Franciscan History, 2013.

Christian, William, Jr. *Local Religion in Sixteenth-Century Spain.* Princeton, N.J.: Princeton University Press, 1981.

Chuchiak, John. "Secrets behind the Screen: Solicitantes in the Colonial Diocese of Yucatan and the Yucatec Maya, 1570–1785." In *Religion in New Spain,* ed. Susan Schroeder and Stafford Poole, pp. 83–109. Albuquerque: University of New Mexico Press, 2007.

Cline, S[arah] L. *The Book of Tributes: Early Sixteenth-Century Nahuatl Censuses from Morelos.* Los Angeles: UCLA Latin American Center Publications, 1993.

———. "Fray Alonso de Molina's Model Testament and Antecedents to Indigenous Wills in Spanish America." In *Dead Giveaways: Indigenous Testaments of Colonial Mesoamerica and the Andes,* ed. Susan Kellogg and Matthew Restall, pp. 13–33. Salt Lake City: University of Utah Press, 1998.

Cline, S. L., and Miguel Leon-Portilla. *Testaments of Culhuacan.* Los Angeles: UCLA Latin American Center Publications and University of California Press, 1984.

Codex Valeriano: Libre des comptes des tributs a payer par les indigenes de San Pablo Teocaltitlan, 1574. México, 1574.

Códice franciscano: Siglo XVI informe de la provincial del santo evangelio al visitador lic. Juan de Ovando. Informe de la provincial de Guadalajara al mismo. Cartas de religiosos, 1533–1569. México: Salvador Chávez Hayhoe, 1941.

Códice Osuna: Reproducción facsimilar de la obra del mismo título, editada en Madrid. Ed. Luis Chávez Orozco. México, D.F.: Ediciones del Institúto Indigenista Interamericano, 1947.

Códice Sierra: Traduccion al español de su texto nahuatl y explicacion de sus pinturas jeroglificas. Ed. Nicolás León. México: Editorial innovación, 1982.

Concilio III provincial mexicano, celebrado en México el año de 1585, confirmado en Roma por el Papa Sixto V, y mandado observer por el gobierno español en diversas reales ordenes. Ed. Mariano Galván Rivera. México: Eugenio Maillefert y Compañía, 1859.

Connell, William F. *After Moctezuma: Indigenous Politics and Self-Government in Mexico City, 1524–1730.* Norman: University of Oklahoma Press, 2011.

Conway, Richard. "Nahua Pictorial Documents, Testaments, and the Defense of Property in Central Mexico." In *Native Wills from the Colonial Americas: Dead Giveaways in a New World.* Ed. Mark Christensen and Jonathan Truitt, pp. 93–118. Salt Lake City: The University of Utah Press, 2016.

Cope, R. Douglas. *The Limits of Racial Domination: Plebeian Society in Colonial Mexico City, 1660–1720.* Madison: University of Wisconsin Press, 1994.

Cruz, Eloy. "De cómo una letra hace la diferencia: Las obras en Náhuatl atribuidas a don Hernando Franco." *Estudios de Cultura Náhuatl* 32 (2001): pp. 257–295.

Curcio-Nagy, Linda. *The Great Festivals of Colonial Mexico City: Performing Power and Identity.* Albuquerque: University of New Mexico Press, 2004.

Dávila Padilla, Agustín. *Historia de la fundación y discurso de la provincia de Santiago de México, de la orden de predicadores, 1596–1625.* México: Editorial Academía Literaria, 1955.

Díaz, Mónica. "The Indigenous Nuns of Corpus Christi: Race and Spirituality." In *Religion in New Spain.* Ed. Susan Schroeder and Stafford Poole, pp. 179–192. Albuquerque: University of New Mexico Press, 2007.

———. *Indigenous Writings from the Convent: Negotiating Ethnic Autonomy in Colonial Mexico.* Tucson: University of Arizona Press, 2010.

Díaz del Castillo, Bernal. *The Conquest of New Spain.* Trans. J. M. Cohen. New York: Penguin, 1963.

Dibble, Charles E. *Historia de la nación mexicana, reproducción a todo color del códice de 1576 (códice Aubin).* Madrid: Ediciones José Porrúa Turanzas, 1963.

———. "The Nahuatlization of Christianity." In *Sixteenth-Century Mexico: The Work of Sahagún,* ed. Munro S. Edmonson, pp. 225–233. Albuquerque: University of New Mexico Press, 1974.

———. "Sahagún's Historia," in *Florentine Codex: General History of the Things of New Spain.* 13 vols. Ed. and trans. Arthur J. O. Anderson and Charles E. Dibble, pp. 9–23. Santa Fe and Salt Lake City: School of American Research and University of Utah, 1982.

Diel, Lori Boornazian. "Women and Political Power: The Inclusion and Exclusion of Noblewomen in Aztec Pictorial Histories." *Res* 47 (Spring, 2005): pp. 82–105.

Diruta, Girolamo. *The Transylvanian (Il Transilvano).* 2 volumes. Ed. Murray C. Bradshaw and Edward J. Soehnlen. Ottawa: Institute of Mediaeval Music, 1984.

Ducey, Michael T. *A Nation of Villages: Riot and Rebellion in the Mexican Huasteca, 1750–1850.* Tucson: University of Arizona Press, 2004.

Durán, Diego. *Book of the Gods and Rites and the Ancient Calendar.* Ed. and trans. Fernando Horcasitas and Doris Heyden. Norman: University of Oklahoma Press, 1971.

Durand-Forest, Jacqueline de. "Cambios económicos y moneda entre los Aztecas." *Estudios de Cultura Náhuatl* 9 (1971): pp. 105–124.

Edgerton, Samuel Y. *Theaters of Conversion: Religious Architecture and Indian Artisans in Colonial Mexico.* Albuquerque: University of New Mexico Press, 2001.

Eire, Carlos M. N. *From Madrid to Purgatory: The Art and Craft of Dying in Sixteenth-Century Spain.* Cambridge: Cambridge University Press, 1995.

Flynn, Maureen. *Sacred Charity: Confraternities and Social Welfare in Spain, 1400–1700.* Ithaca, N.Y.: Cornell University Press, 1989.

French, Katherine L. *The Good Women of the Parish: Gender and Religion after the Black Death.* Philadelphia: University of Pennsylvania Press, 2008.

Gallagher, Ann Miriam. "The Indian Nuns of Mexico City's *Monasterio* of Corpus Christi, 1724–1821." In *Latin American Women: Historical Perspectives*, ed. Asunción Lavrin, pp. 150–172. Westport, Conn.: Greenwood Press, 1978.

Gante, Pedro de. *Doctrina Christiana en lengua Mexicana.* (Edición facsimilar de la de 1553). México: Centro de Estudios Históricos Fray Bernardino de Sahagún, 1981.

———. "Gante's Letter to Charles V," in *Colonial Latin America: A Documentary History*, ed. Kenneth Mills, William B. Taylor, and Sandra Lauderdale Graham, pp. 105–112. Wilmington, Del.: Scholarly Resources, 2002.

Gerhard, Peter. *Guide to the Historical Geography of New Spain.* Rev. ed. Norman: University of Oklahoma Press, 1993.

———. "Pearl Diving in Lower California, 1533–1830." *Pacific Historical Review* 25, no. 3 (August 1956): pp. 239–249.

Gibson, Charles. *The Aztecs under Spanish Rule: A History of the Indians of the Valley of Mexico: 1519–1810.* Stanford, Calif.: Stanford University Press, 1964.

———. *Tlaxcala in the Sixteenth Century.* New Haven, Conn.: Yale University Press, 1952.

Glass, John B. "A Census of Native Middle American Pictorial Manuscripts." In *Handbook of Middle American Indians*, Vol. 14. Ed. Howard F. Cline, pp. 81–252. Austin: University of Texas Press, 1975.

Gómez de Cervantes, Gonzalo. *La vida económica y social de la Nueva España del siglo XVI.* México: Antigua Librería Robredo de J. Porrúa e Hijos, 1944.

Gómez García, Lidia E. "Las fiscalías en la Ciudad de los Ángeles, siglo XVII." In *Los indios y las ciudades de Nueva España*, pp. 173–195. Serie de historia novohispana. México: Universidad Nacional Autónoma, 2010.

Graubart, Karen B. *With Our Labor and Sweat: Indigenous Women and the Formation of Colonial Society in Peru, 1550–1700.* Stanford, Calif.: Stanford University Press, 2007.

Greer, Allan. "Iroquois Virgin: The Story of Catherine Tekakwitha in New France and New Spain." In *Colonial Saints: Discovering the Holy in the Americas*, ed. Allan Greer and Jodi Bilinkoff, pp. 235–250. New York: Routledge, 2003.

Grijalva, Juan de. *Crónica de la orden de N.P.S. Agustín en las provincias de la Nueva España: En cuatro edades desde el año de 1533 hasta el de 1592.* México: Editorial Porrúa, 1985.

Gruzinski, Serge. "Indian Confraternities, Brotherhoods and Mayordomías in Central New Spain: A List of Questions for the Historian and the Anthropologist." In *The Indian Community of Colonial Mexico: Fifteen Essays on Land Tenure, Corporate Organizations, Ideology and Village Politics*, ed. Arij Ouweneel and Simon Miller, pp. 205–223. Amsterdam: CEDLA, 1990.

Haliczer, Stephen. *Between Exaltation and Infamy: Female Mystics in the Golden Age of Spain.* New York: Oxford University Press, 2002.

Haskett, Robert. *Indigenous Rulers: An Ethnohistory of Town Government in Colonial Cuernavaca.* Albuquerque: University of New Mexico Press, 1991.

Hassig, Ross. *Trade, Tribute, and Transportation: The Sixteenth-Century Political Economy of the Valley of Mexico.* Norman: University of Oklahoma Press, 1985.

Hernández, Francisco. *Historia de las plantas de Nueva España.* México: Imprenta Universitaria, 1946.

Hinz, Eike, Claudine Hartau, and Marie-Luise Heimann-Koenen, eds. and trans. *Aztekischer Zensus: Zur indianischen Wirtschaft und Gesellschaft im Marquesado um 1540.* Hannover: Verlag für Ethnologie, 1983.

Hobsbawm, Eric. "Introduction: Inventing Traditions." In *The Invention of Tradition*, ed. Eric Hobsbawm and Terence Ranger. Cambridge: Cambridge University Press, 1992.

Horcasitas, Fernando. *El teatro nahuatl: Épocas novohispana y moderna.* México: Universidad Nacional Autónoma de México, 1974.

Horn, Rebecca. *Postconquest Coyoacan: Nahua-Spanish Relations in Central Mexico, 1519–1650.* Stanford, Calif.: Stanford University Press, 1997.

Jaffery, Nora E. *False Mystics: Deviant Orthodoxy in Colonial Mexico.* Lincoln: University of Nebraska Press, 2005.

Katzew, Ilona. *Casta Paintings: Images of Race in Eighteenth-Century Mexico.* New Haven, Conn.: Yale University Press, 2004.

Keber, Eloise Quiñones. "An Introduction to the Images, Artists, and Physical Features of the *Primeros Memoriales.*" In Bernardino de Sahagún, *Primeros Memoriales: Paleography of Nahuatl Text and English Translation.* Trans. Thelma D. Sullivan, ed. H. B. Nicholson, Arthur J. O. Anderson, Charles E. Dibble, Eloise Quiñones Keber, and Wayne Ruwet, pp. 15–37. Norman: University of Oklahoma Press with Patrimonio Nacional and Real Academia de la Historia, Madrid, 1997.

Kellogg, Susan. "Aztec Inheritance in Sixteenth-Century Mexico City: Colonial Patterns, Prehispanic Influences." *Ethnohistory* 33, no. 3 (Summer 1986): pp. 313–330.

———. "From Parallel and Equivalent to Separate but Unequal: Tenochca Mexica Women, 1500–1700." In *Indian Women of Early Mexico*, ed. Susan Schroeder, Stephanie Wood, and Robert Haskett, pp. 123–144. Norman: University of Oklahoma Press, 1997.

———. "Households in Late Prehispanic and Early Colonial Mexico City: Their Structure and Its Implications for the Study of Historical Demography." *Americas* 44, no. 4 (April 1988): pp. 483–494.

———. "Indigenous Testaments of Early-Colonial Mexico City: Testifying to Gender Differences." In *Dead Giveaways: Indigenous Testaments of Colonial Mesoamerica and the Andes*, ed. Susan Kellogg and Matthew Restall, pp. 37–58. Salt Lake City: University of Utah Press, 1998.

———. *Law and the Transformation of Aztec Culture, 1500–1700.* Norman: University of Oklahoma Press, 1995.

———. *Weaving the Past: A History of Latin America's Indigenous Women from the Prehispanic Period to the Present.* New York: Oxford University Press, 2005.

———. "The Woman's Room: Some Aspects of Gender Relations in Tenochtitlan in the Late Pre-Hispanic Period." *Ethnohistory* 42, no. 4 (Autumn, 1995): pp. 563–576.

Kellogg, Susan, and Matthew Restall. "The Irreplaceable Window: Reflections on the Study of Indigenous Wills." In *Native Wills from the Colonial Americas: Dead Giveaways in a New World*, ed. Mark Christensen and Jonathan Truitt, pp. 242–247. Salt Lake City: University of Utah Press, 2016.

Klor de Alva, Jorge. "Spiritual Conflict and Accommodation in New Spain: Toward a Typology of Aztec Responses to Christianity." In *The Inca and Aztec States: Anthropology and History*, ed. George A. Collier, Renato I. Rosaldo, and John D. Wirth, pp. 345–366. New York: Academic Press, 1982.

Kubler, George. *Mexican Architecture of the Sixteenth Century.* 2 vols. New Haven, Conn.: Yale University Press, 1948.

Las Casas, Bartolomé de. *Apologética historia sumaria: Cuanto a las cualidades, dispusicion, descripcion, cielo y suelo destas tierras, y condiciones naturals, policies, republicas, manera de vivir e costumbres de las gentes destas indias occidentals y meridionales cuyo imperio soberano pertenece a los reyes de castilla.* 2 vols. México: Universidad Nacional Autónoma de México, Instituto de Investigaciones Históricas, 1967.

Lavrin, Asunción. *Brides of Christ: Conventual Life in Colonial Mexico.* Stanford, Calif.: Stanford University Press, 2008.

———. "Confraternities in Colonial Spanish America." In *Nahua Confraternities in Early Colonial Mexico: The 1552 Nahuatl Ordinances of Fray Alonso de Molina, OFM.* Ed. and trans. Barry D. Sell, pp. 23–40. Washington, D.C.: Academy of American Franciscan History, 2002.

———. "Indian Brides of Christ: Creating New Spaces for Indigenous Women in New Spain." *Mexican Studies/Estudios Mexicanos* 15, no. 2 (Summer 1999): pp. 225–260.

Lockhart, James. *The Nahuas after the Conquest: A Social and Cultural History of the Indians of Central Mexico, Sixteenth through Eighteenth Centuries.* Stanford, Calif.: Stanford University Press, 1992.

———. *Nahuatl as Written: Lessons in Older Written Nahuatl, with Copious Examples and Texts*. Stanford, Calif.: Stanford University Press and UCLA Latin American Center, 2001.

———. *Spanish Peru, 1532–1560: A Social History*. 2nd. ed. Madison: University of Wisconsin Press, 1994.

McAndrew, John. *The Open Air Churches of Sixteenth-Century Mexico: Atrios, Posas, Open Chapels, and Other Studies*. Cambridge, Mass.: Harvard University Press, 1965.

McKendrick, Melveena. *Theatre in Spain, 1490–1700*. Cambridge: Cambridge University Press, 1989.

Megged, Amos. "The Religious Context of an 'Unholy Marriage': Elite Alienation and Popular Unrest in the Indigenous Communities of Chiapa, 1570–1680." *Ethnohistory* 46, no. 1 (Winter 1999): pp. 149–172.

———. *Social Memory in Ancient and Colonial Mesoamerica*. Cambridge: Cambridge University Press, 2014.

Mendieta, Gerónimo de. *Historia eclesiástica indiana*. 2 vols. México: Consejo Nacional para la Cultura y las Artes, 1997.

Memarzadeh, Maher. "Medical Practitioners in Early Colonial Mexico." Ph.D. Diss., University of California, Los Angeles, 2005.

Mills, Kenneth, William B. Taylor, and Sandra Lauderdale Graham, eds. *Colonial Latin America: A Documentary History*. Wilmington, Del.: Scholarly Resources, 2002.

Moctezuma, Eduardo Matos, and Felipe Solís Olguín, eds. *Aztecs*. Madrid: Turner at Artes Gráficas, 2002.

Molina, Alonso de. *Confesionario breve, en la lengua Mexicana y castellana*. México, 1565.

———. *Confesionario mayor en la lengua mexicana y castellana (1569)*. México: Universidad Nacional Autónoma de México, 1984.

———. *Vocabulario en lengua Castellana/Mexicana Mexicana/Castellana*. México: Editorial Porrúa, 2001.

Morales, Francisco. "Santoral franciscano en los barrio indígenas de la ciudad de México." *Estudios de Cultura Náhuatl* 24 (1994): pp. 351–385.

Moreno de los Arcos, Roberto. "Los territorios parroquiales de la ciudad arzobispal." *Gaceta del arzobispado: Sancta metropolitana ecclesia mexicana* 22, nos. 9–10 (September–October 1982): pp. 152–173.

Motolinia, Toribio de. *Motolinia's History of the Indians of New Spain*. Trans. Francis Borgia Steck. Washington, D.C.: Academy of American Franciscan History, 1951.

———. *Memoriales; o, Libro de las cosas de la Nueva España y de los naturales de ella*. Ed. Edmundo O'Gorman. México: Universidad Nacional Autónoma de México, 1971.

———. *Historia de los indios de la Nueva España*. Barcelona: Linkgua ediciones, 2006.

Mulhare, Eileen M., and Barry D. Sell. "Bead-Prayers and the Spiritual Conquest of Nahua Mexico: Gante's 'Coronas' of 1553." *Estudios de Cultura Náhuatl* 33 (2002): pp. 217–252.

Mundy, Barbara E. *The Death of Aztec Tenochtitlan, The Life of Mexico City.* Austin: University of Texas Press, 2015.

———. *The Mapping of New Spain: Indigenous Cartography and the Maps of the Relaciones Geográficas.* Chicago: University of Chicago Press, 1996.

———. "Mapping the Aztec Capital: The 1524 Nuremberg Map of Tenochtitlan, Its Sources and Meanings." *Imago Mundi* 50 (1998): pp. 11–33.

Muriel, Josefina. *Hospitales de la Nueva España.* 2 vols. México: Universidad Nacional Autónoma de México, Cruz Roja Mexicana, 1991.

———. *Las indias cacicas de Corpus Christi.* México: Universidad Nacional Autónoma de México, 1963.

Nesvig, Martin Austin. *Ideology and Inquisition: The World of the Censors in Early Mexico.* New Haven, Conn.: Yale University Press, 2009.

Normann, Anne Whited. "Testerian Codices: Hieroglyphic Catechisms for Native Conversion in New Spain." Ph.D. diss., Tulane University, 1985.

O'Hara, Matthew D. *A Flock Divided: Race, Religion, and Politics in Mexico, 1749–1857.* Durham, N.Car.: Duke University Press, 2009.

Oroz, Pedro. *The Oroz Codex: The Oroz Relación, or Relation of the Description of the Holy Gospel Province in New Spain, and the Lives of the Founders and Other Noteworthy Men of Said Province.* Ed. and trans. Angélico Cháves. Washington, D.C.: Academy of American Franciscan History, 1972.

Osowski, Edward W. *Indigenous Miracles: Nahua Authority in Colonial Mexico.* Tucson: University of Arizona Press, 2010.

Palomera, Esteban J. *Fray Diego Valadés O.F.M.: Evangelizador humanista de la Nueva España, su obra.* México: Editorial Jus, 1962.

Perry, Mary Elizabeth. *Gender and Disorder in Early Modern Seville.* Princeton, N.J.: Princeton University Press, 1990.

Peterson, Jeanette Favrot. *The Paradise Garden Murals of Malinalco: Utopia and Empire in Sixteenth-Century Mexico.* Austin: University of Texas, 1993.

Pizzigoni, Caterina. *Testaments of Toluca.* Stanford, Calif.: Stanford University Press, 2006.

Poole, Stafford. "Church Law on the Ordination of Indians and *Castas* in New Spain." *Hispanic American Historical Review* 61, no. 4 (1981): pp. 637–650.

———. *Pedro Moya de Contreras: Catholic Reform and Royal Power in New Spain, 1571–1591.* Berkeley: University of California Press, 1987.

Powers, Karen Vieira. *Women in the Crucible of Conquest: The Gendered Genesis of Spanish American Society, 1500–1600.* Albuquerque: University of New Mexico Press, 2005.

Prescott, William H. *History of the Conquest of Mexico.* New York: Modern Library, 2001.

Rabiela, Teresa Rojas, Elsa Leticia Rea López, and Constantino Medina Lima, eds. *Vidas y bienes olvidados: Testamentos indígenas novohispanos.* 5 vols. Mexico City: Centro de Investigaciones y Estudios Superiores en Antropología Social, 1999.

Recopilación de leyes de los reynos de las indias: Mandadas imprimir, y publicar por la magestad catolica del rey don Carlos II nuestro señor. 4 vols. Madrid, 1681.

Ricard, Robert. "Documents pour l'histoire des franciscains au Mexique." *Revue d'histoire franciscaine* 1(1924): pp. 216–235.

———. *The Spiritual Conquest of Mexico: An Essay on the Apostolate and Evangelizing Methods of the Mendicant Orders in New Spain, 1523–1572.* Trans. Lesley Byrd Simpson. Berkeley: University of California Press, 1966.

Robertson, Donald. *Mexican Manuscript Painting of the Early Colonial Period: The Metropolitan Schools.* Norman: University of Oklahoma Press, 1994.

Rubial García, Antonio. "Icons of Devotion: The Appropriation and Use of Saints in New Spain." Trans. Martin Austin Nesvig trans. In *Local Religion in Colonial Mexico.* ed. Martin Austin Nesvig, pp. 37–61. Albuquerque: University of New Mexico Press, 2006.

Sadie, Stanley, ed. *The New Grove Dictionary of Musical Instruments.* 3 vols. London: Macmillan Press Limited, 1984.

Sahagún, Bernardino de. *Florentine Codex: General History of the Things of New Spain.* 2nd rev. ed. 13 vols. Ed. and trans. Charles E. Dibble and Arthur J. O. Anderson. Santa Fe and Salt Lake City: School of American Research and University of Utah, 1970–1982.

———. *Psalmodia Christiana (Christian Psalmody).* Trans. Arthur J. O. Anderson. Salt Lake City: University of Utah Press, 1993.

Sandstrom, Alan R. *Corn Is Our Blood: Culture and Ethnic Identity in a Contemporary Aztec Indian Village.* Norman: University of Oklahoma Press, 1991.

Schroeder, Susan. *Chimalpahin and the Kingdoms of Chalco.* Tucson: University of Arizona Press, 1991.

———. "Jesuits, Nahuas, and the Good Death Society in Mexico City, 1710–1767." *Hispanic American Historical Review* 80, no. 1 (2000): pp. 43–76.

———. "The Noblewomen of Chalco." *Estudios de Cultura Náhuatl* 22 (1992): pp. 45–86.

———. "Writing Two Cultures: The Meaning of "Amoxtli" (Book) in Nahua New Spain." In *New World, First Nations: Native Peoples of Mesoamerica and the Andes under Colonial Rule*, ed. David Cahill and Blanca Tovías, pp. 13–35. Eastbourne, East Sussex: Sussex Academic Press, 2006.

Schroeder, Susan, Stephanie Wood, and Robert Haskett, eds. *Indian Women of Early Mexico.* Norman: University of Oklahoma Press, 1997.

Schwaller, John Frederick, ed. and trans. "Constitution of the Cofradía del Santíssimo Sacramento of Tula, Hidalgo, 1570." *Estudios de Cultura Náhuatl* 19 (1989): pp. 217–244.

Sedano, Francisco. *Noticias de México: Crónicas de los siglos XVI al XVII.* 3 vols. México: Colección Metropolitana, 1974.

Seijas, Tatiana. *Asian Slaves in Colonial Mexico: From Chinos to Indians.* Cambridge: Cambridge University Press, 2014.

Sell, Barry David. "Friars, Nahuas, and Books: Language and Expression in Colonial Nahuatl Publications." Ph.D. diss., University of California, Los Angeles, 1993.

———. "The Molina Confraternity Rules of 1552." In *Nahua Confraternities in Early Colonial Mexico: The 1552 Nahuatl Ordinances of Fray Alonso de Molina, OFM.* Ed. and trans. Barry D. Sell, pp. 41–68. Washington, D.C.: Academy of American Franciscan History, 2002.

———. *Nahua Confraternities in Early Colonial Mexico: The 1552 Nahuatl Ordinances of fray Alonso de Molina, OFM.* Berkeley, Calif.: Academy of American Franciscan History, 2002.

———, ed. and trans. "Our Lady of Solitude of San Miguel Coyotlan, 1619: A Rare Set of Cofradía Rules in Nahuatl." *Estudios de Cultura Náhuatl* 31 (2000): pp. 331–358.

Sell, Barry D., and Louise M. Burkhart, eds. *Nahuatl Theater,* Vol. 1: *Death and Life in Colonial Nahua Mexico.* Norman: University of Oklahoma Press, 2004.

———, eds. *Nahuatl Theater,* Vol. 4: *Nahua Christianity in Performance.* Norman: University of Oklahoma Press, 2009.

Sell, Barry D., Louise M. Burkhart, and Stafford Poole, eds. *Nahuatl Theater,* Vol. 2: *Our Lady of Guadalupe.* Norman: University of Oklahoma Press, 2006.

Sell, Barry D., Louise M. Burkhart, and Elizabeth R. Wright, eds. *Nahuatl Theater,* Vol. 3: *Spanish Golden Age Drama in Mexican Translation.* Norman: University of Oklahoma Press, 2008.

Sigüenza y Góngora, Carlos de. *Paraíso occidental.* México: Cien de México, 2003.

SilverMoon. "The Imperial College of Tlatelolco and the Emergence of a New Nahua Intellectual Elite in New Spain (1500–1760)." Ph.D. diss., Duke University, 2007.

Socolow, Susan Migden. *The Women of Colonial Latin America.* Cambridge: Cambridge University Press, 2000.

Stevenson, Robert. *Music in Mexico: A Historical Survey.* New York: Thomas Y. Crowell, 1952.

Sumario de las indulgencias y perdones, concedidas a los cofrades del Santísimo Sacramento visitando la iglesia donde está instituida la dicha cofradía son las siguientes. México: Edición Facsimilar, 1992.

Swanson, R. N. *Indulgences in Late Medieval England: Passports to Paradise?* Cambridge: Cambridge University Press, 2007.

Taylor, Larissa. "Molina 1552: A European Perspective." In *Nahua Confraternities in Early Colonial Mexico: The 1552 Nahuatl Ordinances of Fray Alonso de Molina, OFM,* ed. Barry D. Sell, pp. 11–22. Washington, D.C.: Academy of American Franciscan History, 2002.

Taylor, William B. *Drinking, Homicide, and Rebellion in Colonial Mexican Villages*. Stanford, Calif.: Stanford University Press, 1979.

———. *Magistrates of the Sacred: Priests and Parishioners in Eighteenth-Century Mexico*. Stanford, Calif.: Stanford University Press, 1996.

Tezozomoc, Hernando de Alvarado. *Crónica Mexicana*. Madrid: Dastin, 2001.

Torquemada, Juan de. *Monarquía indiana*. 3 vols. México: Editorial Porrúa, 1969.

Toussaint, Manuel. *Arte colonial en México*. México: Universidad Nacional Autonoma de México, Instituto de Investigaciones Esteticas, 1948.

Trexler, Richard C. *Church and Community, 1200–1600: Studies in the History of Florence and New Spain*. Rome: Edizioni di Storia E. Letteratura, 1987.

———. *Reliving Golgotha: The Passion Play of Iztapalapa*. Cambridge, Mass.: Harvard University Press, 2003.

Truitt, Jonathan. "Adopted Pedagogies: Nahua Incorporation of European Music and Theater in Colonial Mexico City." *Americas* 66, no. 3 (January 2010): pp. 311–330.

———. "Courting Catholicism: Nahua Women and the Catholic Church in Colonial Mexico City." *Ethnohistory* 57, no. 3 (Summer 2010): pp. 415–444.

———. "Revelations on Mexico Tenochtitlan: The 1648 Testament of Nicolasa Juana." In *Native Wills from the Colonial Americas: Dead Giveaways in a New World*, ed. Mark Christensen and Jonathan Truitt, pp. 55–67. Salt Lake City: University of Utah Press, 2015.

Turrent, Lourdes. *La conquista musical de México*. México: Fondo de Cultura Económica, 1993.

Van Oss, Adriaan C. *Catholic Colonialism: A Parish History of Guatemala, 1524–1821*. Cambridge: Cambridge University Press, 1986.

Vetancurt, Agustín de. *Teatro mexicano*. México: Editorial Porrúa, 1982.

Vicente, Marta V. "Images and Realities of Work: Women and Guilds in Early Modern Barcelona." In *Spanish Women in the Golden Age: Images and Realities*, ed. Magdalena S. Sánchez and Alain Saint-Saëns, pp. 127–139. Westport: Greenwood Press, 1996.

von Germeten, Nicole. *Black Blood Brothers: Confraternities and Social Mobility for Afro-Mexicans*. Gainesville: University Press of Florida, 2006.

Wake, Eleanor. *Framing the Sacred: The Indian Churches of Early Colonial Mexico*. Norman: University of Oklahoma Press, 2010.

Wood, Stephanie. "Adopted Saints: Christian Images in Nahua Testaments of Late Colonial Toluca." *Americas* 47 (1991): pp. 259–293.

———. "Gender and Town Guardianship in Mesoamerica: Directions for Future Research." *Journal de la Société des Américanistes* 84, no. 2 (1998): pp. 243–276.

———. "The Techialoyan Codices." In *Sources and Methods for the Study of Postconquest Mesoamerican Ethnohistory*, provisional version (e-book), ed. James Lockhart, Lisa Sousa, and Stephanie Wood. Eugene, Or.: Wired Humanities Project, University of Oregon, 2007. http://whp.uoregon.edu/Lockhart/index.html.

Zedillo Castillo, Antonio. *Historia de un hospital: El hospital real de naturales.* México: Instituto Mexicano del Seguro Social, 1984.
Zimmerman, Günter. "Chimalpahin y la iglesia de San Antón Abad en México." In *Traducciones mesoamericanistas: Tomo 1.* México: Sociedad Mexicana de Antropología, 1996.

Index